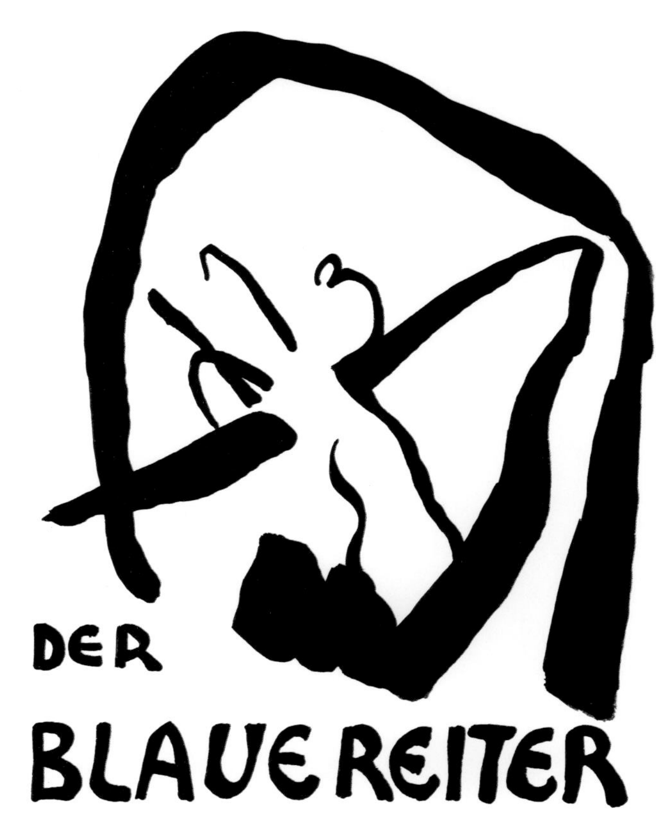
DER
BLAUE REITER

EDITED BY
ULF KÜSTER FOR THE FONDATION BEYELER

KANDINSKY MARC & DER BLAUE REITER

FONDATION **BEYELER**

HATJE
CANTZ

For making the exhibition possible through magnanimous special contributions, the Fondation Beyeler cordially thanks:

Beyeler-Stiftung
Hansjörg Wyss, Wyss Foundation

For their generous support by funding the exhibition, we are indebted to:

L. + Th. La Roche Stiftung
Novartis
Walter Haefner Stiftung

The Fondation Beyeler is deeply grateful to all the lenders who contributed significantly to the success of the exhibition:

ahlers collection, Hanover, Christian Torner
Albright-Knox Art Gallery, Buffalo, Janne Sirén
Bayerische Staatsgemäldesammlungen, Munich, Bernhard Maaz
Bernisches Historisches Museum, Bern, Jakob Messerli
Franz Marc Museum, Kochel am See, Cathrin Klingsöhr-Leroy
Gabriele Münter- und Johannes Eichner-Stiftung, Munich, Isabelle Jansen
Katholische Kirchenstiftung St. Nikolaus, Murnau, Siegbert Schindele
Anne-Marie and Alexander Klee-Coll, Klee Estate Administration, Bern
Kunsthalle Mannheim, Ulrike Lorenz
Kunstmuseum Basel, Bernhard Mendes Bürgi, Josef Helfenstein
Kunstsammlungen Chemnitz, Museum Gunzenhauser, Ingrid Mössinger
Library of Congress, Music Division, Washington, DC, David S. Mao
Merzbacher Kunststiftung, Werner Merzbacher
Münchner Stadtmuseum, Isabella Fehle
Musée national d'art moderne, Centre Pompidou, Paris, Bernard Blistène
Museo Comunale d'Arte Moderna, Commune of Ascona, Mara Folini
Museo Thyssen-Bornemisza, Madrid, Guillermo Solana
Museum Folkwang, Essen, Tobia Bezzola
Museum Ludwig, Cologne, Yilmaz Dziewior
The Museum of Modern Art, New York, Glenn D. Lowry, Ann Temkin
Museum Wiesbaden, Alexander Klar
Oberammergau Museum, Constanze Werner
Peter Eltz GmbH, Salzburg, Peter Graf zu Eltz
Solomon R. Guggenheim Museum, New York, Richard Armstrong
Sprengel Museum Hannover, Reinhard Spieler
Staatliche Kunsthalle Karlsruhe, Pia Müller-Tamm
Staatliche Kunstsammlungen Dresden, Hartwig Fischer, Marion Ackermann, Hilke Wagner
Staatliche Museen zu Berlin, Nationalgalerie, Michael Eissenhauer, Udo Kittelmann
Städel Museum, Frankfurt am Main, Max Hollein, Philipp Demandt, Heinz-Jürgen Bokler
Städtische Galerie im Lenbachhaus, Munich, Matthias Mühling
The State Tretyakov Gallery, Moscow, Zelfira Tregulova
Stiftung Im Obersteg, Basel, Matthias Hagemann
Von der Heydt-Museum Wuppertal, Gerhard Finckh
Walker Art Center, Minneapolis, Fionn Meade

as well as all those who wish to remain anonymous.

For their continued support, the Fondation Beyeler extends thanks to its partners:

accurART
AVC Charity Foundation
AVINA STIFTUNG
Bank J. Safra Sarasin
Bayer
Fondation BNP Paribas Suisse
Gemeinde Riehen
ISS
Kultur Basel-Stadt
kulturelles.bl
Max Kohler Stiftung
Swatch
UBS

CONTENTS

FOREWORD AND ACKNOWLEDGMENTS

SAM KELLER AND ULF KÜSTER

The Fondation Beyeler is devoting an exhibition to one of the most fascinating chapters in art history, which became famous under the name of "Der Blaue Reiter" and exemplifies a central aspect of the development of modern art. Mounting this show at the present time coincides with a number of occasions: one hundred years ago this past March, Franz Marc was killed in action at Verdun, and this December will mark the 150th anniversary of Wassily Kandinsky's birth. There was yet another reason to pursue this project. Since the exhibition at the Kunstmuseum Bern in 1986, thirty years ago, no review of this circle of artists has been presented in Switzerland. It is time to offer a new generation of art lovers the opportunity to witness the transition from figuration to abstraction associated with the Blaue Reiter, initiated by Kandinsky in particular, but also by Marc.

With *Kandinsky, Marc & Der Blaue Reiter*, the Fondation Beyeler is also continuing its series of exhibitions devoted to important art centers. After Venice (2008), Vienna (2010), Paris (2011), and St. Petersburg (2015), the focus is now on Munich, a city that has repeatedly been characterized as Germany's covert capital.

The show is built around two Kandinsky masterpieces in the Beyeler Collection: *Improvisation 10* (1910) and *Fugue* (1914). There were good reasons why Ernst Beyeler—through whose gallery many paintings by the artist passed—decided to keep these two for himself. He viewed *Improvisation 10* as a key work since it marked the beginning of abstraction. And, as a music enthusiast, Beyeler had a special relationship with *Fugue* because of its synaesthetic effect.

The show covers a period that extends from 1908 to 1914. At the time, inspired by the liberal art climate in Munich and the lovely landscapes in the foothills of the Alps around Murnau, an international group of artists set out to fundamentally reform the arts. Their aim was to liberate color from the constrictions of representation, to free line from contour and the plane from the illusion of objectivity. The leading figures were Wassily Kandinsky and Franz Marc, although they did not actually meet in person until early 1911. Both artists were revolutionaries who, frequently in face of vitriolic opposition, pursued their ideas undeterred. Further major figures represented in the exhibition include Alexei von Jawlensky, August Macke, and naturally Gabriele Münter, whose aperçu about how she had advanced in Murnau "from copying nature . . . to feeling the content of things—abstracting—conveying an extract" perfectly summed up the contemporaneous developments in art.

The striking catchword "Der Blaue Reiter," signaling a departure into uncharted territory, was originally the title of the legendary almanac published by Kandinsky and Marc in 1912. The volume contained essays and imagery by a range of writers and artists from various cultures and eras. Not a manifesto in the narrower sense, the almanac's conglomeration of heterogeneous works of European and non-European art, as well as so-called fine art and folk art, was manifesto enough in itself. Both Kandinsky and Marc were convinced that an "internal necessity" existed in art, a kind of soul mating of forms of expression that far transcended the restrictive boundaries of the Western art tradition.

During the preparations for the show, we discovered just how open and international Kandinsky's and Marc's definition of art really was. In a draft of the preface to the almanac, the two editors stated a credo that is still valid today: "The whole work, called art, knows no borders or nations, only humanity."

The openness of the thinking of individuals like Kandinsky and Marc stood in sharp contrast to the nationalistic trends in Europe of the early twentieth century. These led to World War I and to the abrupt end of the liberal approach to art embodied by the Blaue Reiter.

Our own period, too, is marked by growing national egotism and concerns about foreign, unconventional influences. *Kandinsky, Marc & Der Blaue Reiter* offers a good opportunity to recall the uncertain ground on which liberal, independent thinking and the freedom of art stand.

A project of this kind would not be possible without the generosity of numerous lenders. We wish to thank the private and institutional lenders who went to great lengths to provide their support. For advice and assistance we are especially grateful to Paloma Alarcó, Susan Davidson, Alexander Eiling, Peter Graf zu Eltz, Gudrun Föttinger, Stefan Frey, Itzhak Goldberg, Claire Angela Häfliger, Carl-Heinz Heuer, Annegret Hoberg, Jessica Horsley, Isabelle Jansen, Angelica Jawlensky-Bianconi, Oliver Kase, Sofia Komarova, Eberhard W. Kornfeld, Annette Krämer, Felix Krämer, Denise Marroquin, Henriette Mentha, Lara Rath, Cora Rosevear, Masha Shaluieva, Christine E. Stauffer, Alban von Stockhausen, Anna Szech, Manfred Wegner, and Wolfgang Wittrock.

We are also greatly indebted to the authors of the scholarly catalogue essays: Oskar Bätschmann, Andreas Beyer, Cathrin Klingsöhr-Leroy, and Marta Ruiz del Árbol, as well as to Fiona Hesse, who aided the project in her curatorial role as well. For the design of the catalogue we thank Heinz Hiltbrunner and Hatje Cantz Verlag for their unfailing collaboration.

That the Fondation Beyeler is able to realize its exhibition program is to a great extent indebted to the Beyeler-Stiftung and the Wyss Foundation, and to support from the Cantons of Basel-Stadt and Basel-Land, the Municipality of Riehen, and numerous sponsors and patrons.

The exhibition has also enjoyed the generous support of the L. + Th. La Roche Stiftung, Novartis, and the Walter Haefner Stiftung.

It is our hope that the visitors to the exhibition are inspired by the openness and enthusiasm of those who championed the Blaue Reiter and can experience the fascinating awakening of art before 1914.

THE FORM OF COLOR:
KANDINSKY'S REVIVAL OF THE ARTS

OSKAR BÄTSCHMANN

THE TRIANGLE

For his book *Über das Geistige in der Kunst* (*On the Spiritual in Art*), published in December 1911 but dated 1912, Wassily Kandinsky initially designed a cover bearing the subtitle "*Farbensprache*" (The language of color). This design (fig. 1) shows the title in white against a brown background and, in the center, a triangle containing various irregular inner forms in red, violet, ocher, yellow, and blue, and a black spot. Blue shapes with black inclusions fill the two lower corners, and a blue shape with a yellow sail tops the triangle. From the base to the right side a red band heightened in white tapers upward, crossing a black form accompanied by flecks of ocher on white and extending to the sail. The left side of the triangle is occupied by an organoid, white plane with red, and black dots, bulging toward the black shape.[1]

According to theosophical principles, the triangle demonstrated hierarchy and progress in the "spiritual life." In *Über das Geistige in der Kunst* Kandinsky wrote: "The spiritual life can be accurately represented by a diagram of a large acute triangle divided into unequal parts, with the most acute and smallest division at the top. The farther down one goes, the larger, broader, more extensive, and deeper become the divisions of the triangle."[2] Kandinsky envisioned a shift in the mystical triangle forward and upward, enabling a section to rise to a higher level of understanding. With great pathos he imagined a lone seer and his place in the scheme of things: "At the apex of the topmost division there stands sometimes only a single man. His joyful vision is like an inner, immeasurable sorrow. Those who are closest to him do not understand him and in their indignation, call him deranged: a phoney or a candidate for the madhouse."[3] This lack of understanding is illustrated in the title woodcut (fig. 2). On a semicircle stands an upright figure wearing a sash; to the left a mushroom-like, bent form touches a deceptive star. In between these are two half figures and a doglike shape lying on its back on a black field. As an example of the misunderstood artist, Kandinsky cites Ludwig van Beethoven, the supposedly reviled composer, who was celebrated as an artist god by the Vienna Secession in 1902 in a magnificent presentation that included Max Klinger's multicolor *Beethoven* monument (fig. 3) and Gustav Klimt's opulent *Beethoven Frieze*.[4]

Kandinsky's hierarchical triangle is occupied by various artists on each level. Some gaze up to the next higher section like prophets, pass the "spiritual bread," and extend the triangle forward and upward. Others pander to lower urges and deceive the public. These negative artists of the "great, dead black expanse" cause the spiritual triangle to decay.[5] Franz Marc shared this view of things, explaining why people were angered by "this stringent and melancholic painter prophet," namely Kandinsky, who had put an end to the comfortable life and the "fine tradition."[6]

In Kandinsky's eyes, people in the nineteenth century had pursued material goods and technological progress, and demeaned seers or wise men as "mentally abnormal."[7] He imagined the nadir in the form of an exhibition in which artists satisfied their vanity, ambition, and greed, and from which the public, bored, turned away. This amounted to a critique of the contemporary art business as a whole, which Kandinsky believed destroyed "inner sounds," was a "dissipation of the artist's powers," and frustrated viewers.[8] This, he thought, was a result of materialism, which had "turned the life of the universe into an evil, purposeless game." He envisioned a revival as a dim light that "glimmers, like a tiny point in an enormous circle of blackness," representing hope in a new epoch of spirituality.[9]

INNER RENAISSANCE

In *Über das Geistige in der Kunst* Kandinsky listed the signs of a "spiritual turning-point" in literature, music, and painting. In the case of literature, he referred to Maurice Maeterlinck; in that of music,

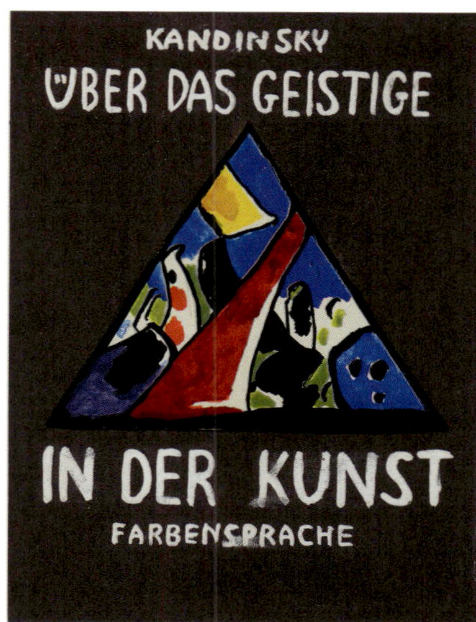

Fig. 1 Wassily Kandinsky, Study for the cover of *Über das Geistige in der Kunst* (*On the Spiritual in Art*), ca. 1910, gouache and India ink on paper, 17.5 x 13.3 cm, Städtische Galerie im Lenbachhaus, Munich

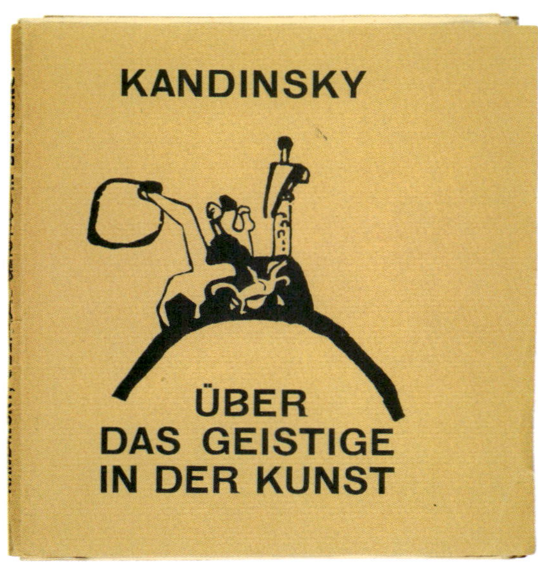

Fig. 2 Wassily Kandinsky, *Über das Geistige in der Kunst* (*On the Spiritual in Art*), Munich, 1912 (published December 1911)

especially to Arnold Schoenberg and his *Harmonielehre* (*Theory of Harmony*).[10] As examples of the search for "the internal in the world of the external,'" he named Dante Gabriel Rossetti, Arnold Böcklin, and Giovanni Segantini, and for the "new laws of form," Paul Cézanne.[11] Then Kandinsky mentioned two new names: Henri Matisse and Pablo Picasso. The former, wrote Kandinsky, required only the intrinsic means of painting, "color and form," to express "the 'divine,'" yet he still relied on the conventional idea of beauty. About Picasso we read: "In his latest works (1911), he arrives at the destruction of the material object by a logical path, not by dissolving it, but by breaking it up into its individual parts and scattering these parts in a constructive fashion over the canvas." By eliminating color in favor of form, Picasso was more radical than Matisse, averred Kandinsky in his formula: "Matisse—color. Picasso—form. Two great pointers toward one great goal."[12]

A promotional brochure (fig. 4) produced by the editors of *Der Blaue Reiter* (*The Blaue Reiter Almanac*) in 1911 announced the aim of the first exhibition as predicting the "great revolution" on the basis of signs of a "new inner renaissance."[13] Several mentions were made of the apparent turn from the "external" to the "internal," that is, to the constructive nature of form, the "inwardness of nature," the "inner link" with earlier epochs, and the "inner aspirations in every internally sounding form."

Kandinsky's hope for a revolution (fig. 5) derived from the Theosophical Society, founded by Helena P. Blavatsky and others in New York in 1875. Its hierarchical division into a section whose membership was open to anyone, a higher section for adepts, and a supreme section composed of masters of the occult, led to continual conflicts within this esoteric association.[14] Still, Kandinsky viewed it as "one of the greatest spiritual movements," and saw a parallel between Blavatsky's connection with Indian philosophy and an involvement with the art of the "savages." Though he remained skeptical about theosophical promises, he supported the intellectual thrust of the movements, which would cast "a note of salvation that reaches the desperate hearts of many who are enveloped in darkness and night."[15] In Kandinsky's eyes, theosophy represented the spiritual counterforce to socialism, capitalism, materialism, and positivism.

Kandinsky's reliance on Blavatsky and the early Rudolf Steiner has been carefully analyzed by Sixten Ringbom and others.[16] A connection between his art theory of the 1910s and theosophy is generally accepted; yet its effects on painting and the theory's links with Goethe's color theory, the philosophy of Henri Bergson, and the Mir iskusstva group remain controversial.[17] Interestingly, Blavatsky's 1889 book, *The Key to Theosophy,* translated into German as *Schlüssel zur Theosophie* (1893), includes a chapter titled "The Abstract and the Concrete," describing the contrast between "Divine Wisdom" and the wisdom accessible to human beings.[18] It requires some effort to imagine the intellectual Kandinsky in the company of clairvoyants, table levitators, and spiritualists. Yet he was evidently interested in what was known as "thoughtography" (psychic photography) and referred to scholars who had conducted scientific research of "puzzling facts" at spiritualist séances in St. Petersburg, London, and Paris.[19] The artist had known about these since his stay in Paris in 1906–07.[20] He shared these esoteric interests with his partner Gabriele Münter until 1914, although he never became a member of the Theosophical Society.[21] Marc considered Kandinsky an expert on occult knowledge; when he wrote a newspaper article on the secrets of the Great Pyramid of Giza in 1911, he asked Kandinsky whether its surveying had been done "in a spiritualistic way."[22]

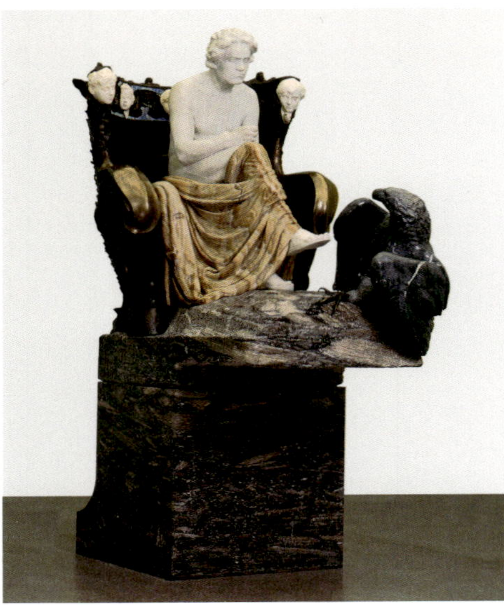

Fig. 3 Max Klinger, *Beethoven,* 1902, various colored stones and bronze with inlays of glass, metal, ivory, and gems, height 3.1 m, Museum der bildenden Künste, Leipzig

The question whether theosophical color theory played a role for Kandinsky cannot be answered with any certainty.[23] The only secure parallel is the fact that he associated the color black with evil, darkness, and death, and white with life. In his essay "Über die Formfrage" (On the Question of Form), published in *Der Blaue Reiter* almanac in 1912, he contrasted the force of the good, described as "the white, fructifying ray," to that of the destructive, "black, death-dealing hand."[24] At the time, the Black Hand, a secret terrorist society organized by officers in the Serbian army, had been responsible for a number of assassinations.[25] In Kandinsky's eyes, the "black hand" had destroyed evolution and freedom.[26] In the essay "Rückblicke" (Reminiscences), written for the catalogue of the 1913 Berlin exhibition, he recalled a trip he took as a three-year-old with his parents to Florence, where he was struck by the eerie black of a carriage, the water, and a boat: "And then the whole of Italy is colored by two memories in black."[27]

Charles Webster Leadbeater, for a time a leading member of the Theosophical Society, prefaced his 1902 book, *Man Visible and Invisible,* with a key to the meaning of colors (fig. 6), which he had arrived at by means of clairvoyance.[28] Moral and spiritual qualities are associated with the twenty-five color fields. Light yellow, for example, is linked with "Highest Intellect," and a somewhat darker yellow with "Strong Intellect." "Selfish Affection" is associated with black-red, and "Malice" with black.[29] The author employed these definitions of color in his characterizations of human types by means of oval "auras" that had been revealed to him. Kandinsky, by contrast, was less interested in moral interpretations of color than in its sounds (*Klänge*) and the "vibrating" of the human soul.[30]

PSYCHIC EFFECTS

In 1904, when he began work on his color theory, Kandinsky noted the assumption that "physical laws" also had "psychic consequences." As he saw it, physical laws included the common oppositions of primary and secondary colors—the contrasting pairs 1) red-green, 2) orange-blue, and 3) yellow-violet. He associated the following psychic effects with these pairs: 1) strength, power, 2) enthusiasm, elation, and 3) sickness, melancholy.[31] Color, Kandinsky believed, took effect through the eye and affected all of the senses: hearing, taste, touch, and smell.[32] A synaesthetic, Kandinsky experienced colors and tones as interchangeable, and expressed their close relationship by calling both sounds and their perception "spiritual vibrations."

Synaesthesia had become a fad in the last quarter of the nineteenth century. In 1883 Arthur Rimbaud published his famous sonnet *Voyelles* in the revue *Lutèce,* describing the association of colors with vowels (black with A, white with E, etc.). That same year, Francis Galton's book *Inquiries into Human Faculty and Its Development* was published in London, a discussion of "colour associations with letters" based on the work of Dr. James Key and a female clairvoyant.[33] Karl Scheffler, a respected German critic who could scarcely be suspected of esotericism, nonetheless stated in his essay "Notizen über die Farbe" (Notes on color), which Kandinsky quoted in 1912, that every sensitive person "tacitly relies on his own color symbolism," sensing the "vowels as colored," that is, A as white, E as gray, etc. Regarding the effects of colors, Scheffler referred to experiments devoted to "influencing mental patients by means of color stimuli."[34] The critic's description of synaesthetic perception as "color symbolism" reflects a conceptual fuzziness much like that of Kandinsky when he uses the term "language of color" for the psychic effects of color.

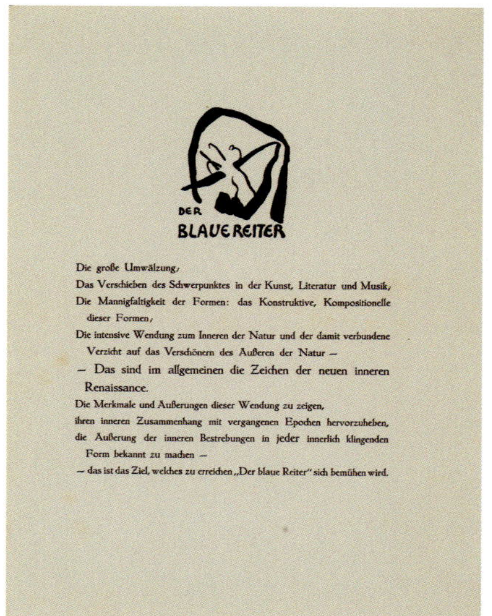

DER BLAUE REITER

Die große Umwälzung,
Das Verschieben des Schwerpunktes in der Kunst, Literatur und Musik,
Die Mannigfaltigkeit der Formen: das Konstruktive, Kompositionelle dieser Formen,
Die intensive Wendung zum Inneren der Natur und der damit verbundene Verzicht auf das Verschönern des Äußeren der Natur –
– Das sind im allgemeinen die Zeichen der neuen inneren Renaissance.
Die Merkmale und Äußerungen dieser Wendung zu zeigen,
ihren inneren Zusammenhang mit vergangenen Epochen hervorzuheben,
die Äußerung der inneren Bestrebungen in jeder innerlich klingenden Form bekannt zu machen –
– das ist das Ziel, welches zu erreichen „Der blaue Reiter" sich bemühen wird.

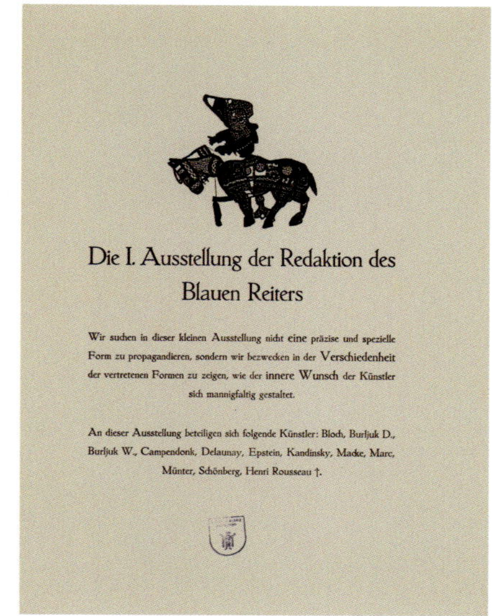

Die I. Ausstellung der Redaktion des Blauen Reiters

Wir suchen in dieser kleinen Ausstellung nicht eine präzise und spezielle Form zu propagandieren, sondern wir bezwecken in der Verschiedenheit der vertretenen Formen zu zeigen, wie der innere Wunsch der Künstler sich mannigfaltig gestaltet.

An dieser Ausstellung beteiligen sich folgende Künstler: Bloch, Burljuk D., Burljuk W., Campendonk, Delaunay, Epstein, Kandinsky, Macke, Marc, Münter, Schönberg, Henri Rousseau †.

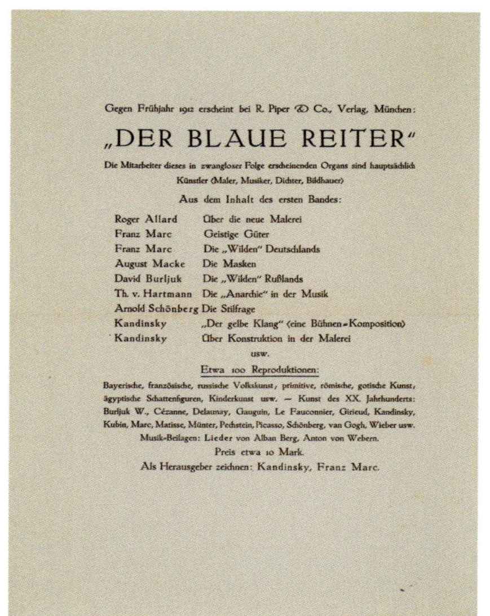

Gegen Frühjahr 1912 erscheint bei R. Piper & Co., Verlag, München:

„DER BLAUE REITER"

Die Mitarbeiter dieses in zwangloser Folge erscheinenden Organs sind hauptsächlich Künstler (Maler, Musiker, Dichter, Bildhauer)

Aus dem Inhalt des ersten Bandes:

Roger Allard — Über die neue Malerei
Franz Marc — Geistige Güter
Franz Marc — Die „Wilden" Deutschlands
August Macke — Die Masken
David Burljuk — Die „Wilden" Rußlands
Th. v. Hartmann — Die „Anarchie" in der Musik
Arnold Schönberg — Die Stilfrage
Kandinsky — „Der gelbe Klang" (eine Bühnen-Komposition)
Kandinsky — Über Konstruktion in der Malerei
usw.

Etwa 100 Reproduktionen:

Bayerische, französische, russische Volkskunst, primitive, römische, gotische Kunst, ägyptische Schattenfiguren, Kinderkunst usw. – Kunst des XX. Jahrhunderts: Burljuk W., Cézanne, Delaunay, Gauguin, Le Fauconnier, Girieud, Kandinsky, Kubin, Marc, Matisse, Münter, Pechstein, Picasso, Schönberg, van Gogh, Wieber usw.
Musik-Beilagen: Lieder von Alban Berg, Anton von Webern.
Preis etwa 10 Mark.
Als Herausgeber zeichnen: Kandinsky, Franz Marc.

Fig. 4 Promotional brochure for the first exhibition and the almanac of *Der Blaue Reiter*, 1911, text "Die grosse Umwälzung" (The Great Revolution) by Wassily Kandinsky, Städtische Galerie im Lenbachhaus, Munich

Chromotherapy was a well-known treatment method for nervous disorders. Kandinsky used the invigorating effect of red light and the paralyzing effect of blue as an argument for the power of colors, "which can influence the entire human body as a physical organism."[35] In his chapter "Wirkung der Farbe" (Effects of Color; fig. 7), such ideas are condensed in the question whether color abets "a high level of development" of human beings through the "psychological effect" of beauty, joy, stimulus, etc.[36] Then he explains, "Color is the keyboard. The eye is the hammer. The soul is the piano, with its many strings," and the artist sets the soul in vibration by striking the keys. From this Kandinsky confidently concludes: "Thus it is clear that the harmony of colors can only be based upon the principle of purposefully touching the human soul."[37] A quotation from Shakespeare's *The Merchant of Venice* cautioning against the individual who "hath no music in himself," serves Kandinsky as a confirmation of his general assumption that musical sounds have direct access to the soul.[38]

The following chapter, "Formen- und Farbensprache" (The Language of Forms and Colors), links music and painting, quoting a statement of Goethe's that "there must be a thorough-bass of painting."[39] This prophecy, Kandinsky believed, was the point of departure for a path on which painting would finally achieve "purely pictorial composition," for which two means were available:

1. Color
2. Form

Form could "exist *per se,*" either as the depiction of a real or unreal object, or as a "purely abstract dividing up of a space, of a surface." Color, as paint matter, could not exist without delineation, or as Kandinsky put it, "color cannot extend without limits." A color without boundaries could only be imagined or seen "in one's mind's eye."[40]

Kandinsky was unable to precisely characterize the reciprocal effects of form and color: "A triangle filled with yellow, a circle with blue, a square with green, then again a triangle with green, a circle with yellow, a square with blue, etc. These are all completely different entities, having completely different effects."[41] The effect of colors could be heightened or diminished by form. Form, in turn, was not something external or superficial, as Kandinsky explained: "Form is, therefore, the expression of inner content." At this point he repeated the metaphor of the piano: "the artist is the hand that purposefully sets the human soul vibrating by pressing this or that key (= form)."[42] Like color, form had a sound, even a principal sound and variations on it.[43] The possibilities of combining colors and forms, Kandinsky said, were "infinite."[44]

As in the case of color, the harmony of forms was based on "the purposeful touching of the human soul."[45] To compose a work, Kandinsky combined its effect with "the principle of internal necessity." This principle was evoked for a third time in connection with the "object." Here, again, Kandinsky referred to the piano: "So it is clear that the choice of object (= a contributory element in the harmony of form) must be based only upon the principle of the purposeful touching of the human soul."[46]

In other words, a threefold emphasis was placed on the principle of "internal necessity" and its fulfilment through the principle of "the purposeful touching of the human soul," something that could not

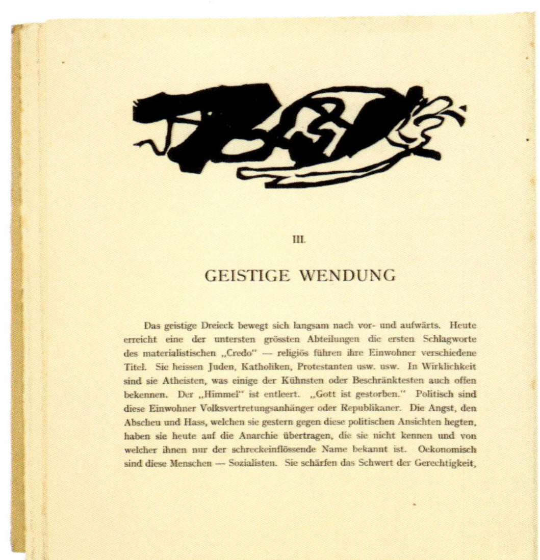

III.

GEISTIGE WENDUNG

Das geistige Dreieck bewegt sich langsam nach vor- und aufwärts. Heute erreicht eine der untersten grössten Abteilungen die ersten Schlagworte des materialistischen „Credo" — religiös führen ihre Einwohner verschiedene Titel. Sie heissen Juden, Katholiken, Protestanten usw. usw. In Wirklichkeit sind sie Atheisten, was einige der Kühnsten oder Beschränktesten auch offen bekennen. Der „Himmel" ist entleert. „Gott ist gestorben." Politisch sind diese Einwohner Volksvertretungsanhänger oder Republikaner. Die Angst, den Abscheu und Hass, welchen sie gestern gegen diese politischen Ansichten hegten, haben sie heute auf die Anarchie übertragen, die sie nicht kennen und von welcher ihnen nur der schreckeinflössende Name bekannt ist. Oekonomisch sind diese Menschen — Sozialisten. Sie schärfen das Schwert der Gerechtigkeit,

Fig. 5 Wassily Kandinsky, *Über das Geistige in der Kunst* (*On the Spiritual in Art*), Munich, 1912 (published December 1911), first page of chapter III, "Geistige Wendung" (Spiritual Turning-Point)

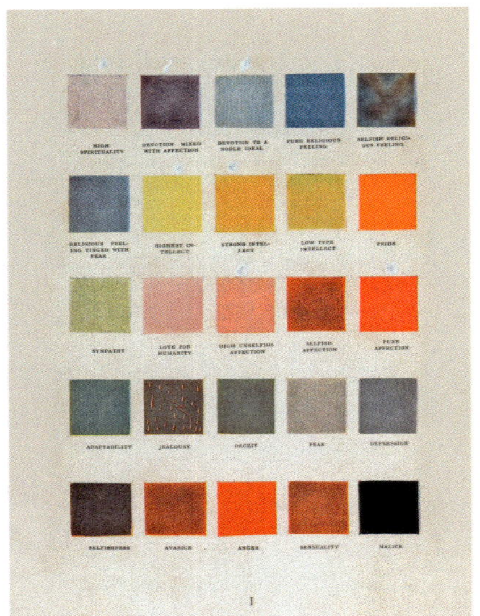

Fig. 6 Charles W. Leadbeater, *Man Visible and Invisible: Examples of Different Types of Men as Seen by Means of Trained Clairvoyance*, London, 1902, frontispiece (plate I) "Signification of the Colours"

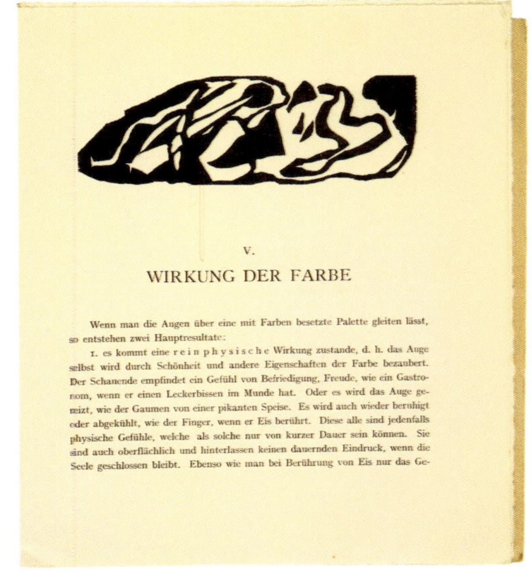

V.

WIRKUNG DER FARBE

Wenn man die Augen über eine mit Farben besetzte Palette gleiten lässt, so entstehen zwei Hauptresultate:

1. es kommt eine r e i n p h y s i s c h e Wirkung zustande, d. h. das Auge selbst wird durch Schönheit und andere Eigenschaften der Farbe bezaubert. Der Schauende empfindet ein Gefühl von Befriedigung, Freude, wie ein Gastronom, wenn er einen Leckerbissen im Munde hat. Oder es wird das Auge gereizt, wie der Gaumen von einer pikanten Speise. Es wird auch wieder beruhigt oder abgekühlt, wie der Finger, wenn er Eis berührt. Diese alle sind jedenfalls physische Gefühle, welche als solche nur von kurzer Dauer sein können. Sie sind auch oberflächlich und hinterlassen keinen dauernden Eindruck, wenn die Seele geschlossen bleibt. Ebenso wie man bei Berührung von Eis nur das Ge-

Fig. 7 Wassily Kandinsky, *Über das Geistige in der Kunst* (*On the Spiritual in Art*), Munich, 1912 (published December 1911), first page of chapter V, "Wirkung der Farbe" (Effects of Color)

occur under the conditions of a materialistic relationship between art and the public. The "internal necessity" of artistic activity and the resulting work would serve as an antidote to subjectivity, the artist's arbitrary decisions, and decorative tendencies.[47] According to Kandinsky, this "internal necessity" arose from three "mystical sources": a) the artist's personality; b) his or her present situation or epoch; and c) from art itself, that is, the "eternally artistic."[48] In his essay "Malerei als reine Kunst" (Painting as Pure Art), published in Herwarth Walden's periodical *Der Sturm* in September 1913, Kandinsky elevated "internal necessity" to the "only unalterable law of art."[49]

FORM—COLOR

The issue of form and color was being widely discussed around 1900. In 1893 Adolf von Hildebrand published his successful book *Das Problem der Form in der bildenden Kunst* (*The Problem of Form in Painting and Sculpture*).[50] Heinrich Wölfflin, who moved from Berlin to Munich in 1912, postulated in "Das Problem des Stils in der bildenden Kunst" (The problem of style in visual art), an academy lecture of 1911, that a distinction should be made between the "current of the substantial" and "the generally visual form in which the substantial [was shaped] for the purpose of perception."[51] In Munich Wölfflin expanded this hypothesis in his 1915 book *Kunstgeschichtliche Grundbegriffe* (*Principles of Art History*).[52] Marc wrote about the original unity of form, color, and object in 1912–13: "Earlier everything was one form color object; then color and object began to separate—Impressionism, until people succeeded in bringing out form per se as well, now we have all three elements."[53] According to Marc, these would be "three worlds that intersect." In his March 1912 essay "Die konstruktiven Ideen der neuen Malerei" (The constructive ideas of the new painting), Marc contrasted habitual perception to the "shaping impulse of the artist" who followed the laws that were "the only ones that determine people's inner life." In agreement with Kandinsky, Marc wrote of the new painting: "Today's art turns directly to this inner life with its expressive forms and by so doing divests its works of the external shell in which their predecessors, following the intellectual tendency of their period, enclosed them."[54] Marc accused the general public of not distinguishing between the "imitative impulse" and "creative impulse," which he blamed on the "corrupted art concepts of the nineteenth century." In order to distinguish between "strong" and "weak" pictures, it was instructive to turn to Japanese art, which would provide the basis for the establishment of a "nation of the soul" (*Seelenstaat*). Surprisingly, Marc saw attempts in this direction in Wilhelm Worringer's 1908 book *Abstraktion und Einfühlung* (*Abstraction and Empathy*) and in Kandinsky's theory of harmony, in which the "currently conceivable laws governing the effects of forms and colors are formulated."[55] Marc defended himself against the impression that the point of the exercise was "stylization," and averred that "the authentic artist has at all times proceeded from constructive visual ideas (of inspiration) that are as old as art itself; what is new is their current, sheer *application,* which brooks of no 'foreign body' within the picture, of which the art of our predecessors likely occasionally had too many."[56] In conclusion, Marc assured his readers that it was impossible to "discuss the multifarious laws of 'intrinsic construction' in this context," since the attempts to do so were still too various, and their character that of an "arcane science whose logic is still almost as unfathomable to its priests as to the general public."[57] His hope in the future is couched as a prophecy: "Through the de-sensualization [*Entsinnlichung*] and overcoming of substance, the ancient belief in color will increase in ecstatic fire and inwardness, as theism once did as a result of a rejection of idolatry."[58]

The discussion of the psychic effects of color as the elementary basis of painting takes up more than twenty pages in *Über das Geistige in der Kunst*.[59] First Kandinsky associates opposing psychic effects with the primary and secondary colors, as well as white and black. These

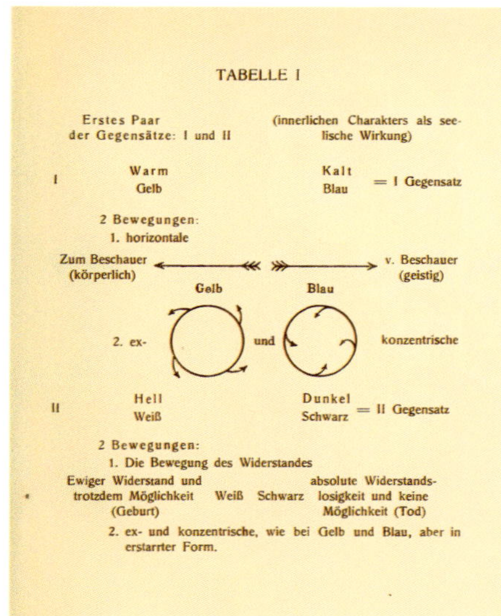

Fig. 8 Wassily Kandinsky, *Über das Geistige in der Kunst* (*On the Spiritual in Art*), Munich, 1912 (published December 1911), Table I, "Erstes Paar der Gegensätze" (First Pair of Opposites)

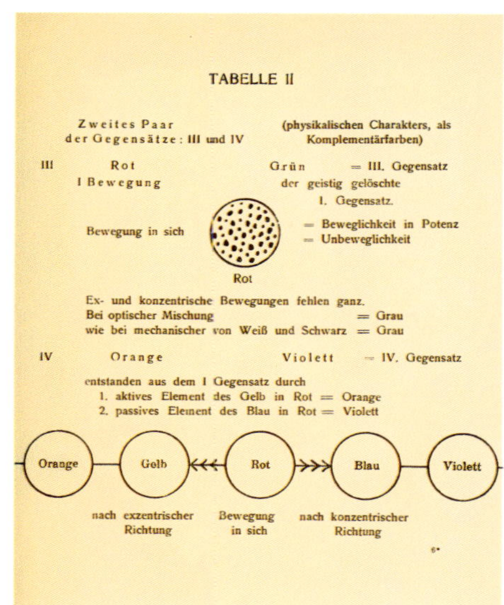

Fig. 9 Wassily Kandinsky, *Über das Geistige in der Kunst* (*On the Spiritual in Art*), Munich, 1912 (published December 1911), Table II, "Zweites Paar der Gegensätze" (Second Pair of Opposites)

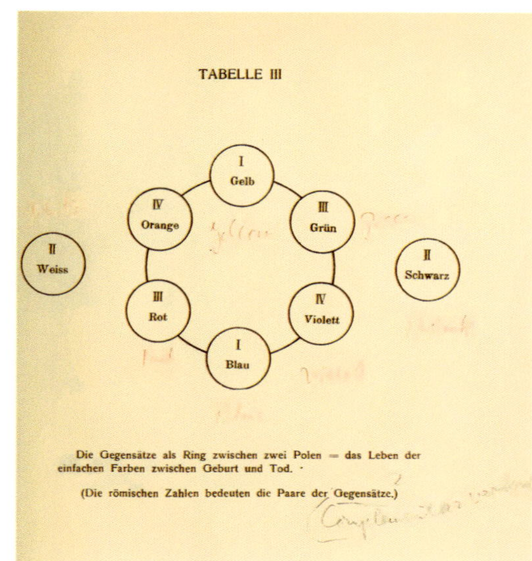

Fig. 10 Wassily Kandinsky, *Über das Geistige in der Kunst* (*On the Spiritual in Art*), Munich, 1912 (published December 1911), Table III, "Die Gegensätze als Ring zwischen zwei Polen" (The Pairs of Opposites Represented As a Ring between Two Poles)

opposites are schematically illustrated in Table I (fig. 8). Yellow and blue represent the strongest antitheses of warm and cold, as well as movement with respect to the "spectator": yellow, for instance, moves outward toward us, sometimes stridently, and sounds like a trumpet or fanfare. Blue, the color of sky or heaven, unfolds a concentric motion to figure as "the element of tranquility," and its sound, depending on its lightness or darkness, corresponds to a flute or cello. The balance between these "diametrically opposed" colors is established by green, whose calmness may be so marked as to be wearisome: "This green is like a fat, extremely healthy cow, lying motionless, fit only for chewing the cud, regarding the world with stupid, lackluster eyes."[60] When green rises to yellow, "it comes alive, full of joy and youth"; when it descends to blue, "it becomes serious and, so to speak, pensive."[61] Kandinsky then goes on to explain the contrast of light and dark, and the varying character of nothingness, or silence, in white (as before birth) and black (as death).[62]

Table II (fig. 9) records the opposites of physical character, as associated with the complementary colors. Red and green represent the contrast between motion and stasis. Red, the rich color with many gradations, is viewed as unbounded and warm, having the "effect of a highly lively, living, turbulent color," which lacks the "rather light-minded character" of yellow. A light, warm red triggers "feelings of power, energy, striving, determination, joy, triumph," and has the "sound of a fanfare, in which the tuba can also be heard."[63] Mixing red with blue results in a violent cooling off and produces "a tone that is avoided and decried by artists . . . as muddy," a judgement Kandinsky rejects because such mixtures, like all colors, have their "own inner sound."[64] Finally, he addresses the formation of orange out of warm red, and of violet from cold red by moving toward yellow and blue respectively, describing them as the "last pair of opposites."[65]

In Table III (fig. 10) the oppositions are arranged in a circle between the "two great possibilities of silence," white and black. The commentary reads: "The six colors that constitute the three great pairs of opposites confront us like a great circle, like a snake biting its own tail (the symbol of infinity and of eternity)."[66]

Komposition V (*Composition V;* fig. 11) was executed in 1911, at a point when Kandinsky was making the final revisions to his book. When the Neue Künstlervereinigung München (New Artists' Association of Munich) did not accept the painting for their show, Kandinsky cancelled his membership and exhibited the work at the *Blaue Reiter* show in 1911 and subsequent exhibitions.[67] In 1914 he wrote: "To my way of feeling, at that point still entirely unconscious, the highest tragedy was cloaked in the greatest coldness."[68] In the painting, expansive white and icy blue areas, accented only by scattered warm contrasts, comprise the lower part of the composition. In the upper part the relationship between warm and cold is reversed, with brown, yellow, and red violently chasing each other. A sinuous, black line extends downward, looping across the surface and into the cold zone. Further zigzag or curving black lines set the white and blue areas in restless motion.

THE SOUND OF PAINTING

While *Über das Geistige in der Kunst* is chiefly devoted to color, *Der Blaue Reiter* contains Kandinsky's major essay "Über die Formfrage."[69] The artist believed in the Pythagorean music of the spheres, described in the *Brockhaus* encyclopedia of 1908 as the: "Song of the spheres, harmony of the spheres, music of the spheres: according to the hypothesis of Pythagoras and his school, the sounds of the planets, inaudible to mortals, said to be the higher the farther their orbit, and the lower the closer."[70] In Part I of Goethe's tragedy *Faust* (1808), the archangel Raphael begins the "Prologue in Heaven"

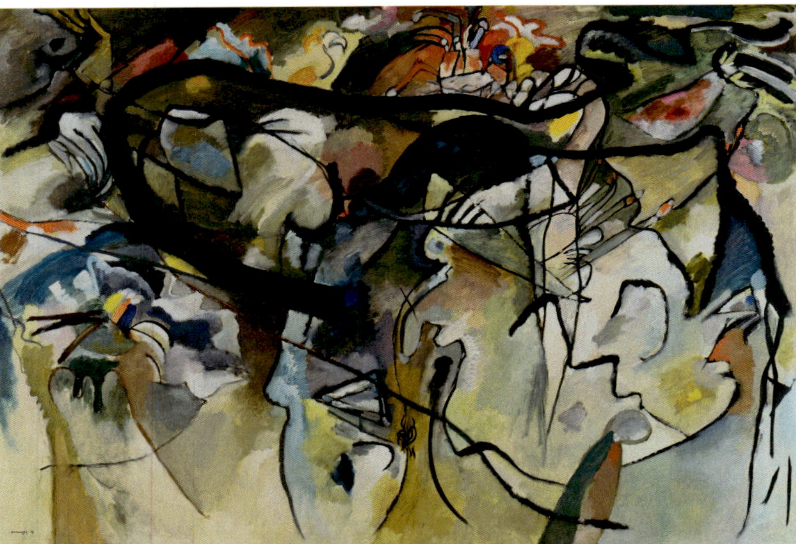

Fig. 11 Wassily Kandinsky, *Komposition V* (*Composition V*), 1911, oil on canvas, 190 x 275 cm, private collect on

with the words, "The sun contends in age-old fashion / With brother spheres in hymnic sound, / And in far-thundering progression / Discharges his appointed round." In accordance with his belief in cosmic harmonies, Kandinsky asserted: "The world sounds. It is a cosmos of spiritually effective beings. Thus, dead matter is living spirit."[71]

As in other contexts, Kandinsky assumed an opposition between internal and external in the case of sound. While "external necessity" has a negative connotation for the artist, representing ambition and greed, "internal necessity" is the reason and justification for every means of expression, forms, and colors: "rather, of prime importance in the question of form is whether or not form has arisen out of internal necessity."[72] If it hasn't, neither form nor color could possess an "inner sound." In "Über die Formfrage," Kandinsky used a letter of the alphabet, a dash, and a line to explain the contrast between the "practical-purposive" and the "pure, inner sound." For instance, when a line is liberated from the necessity of "indicating an object, and itself functions as a thing, its inner sound is not weakened by being forced to play an incidental role, and assumes its full, inner power."[73]

The precondition for this is the divorcing of painterly means from their role as handmaiden, which they play for as long as form serves to indicate an object and color its hue. A further process is described in terms of the "outer shell of the object," whose soul sounds out strongest when "external, palatable beauty can no longer distract us."[74] To perceive its "inner sound," a viewer would have to develop an enabling capacity and receptiveness. As Kandinsky explained, a viewer would submit to "the effect of the practical-purposive" as long as he or she perceived a line as "a means of delineating an object"; yet as soon as an object was perceived as merely secondary and line in terms of its "purely pictorial significance," "the soul of the spectator is ready to experience the pure, inner sound of this line."[75]

Kandinsky's writings are apparently intended to assist the viewer, or better, the public at large. Such concepts as "vibration of the human soul," or "the language of color" and its "psychic effects" reflect a concern with reception. The communicating link between form, color, artist, and public is the sound or ring of painterly means.

In his 1913 essay "Malerei als reine Kunst," Kandinsky schematically distinguished "periods" in painting: a) a devotion to "the transitory corporeal element" as origin; b) a general diminishing of practical purpose in favor of the "spiritual element" as representing development; and c) "pure art" as the goal.[76] A painting like *Murnau—Kohlgruberstrasse* (cat. p. 67) can be seen as representing the artist's developmental phase. Here, color and color contrasts possess an autonomous value that goes beyond their purpose of indicating the field, street, trees, or church. For instance, a blue line beginning in the floating dark blue shape on the right crosses the whitish yellow of the street and flows to the blue area from which two lines emerge, one leading upward between white and green and the other following a tree trunk upward.

A condition for the "exclusion of the practical element, of subject matter," Kandinsky stated, was the replacement of this element by one of equal weight, that is, construction as the "purely artistic form, which can confer upon the painting the strength necessary for independent life, and which is also able to raise the picture to the level of a spiritual subject."[77] Kandinsky imagined the emergence of a work of art as the creation of a living creature or being. In *Über das Geistige in der Kunst,* he wrote: "In a mysterious, puzzling, and mystical way, the true work of art arises 'from out of the artist.' Once released from him, it assumes its own independent life, takes on a personality, and becomes a self-sufficient, spiritually breathing subject that also leads a real material life: it is a being."[78] Similar statements are found in "Über die Formfrage."[79] In the preface to the second, 1913 edition of the exhibition catalogue from 1912 Kandinsky stated: "My goal

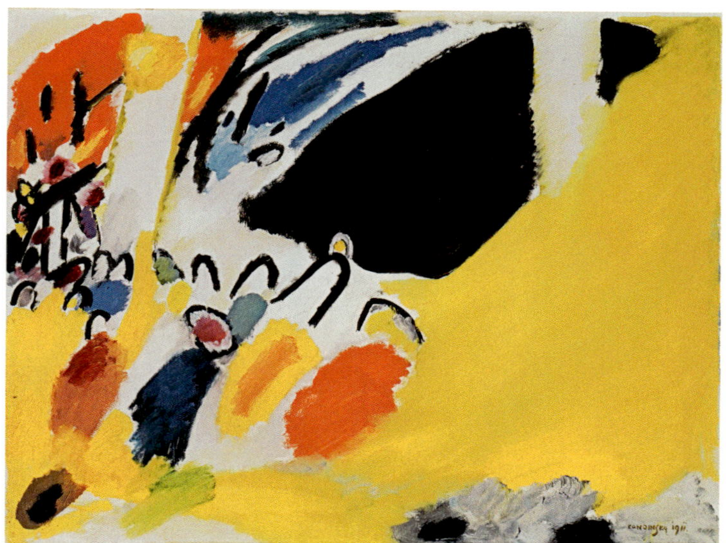

Fig. 12 Wassily Kandinsky, *Impression III (Konzert)* (*Impression III [Concert]*), 1911, oil on canvas, 77.5 x 100 cm, Städtische Galerie im Lenbachhaus, Munich

is to use painterly means, which I love more than any other means of art, to create pictures of a kind that lead their own, independent, intensive life as purely painterly beings."[80] This is an example of the artist's perennial dream of creating, like Pygmalion, a living work. It was confirmed by Kandinsky's nephew, Alexandre Kojève, in a pamphlet of 1936, in which he relied on the concept of "concrete painting" advanced by Theo van Doesburg. Kojève alleged that each of Kandinsky's paintings was "a real, complete, that is, concrete universe, self-contained and self-sufficient," in contrast to works based on the various types of imitation.[81]

Kandinsky declared music—a "pure art"—to be the model for painting. In the 1911 book *Kampf um die Kunst* (The Battle for Art), he concluded his article with a prophecy similar to that contained in *Über das Geistige in der Kunst*:

> *After music, painting will be the second of the arts to be unthinkable without construction, which even today is already the case. Thus painting will attain to the higher level of pure art, upon which music has already stood for several centuries. This will be the great aim of all "young artists," or "fauves," of every spiritually great country. And there is no power capable of halting this progress of art. Before this lofty striving, the greatest hindrance appears no more than a leaf in the face of the oncoming storm.*[82]

On January 2, 1911, Kandinsky, Gabriele Münter, Franz Marc, Maria Franck, Alexei von Jawlensky, and Marianne von Werefkin attended a soiree of chamber music by Arnold Schoenberg in Munich. A week and a half later, Marc, in a letter to August Macke dated January 14, reported that he had encouraged the Neue Künstlervereinigung München to go to the concert, because he had "smelled the roast" of public opprobrium. Marc was nevertheless disturbed by Schoenberg's atonal consonances and dissonances, which reminded him of Kandinsky's compositions, whose "jumping spots" seemed to stand as much alone as Schoenberg's notes. At this point Marc came up with the basically despairing idea of placing complementary colors not next to one another but at greater distances apart, and scattering them across the entire picture plane. In addition, he hoped to do this "instinctively," going on to report of Maria Franck's failed attempt to draw parallels between musical keys and color tones.[83]

Kandinsky digested the acoustic and optical impressions he gained at the chamber music performance in his painting *Impression III (Konzert)* (*Impression III [Concert];* fig. 12). The dominant color is yellow, sweeping up to the right corner, amplified by small areas of red, yellow, and blue running in the same direction, and the black trapezoid, preceded by a small, black shape divided by white. Various black lines mark a parallel or countermovement to these dynamics of color.[84] This impression may have contributed to the subsequent misunderstanding that Kandinsky was out to "paint music." In 1913 he expressly denied any such intention: "I personally am unable to paint music, since I believe any such kind of painting to be basically impossible, basically unattainable."[85] In the lecture he sent to his 1914 exhibition in Cologne, Kandinsky repeated this denial of wishing "to paint music or states of mind, not to mention attempting to determine the future."[86] Instead of imitating music, he said, painting should analogously achieve a "vibration of the human soul" through its autonomous means of color and form. He defined nothing as absolute, neither form, color, nor composition. Whether forms, colors, and objects emerged from inner necessity was determined solely by their source in a "true artist" and their presence in a "true art work."[87] The "inner sound" of forms and colors was a precondition of the work, although its perception demanded the viewer's ability to feel the vibrations and understand the work as an "independent being." Kandinsky's art theory achieved a turn from a hierarchical "mystical triangle" to a horizontal triangular relationship between artist, work, and public.

1 Repr. in *Der Blaue Reiter,* exh. cat. Kunstmuseum Bern (Bern, 1986), cat. no. 95, p. 94.
2 Wassily Kandinsky, *Über das Geistige in der Kunst: insbesondere in der Malerei,* with an introduction by Max Bill and a foreword and annotation on the rev. new ed. by Jelena Hahl-Fontaine (Munich, 1912; 5th ed., Zurich, 2016), p. 33. English trans.: "On the Spiritual in Art," in *Kandinsky: Complete Writings on Art,* ed. Kenneth C. Lindsay and Peter Vergo (Boston, 1982; new, repr. ed., New York, 1994), p. 133.
3 Kandinsky 1994 (see note 2), pp. 133–34.
4 See Georg Bussmann, "Der Zeit ihre Kunst: Max Klingers 'Beethoven' in der 14. Ausstellung der Wiener Sezession," in *Max Klinger, 1857–1920,* ed. by Dieter Gleisberg, exh. cat. Städtische Galerie im Städelschen Kunstinstitut, Frankfurt am Main; Von der Heydt-Museum Wuppertal (Leipzig, 1992), pp. 38–49.
5 Kandinsky 1994 (see note 2), pp. 134–35, esp. p. 134.
6 Franz Marc, *Schriften,* ed. by Klaus Lankheit (Cologne, 1978), p. 200, Aphorism 53. See also Annegret Hoberg, "Kandinsky, Marc und das Sendungsbewusstsein der Avantgarde," in *Der Blaue Reiter: Marc, Macke, Kandinsky, Münter, Jawlensky aus dem Lenbachhaus München,* ed. Stiftung Frieder Burda, Helmut Friedel, and Annegret Hoberg, exh. cat. Museum Frieder Burda, Baden-Baden (Baden-Baden and Ostfildern, 2009), pp. 55–69.
7 Kandinsky 1994 (see note 2), p. 135.
8 Ibid., pp. 129–31, esp. p. 130. Which of the many exhibitions is meant cannot be determined; yet it is safe to assume that the 1909 *Internationale Kunstausstellung* (*International Art Exhibition*) at the Königliche Glaspalast (Royal Glass Palace) in Munich was one of the models. This was organized by the Munich Art League and Munich Secession.
9 Ibid., pp. 127–29, esp. p. 128.
10 Arnold Schoenberg, *Harmonielehre* (Leipzig, 1911). English ed.: Arnold Schoenberg, *Theory of Harmony,* trans. Roy E. Carter (Berkeley, 1979).
11 Kandinsky 1994 (see note 2), pp. 145–52, here 151.
12 Ibid., pp. 151–52.
13 Wassily Kandinsky, "Die grosse Umwälzung," text of the promotional brochure for the first exhibition and the almanac of *Der Blaue Reiter*, 1911
14 See Marty Bax, "Die Theosophische Gesellschaft," in *Okkultismus und Avantgarde: Von Munch bis Mondrian 1900–1915,* exh. cat. Schirn Kunsthalle, Frankfurt am Main (Ostfildern, 1995), pp. 32–37.
15 Kandinsky 1994 (see note 2), pp. 143–45.; with quotation from H. P. Blavatsky, *The Key to Theosophy: Being a Clear Exposition, in the Form of Question and Answer of the Ethics, Science, and Philosophy* (1889; repr., Pasadena, 1972), p. 238.
16 See esp. Sixten Ringbom, *The Sounding Cosmos: A Study in the Spiritualism of Kandinsky and the Genesis of Abstract Painting* (Åbo, 1970). See also the critique by Felix Thürlemann, *Kandinsky über Kandinsky: Der Künstler als Interpret eigener Werke* (Bern, 1986), pp. 81–84.
17 Reinhard Zimmermann, *Die Kunsttheorie von Wassily Kandinsky,* 2 vols. (Berlin, 2002), vol. 1, pp. 449–62 (brief review); and Reinhard Zimmermann, "Der Bauhaus-Künstler Kandinsky—ein Esoteriker?," in *Das Bauhaus und die Esoterik: Johannes Itten, Wassily Kandinsky, Paul Klee,* ed. Christoph Wagner, exh. cat. Gustav-Lübcke-Museum, Hamm; Museum im Kulturspeicher, Würzburg (Bielefeld, 2005), pp. 47–54.
18 Blavatsky 1972 (see note 15), "The Abstract and the Concrete," pp. 32–35.
19 Kandinsky 1994 (see note 2), p. 143; see also Veit Loers, "'Das Kombinieren des Verschleierten und des Blossgelegten'—Kandinsky und die Gedankenfotografie," in exh. cat. Frankfurt am Main 1995 (see note 14), pp. 245–53.
20 Jonathan David Fineberg, *Kandinsky in Paris, 1906–1907* (Ann Arbor, MI, 1984), pp. 59–80, 93–99.
21 See Zimmermann 2002 (see note 17), p. 47, with information on the esoteric literature in Münter's library.
22 Franz Marc, letter to Wassily Kandinsky, July 27, 1911, in Wassily Kandinsky and Franz Marc, *Briefwechsel: Mit Briefen von und an Gabriele Münter und Maria Marc,* ed., introduction, and annotation by Klaus Lankheit (Munich, 1983), p. 48.
23 See John Gage, "The morality of colour," in *Colour and Culture: Practice and Meaning from Antiquity to Abstraction* (London, 1993), pp. 204–11. Zimmermann found few signs of a straightforward influence of theosophical color theory on Kandinsky's art theory, see Zimmerman 2002 (see note 17), pp. 455–60.
24 Wassily Kandinsky, "Über die Formfrage," in *Der Blaue Reiter,* ed. Wassily Kandinsky and Franz Marc (Munich, 1912), pp. 74–100. English trans.: "On the Question of Form," *The Blaue Reiter Almanac,* ed. Wassily Kandinsky and Franz Marc, in *Kandinsky: Complete Writings on Art,* ed. by Kenneth C. Lindsay and Peter Vergo (Boston, 1982; new, repr. ed., New York, 1994), pp. 235–57, here 235–36.
25 Christopher Clark, *The Sleepwalkers: How Europe Went to War in 1914* (London et al., 2012).
26 Kandinsky 1994 ("On the Question of Form"; see note 24), pp. 235–36.
27 Wassily Kandinsky, "Rückblicke," in *Kandinsky: 1901–1913,* exh. cat. Galerie Der Sturm, Berlin (Berlin, 1913), p. iii. English trans.: "Reminiscences," in *Kandinsky: Complete Writings on Art,* ed. by Kenneth C. Lindsay and Peter Vergo (Boston, 1982; new, repr. ed., New York, 1994), pp. 357–82, here p. 358.
28 Charles W. Leadbeater, "Signification of the Colours," in *Man Visible and Invisible: Examples of Different Types of Men as Seen by Means of Trained Clairvoyance* (1902; 2nd rev. ed., London, 1920), plate 1.
29 Charles W. Leadbeater, "Colours and their Meaning," in ibid., pl. I, and pp. 80–86.
30 Kandinsky 1994 (see note 2), pp. 161–65; see also John Gage, "Colour in Theosophy and in Kandinsky," in *Colour and Meaning: Art, Science and Symbolism* (London, 1999), pp. 242–43.
31 Wassily Kandinsky, "Definieren der Farben" [1904], in *Gesammelte Schriften,* ed. Helmut Friedel (Munich, 2007), pp. 248–58.
32 Ibid., pp. 250–51.
33 Francis Galton, "Colour Associations," in *Inquiries into Human Faculty and Its Development* (London, 1883), pp. 145–54; see pl. V, "Colour associations by Dr. James Key."
34 Karl Scheffler, "Notizen über die Farbe," *Dekorative Kunst* 7 (February 1901), pp. 183–96; Kandinsky 1994 (see note 2), p. 161.
35 Kandinsky 1994 (see note 2), p. 159.
36 Ibid., pp. 156–60, esp. 157.
37 Ibid., p. 160.
38 Ibid., p. 161.
39 Ibid., p. 162; the preface to the second German edition promises a forthcoming "Harmonielehre in der Malerei" (Theory of harmony in painting).
40 Ibid.
41 Ibid., p. 163.
42 Ibid., p. 165.
43 See entries for 1912–1914, in Kandinsky 2007 (see note 31), pp. 559–78.
44 Kandinsky 1994 (see note 2), p. 163.
45 Ibid., p. 165.
46 Ibid., p. 169.

47 Zimmermann 2002 (see note 17), vol. 1, pp. 124–28; vol. 2, pp. 292–301.
48 Kandinsky 1994 (see note 2), pp. 173–76, esp. p. 173.
49 Wassily Kandinsky, "Malerei als reine Kunst," *Der Sturm* 4, nos. 178–79 (1913), pp. 98–99. Engl. trans.: "Painting as Pure Art," in *Kandinsky: Complete Writings on Art,* ed. by Kenneth C. Lindsay and Peter Vergo (Boston, 1982; new, repr. ed., New York, 1994), pp. 349–54, here p. 350.
50 Adolf von Hildebrand, *Das Problem der Form in der bildenden Kunst* (Strasbourg, 1893). English ed.: *The Problem of Form in Painting and Sculpture,* trans. and rev. Max Meyer and Robert Morris Ogden (New York, 1907).
51 Heinrich Wölfflin, "Das Problem des Stils in der bildenden Kunst," *Sitzungsberichte der Königlich Preussischen Akademie der Wissenschaften* 31 (1912), pp. 572–78, here p. 573.
52 Heinrich Wölfflin, *Kunstgeschichtliche Grundbegriffe: Das Problem der Stilentwickelung in der neueren Kunst* (Munich, 1915). Engl. ed.: *Principles of Art History: The Problem of the Development of Style in Later Art,* trans. Jonathan Blower, ed. and with essays by Evonne Levy and Tristan Weddigen (Los Angeles, 2015).
53 Marc 1978 (see note 6), p. 110.
54 Ibid., p. 106.
55 Ibid., p. 107.
56 Ibid., p. 108.
57 Ibid.
58 Ibid., p. 200; Aphorism no. 54.
59 In the 1912 German ed., pp. 71–95; cf. Kandinsky 2016 [1912] (see note 2), pp. 89–112; English ed.: Kandinsky 1994 (see note 2), pp. 177–93.
60 Kandinsky 1994 (see note 2), pp. 182–83.
61 Ibid., p. 183.
62 Ibid., pp. 183–86.
63 Ibid., pp. 186–87.
64 Ibid., p. 187.
65 Ibid., pp. 188–89.
66 Ibid., p. 189.
67 As a young collector Josef Müller from Solothurn acquired the painting in 1914; see exh. cat. Bern 1986 (see note 1), cat. no. 55, pp. 62–63.
68 Wassily Kandinsky, *Die gesammelten Schriften,* ed. Hans K. Roethel and Jelena Hahl-Koch (Bern, 1980), vol. 1, p. 57. For Kandinsky's own interpretation, see Thürlemann 1986 (see note 16); and Barbara Mackert-Riedel, *Wassily Kandinsky über eigene Bilder: Zum Problem der Interpretation moderner Malerei* (Weimar, 2003).
69 Kandinsky 1994 ("On the Question of Form"; see note 24), pp. 235–57. See also draft by Kandinsky, in Kandinsky 2007 (see note 31), pp. 453–57.
70 Entry on "Sphärengesang," in *Brockhaus' Konversations-Lexikon* (14th ed., Leipzig, 1908), vol. 15, p. 147.
71 Kandinsky 1994 ("On the Question of Form"; see note 24), p. 250.
72 Ibid., p. 239.
73 Ibid., pp. 246–48, here p. 247.
74 Ibid., p. 243.
75 Ibid., p. 247.
76 Kandinsky 1994 ("Painting as Pure Art"; see note 49), p. 351.
77 Ibid., 353.
78 Kandinsky 1994 (see note 2), p. 210.
79 Kandinsky 1994 ("On the Question of Form"; see note 24), p. 253.
80 Kandinsky 1980 (see note 68), p. 26.
81 Alexandre Kojève, *Die konkrete Malerei Kandinskys,* trans. and ed. Hans Jörg Glattfelder (Bern, 2005), pp. 32–37, 43.
82 Wassily Kandinsky, untitled essay, in *Im Kampf um die Kunst: Die Antwort auf den "Protest deutscher Künstler": Mit Beiträgen deutscher Künstler, Galerieleiter, Sammler und Schriftsteller* (Munich, 1911), pp. 73–75. English trans.: "The Battle for Art," in *Kandinsky: Complete Writings on Art,* ed. by Kenneth C. Lindsay and Peter Vergo (Boston, 1982; new, repr. ed., New York, 1994), pp. 106–08, here pp. 107–08.
83 Franz Marc, letter to August Macke, January 14, 1911, in August Macke and Franz Marc, *Briefwechsel* (Cologne, 1964), pp. 39–42.
84 *Der Blaue Reiter im Lenbachhaus München,* ed. by Helmut Friedel and Annegret Hoberg (Munich, 2000), no. 18.
85 Kandinsky in 1913 (see note 68), p. 25. English trans.: "Postscript," in *Kandinsky: Complete Writings on Art,* ed. by Kenneth C. Lindsay and Peter Vergo (Boston, 1982; new, repr. ed., New York, 1994), p. 345.
86 Johannes Eichner, *Kandinsky und Gabriele Münter: Von Ursprüngen moderner Kunst* (Munich, n.d. [1957]), pp. 109–16.
87 See Kandinsky 2007 (see note 31), pp. 493–95.

THINKING IN PICTURES: WHAT FRANZ MARC AND WASSILY KANDINSKY HAVE IN COMMON WITH ABY WARBURG

ANDREAS BEYER

Everywhere, forms speak in a sublime language right in the face of European aesthetics. August Macke, "Masks," 1912

Nowadays, we automatically assume that art in itself encourages insight, that it "speaks" self-referentially or by showing, and, like criticism and scholarship, that it plays a part in the general discourse about what it engenders and the ideas it inspires. This is due in large part, if not causally, to Der Blaue Reiter (The Blue Rider). This name stands as a synonym for the two exhibitions arranged by Wassily Kandinsky and Franz Marc in Munich in 1911 and 1912, after they had left the Neue Künstlervereinigung München (New Artists' Association Munich) there. The name has also come to stand for the group of like-minded artists who gathered around these two. First and foremost, however, the Blaue Reiter represents an "editorship." Kandinsky and Marc "signed" the two shows and in May 1912 published an almanac under the name, a yearbook that was to be the first in a series. In fact, however, this issue was to remain the only one. Reprinted in 1914, it can be viewed without reservation as a foundational manifesto of modernism.[1]

The manuscript has been continually lauded as such ever since. In addition, its involvement in the intellectual and artistic movements since Classicism and Romanticism, its derivation from both French Symbolism and Russian mysticism, its reliance on aesthetic and philosophical approaches of the late nineteenth century, especially those of Richard Wagner and Friedrich Nietzsche, have long been recognized. Its intellectual dependence on contemporaneous thinking, on Sigmund Freud's depth psychology, Henri Bergson's vitalistic philosophy, and Wilhelm Worringer's *Abstraktion und Einfühlung* (*Abstraction and Empathy*) of 1908, has also been justly emphasized.[2] From the standpoint of contemporary art history, increasingly marked by visual theory, the book's very design lends it a singular significance. It is the employment of imagery, the illustrations, their distribution and arrangement, that made Kandinsky and Marc, along with their contemporary, the Hamburg art historian and cultural theorist Aby Warburg, pioneers of what might be called "thinking in pictures." It reflected, moreover, the anthropological conviction that human beings possessed an innate need for imagery, and concomitantly, that the limits of European aesthetics should be overcome to enable an egalitarian perception of foreign or so-called primitive imagery. In all of these respects, *Der Blaue Reiter* proved to be as historically pioneering as it is still relevant today.

In a famous letter to Marc dated June 19, 1911, Kandinsky concisely sketched the basic ideas behind their project:

> *A kind of almanac (yearbook) with reproductions and articles . . . and a* chronicle!! *that is, reports on exhibitions reviewed by artists, and artists alone. In the book the entire year must be reflected; and a link to the past as well as a ray to the future must give this mirror its full life. . . . We will put an Egyptian work beside a small Zeh [drawings by two children of the Munich architect August Zeh, an acquaintance of Kandinsky's], a Chinese work beside a Rousseau, a folk print beside a Picasso, and the like! . . . The book could be called "The Chain" or some other title. . . .*[3]

In fact, this letter represents the "birth certificate"[4] of *Der Blaue Reiter,* and it was the comparative method outlined here of placing imagery of all genres, regions, and eras in a new constellation with interacting relationships that made this group a visual cultural experiment *avant la lettre*.

In a note written for the subscription prospectus in mid-January 1912, Marc expanded programmatically on this aspect:

> *Today art is moving in a direction of which our fathers would never even have dreamed. . . . We know that the basic ideas of what we feel and create today have existed before us, and we are emphasizing that in essence they are not new. . . . The first volume here-*

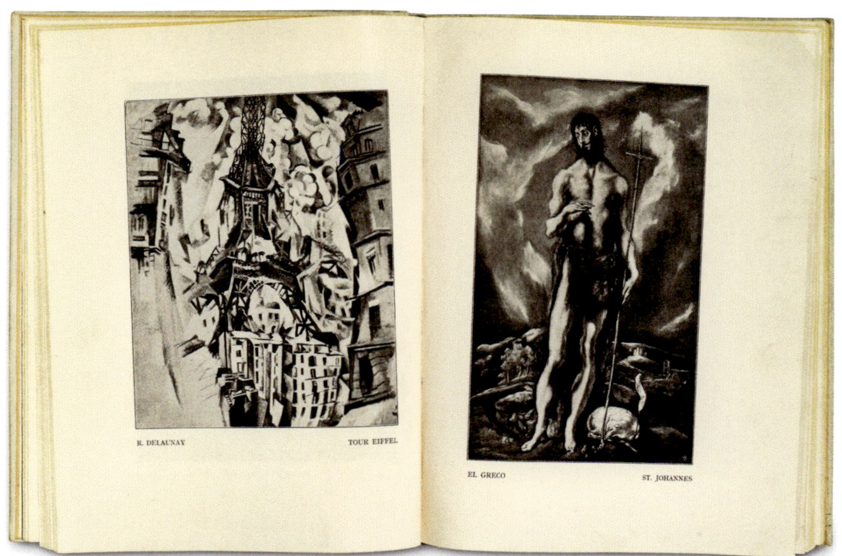

Fig. 1 Double-page spread from *Der Blaue Reiter* almanac (Munich, 1912) juxtaposing Robert Delaunay, *Tour Eiffel* (*Eiffel Tower,* 1911; destroyed 1945) and El Greco, *St. John the Baptist* (ca. 1605; today Pushkin Museum, Moscow), both formerly in the Koehler Collection, Berlin

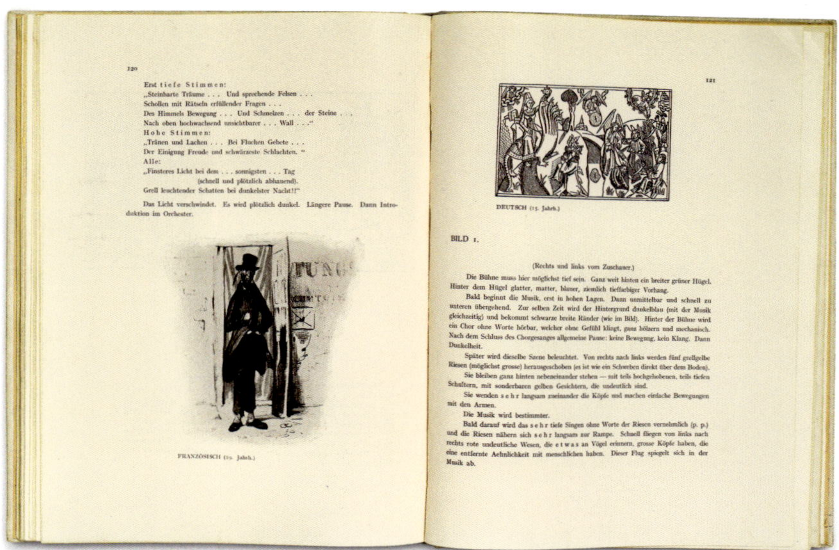

120

Erst tiefe Stimmen:
„Steinharte Träume . . . Und sprechende Felsen . . .
Schollen mit Rätseln erfüllender Fragen . . .
Des Himmels Bewegung . . . Und Schmelzen . . . der Steine . . .
Nach oben hochwachsend unsichtbarer . . . Wall . . ."
Hohe Stimmen:
„Tränen und Lachen . . . Bei Fluchen Gebete . . .
Der Einigung Freude und schwärzeste Schlachten."
Alle:
„Finsteres Licht bei dem . . . sonnigsten . . . Tag
(schnell und plötzlich abhauend).
Grell leuchtender Schatten bei dunkelster Nacht!!"

Das Licht verschwindet. Es wird plötzlich dunkel. Längere Pause. Dann Introduktion im Orchester.

FRANZÖSISCH (19. Jahrh.)

121

DEUTSCH (15. Jahrh.)

BILD 1.

(Rechts und links vom Zuschauer.)

Die Bühne muss hier möglichst tief sein. Ganz weit hinten ein breiter grüner Hügel. Hinter dem Hügel glatter, matter, blauer, ziemlich tieffarbiger Vorhang.

Bald beginnt die Musik, erst in hohen Lagen. Dann unmittelbar und schnell zu unteren übergehend. Zur selben Zeit wird der Hintergrund dunkelblau (mit der Musik gleichzeitig) und bekommt schwarze breite Ränder (wie im Bild). Hinter der Bühne wird ein Chor ohne Worte hörbar, welcher ohne Gefühl klingt, ganz hölzern und mechanisch. Nach dem Schluss des Chorgesanges allgemeine Pause: keine Bewegung, kein Klang. Dann Dunkelheit.

Später wird dieselbe Szene beleuchtet. Von rechts nach links werden fünf grellgelbe Riesen (möglichst grosse) herausgeschoben (es ist wie ein Schweben direkt über dem Boden).

Sie bleiben ganz hinten nebeneinander stehen — mit teils hochgehobenen, teils tiefen Schultern, mit sonderbaren gelben Gesichtern, die undeutlich sind.

Sie wenden sehr langsam zueinander die Köpfe und machen einfache Bewegungen mit den Armen.

Die Musik wird bestimmter.

Bald darauf wird das sehr tiefe Singen ohne Worte der Riesen vernehmlich (p. p.) und die Riesen nähern sich sehr langsam zur Rampe. Schnell fliegen von links nach rechts rote undeutliche Wesen, die etwas an Vögel erinnern, grosse Köpfe haben, die eine entfernte Aehnlichkeit mit menschlichen haben. Dieser Flug spiegelt sich in der Musik ab.

Fig. 2 Double-page spread from *Der Blaue Reiter* almanac (Munich, 1912) juxtaposing a lithograph (19th cent.) from an album owned by Franz Marc (then regarded as French, but probably from the printing workshop of J. Scholz, Mainz), and Anton Koberger's woodcut *The Whore of Babylon* (1483) as reproduced in Wilhelm Worringer's *Die altdeutsche Buchillustration,* Munich, 1912

with announced . . . includes the latest movements in French, German, and Russian painting. It reveals subtle connections with Gothic and primitive art, with Africa and the vast Orient, with the highly expressive, spontaneous folk and children's art, and especially with the most recent musical movements in Europe and the new ideas for the theater of our time.[5]

By confronting or juxtaposing imagery that on first sight was entirely heterogeneous, this method was intended not so much to illustrate derivations as to highlight analogies or constants and let pictures communicate with other pictures. This may not make *Der Blaue Reiter* an example of the crisis of language described at the start of the century, as in Hugo von Hofmannsthal's "Brief des Lord Chandos" (Letter of Lord Chandos, 1902),[6] because the artists involved also figured as authors, and quite liberally so. It is just that the imagery was accorded a no less expressive, independent level of discourse than the text, particularly by synthetic comparison, which is why *Der Blaue Reiter* can be understood as attesting to the "demise of conventional semantics . . . and traditional symbolic-allegorical relations of word and picture."[7]

By the start of the century, this type of "comparative vision" had become established in academic practice, thanks to the art historian Heinrich Wölfflin, who was active in Switzerland and Germany.[8] Yet indicatively, artists also concurrently turned to this method of approaching images comparatively. Even prior to June 1911, Marc, in a letter to his artist friend August Macke, saying he would supply an essay for the volume *Im Kampf um die Kunst* (The Battle for Art), mentioned that it would include "a juxtaposition of reproductions."[9] That same day he wrote to Kandinsky, "I am thinking, for instance, of a juxtaposition of reproductions, Maillol next to Taschner and Flossmann, Cézanne next to Groeber, Nissl, Renoir nude next to Münzer and Putz, Picasso next to Greiner and Stuck, Derain next to Buttersack and Dill, Matisse next to Erler and Habermann, etc."[10]

In general, Macke seems to have supplied a considerable impulse, as Marc recalled when he announced to Macke, this time regarding the design of *Der Blaue Reiter,* in September 1911: "Especially, much should be explained by means of comparative material—your old plans to conduct comparative art history have their place here. We will include glass painting, French and Russian folk prints, beside others' and our new things, occasionally interspersing 'Munich modern painting' by way of comparison."[11] And to Hugo von Tschudi, in a letter of October 24, 1911, he explained an underlying principle of the publication, which "should be so rich in comparative illustrational material, since the value of comparison does not lie in the single image."[12]

The initially confusing abundance of the book's imagery was itself evident in the list of 141 reproductions at the end of the volume.[13] The selection was apparently made as intuitively as it was associatively: "With a divining rod we searched through the art of the past and the present," wrote Marc in the preface to the second edition.[14] The editorial challenge posed by this amassing of visual material, as well as its methodological boldness, are indicated by a further statement of Kandinsky's that seems to reflect a fear of his own courage: "The amount of reproductions we have is truly frightening."[15] Moreover, *Der Blaue Reiter* was a proving ground for a montage of elements that were heterogeneous in terms of conventional aesthetics, anticipating what Theodor W. Adorno would later disparage as the "fraying of [boundaries between] the arts."[16]

It is fundamentally true, however, that the long tradition of almanacs and atlases, as well as that of encyclopedias, especially in the nineteenth century, likewise employed comparative illustrations, occasionally even giving precedence to visual over linguistic argumentation. Uwe Fleckner has pointed out the great number of handbooks that presented readers "a cartography of visually explored fields," at the same time adding, however, that these "in no way developed any sort of independent visual argumentation."[17] In fact, these image plates

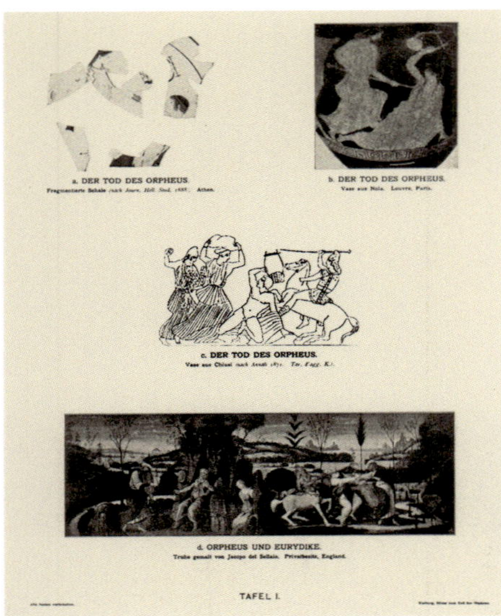

Fig. 3 Aby Warburg, *Der Tod des Orpheus* (*The Death of Orpheus*), picture plate from Warburg's lecture "Dürer und die italienische Antike" (Dürer and Italian Antiquity), Hamburg, n.d. [1905], plate 1

aimed primarily at homogeneous, coherent illustration, were designed as correlates to the accompanying text, and did not rely on the intrinsic value and logic of visual narration. Hence, we can say that the visual strategy of *Der Blaue Reiter* relied on entirely new foundations.[18] This not least because reproductions permitted the use of excerpts, or the altering or adapting of size relationships. Felix Thürlemann has emphasized that the editors of *Der Blaue Reiter* used "the new potentials provided by the manipulation of photographic reproductions with great consistency to create a new visual discourse."[19]

Only in rare cases does the placement of a reproduction in *Der Blaue Reiter* correspond to the accompanying text. Evident text-image relationships are found only in the essays by Macke, Marc, and Kandinsky. These usually remain covert or are linked solely through passages quite distant from one another, leading to an innovative trust in the discursive independence of pictures.[20] Sheer visual confrontations were staged by the editors by placing Vincent van Gogh's *Dr. Paul Gachet* (1890), for instance, alongside a detail from a Japanese woodblock print (19th cent.; pp. 56–57); Robert Delaunay's *Tour Eiffel* (*Eiffel Tower,* 1911) alongside El Greco's *St. John the Baptist* (ca. 1605; fig. 1); Oskar Kokoschka's *Else Kupfer* (ca. 1911) alongside Henri Rousseau's *Portrait de la seconde femme de l'artiste* (*Portrait of the Artist's Second Wife with a Lamp,* 1900–03); and a French nineteenth-century print alongside a fifteenth-century German woodcut (fig. 2).

Kandinsky explained this only apparently aleatory combination practice in terms of what he considered to be the generally valid, inherent arrangement requirements of works of art:

> *If the reader of this book is temporarily able to banish his own wishes, thoughts, and feelings, and then leafs through the book, passing from a votive picture to Delaunay, from Cézanne to a Russian folk-print, from a mask to Picasso, from a glass picture to Kubin, etc., etc., then his soul will experience a multitude of vibrations and enter into the realm of art. Then he will find here not irritating insufficiency and annoying mistakes, but rather will arrive spiritually not at a minus, but at a plus. These vibrations and the plus that derives from them will be a kind of enrichment of the soul that cannot be attained by any other means than those of art. Later, the reader can, with the artist, go over to objective observations, to scientific analysis. He will find that all the examples given here obey one single inner call—composition—and that they all rest upon the same inner basis—construction.*[21]

What Kandinsky characterizes as the inner necessity of all imagery is for Macke an "intellectual equality." In his essay "Die Masken" (Masks) he correspondingly wrote:

> *Does Van Gogh's portrait of Dr. Gachet not originate from a spiritual life similar to the amazed grimace of a Japanese juggler cut in a wood block? The mask of the disease demon from Ceylon is the gesture of horror of a primitive race by which their priests conjure sickness. The grotesque embellishments found on a mask have their analogies in Gothic monuments and in the almost unknown buildings and inscriptions in the primeval forests of Mexico. What the withered flowers are for the portrait of the European doctor, so are the withered corpses for the mask of the conjurer of disease. The cast bronzes of the Negroes from Benin in West Africa (discovered in 1889), the idols from the Easter Islands in the remotest Pacific, the cape of a chieftain from Alaska, and the wooden masks from New Caledonia speak the same powerful language as the chimeras of Notre-Dame and the tombstones in Frankfurt Cathedral. Everywhere, forms speak in a sublime language right in the face of European aesthetics.*[22]

When we recall that around the same time, in Germany, France, and elsewhere, art was being degraded to an instrument of nationalistic ideologies, Macke's not only non-nationalistic but also anti-Eurocentric appeal reflects an independence of visual thought that can hardly be overestimated.[23]

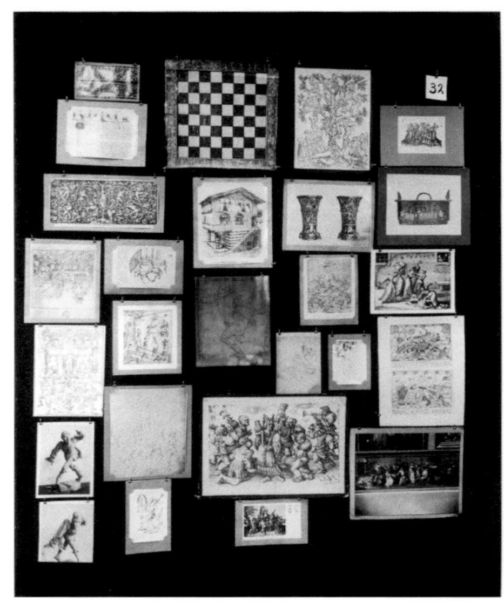

Fig. 4 Aby Warburg, Plate 32 from the *Mnemosyne Atlas* (1924–29), 1926 (lost)

Marc, too, sees the commonality of the images gathered in *Der Blaue Reiter* as resting in something "genuine," recognizable by an "inner life [that] guarantees its truth. All works of art created by truthful minds without regard for the work's conventional exterior remain genuine for all times."[24] In his essay "Zwei Bilder" (Two Pictures) Marc programmatically sums up:

> *We will make this as difficult as possible for ourselves, never fearing the ordeal by fire that will result from placing our works, which point to the future and are still unproved, beside the works of older, proved cultures. We believe that nothing can illustrate our ideas better than such comparisons. Genuine art can always be compared with genuine art, however different the expression may be.*[25]

Works correlated in this way have been described as "visual rhymes" that, regardless of their individual character, set a "process of meaning formation" in motion.[26] This is a practice of "showing," of demonstrating and juxtaposing that relies on the self-expressive power of imagery. If we follow the current visual culture debates, the pathfinding role of *Der Blaue Reiter* becomes immediately apparent.[27]

When Kandinsky spoke of the idea of a synthetic book "that should expunge old, narrow notions and bring down the walls between the arts,"[28] this was a surprising prelude to a global understanding of art that would seem possible only today, under the premise of a postcolonial view. Macke, made privy to the project in September 1911 and asked to contribute to *Der Blaue Reiter,* outlined this expansive conception in a letter to Gabriele Münter, dated September 25, 1911:

> *I compiled a few important things which will be hard to abandon. "Justification of Peasant Art," or "Character in Pottery Ornaments," "Artistic Trends in African Secret Societies," "Masks and Puppet Plays among the Greeks, Japanese, Siamese," "Mystery Plays among Heathens and Early Christians," "Living and Dead Ornament," "Bare Facts in Art," etc. All these things make my head bubble in confusion. Whenever I pick out something intelligent, I like to write it down."*[29]

What Macke unfolds here is the conception of a visual policy that encompasses continents and epochs that have developed analogous forms, and that qualifies or even questions the primacy of European art history.[30] The point is not issues of influence, "stylistic impulses," or a romantically inspired yearning for the elemental or primal, but rather an egalitarian view, internal structural links, and an equal aesthetic status. The ideal space of a publication like *Der Blaue Reiter* permitted this kind of equality, for which, as Felix Thürlemann has noted, the theoretical discourse attests just as much as the systematic impartiality with which the visual discourse was put into practice.[31]

That a comparable unfolding of visual argumentation was difficult or impossible to achieve in museums or exhibitions is something that became apparent even at the Blaue Reiter's first Munich show, which was hung conventionally and evinced no juxtapositions of the kind seen in the almanac.[32] The standard gallery hanging of the period, based on counterparts—that is, symmetrical arrangements of works with the same format and related subjects—may actually have initially determined the juxtapositions in *Der Blaue Reiter*. This is indicated by the repeated use of the term "*Pendant,*" or counterpart, in the relevant correspondence between Marc and Kandinsky.[33] Still, the editors of the almanac eventually arrived at an arrangement, the radicalism of which could only be realized in the form of a book or catalogue, and which thus can be viewed as a kind of alternative to the contemporaneous hanging practice.[34]

Uwe Fleckner has pointed out that this type of visual essay, based in whole or part on the expressive power of imagery and form, had a parallel at most in the visual plates conceived by Aby Warburg, beginning in 1905 at the latest. These served Warburg as comparative examples supplementing his lectures based on slides. As in the case of his lecture "Dürer und die italienische Antike" (Dürer and Italian Antiquity; fig. 3), these were fragments of his "Atlas zur Geschichte der wandernden antikisierenden Gebärdensprache" (Atlas of the historical development of the classicizing visual language). This work, in turn, ultimately led to the unfinished project to which he devoted all his energy in the last years of his life: the *Mnemosyne Atlas,* which traces the sources and development of the pictorial tradition. This undertaking has in recent decades become the subject of intense exploration and ongoing fascination among art and cultural historians (fig. 4).[35] Despite all the differences in layout and disposition—Warburg's plates were literally expansive and did largely without text—the arrangement of the illustrations in *Der Blaue Reiter* can be compared to the visual rhetoric Warburg developed concurrently on his own. The fact that this thinking in pictures truly aimed in the same direction is indicated by the circumstance that Kandinsky would later on, while a teacher at the Bauhaus, employ a combination of visual materials that corresponded in a baffling way to Warburg's.[36] Kandinsky's estate at the Centre Pompidou in Paris includes around two hundred surviving reproductions that he cut out of magazines, newspapers, and books and arranged in ensembles (figs. 5 and 6). These plates were used during lectures or instruction and have in part also survived in the form of notes, such as for the summer of 1931, when Kandinsky worked on the subject of "art—science—technology—nature." Under the rubric of "technology" he gathered the following motifs: "lots of sailing ships, benz phaeton from 1890s (incipient auto form), junkers airplane—L5, motor from a four cylinder motorcar, junkers high-altitude motor—5,000 m high, rotary engine and human being, zschornewitz-golpa [a modern power plant]—aerial photograph, dentist's room, coburg castle," for art, "van dyck, corinth, daumier, kirchner, nolde, juan gris—human figure, pissarro, miro—landscape," and for nature, "a giraffe."[37]

Kandinsky and Marc referred to their book as an "almanac." This was also the subtitle that was to appear on the title page, yet was omitted at the request of the publisher, Reinhard Piper. Piper likely realized that this concept could have obligated him to produce a no less costly series.[38] In fact, work had already begun on a second edition, which, however, never materialized.[39] The term "almanac" typically refers to a periodical publication; still, it derives from the tradition of books of astronomical plates and illustrated text anthologies, and hence was quite appropriate. As Kandinsky later recalled, the choice of the final title, *Der Blaue Reiter,* emerged from a whim: "we both loved blue, Marc liked horses, I riders."[40] The suggestion he made in the June 19, 1911 letter to Marc, cited above, to call the book "*Die Kette*" (The Chain) was of course much more programmatic. In fact, the theoretical arguments in *Der Blaue Reiter,* like the visual discourse developed there, are expressions of a visual thinking that views formal invention in terms of manifold "concatenations," unhierarchical in both temporal and formal regards. This emphasis on relationships and continuity also characterizes the metaphor of the "visual vehicle" introduced by Warburg,[41] which describes a more than just physical migration of imagery among far distant visual cultures, and this beyond all positivism, schematism, or idealism.[42] Though a copy of *Der Blaue Reiter* has not been found in the Warburg Library, Warburg did acquire a painting by Marc in 1913, *Stute mit Fohlen* (*Mare with Foals,* 1912; cat. p. 103), and he viewed himself as being allied with the avant-garde.[43] On the occasion of the inauguration of his Hamburg library, the Kulturwissenschaftliche Bibliothek, at Heilwigstrasse 116, in May 1926, Warburg had intended to hang the painting over the door to the main room, something that apparently was not realized.[44] It would have formed the counterpart to the inscription carved in stone over the inner entrance door: MNEMOSYNE (Greek "memory"). What to Warburg constituted the "posthumous life" of forms was to Kandinsky and Marc their reflection. With their consistent negation of space and time, their far-reaching detachment of visual creations from their original context and placement in an autonomous aesthetic universe that was simultaneously a space for reflection, the two artists lived out an attitude that is yet to be matched by so-called visual culture.

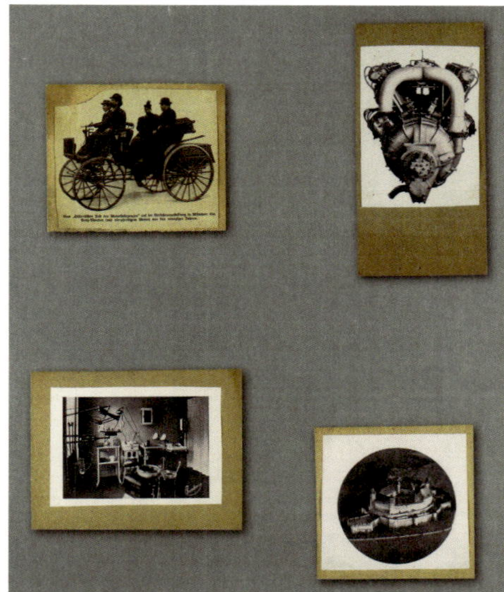

Fig. 5 Wassily Kandinsky, Picture plate for his lectures at the Bauhaus "kunst—wissenschaft—technik—natur" (art—science—technology—nature) with the subject technology, 1931, Musée national d'art moderne, Centre Pompidou, Paris

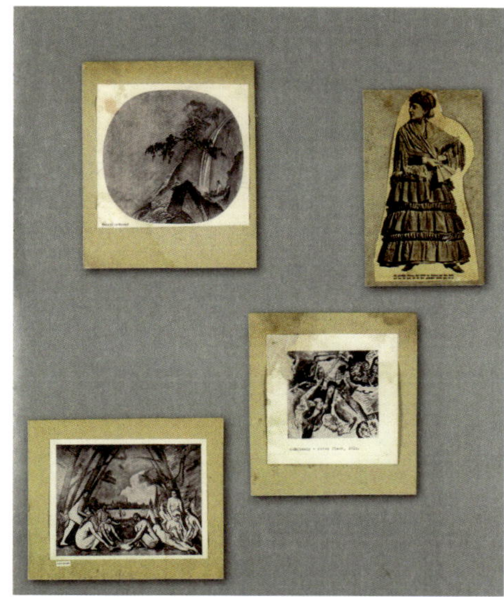

Fig. 6 Wassily Kandinsky, Picture plate for his lectures at the Bauhaus "kunst—wissenschaft—technik—natur" (art—science—technology—nature) with the subject art, 1931, Musée national d'art moderne, Centre Pompidou, Paris

1 Wassily Kandinsky and Franz Marc, eds., *Der Blaue Reiter* (Munich, 1912); English ed.: *The Blaue Reiter Almanac,* documentary edition, ed. and with an introduction by Klaus Lankheit, trans. Henning Falkenstein with assistance of Manug Terzian and Gertrude Hinderlie (New York, 1974; repr., Boston, 2005). See also *Der Blaue Reiter und das Neue Bild: Von der "Neuen Künstlervereinigung München" zum "Blauen Reiter,"* ed. Annegret Hoberg and Helmut Friedel, exh. cat. Städtische Galerie im Lenbachhaus, Munich (Munich, 1999).

2 See Klaus Lankheit, "A History of the Almanac," in Kandinsky and Marc 2005 (see note 1), p. 36; and Jessica Horsley, *Der Almanach des* Blauen Reiters *als Gesamtkunstwerk: Eine interdisziplinäre Untersuchung* (Frankfurt am Main et. al, 2006). See also Felix Thürlemann, *Kandinsky über Kandinsky: Der Künstler als Interpret eigener Werke* (Bern, 1986); Matthias Haldemann, *Kandinskys Abstraktion: Die Entstehung und Transformation seines Bildkonzepts* (Munich, 2001); and Reinhard Zimmermann, *Die Kunsttheorie von Wassily Kandinsky* (Berlin, 2002).

3 Wassily Kandinsky and Franz Marc, *Briefwechsel: Mit Briefen von und an Gabriele Münter und Maria Marc,* ed., introduction, and annotation by Klaus Lankheit (Munich, 1983), p. 40–41. Engl. translation in Lankheit 2005 (see note 2), pp. 15–16.

4 Lankheit 2005 (see note 2), p. 16.

5 Franz Marc, *Der Blaue Reiter,* subscription prospectus, written mid-January 1912; quoted in Kandinsky and Marc 2005 (see note 1), p. 252.

6 Originally published as *Ein Brief* in 1902. See Hugo von Hofmannsthal, *The Lord Chandos Letter and Other Writings,* ed. Joel Rotenberg (New York, 2005).

7 Ulrich Raulff, *Wilde Energien: vier Versuche zu Aby Warburg,* Göttinger Gespräche zur Geschichtswissenschaft 9 (Göttingen, 2003), p. 13.

8 See Lena Bader, et al., eds., *Vergleichendes Sehen* (Munich, 2010).

9 Franz Marc, letter to August Macke, April 12, 1911, in August Macke and Franz Marc, *Briefwechsel 1910–1914*, ed. Karl-Maria Guth, complete new ed. (Berlin, 2014), p. 51. See Horsley 2006 (see note 2), p. 360.

10 Franz Marc, letter to Wassily Kandinsky, April 12, 1911, in Kandinsky and Marc 1983 (see note 3), p. 28.

11 Franz Marc, letter to August Macke, September 8, 1911, in Macke and Marc 2014 (see note 9), p. 72. See also Sigrid Köllner, *Der Blaue Reiter und die "Vergleichende Kunstgeschichte,"* diss., Universität Karlsruhe, 1984, p. 3.

12 Franz Marc, letter to Hugo von Tschudi, October 24, 1911, quoted in *Der Blaue Reiter,* exh. cat. Kunstmuseum Bern (Bern, 1986), p. 196.

13 "Notes on the Illustrations," in Kandinsky and Marc 2005 (see note 1), pp. 267–81.

14 Franz Marc, "Preface to the Second Edition," in ibid., p. 258.

15 Wassily Kandinsky, second postscript of a letter to Franz Marc, October, 29, 1911, in Kandinsky and Marc 1983 (see note 3), p. 69. Regarding the abundance of visual material in the almanac and its sources, see Helmut Friedel and Isabelle Jansen, eds., *"Die Blaue Reiterei stürmt voran": Bildquellen für den Almanach Der Blaue Reiter: Die Sammlung von Wassily Kandinsky und Gabriele Münter,* ed. Helmut Friedel, Isabelle Jansen, and the Gabriele Münter- und Johannes Eichner-Stiftung, exh. cat. Münter-Haus, Murnau (Munich, 2012).

16 See Georges Didi-Huberman, "Was zwischen zwei Bildern passiert: Anachronie, Montage, Allegorie, Pathos," in Bader et al. 2010 (see note 8), pp. 542–43.

17 Uwe Fleckner, "Ohne Worte: Aby Warburgs Bildkomparatistik zwischen wissenschaftlichem Atlas und kunstpublizistischem Experiment," in *Aby Warburg: Bilderreihen und Ausstellungen,* ed. Fleckner and Isabella Woldt (Berlin, 2012), pp. 2–4. See also Andreas Beyer, et al., *Interpositions: Montage d'images et production de sens* (Paris, 2014); and Hubert Locher, *Kunstgeschichte als historische Theorie der Kunst 1750–1950* (Munich, 2001), pp. 203–97.

18 On this topic, see also Lankheit 2005 (see note 2), pp. 38–39, and note 21; and Felix Thürlemann, "Famose Gegenklänge: Der Diskurs der Abbildungen im Almanach "Der Blaue Reiter," in exh. cat. Bern 1986 (see note 12), pp. 210–22.

19 Thürlemann 1986 (see note 18), p. 211.

20 On the distribution of the illustrations in the almanac, see Horsley 2006 (see note 2), pp. 352–62; and Thürlemann 1986 (see note 18), p. 212.

21 Wassily Kandinsky, "Über die Formfrage," in Kandinsky and Marc 1912 (see note 1), p. 99; English ed.: "On the Question of Form," in *Kandinsky: Complete Writings on Art*, ed. Kenneth C. Lindsay and Peter Vergo (Boston, 1982; new, repr. ed., New York, 1994), p. 256.

22 August Macke, "Die Masken," in Kandinsky and Marc 1912 (see note 1), pp. 24–26; English ed.: "Masks," in Kandinsky and Marc 2005 (see note 1), pp. 88–89.

23 Michela Passini, *La Fabrique de l'art national: Le nationalisme et les origines de l'histoire de l'art en France et en Allemagne 1870–1933* (Paris, 2012).

24 Franz Marc, "Zwei Bilder," in Kandinsky and Franz Marc 1912 (see note 1), p. 10; English ed.: "Two Pictures," in Kandinsky and Marc 2005 (see note 1), p. 67.

25 Ibid., in Kandinsky and Franz Marc 1912 (see note 1), p. 8; in Kandinsky and Marc 2005 (see note 1), p. 65.

26 See Thürlemann 1986 (see note 18), pp. 218–21, as well as Thürlemann's suggested analogy with "creative metaphor formation" in literature.

27 See Gottfried Boehm, et al., *Zeigen: Die Rhetorik des Sichtbaren* (Munich, 2010).

28 Wassily Kandinsky, "Franz Marc," in Wassily Kandinsky, *Essays über Kunst und Künstler,* ed. and annotated by Max Bill (Stuttgart, 1955), p. 189.

29 August Macke, letter to Gabriele Münter, September 25, 1911. Quoted in Lankheit 2005 (see note 2), p. 19.

30 See also Thürlemann 1986 (see note 18), p. 221.

31 Ibid., p. 220.

32 See Horsley 2006 (see note 2), pp. 361–62.

33 Thürlemann 1986 (see note 18), p. 218.

34 In fact, a comparative hanging that spanned cultures and epochs was already occasionally found at the time in exhibitions and private collections. This phenomenon still remains largely uninvestigated. See Köllner 1984 (see note 11), pp. 149–62; and Fleckner 2012 (see note 17), p. 5.

35 Aby Warburg, *Der Bilderatlas Mnemosyne,* ed. by Martin Warnke with the assistance of Claudia Brink (Berlin, 2000); also Fleckner 2012 (see note 17), pp. 1–18.

36 Angelika Weissbach, "Majestät geruht zu trinken und andere Zufälle—Kandinskys 'Bilder-Atlas' für seinen Unterricht am Bauhaus," in *Wassily Kandinsky: Lehrer am Bauhaus,* ed. Magdalena Droste, exh. cat. Bauhaus-Archiv/Museum für Gestaltung (Berlin, 2014), pp. 134–36.

37 See ibid., p. 144.

38 Lankheit 2005 (see note 2), p. 26.

39 Ibid., pp. 29–35.

40 Wassily Kandinsky, "'Der Blaue Reiter' (Rückblick)," *Das Kunstblatt* 14 (1930), p. 59 note. See also Lankheit 2005 (see note 2), p. 18 and note 8.

41 "The Flanders tapestry is the first, still colossal type of the automobile [*sic*] visual vehicle, which, removed from the wall, was a precursor of sheets of paper printed with imagery, not only in terms of its mobility but in terms of its technique designed for multiple reproduction. [These sheets], copper engravings and woodcuts, made the exchange of expressive values between north and south into a vital process in the circulation of European style generation." Aby Warburg, "Introduction," in Warburg 2000 (see note 35), p. 5.

42 Georges Didi-Huberman, *L'Image survivante: Histoire de l'art et temps des fantômes selon Aby Warburg* (Paris, 2002). See also Fleckner 2012 (see note 17), p. 4. On the fundamental debate over Warburg's supposedly uncritical, Eurocentric reception of non-European cultures, see Claudia Wedepohl, "Nachwort," in Aby Warburg, *Schlangenritual: Ein Reisebericht* (Berlin, 2011), pp. 129–40; here pp. 137–38.

43 See Annegret Hoberg and Isabelle Jansen, *Franz Marc: Werkverzeichnis,* vol. 1, *Gemälde* (Munich, 2004), no. 194; and Carl Georg Heise, *Persönliche Erinnerungen an Aby Warburg,* ed. and annotated by Björn Biester and Hans-Michael Schäfer (Wiesbaden, 2005), pp. 16–17. See also Karen Michels and Charlotte Schoell-Glass, eds., *Aby Warburg: Tagebuch der Kulturwissenschaftlichen Bibliothek Warburg* (Berlin, 2001), p. 325: "It's exactly the same as back then, regarding the acquisition of the Marc painting: now everybody is for it, but back then it was 'a waste of money.'"

44 On this topic, see Aby Warburg, letter to his wife, Mary, April 22, 1926; Warburg Institute Archive, Family Correspondence; reference thanks to Claudia Wedepohl, London.

KANDINSKY, MARC, AND DER BLAUE REITER: THE ALMANAC

ULF KÜSTER

Der Blaue Reiter (The Blue Rider) is the title of an almanac edited by Wassily Kandinsky and Franz Marc and published by Piper Verlag in Munich in May 1912. The almanac gathered together writings by mostly contemporaneous artists, who included, apart from the editors, August Macke and David Burliuk, among others. These were augmented by illustrations of European and non-European works of fine art, but also folk art and "music supplements."

The publication was preceded by two exhibitions, organized by Kandinsky and Marc. *Die Erste Ausstellung der Redaktion Der Blaue Reiter* (*First Exhibition of the Editors of Der Blaue Reiter*), was held in 1911 at the Galerie Thannhauser in Munich, and comprised works by the artists who contributed to the almanac. It subsequently traveled to various cities in Germany and Europe. The following show, held at the Munich gallery of Hans Goltz in February to April 1912, was *Die Zweite Ausstellung der Redaktion Der Blaue Reiter: Schwarz-Weiss* (*Second Exhibition of the Editors of Der Blaue Reiter: Black and White*) and featured exclusively works on paper. Here, the number of artists represented was considerably expanded, such as by members of the Brücke (Bridge) artists' group, which had been founded in Dresden in 1905.

Yet the Blaue Reiter was not an association of artists who worked together and developed a specific style, as did the members of the Brücke. Rather, the publication of the almanac might better be described as a reaction to the constricting statutes of an artists' association. In early December 1911, as preparations for the almanac were underway, Kandinsky, his partner Gabriele Münter, and Marc left the Neue Künstlervereinigung München (New Artists' Association Munich), a progressive group co-founded in 1909 by Kandinsky and Münter. As the variety of the almanac suggests, one of its messages was an emphasis on artistic individualism, just the opposite of the idea of an artists' group.

Der Blaue Reiter (*The Blaue Reiter Almanac*) has since taken on the status of a founding manifesto of modernism.[1] Yet it was not a programmatic pamphlet like the *Futurist Manifesto,* issued by Filippo Tommaso Marinetti in 1909. The reason for the almanac's importance does not become evident until we view it as a whole. The point is not only the content of the writings it includes but also their relationship to one another and to the illustrations, whose arrangement in turn tells a story in itself. Then there are the notes to musical compositions by Arnold Schoenberg, Alban Berg, and Anton von Webern. Schoenberg's setting of the poem "Herzgewächse" (Heart's Foliage) by Maurice Maeterlinck was even reproduced as a facsimile of the composer's handwritten version. Though never expressly mentioned, the volume was based on the idea of the total or interdisciplinary work of art, combining visual art, literature, and music.[2]

While the message of the almanac amounted to a synopsis of all of its parts, this is never expressed as a program. The renewal of art envisioned by Kandinsky and Marc was to take place in an open and unrestricted manner. The thrust is well expressed in Kandinsky's famous letter to Marc of June 19, 1911, in which he outlines his plans for the almanac:

> *A kind of almanac (yearbook) with reproductions and articles . . . and a* chronicle!! *that is, reports on exhibitions reviewed by artists, and artists alone. In the book the entire year must be reflected; and a link to the past as well as a ray to the future must give this mirror its full life. . . . We will put an Egyptian work beside a small Zeh [drawings by two children of the Munich architect August Zeh, an acquaintance of Kandinsky's], a Chinese work beside a Rousseau, a folk print beside a Picasso, and the like! . . . The book could be called "The Chain," or some other title. . .* .[3]

As the references to a mirror of the present day, "a link to the past," and a "ray to the future" indicate, the two editors' project was based on a notion of historical and future relationships among the arts. The seemingly most diverse things would be combined, such as art from Antiquity and children's drawings, or non-European art and contemporary European art. What Kandinsky and Marc purposely left out was nineteenth-century art and works marked by academic principles from the Renaissance onward. Without referring to the almanac, Marc explained this to his friend Macke on January 14, 1911, after visiting the Ethnological Museum of Berlin:

> *I find it such a matter of course that we seek a rebirth of our artistic feeling in the cold, early light of artistic intelligence [i.e. works from Cameroon and Inca art] rather than in cultures that have already run through a thousand-year course, such as the Japanese and the Italian Renaissance.*[4]

The mention of an early "artistic intelligence" in connection with non-European art might sound condescending to us today; the sculptures from Cameroon also derive from a very long tradition. What was important to Marc was the idea of creating a connection (Kandinsky spoke of a "link" in the letter quoted above) with the roots of a primal and unsullied art. In Kandinsky's essay printed in the almanac, "Über die Formfrage" (On the Question of Form), his rejection of traditional, naturalistic approaches to the figure and space as represented by nineteenth-century academic art becomes apparent in his naming of Henri Rousseau—who roundly rejected the academicism of his day—as a protagonist of "Great Realism" as opposed to "Great Abstraction."[5] Rousseau, correspondingly, was the artist whose work was most frequently reproduced in the almanac.[6]

According to Kandinsky, the publication's name was decided on over coffee in the arbor of the Marcs' home in Sindelsdorf, Upper Bavaria: "we both loved blue, Marc liked horses, I riders. So the name came by itself."[7] The woodcut on the almanac's cover, a stylized rider on a horse, was created by Kandinsky. For the first edition in board covers it was printed from a blue block, and for the edition bound in cloth from a blue and a light red one (cat. pp. 28–29). The rider in a blue jacket is truly a *blue* rider, and the horse too is blue, perhaps an homage on Kandinsky's part to the blue horses of his co-editor. The image shows the horse and rider in mid-leap—surely a reference to the dynamic advance of the New Art. The fact that a horse and rider were chosen at all, these not really being a symbol of progress at the start of the twentieth century, once more suggests the notion of a "link to the past."

A further important aspect of *Der Blaue Reiter* almanac that, although not expressly mentioned in the book, becomes apparent from the character of the publication as a whole: the international nature of art that Marc and Kandinsky championed. As editors they advanced this in an unpublished preface that remains valid far beyond its time:

> *It should be almost superfluous to emphasize specifically that in our case the principle of internationalism is the only one possible. However, in these times we must say that an individual nation is only one of the creators of all art; one alone can never be a whole. As with a personality, the national element is automatically reflected in each great work. But in the last resort this national coloration is merely incidental. The whole work, called art, knows no borders or nations, only humanity.*[8]

So what are the special traits of this new "whole work, called art"? Perhaps it is worth recalling that the almanac was published at a time when Kandinsky's art in particular, but Marc's as well, was in the process of moving from figuration to abstraction, or nonobjectivity. The publication served as a kind of legitimation of this development.[9] So any exhibition that deals with this subject should concern itself with not only the almanac but also the artistic transformation of those on whose ideas it rested.

The new imagery was intended to find its place in the development of an art in which individual works—despite all their differences—would be linked, on the level of the "spiritual," by an "internal necessity." In the essay "Über die Formfrage" mentioned above, Kandinsky explained that the form of a work was "the external expression of inner content," but that "of prime importance in the question of form is whether or not form has arisen out of internal necessity."[10] What "The Spiritual in Art,"[11] or the "great spirituality"[12] was, remained subjective. Basically, it was a matter of explaining that despite all external differences, there was something akin to a spiritual affinity among all artists and within all of art. Linked to this was the question of good and less good art. This question dominated the discussion about art, independently of its content, from the onset of modernism. The *Blaue Reiter* editors' attempt to develop subjective categories for "good art" did not succeed. Still, this very failure seems to shed light on the traits that good art must have, which might indeed be called a "spiritual" quality or "internal necessity."

1 See the essay by Andreas Beyer in the present catalogue: "Thinking in Pictures: What Franz Marc and Wassily Kandinsky Have in Common with Aby Warburg," pp. 18–23.

2 For a general discussion, see Jessica Horsley, *Der Almanach des* Blauen Reiters *als Gesamtkunstwerk: Eine interdisziplinäre Untersuchung* (Frankfurt am Main et al., 2006), pp. 351–84, esp. pp. 351–52.

3 Wassily Kandinsky, letter to Franz Marc, June 19, 1911, in Wassily Kandinsky and Franz Marc, *Briefwechsel: Mit Briefen von und an Gabriele Münter und Maria Marc*, ed., introduction, and annotation by Klaus Lankheit (Munich, 1983), pp. 39–41, here pp. 40–41; English trans.: Klaus Lankheit, "A History of the Almanac," in *The Blaue Reiter Almanac,* ed. Wassily Kandinsky and Franz Marc, documentary edition, ed. and with an introduction by Klaus Lankheit, trans. Henning Falkenstein with assistance of Manug Terzian and Gertrude Hinderlie (New York, 1974; repr. Boston, 2005), pp. 15–16.

4 Franz Marc, letter to August Macke, January 14, 1911, in August Macke and Franz Marc, *Briefwechsel 1910–1914*, ed. Karl-Maria Guth, complete new ed. (Berlin, 2014), pp. 38–41, here p. 38.

5 Wassily Kandinsky, "Über die Formfrage," in *Der Blaue Reiter,* ed. Wassily Kandinsky and Franz Marc (Munich, 1912), pp. 74–100; English ed.: "On the Question of Form," in *Kandinsky: Complete Writings on Art,* ed. Kenneth C. Lindsay and Peter Vergo (Boston, 1982; new, repr. ed., New York, 1994), pp. 242 and 252.

6 Kandinsky and Marc 2005 (see note 3), figs. 82, 86, 92, 95, 103, 104, 111.

7 Wassily Kandinsky, "Der Blaue Reiter (Rückblick)" in *Das Kunstblatt* 14 (1930), p. 59 note; English trans.: Lankheit 2005 (see note 3), p. 18 and note 8.

8 Wassily Kandinsky and Franz Marc, unpublished manuscript, probably October 1911. A typewritten version is preserved at the Estate of August Macke and a handwritten one at the Estate of Gabriele Münter, from which the present quotation is taken. In *"Die Blaue Reiterei stürmt voran": Bildquellen für den Almanach Der Blaue Reiter: Die Sammlung von Wassily Kandinsky und Gabriele Münter,* ed. Helmut Friedel, Isabelle Jansen, and the Gabriele Münter- und Johannes Eichner-Stiftung, exh. cat. Münter-Haus, Murnau (Munich, 2012), pp. 87–89, here p. 89. English trans.: Wassily Kandinsky and Franz Marc, "Almanac: *Der Blaue Reiter,*" in Kandinsky and Marc 2005 (see note 3), p. 251.

9 See the remark by Itzhak Goldberg regarding the connection between degree of recognition and theoretical statement in Kandinsky by contrast to Jawlensky, in Itzhak Goldberg, *Jawlensky, ou, le visage promis,* with a preface by Marie-José Mondzain (Paris, 1998), p. 43.

10 Kandinsky 1912 (see note 5), pp. 75, 78; English ed.: Kandinsky 1994 (see note 5), pp. 237 and 239.

11 The title of a famous essay by Kandinsky, published shortly before the almanac: Wassily Kandinsky, *Über das Geistige in der Kunst: insbesondere in der Malerei*, with an introduction by Max Bill and a foreword and annotation on the rev. new ed. by Jelena Hahl-Fontaine (Munich, 1912; 5th ed., Zurich, 2016); English ed.: "On the Spiritual in Art," in *Kandinsky: Complete Writings on Art,* ed. Kenneth C. Lindsay and Peter Vergo (Boston, 1982; new, repr. ed., New York, 1994), pp. 119–219.

12 Wassily Kandinsky and Franz Marc, from the unpublished preface of October 1911, see Friedel and Jansen 2012 (see note 8), p. 87; English trans: Kandinsky and Marc 2005 (see note 8), p. 250.

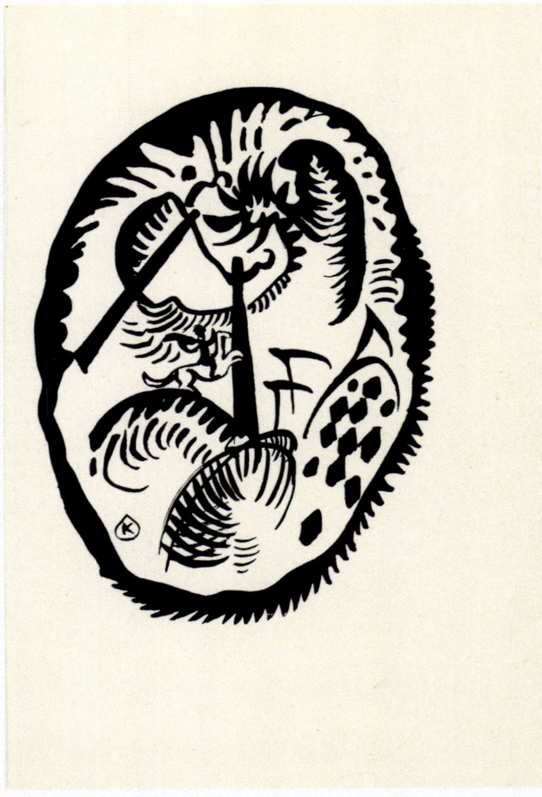

Wassily Kandinsky, Vignette for *Der Blaue Reiter* almanac, 1911, print on paper (chemitype) after an India ink drawing, 14.5 x 10.7 cm, Musée national d'art moderne, Centre Pompidou, Paris, Bequest of Nina Kandinsky, 1981

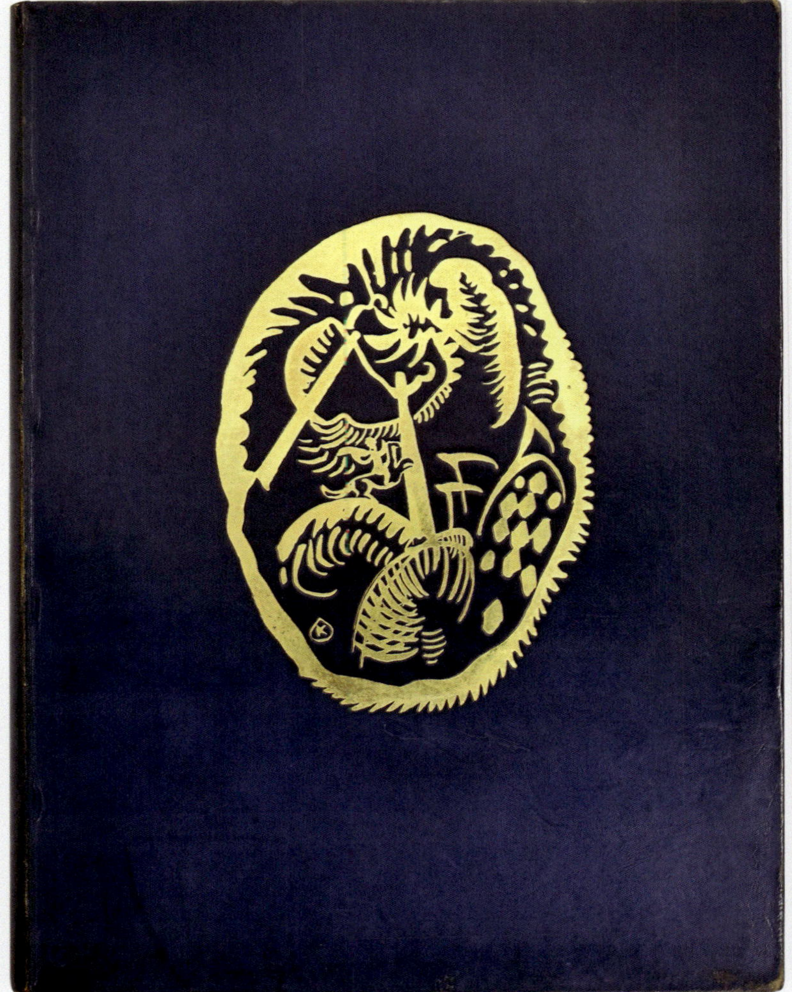

Wassily Kandinsky and Franz Marc, *Der Blaue Reiter* almanac, Munich, 1912, deluxe first edition (no. 21 of 50), bound in blue morocco, vignette tooled in gold on the front cover, 29 x 22.2 cm, ahlers collection

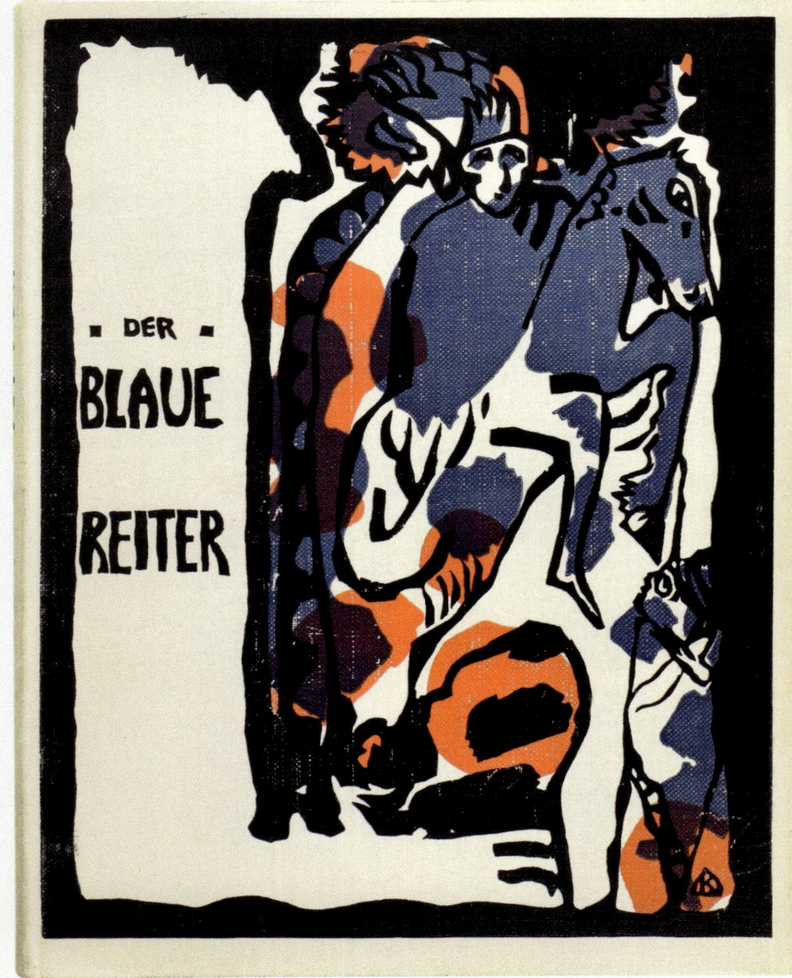

Wassily Kandinsky and Franz Marc, *Der Blaue Reiter* almanac, Munich, 1912, first standard edition, bound in cloth, galvano print of the color woodcut in red, blue, and black on the front cover and the vignette on the back, 29.5 x 23 cm, ahlers collection

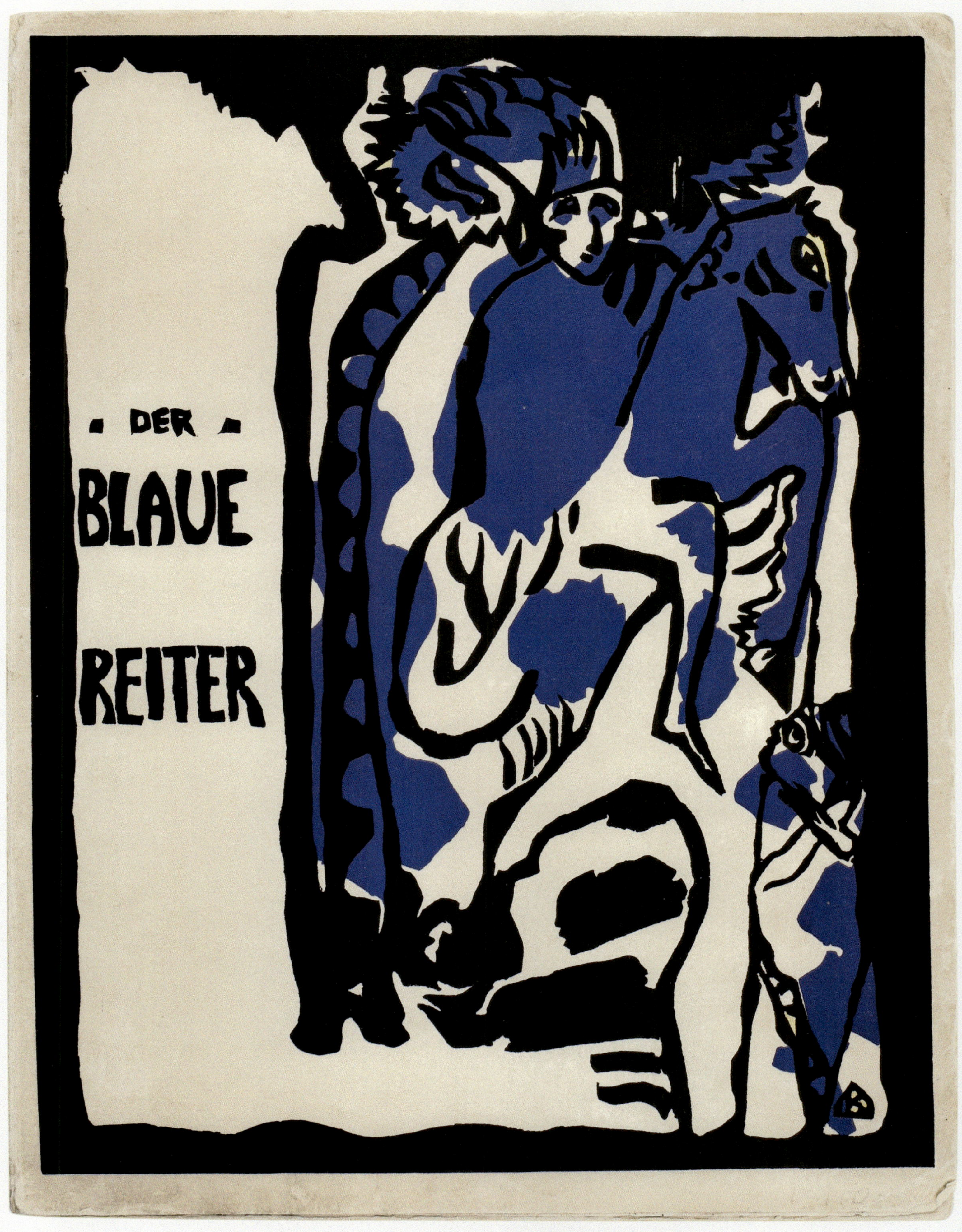

Wassily Kandinsky and Franz Marc, *Der Blaue Reiter* almanac, Munich, 1912, first standard edition, in board covers, galvano print of the color woodcut in blue and black on the front cover and the vignette on the back, 29.5 x 22.3 cm, ahlers collection

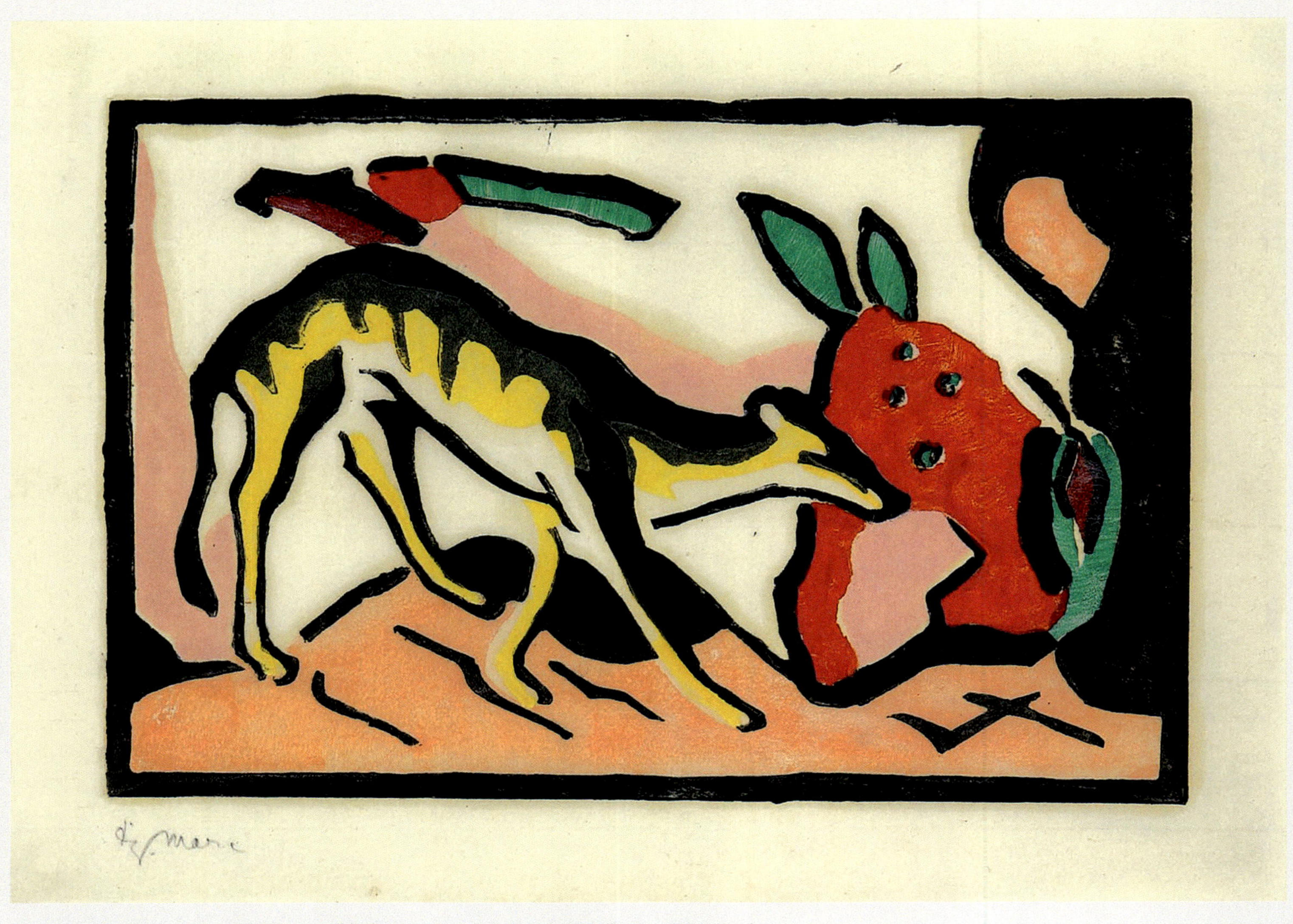

Franz Marc, *Fabulous Beast*, 1912, color woodblock print, 14.5 x 21.7 cm, private collection, Switzerland

One of the illustrations in Franz Marc's essay "Geistige Güter" (Spiritual Treasures) shows a *Chinese Painting* from the author's own collection of Far Eastern art. The vignette of a horse is from his own hand. It forms a caesura in the text, after which Marc turns to the deceased director general of the Bavarian State Collections of Paintings, Hugo von Tschudi, who supported the Blaue Reiter artists from early on. The almanac is dedicated to him.

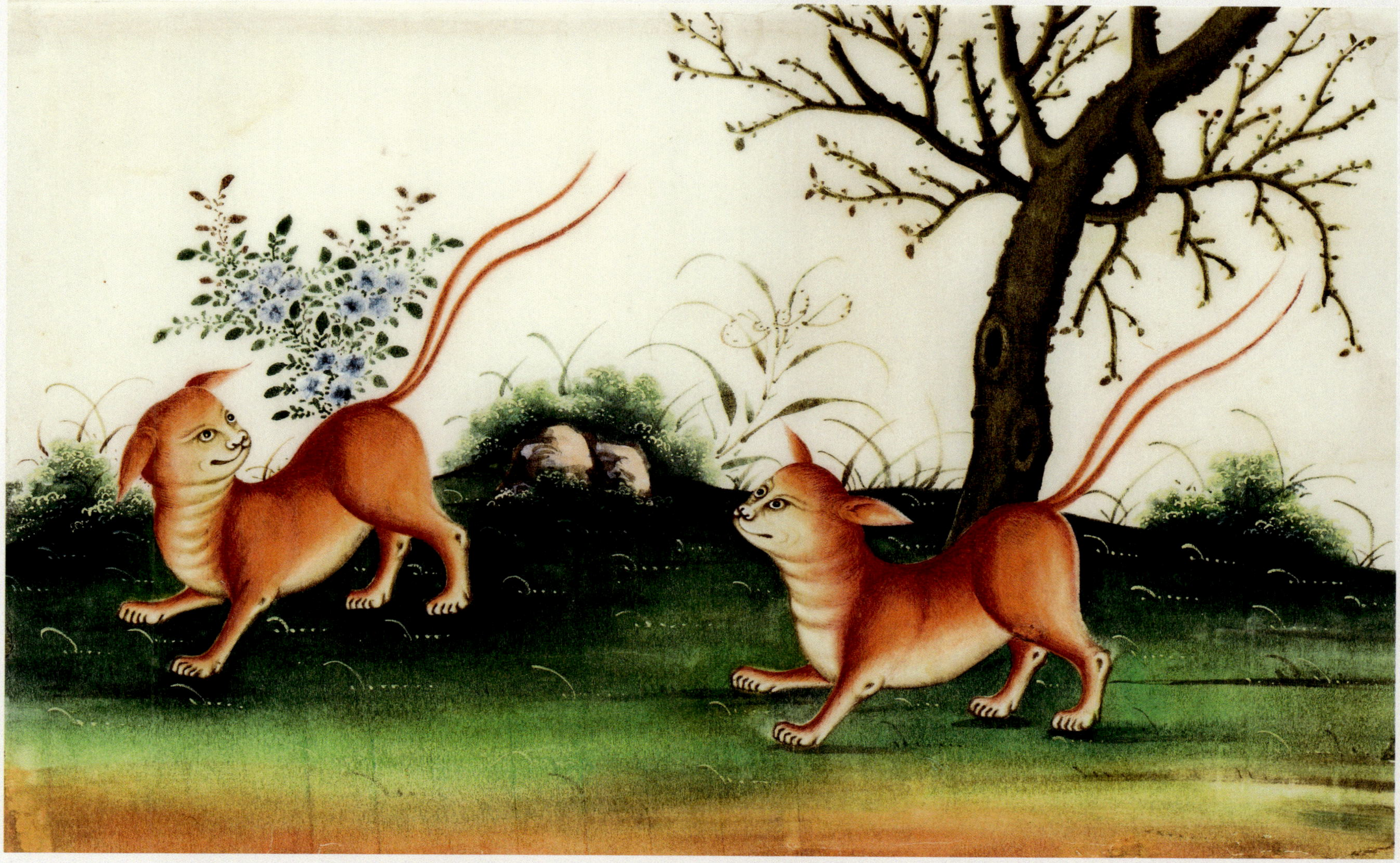

Mythical Creatures, China (?), 18th–19th cent., gouache on paper, 20.5 x 33 cm, Franz Marc Museum, Kochel am See, Franz Marc Stiftung, on permanent loan from the community of Maria Marc's heirs

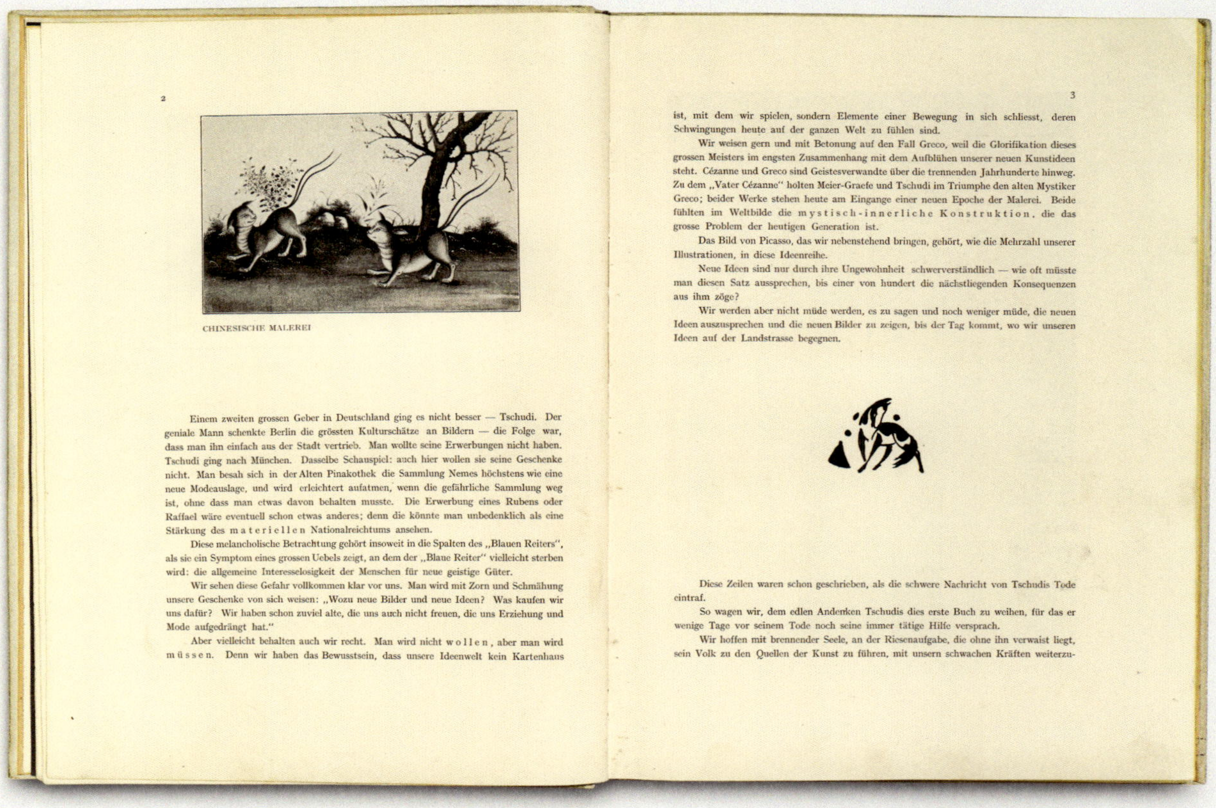

2

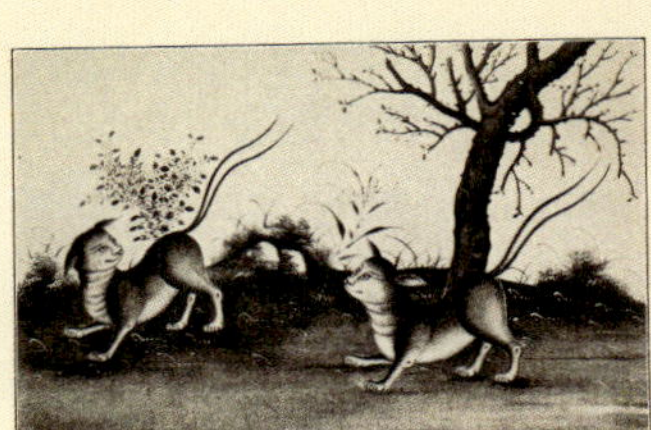

CHINESISCHE MALEREI

Einem zweiten grossen Geber in Deutschland ging es nicht besser — Tschudi. Der geniale Mann schenkte Berlin die grössten Kulturschätze an Bildern — die Folge war, dass man ihn einfach aus der Stadt vertrieb. Man wollte seine Erwerbungen nicht haben. Tschudi ging nach München. Dasselbe Schauspiel: auch hier wollen sie seine Geschenke nicht. Man besah sich in der Alten Pinakothek die Sammlung Nemes höchstens wie eine neue Modeauslage, und wird erleichtert aufatmen, wenn die gefährliche Sammlung weg ist, ohne dass man etwas davon behalten musste. Die Erwerbung eines Rubens oder Raffael wäre eventuell schon etwas anderes; denn die könnte man unbedenklich als eine Stärkung des materiellen Nationalreichtums ansehen.

Diese melancholische Betrachtung gehört insoweit in die Spalten des „Blauen Reiters", als sie ein Symptom eines grossen Uebels zeigt, an dem der „Blaue Reiter" vielleicht sterben wird: die allgemeine Interesselosigkeit der Menschen für neue geistige Güter.

Wir sehen diese Gefahr vollkommen klar vor uns. Man wird mit Zorn und Schmähung unsere Geschenke von sich weisen: „Wozu neue Bilder und neue Ideen? Was kaufen wir uns dafür? Wir haben schon zuviel alte, die uns auch nicht freuen, die uns Erziehung und Mode aufgedrängt hat."

Aber vielleicht behalten auch wir recht. Man wird nicht wollen, aber man wird müssen. Denn wir haben das Bewusstsein, dass unsere Ideenwelt kein Kartenhaus

3

ist, mit dem wir spielen, sondern Elemente einer Bewegung in sich schliesst, deren Schwingungen heute auf der ganzen Welt zu fühlen sind.

Wir weisen gern und mit Betonung auf den Fall Greco, weil die Glorifikation dieses grossen Meisters im engsten Zusammenhang mit dem Aufblühen unserer neuen Kunstideen steht. Cézanne und Greco sind Geistesverwandte über die trennenden Jahrhunderte hinweg. Zu dem „Vater Cézanne" holten Meier-Graefe und Tschudi im Triumphe den alten Mystiker Greco; beider Werke stehen heute am Eingange einer neuen Epoche der Malerei. Beide fühlten im Weltbilde die mystisch-innerliche Konstruktion, die das grosse Problem der heutigen Generation ist.

Das Bild von Picasso, das wir nebenstehend bringen, gehört, wie die Mehrzahl unserer Illustrationen, in diese Ideenreihe.

Neue Ideen sind nur durch ihre Ungewohnheit schwerverständlich — wie oft müsste man diesen Satz aussprechen, bis einer von hundert die nächstliegenden Konsequenzen aus ihm zöge?

Wir werden aber nicht müde werden, es zu sagen und noch weniger müde, die neuen Ideen auszusprechen und die neuen Bilder zu zeigen, bis der Tag kommt, wo wir unseren Ideen auf der Landstrasse begegnen.

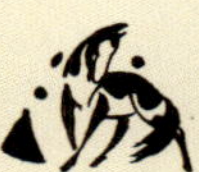

Diese Zeilen waren schon geschrieben, als die schwere Nachricht von Tschudis Tode eintraf.

So wagen wir, dem edlen Andenken Tschudis dies erste Buch zu weihen, für das er wenige Tage vor seinem Tode noch seine immer tätige Hilfe versprach.

Wir hoffen mit brennender Seele, an der Riesenaufgabe, die ohne ihn verwaist liegt, sein Volk zu den Quellen der Kunst zu führen, mit unsern schwachen Kräften weiterzu-

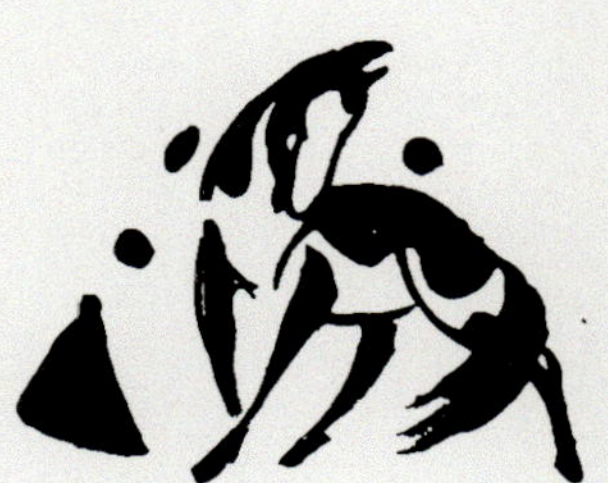

From the beginning of their Murnau period, Gabriele Münter and Wassily Kandinsky collected folk paintings on glass and mirrors. Their simplified depictions and flat colors may well have influenced Kandinsky's declaration that "of prime importance in the question of form is whether or not form has arisen out of internal necessity." The mirror painting of the *Death of Saint Joseph* is juxtaposed with *La Femme à la mandoline au piano* (*Woman with Mandolin at the Piano*) by Pablo Picasso, whose facetted Cubist forms, according to Marc, introduce "mystical inner construction" into the "sequence of ideas," and in Kandinsky's eyes illustrate the "complete destruction of the material relationship."

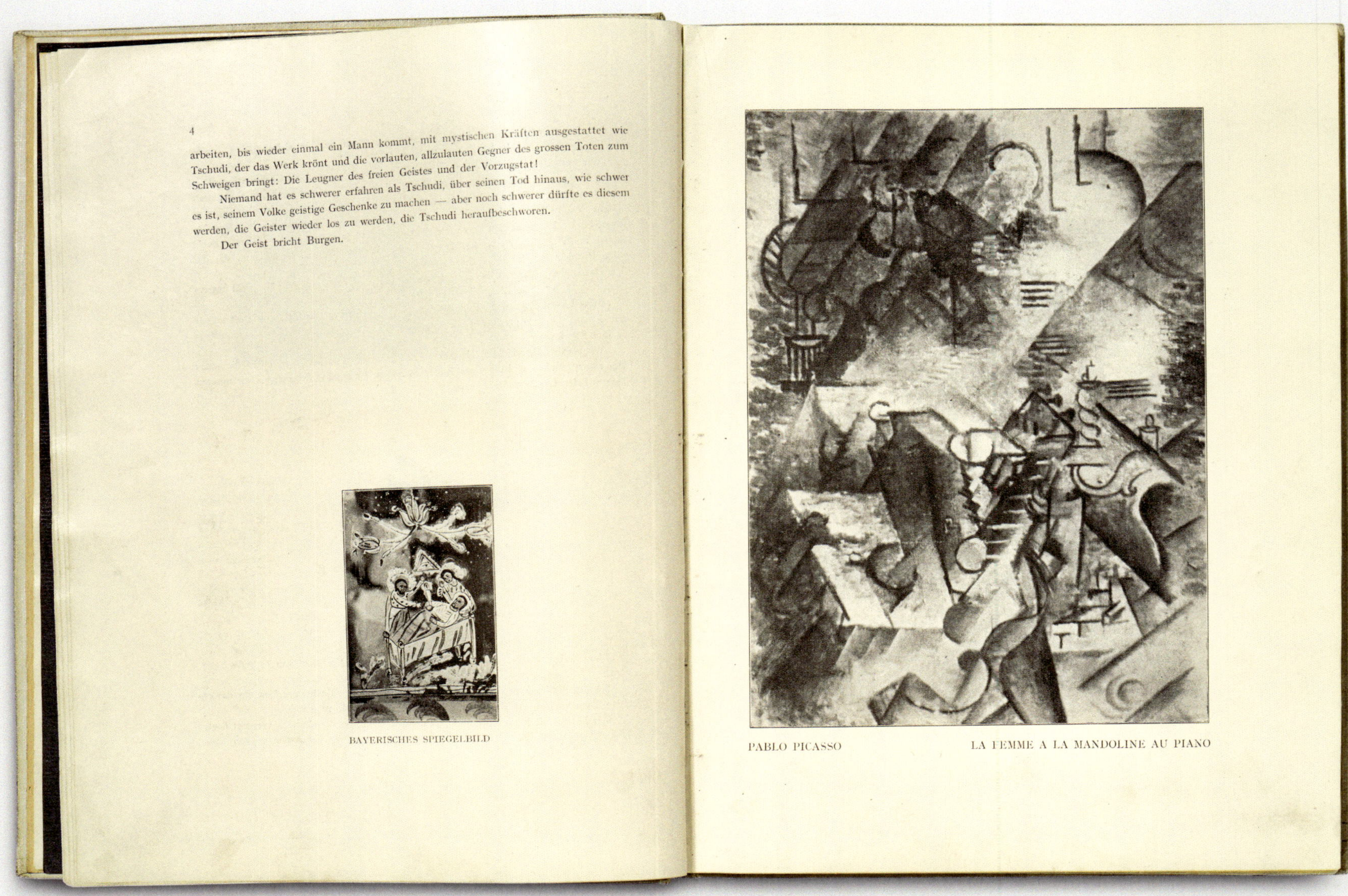

4

arbeiten, bis wieder einmal ein Mann kommt, mit mystischen Kräften ausgestattet wie Tschudi, der das Werk krönt und die vorlauten, allzulauten Gegner des grossen Toten zum Schweigen bringt: Die Leugner des freien Geistes und der Vorzugstat!

Niemand hat es schwerer erfahren als Tschudi, über seinen Tod hinaus, wie schwer es ist, seinem Volke geistige Geschenke zu machen — aber noch schwerer dürfte es diesem werden, die Geister wieder los zu werden, die Tschudi heraufbeschworen.

Der Geist bricht Burgen.

BAYERISCHES SPIEGELBILD

PABLO PICASSO LA FEMME A LA MANDOLINE AU PIANO

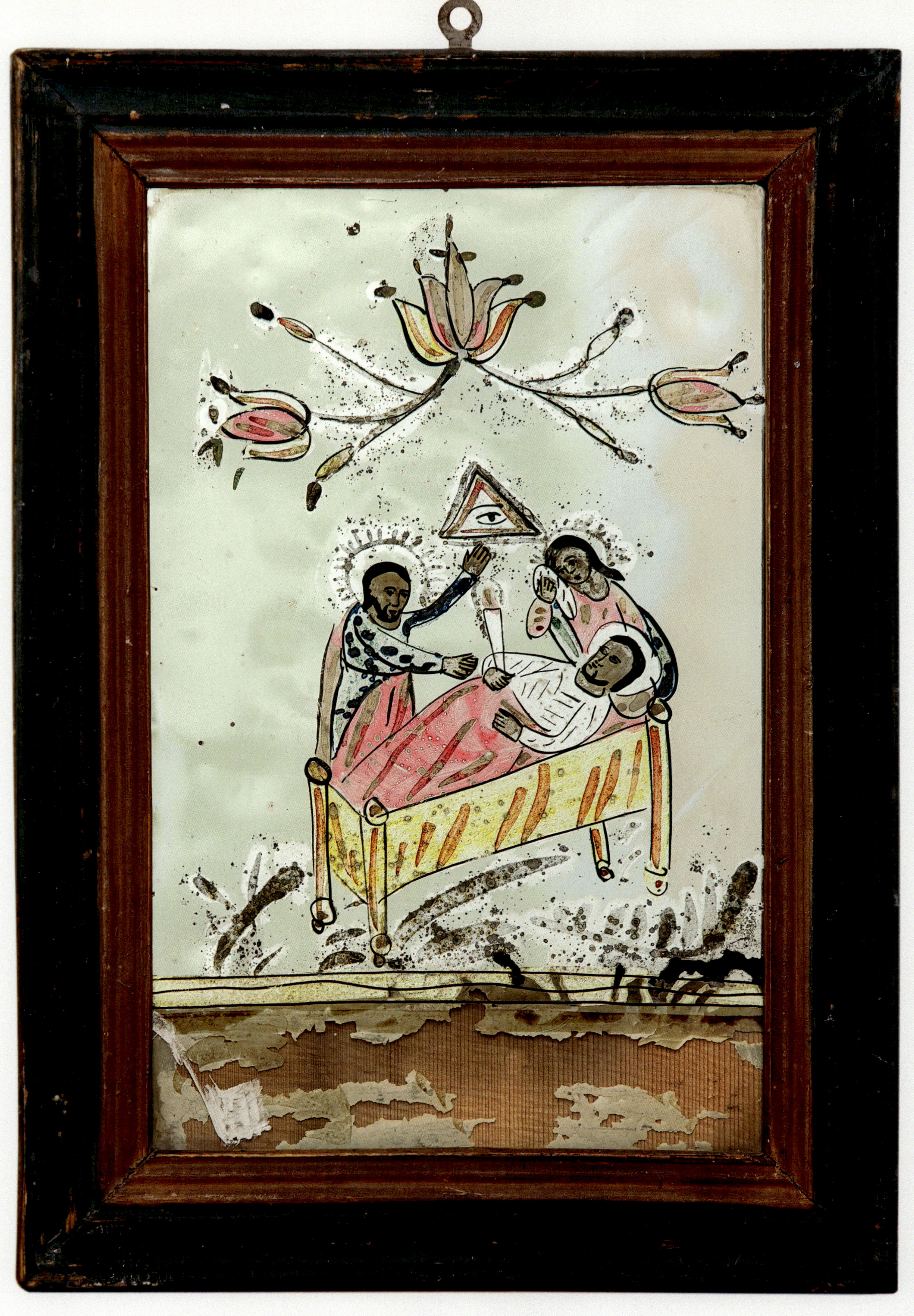

Death of Saint Joseph, Raimundsreut (Bavaria), 1775–1800, mirror painting, 32.6 x 22.8 cm, Oberammergau Museum

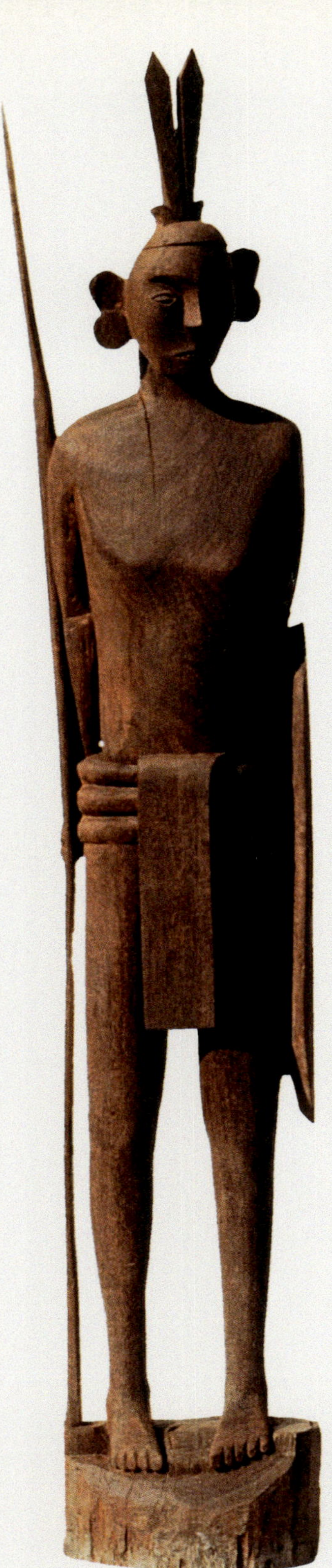

Ancestral figure of the Dayak, South Borneo, ca. 1900, palisander, 190 x 39 x 33 cm, Bernisches Historisches Museum, Bern

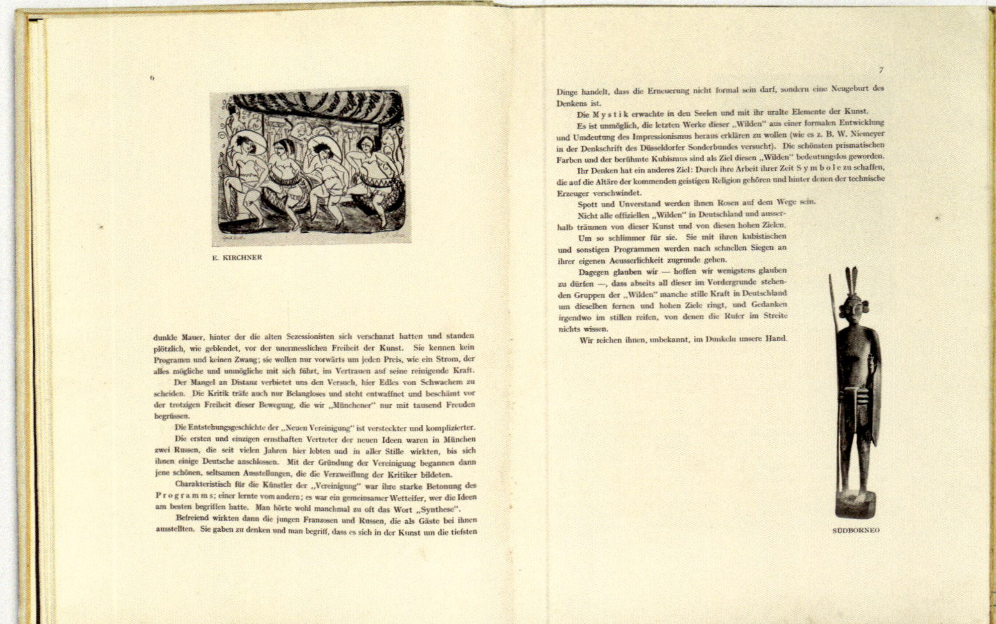

6

E. KIRCHNER

dunkle Mauer, hinter der die alten Sezessionisten sich verschanzt hatten und standen plötzlich, wie geblendet, vor der unermesslichen Freiheit der Kunst. Sie kennen kein Programm und keinen Zwang; sie wollen nur vorwärts um jeden Preis, wie ein Strom, der alles mögliche und unmögliche mit sich führt, im Vertrauen auf seine reinigende Kraft.

Der Mangel an Distanz verbietet uns den Versuch, hier Edles von Schwachem zu scheiden. Die Kritik träfe auch nur Belangloses und steht entwaffnet und beschämt vor der trotzigen Freiheit dieser Bewegung, die wir „Münchener" nur mit tausend Freuden begrüssen.

Die Entstehungsgeschichte der „Neuen Vereinigung" ist versteckter und komplizierter.

Die ersten und einzigen ernsthaften Vertreter der neuen Ideen waren in München zwei Russen, die seit vielen Jahren hier lebten und in aller Stille wirkten, bis sich ihnen einige Deutsche anschlossen. Mit der Gründung der Vereinigung begannen dann jene schönen, seltsamen Ausstellungen, die die Verzweiflung der Kritiker bildeten.

Charakteristisch für die Künstler der „Vereinigung" war ihre starke Betonung des Programms; einer lernte vom andern; es war ein gemeinsamer Wetteifer, wer die Ideen am besten begriffen hatte. Man hörte wohl manchmal zu oft das Wort „Synthese".

Befreiend wirkten dann die jungen Franzosen und Russen, die als Gäste bei ihnen ausstellten. Sie gaben zu denken und man begriff, dass es sich in der Kunst um die tiefsten

7

Dinge handelt, dass die Erneuerung nicht formal sein darf, sondern eine Neugeburt des Denkens ist.

Die Mystik erwachte in den Seelen und mit ihr uralte Elemente der Kunst.

Es ist unmöglich, die letzten Werke dieser „Wilden" aus einer formalen Entwicklung und Umdeutung des Impressionismus heraus erklären zu wollen (wie es z. B. W. Niemeyer in der Denkschrift des Düsseldorfer Sonderbundes versucht). Die schönsten prismatischen Farben und der berühmte Kubismus sind als Ziel diesen „Wilden" bedeutungslos geworden.

Ihr Denken hat ein anderes Ziel: Durch ihre Arbeit ihrer Zeit Symbole zu schaffen, die auf die Altäre der kommenden geistigen Religion gehören und hinter denen der technische Erzeuger verschwindet.

Spott und Unverstand werden ihnen Rosen auf dem Wege sein.

Nicht alle offiziellen „Wilden" in Deutschland und ausserhalb träumen von dieser Kunst und von diesen hohen Zielen.

Um so schlimmer für sie. Sie mit ihren kubistischen und sonstigen Programmen werden nach schnellen Siegen an ihrer eigenen Aeusserlichkeit zugrunde gehen.

Dagegen glauben wir — hoffen wir wenigstens glauben zu dürfen —, dass abseits all dieser im Vordergrunde stehenden Gruppen der „Wilden" manche stille Kraft in Deutschland um dieselben fernen und hohen Ziele ringt, und Gedanken irgendwo im stillen reifen, von denen die Rufer im Streite nichts wissen.

Wir reichen ihnen, unbekannt, im Dunkeln unsere Hand.

SÜDBORNEO

Paul Gauguin and Henri Matisse themselves esteemed and collected what was known as primitive art. In the almanac, objects from Asia and Africa, Russian and Bavarian folk art, children's drawings, and amateur paintings were illustrated on equal terms alongside contemporary European art. The juxtaposition of a lithograph by Ernst Ludwig Kirchner and an ancestral figure of the Dayak from the Historical Museum in Bern apparently relates to the concept of "the savage." This savage quality, which, in the early twentieth century, was still seen in negative terms when applied to non-European peoples, was often purposely quoted by European artists, including Kirchner. In Marc's almanac essay "Die 'Wilden' Deutschlands" (The "Savages" of Germany), we read: "In this time of the great struggle for a new art we fight like disorganized 'savages,'" by which Marc meant especially the Brücke artists.

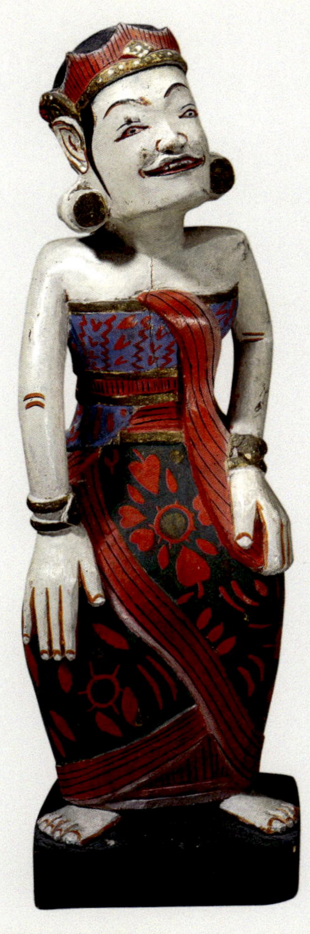

Female figure, Gianyar, Bali, ca. 1900, painted wood, 31.5 x 9 x 9 cm, Bernisches Historisches Museum, Bern

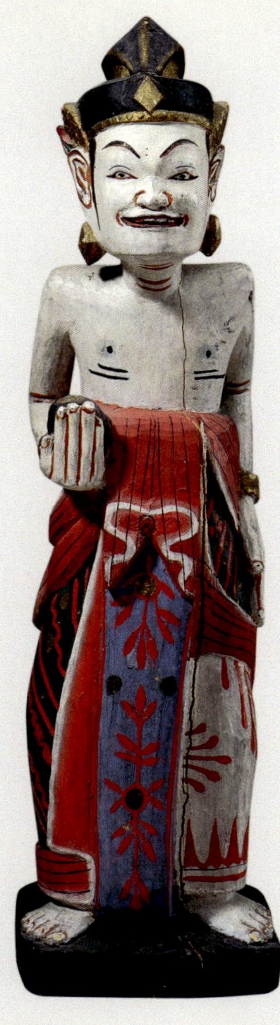

Male figure, Gianyar, Bali, ca. 1900, painted wood, 33 x 8.5 x 8.5 cm, Bernisches Historisches Museum, Bern

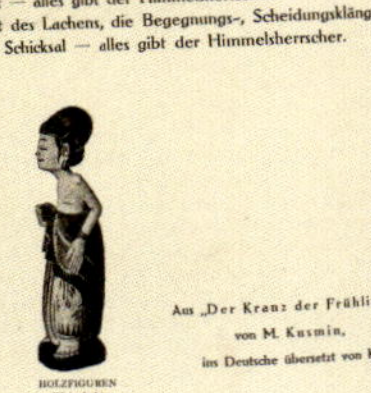

It is not surprising to find an early work by Paul Cézanne prefacing Roger Allard's article "Die Kennzeichen der Erneuerung in der Malerei" (Signs of Renewal in Painting). The almanac's editors viewed Cézanne as the father of modern art. His depiction of Autumn is set off by a poem on spring by Mikhail Kuzmin on the opposite page. Whether the Balinese wooden figures flanking the poem were chosen for their formal analogies or for correspondences in "expressions of their inner lives," which Macke ascribed to Cézanne's work, remains an open question. The transition from one image to the next, Kandinsky hoped, would trigger in the viewer's mind "many vibrations and he will enter the sphere of art."

The quotation from Goethe on the left and the essay by the composer Thomas von Hartmann that begins on the right-hand page both deal with the subject of music. The lack of a "thorough bass" in painting, lamented by Goethe, was understood as a challenge to contemporary artists. The arrangement of the illustrations is based on purely formal principles. The figure on the left, then believed to date from the late medieval period, has since been identified as a nineteenth-century imitation. The composition is framed by this figure, leaning to the right, as well as by the mother and child leaning to the left. The position of the initial "Ü" echoes the silhouette of the Balinese figure.

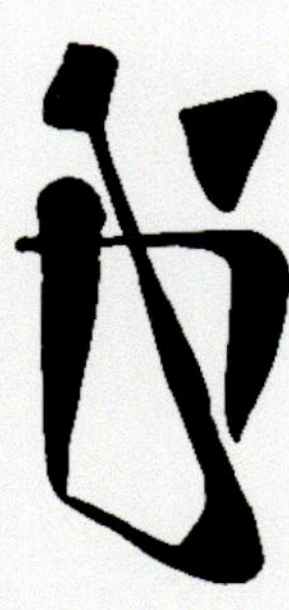

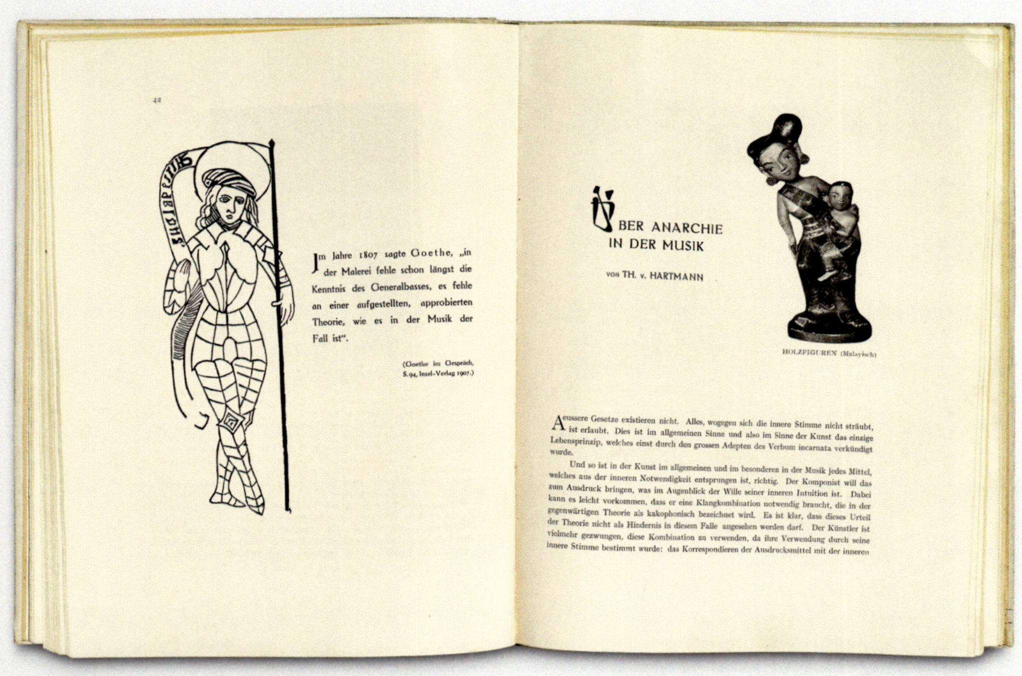

42

Im Jahre 1807 sagte Goethe, „in der Malerei fehle schon längst die Kenntnis des Generalbasses, es fehle an einer aufgestellten, approbierten Theorie, wie es in der Musik der Fall ist".

(Goethe im Gespräch, S. 94, Insel-Verlag 1907.)

ÜBER ANARCHIE IN DER MUSIK

von TH. v. HARTMANN

HOLZFIGUREN (Malayisch)

Aeussere Gesetze existieren nicht. Alles, wogegen sich die innere Stimme nicht sträubt, ist erlaubt. Dies ist im allgemeinen Sinne und also im Sinne der Kunst das einzige Lebensprinzip, welches einst durch den grossen Adepten des Verbum incarnata verkündigt wurde.

Und so ist in der Kunst im allgemeinen und im besonderen in der Musik jedes Mittel, welches aus der inneren Notwendigkeit entsprungen ist, richtig. Der Komponist will das zum Ausdruck bringen, was im Augenblick der Wille seiner inneren Intuition ist. Dabei kann es leicht vorkommen, dass er eine Klangkombination notwendig braucht, die in der gegenwärtigen Theorie als kakophonisch bezeichnet wird. Es ist klar, dass dieses Urteil der Theorie nicht als Hindernis in diesem Falle angesehen werden darf. Der Künstler ist vielmehr gezwungen, diese Kombination zu verwenden, da ihre Verwendung durch seine innere Stimme bestimmt wurde: das Korrespondieren der Ausdrucksmittel mit der inneren

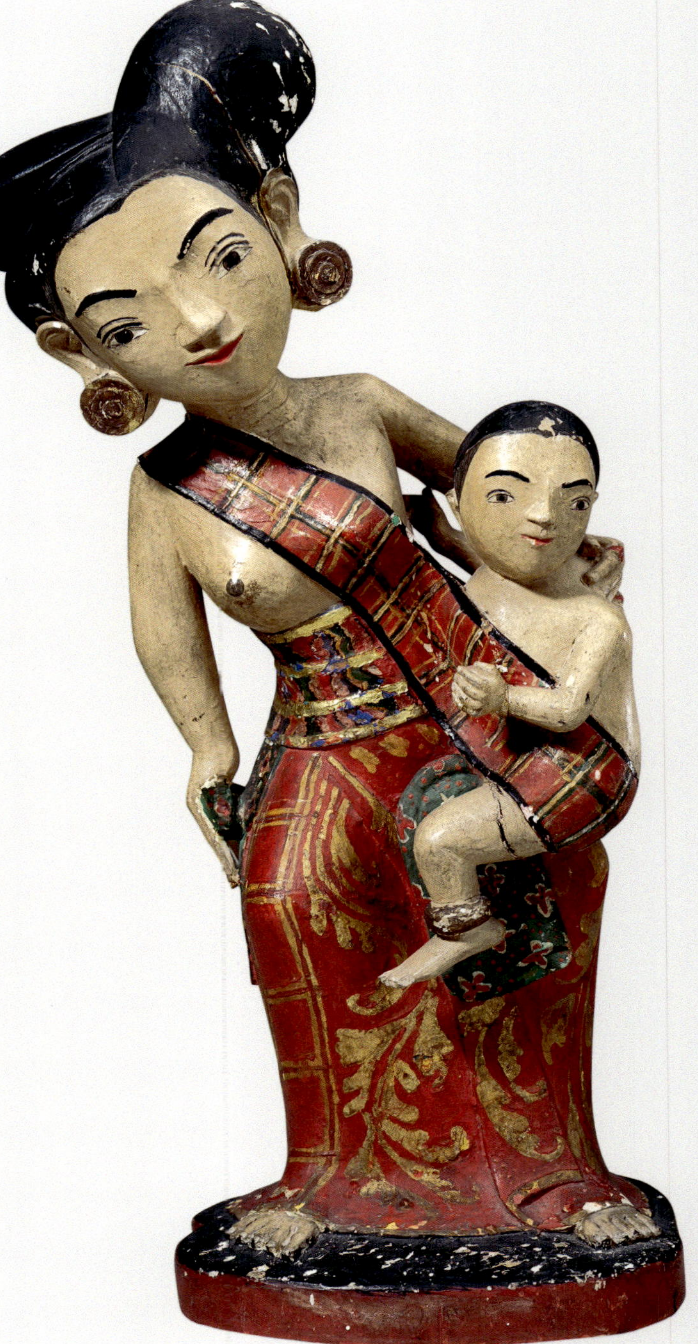

Mother and child, Gianyar, Bali, ca. 1900, painted wood, 53.7 x 28.5 x 19 cm, Bernisches Historisches Museum, Bern

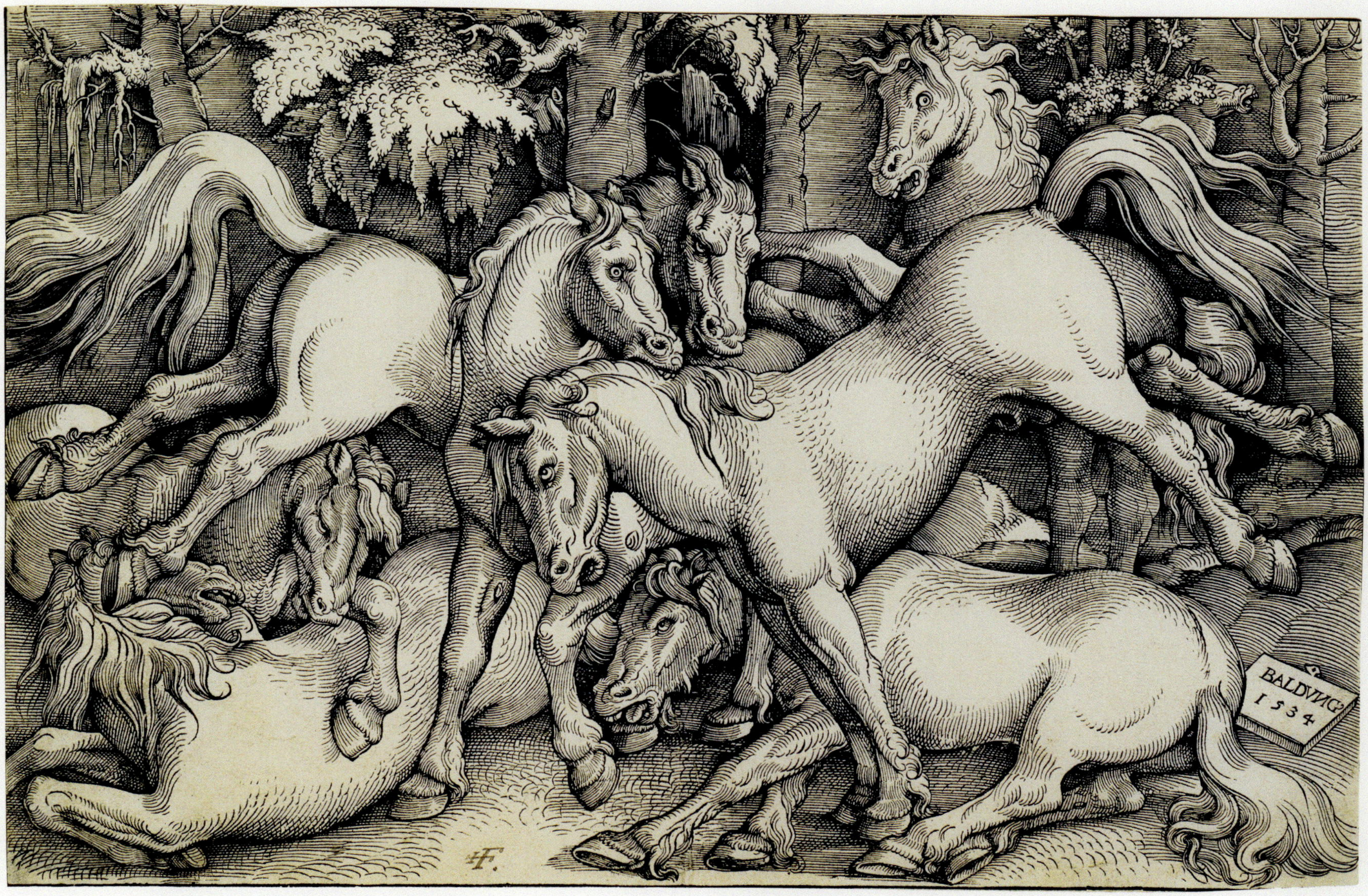

Hans Baldung Grien, *Fighting Horses in a Forest Clearing*, 1534, woodcut on handmade paper, 21.3 x 32.1 cm, ahlers collection

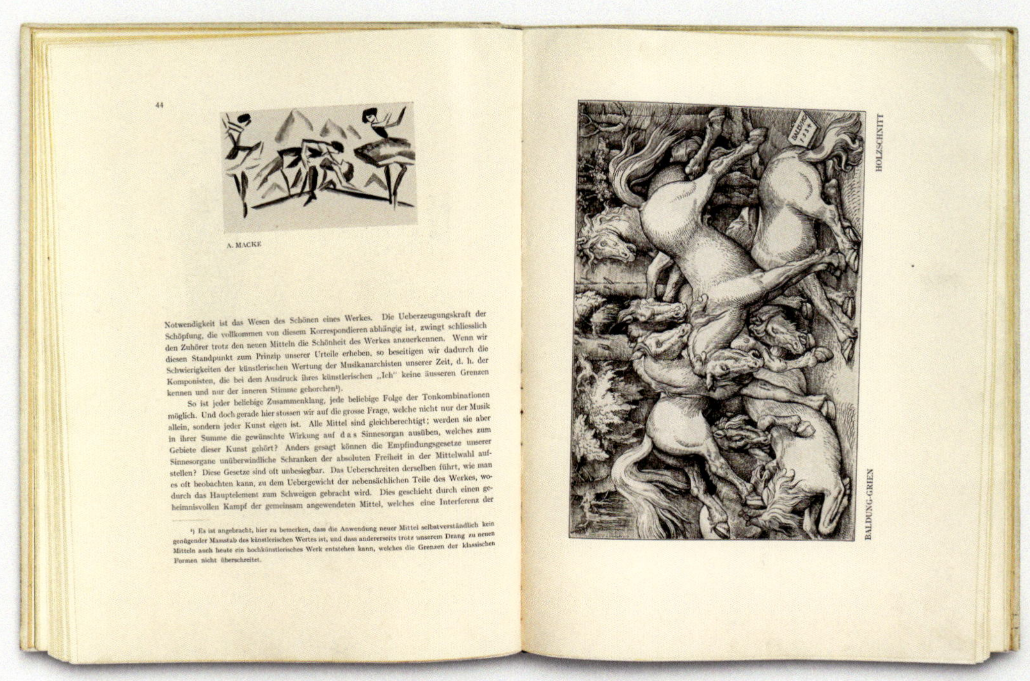

44

A. MACKE

Notwendigkeit ist das Wesen des Schönen eines Werkes. Die Ueberzeugungskraft der Schöpfung, die vollkommen von diesem Korrespondieren abhängig ist, zwingt schliesslich den Zuhörer trotz den neuen Mitteln die Schönheit des Werkes anzuerkennen. Wenn wir diesen Standpunkt zum Prinzip unserer Urteile erheben, so beseitigen wir dadurch die Schwierigkeiten der künstlerischen Wertung der Musikanarchisten unserer Zeit, d. h. der Komponisten, die bei dem Ausdruck ihres künstlerischen „Ich" keine äusseren Grenzen kennen und nur der inneren Stimme gehorchen¹).

So ist jeder beliebige Zusammenklang, jede beliebige Folge der Tonkombinationen möglich. Und doch gerade hier stossen wir auf die grosse Frage, welche nicht nur der Musik allein, sondern jeder Kunst eigen ist. Alle Mittel sind gleichberechtigt; werden sie aber in ihrer Summe die gewünschte Wirkung auf d a s Sinnesorgan ausüben, welches zum Gebiete dieser Kunst gehört? Anders gesagt können die Empfindungsgesetze unserer Sinnesorgane unüberwindliche Schranken der absoluten Freiheit in der Mittelwahl aufstellen? Diese Gesetze sind oft unbesiegbar. Das Ueberschreiten derselben führt, wie man es oft beobachten kann, zu dem Uebergewicht der nebensächlichen Teile des Werkes, wodurch das Hauptelement zum Schweigen gebracht wird. Dies geschieht durch einen geheimnisvollen Kampf der gemeinsam angewendeten Mittel, welches eine Interferenz der

¹) Es ist angebracht, hier zu bemerken, dass die Anwendung neuer Mittel selbstverständlich kein genügender Masstab des künstlerischen Wertes ist, und dass andererseits trotz unserem Drang zu neuen Mitteln auch heute ein hochkünstlerisches Werk entstehen kann, welches die Grenzen der klassischen Formen nicht überschreitet.

HOLZSCHNITT

BALDUNG-GRIEN

Hans Baldung Grien's famous woodcut of battling stallions may represent a consciously chosen contrast to Marc's approach to the subject of the horse. As Kandinsky notes in "Über die Formfrage" (On the Question of Form), the "greatest external difference becomes the greatest internal equality."

Robert Delaunay's depiction of Paris *La Fenêtre sur la ville* (*The City No. 2*) illustrates the last page of the almanac's essay by Erwin Ritter von Busse on "Die Kompositionsmittel bei Robert Delaunay" (Robert Delaunay's Methods of Composition). Here the author sums up Delaunay's development as achieving an ability "to extend [his] ideas to everything that the eye and mind can conceive: the inherent laws of everything that exists and its subjective understanding and representation."

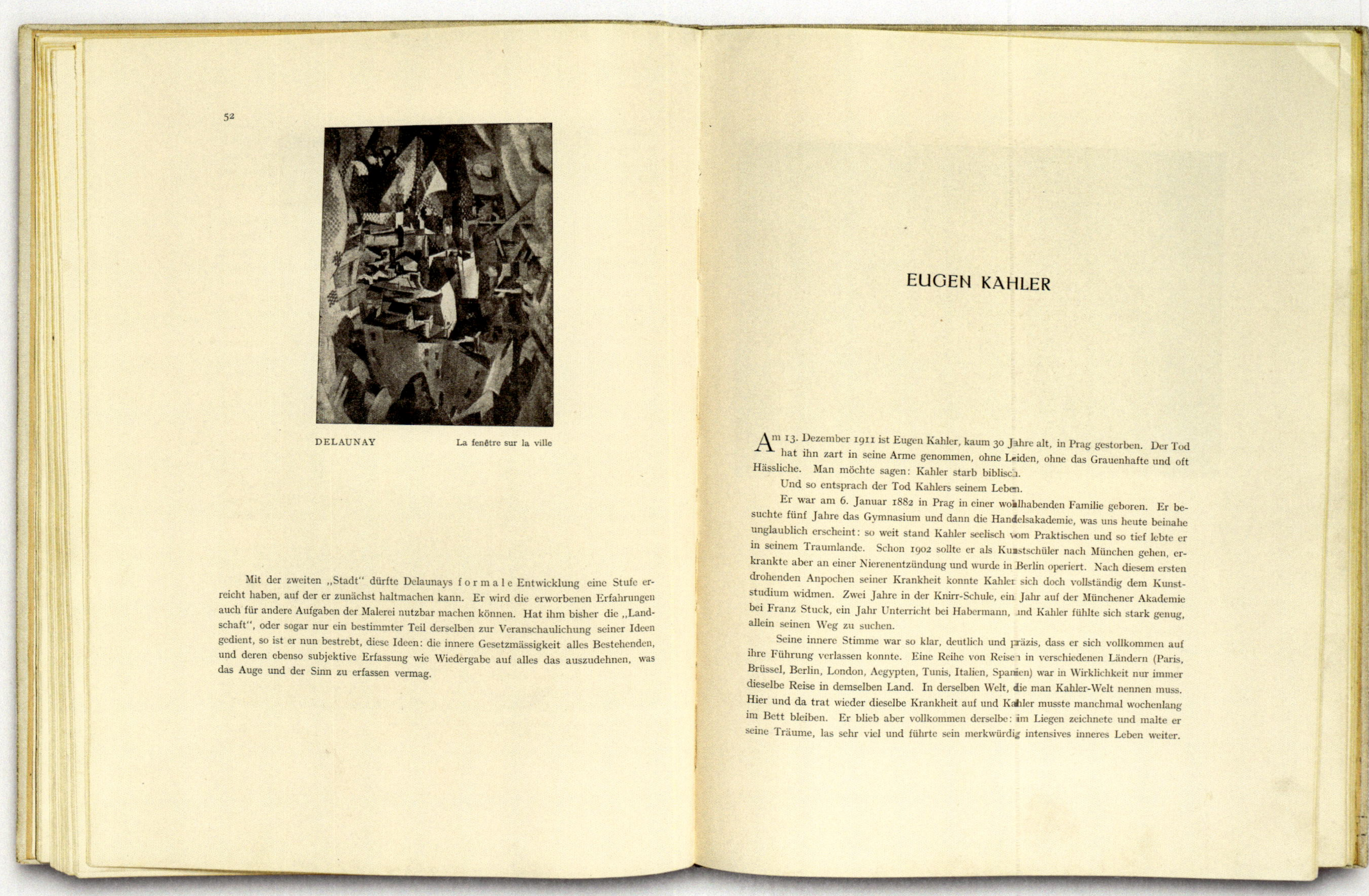

52

DELAUNAY La fenêtre sur la ville

Mit der zweiten „Stadt" dürfte Delaunays formale Entwicklung eine Stufe erreicht haben, auf der er zunächst haltmachen kann. Er wird die erworbenen Erfahrungen auch für andere Aufgaben der Malerei nutzbar machen können. Hat ihm bisher die „Landschaft", oder sogar nur ein bestimmter Teil derselben zur Veranschaulichung seiner Ideen gedient, so ist er nun bestrebt, diese Ideen: die innere Gesetzmässigkeit alles Bestehenden, und deren ebenso subjektive Erfassung wie Wiedergabe auf alles das auszudehnen, was das Auge und der Sinn zu erfassen vermag.

EUGEN KAHLER

Am 13. Dezember 1911 ist Eugen Kahler, kaum 30 Jahre alt, in Prag gestorben. Der Tod hat ihn zart in seine Arme genommen, ohne Leiden, ohne das Grauenhafte und oft Hässliche. Man möchte sagen: Kahler starb biblisch.

Und so entsprach der Tod Kahlers seinem Leben.

Er war am 6. Januar 1882 in Prag in einer wohlhabenden Familie geboren. Er besuchte fünf Jahre das Gymnasium und dann die Handelsakademie, was uns heute beinahe unglaublich erscheint: so weit stand Kahler seelisch vom Praktischen und so tief lebte er in seinem Traumlande. Schon 1902 sollte er als Kunstschüler nach München gehen, erkrankte aber an einer Nierenentzündung und wurde in Berlin operiert. Nach diesem ersten drohenden Anpochen seiner Krankheit konnte Kahler sich doch vollständig dem Kunststudium widmen. Zwei Jahre in der Knirr-Schule, ein Jahr auf der Münchener Akademie bei Franz Stuck, ein Jahr Unterricht bei Habermann, und Kahler fühlte sich stark genug, allein seinen Weg zu suchen.

Seine innere Stimme war so klar, deutlich und präzis, dass er sich vollkommen auf ihre Führung verlassen konnte. Eine Reihe von Reisen in verschiedenen Ländern (Paris, Brüssel, Berlin, London, Aegypten, Tunis, Italien, Spanien) war in Wirklichkeit nur immer dieselbe Reise in demselben Land. In derselben Welt, die man Kahler-Welt nennen muss. Hier und da trat wieder dieselbe Krankheit auf und Kahler musste manchmal wochenlang im Bett bleiben. Er blieb aber vollkommen derselbe: im Liegen zeichnete und malte er seine Träume, las sehr viel und führte sein merkwürdig intensives inneres Leben weiter.

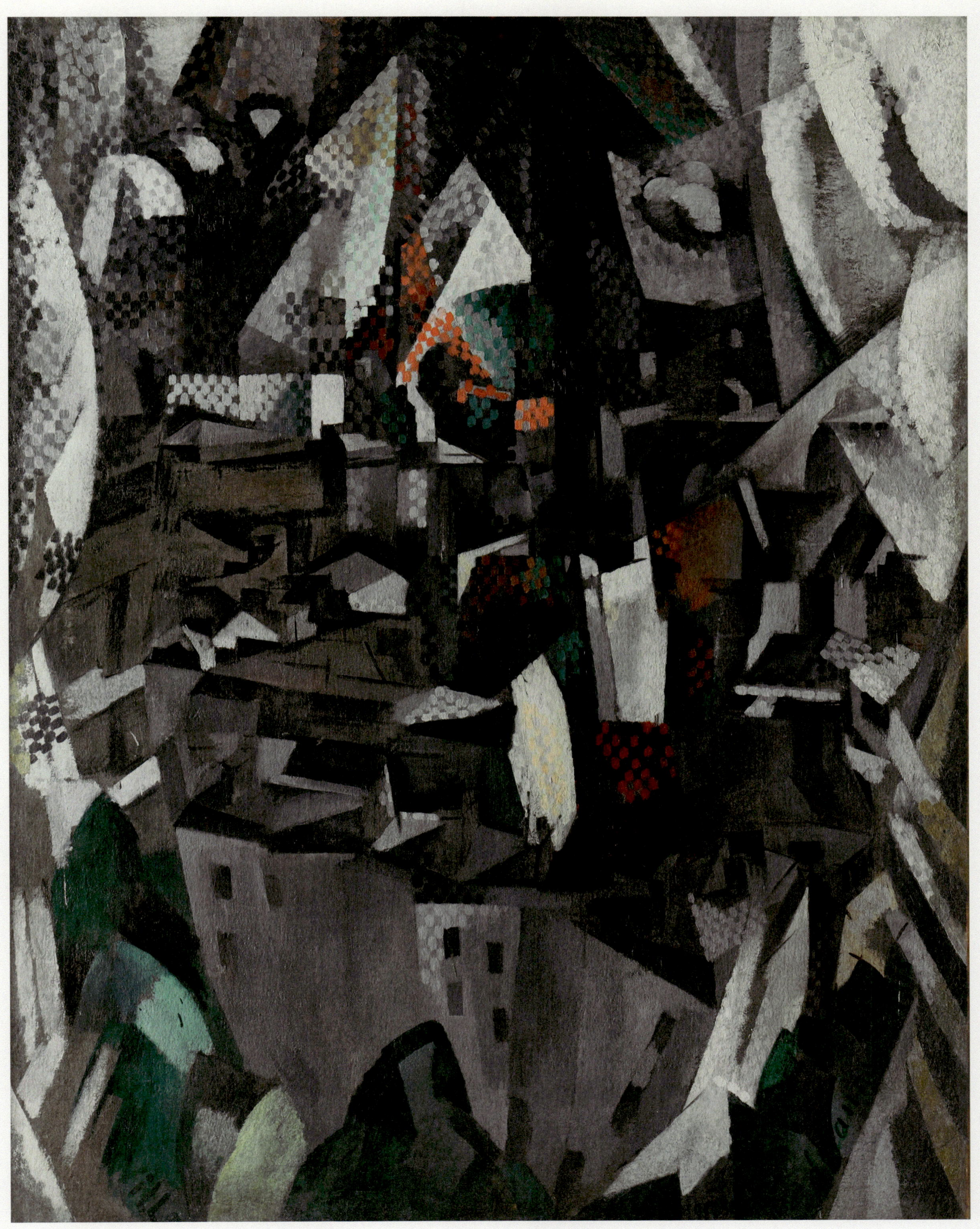

Robert Delaunay, *The City No. 2*, 1910, oil on canvas, 146 x 114 cm,
Musée national d'art moderne, Centre Pompidou, Paris, purchase, 1947

In the almanac Kandinsky memorialized his fellow artist Eugen von Kahler, who had died prematurely. This obituary was likely the first publication about Kahler, who passed away in December 1911, shortly before the opening of the first exhibition of the Blaue Reiter.

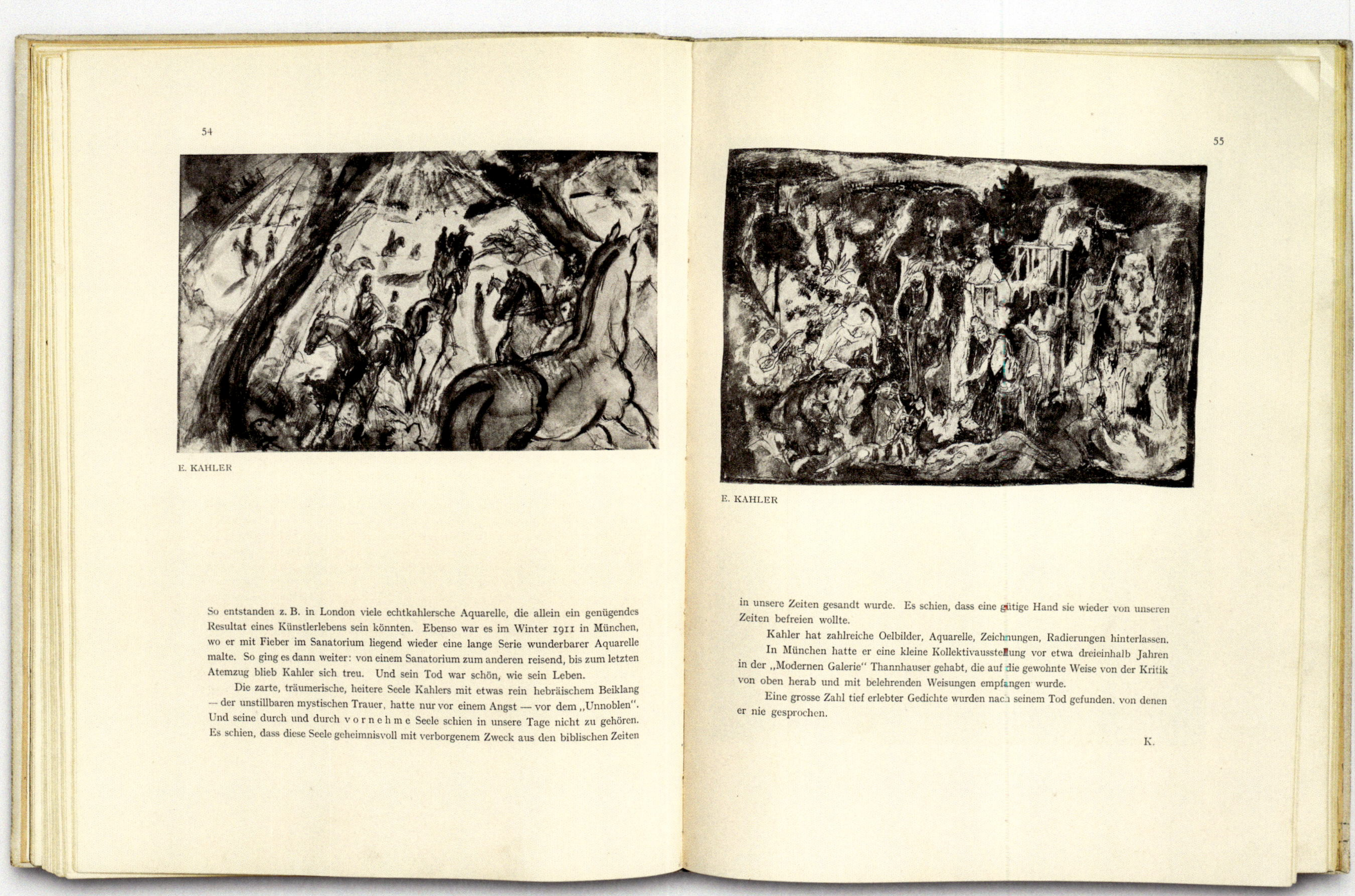

54

E. KAHLER

So entstanden z. B. in London viele echtkahlersche Aquarelle, die allein ein genügendes Resultat eines Künstlerlebens sein könnten. Ebenso war es im Winter 1911 in München, wo er mit Fieber im Sanatorium liegend wieder eine lange Serie wunderbarer Aquarelle malte. So ging es dann weiter: von einem Sanatorium zum anderen reisend, bis zum letzten Atemzug blieb Kahler sich treu. Und sein Tod war schön, wie sein Leben.

Die zarte, träumerische, heitere Seele Kahlers mit etwas rein hebräischem Beiklang — der unstillbaren mystischen Trauer, hatte nur vor einem Angst — vor dem „Unnoblen". Und seine durch und durch v o r n e h m e Seele schien in unsere Tage nicht zu gehören. Es schien, dass diese Seele geheimnisvoll mit verborgenem Zweck aus den biblischen Zeiten

55

E. KAHLER

in unsere Zeiten gesandt wurde. Es schien, dass eine gütige Hand sie wieder von unseren Zeiten befreien wollte.

Kahler hat zahlreiche Oelbilder, Aquarelle, Zeichnungen, Radierungen hinterlassen.

In München hatte er eine kleine Kollektivausstellung vor etwa dreieinhalb Jahren in der „Modernen Galerie" Thannhauser gehabt, die auf die gewohnte Weise von der Kritik von oben herab und mit belehrenden Weisungen empfangen wurde.

Eine grosse Zahl tief erlebter Gedichte wurden nach seinem Tod gefunden, von denen er nie gesprochen.

K.

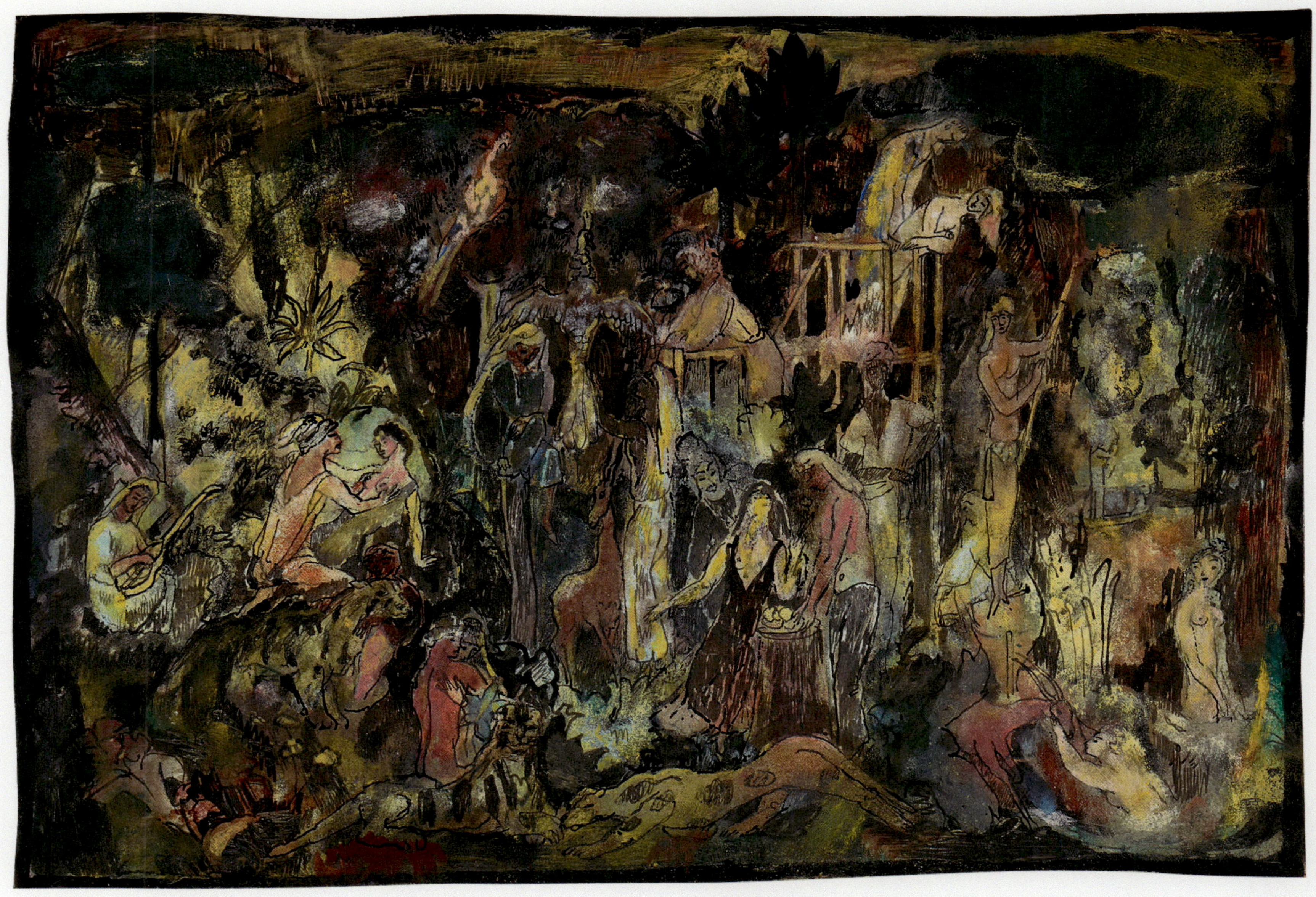

Eugen von Kahler, *Love Garden,* 1910–11, opaque colors and India ink on paper (on cardboard), 19 x 27 cm, Städtische Galerie im Lenbachhaus, Munich

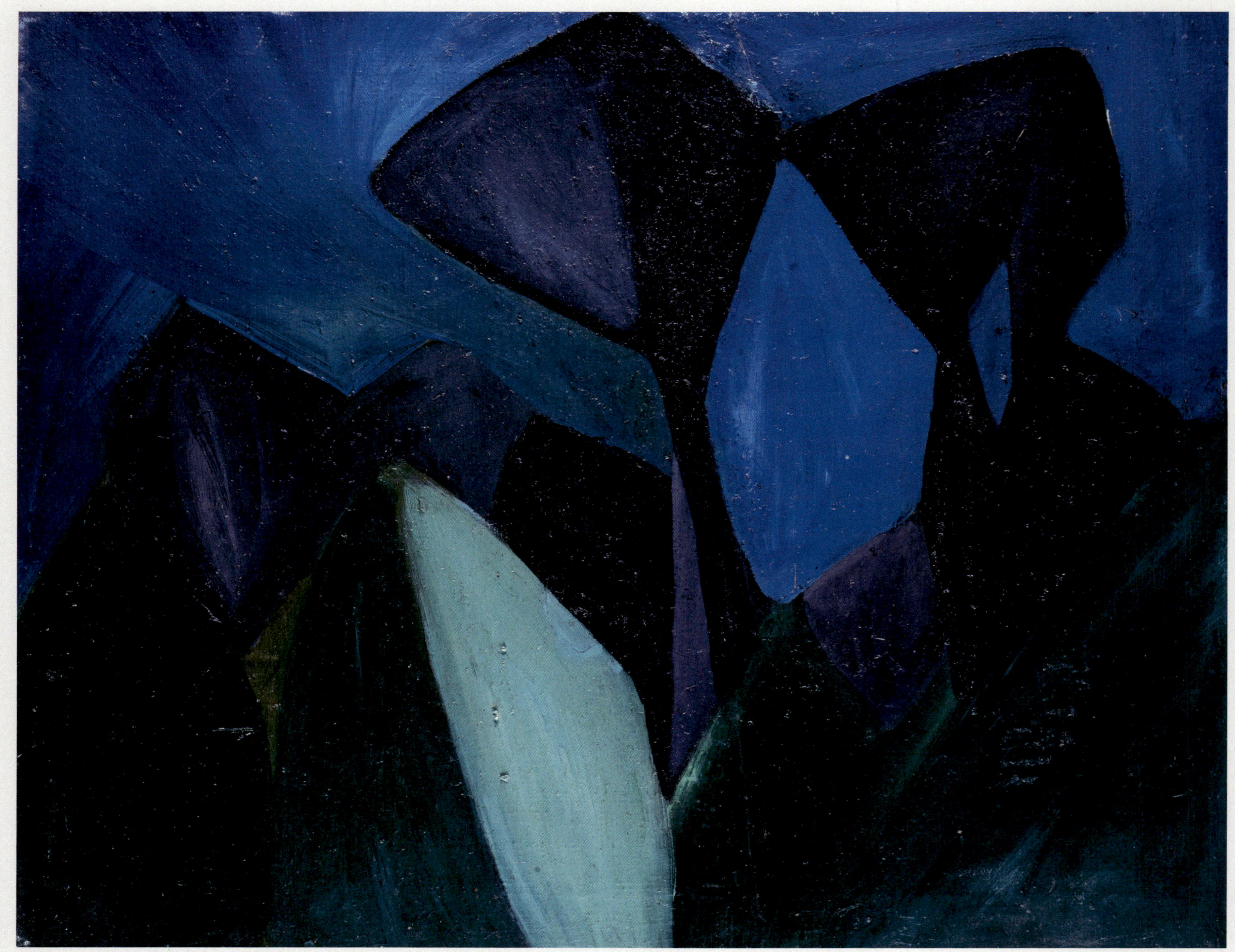

Wladimir Burliuk, *The Trees*, 1911, oil on canvas, 64 x 84 cm,
Gabriele Münter- und Johannes Eichner-Stiftung, Munich

The brothers David and Wladimir Burliuk were friends of Kandinsky's, who championed their work. Wladimir Burliuk's *Landschaft* (*Landscape*) was apparently part of Kandinsky's collection. Another painting by Wladimir Burliuk, *Die Bäume* (*The Trees*), was probably shown in the first Blaue Reiter exhibition under the title *Landschaft* (*Landscape*). David Burliuk wrote the essay "Die 'Wilden' Russlands" (The "Savages" of Russia) for the almanac.

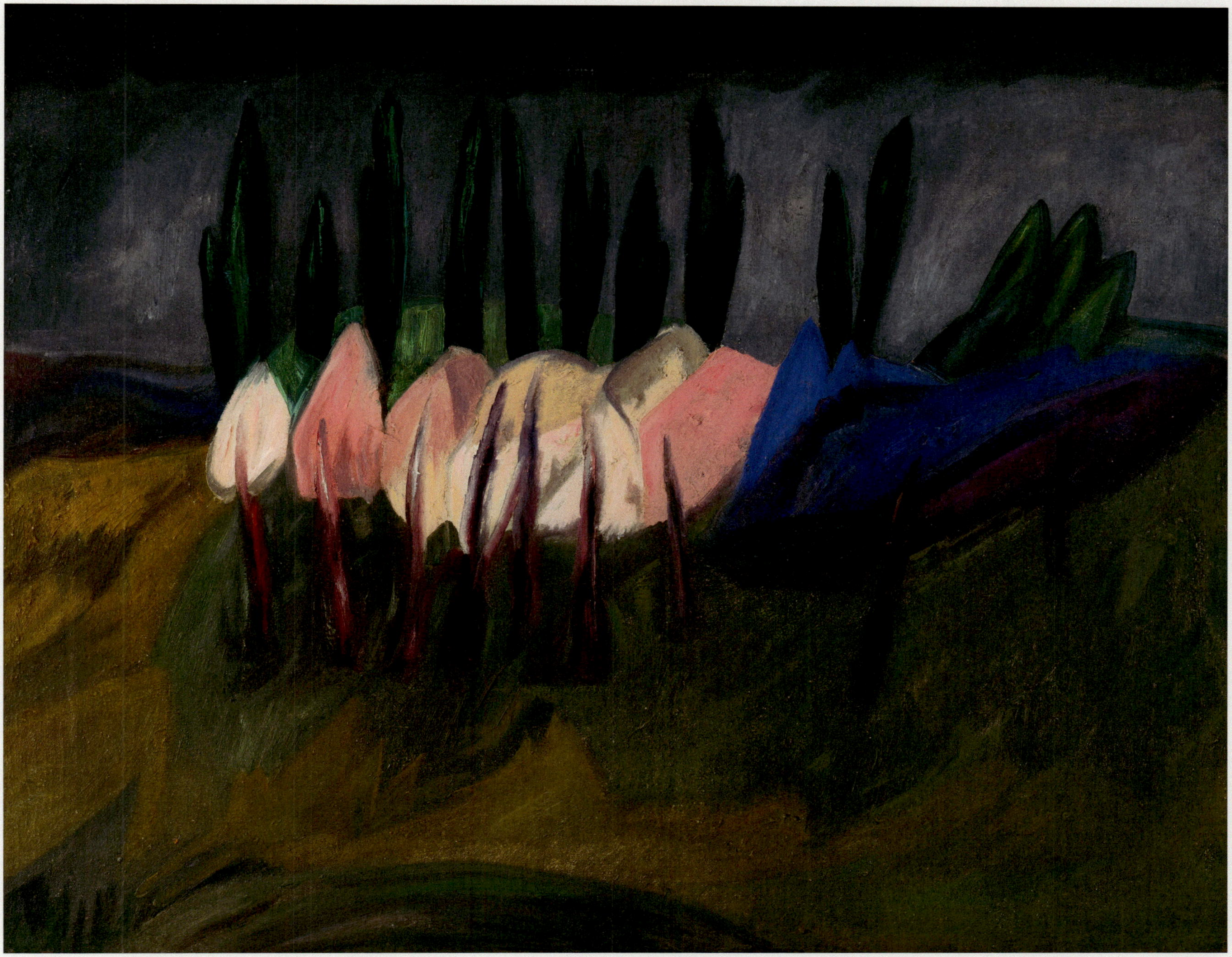

Wladimir Burliuk, *Landscape (Blossoming Trees in Spring)*, 1911, oil on canvas, 73.2 x 92.5 cm, private collection

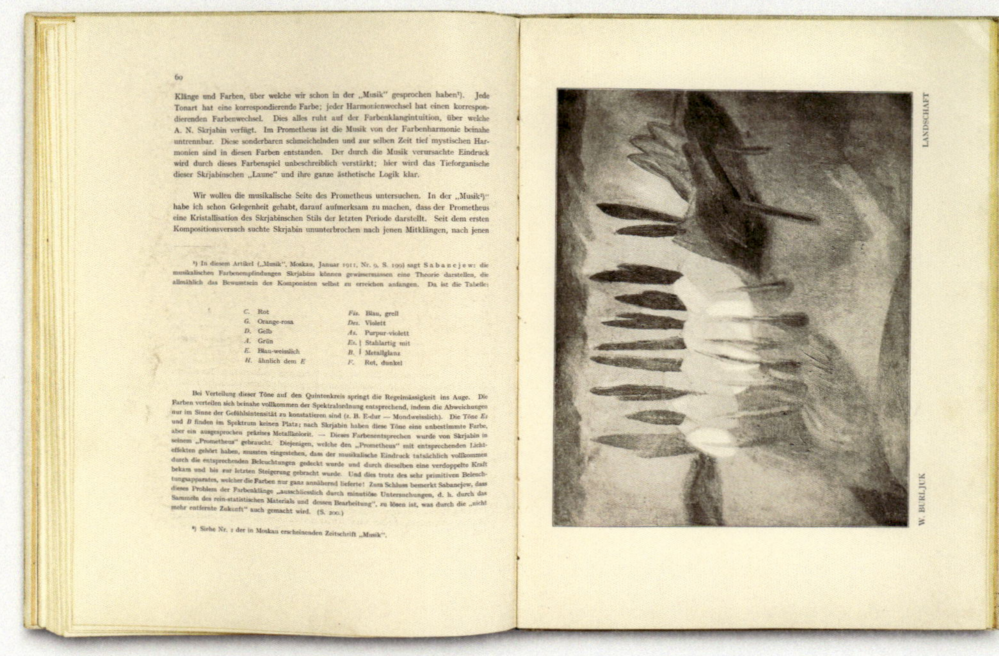

69

Klänge und Farben, über welche wir schon in der „Musik" gesprochen haben[1]). Jede Tonart hat eine korrespondierende Farbe; jeder Harmonienwechsel hat einen korrespondierenden Farbenwechsel. Dies alles ruht auf der Farbenklangintuition, über welche A. N. Skrjabin verfügt. Im Prometheus ist die Musik von der Farbenharmonie beinahe untrennbar. Diese sonderbaren schmeichelnden und zur selben Zeit tief mystischen Harmonien sind in diesen Farben entstanden. Der durch die Musik verursachte Eindruck wird durch dieses Farbenspiel unbeschreiblich verstärkt; hier wird das Tieforganische dieser Skrjabinschen „Laune" und ihre ganze ästhetische Logik klar.

Wir wollen die musikalische Seite des Prometheus untersuchen. In der „Musik[2])" habe ich schon Gelegenheit gehabt, darauf aufmerksam zu machen, dass der Prometheus eine Kristallisation des Skrjabinschen Stils der letzten Periode darstellt. Seit dem ersten Kompositionsversuch suchte Skrjabin ununterbrochen nach jenen Mitklängen, nach jenen

[1]) In diesem Artikel („Musik", Moskau, Januar 1911, Nr. 9, S. 199) sagt Sabancjew: die musikalischen Farbenempfindungen Skrjabins können gewissermassen eine Theorie darstellen, die allmählich das Bewusstsein des Komponisten selbst zu erreichen anfangen. Da ist die Tabelle:

C.	Rot	*Fis.*	Blau, grell
G.	Orange-rosa	*Des.*	Violett
D.	Gelb	*As.*	Purpur-violett
A.	Grün	*Es.*	Stahlartig mit
E.	Blau-weisslich	*B.*	Metallglanz
H.	ähnlich dem *E*	*F.*	Rot, dunkel

Bei Verteilung dieser Töne auf den Quintenkreis springt die Regelmässigkeit ins Auge. Die Farben verteilen sich beinahe vollkommen der Spektralordnung entsprechend, indem die Abweichungen nur im Sinne der Gefühlsintensität zu konstatieren sind (z. B. E-dur — Mondweisslich). Die Töne *Es* und *B* finden im Spektrum keinen Platz; nach Skrjabin haben diese Töne eine unbestimmte Farbe, aber ein ausgesprochen präzises Metallkolorit. — Dieses Farbenentsprechen wurde von Skrjabin in seinem „Prometheus" gebraucht. Diejenigen, welche den „Prometheus" mit entsprechenden Lichteffekten gehört haben, mussten eingestehen, dass der musikalische Eindruck tatsächlich vollkommen durch die entsprechenden Beleuchtungen gedeckt wurde und durch dieselben eine verdoppelte Kraft bekam und bis zur letzten Steigerung gebracht wurde. Und dies trotz des sehr primitiven Beleuchtungsapparates, welcher die Farben nur ganz annähernd lieferte! Zum Schluss bemerkt Sabanejew, dass dieses Problem der Farbenklänge „ausschliesslich durch minutiöse Untersuchungen, d. h. durch das Sammeln des rein-statistischen Materials und dessen Bearbeitung", zu lösen ist, was durch die „nicht mehr entfernte Zukunft" auch gemacht wird. (S. 200.)

[2]) Siehe Nr. 1 der in Moskau erscheinenden Zeitschrift „Musik".

LANDSCHAFT

W. BURLJUK

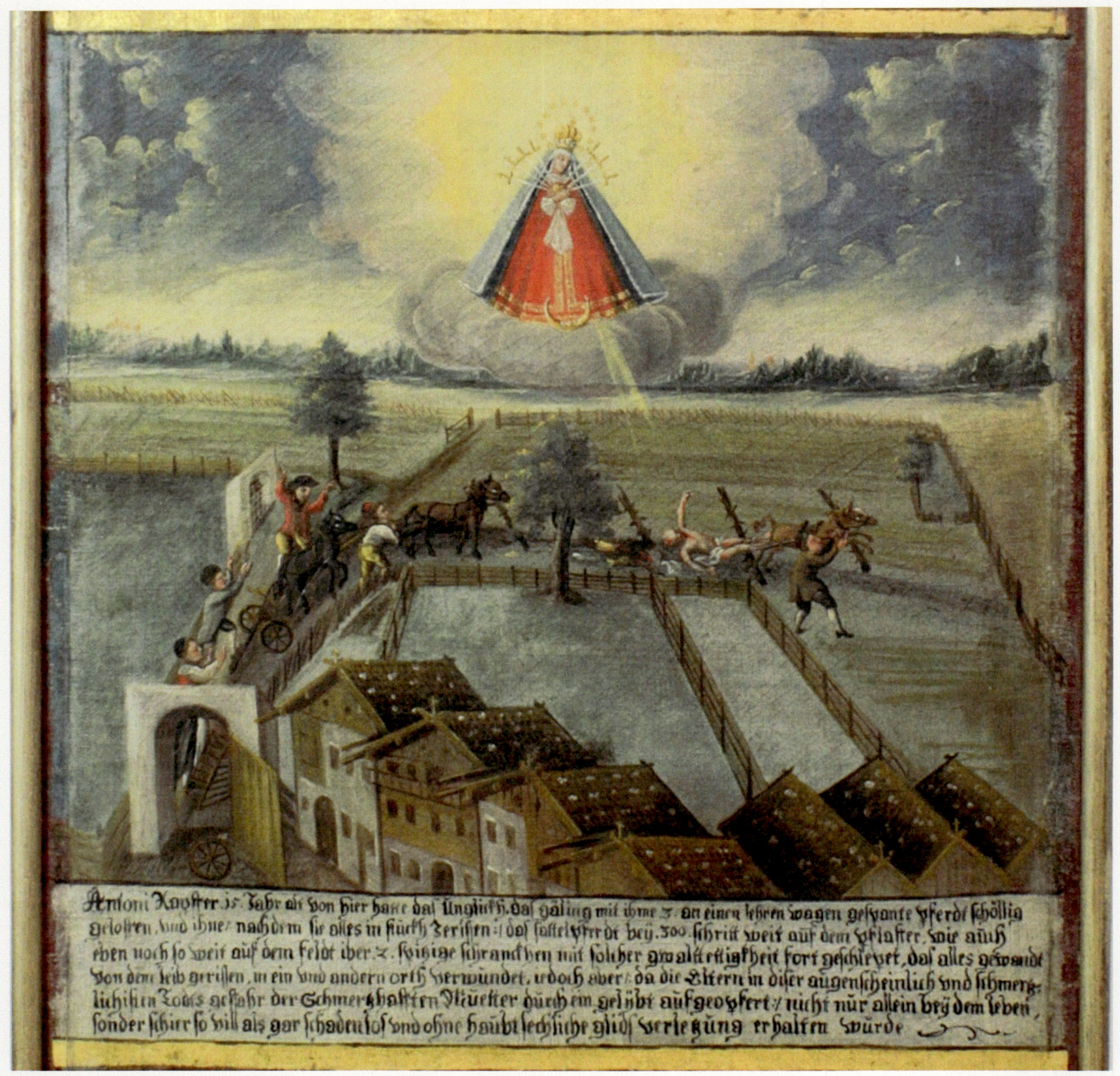

Votive painting donated by Anton Kapfer to the Murnau Lady of Sorrows church, ca. 1756–66, oil on canvas, 50 x 50 cm, Katholische Kirchenstiftung St. Nikolaus, Murnau

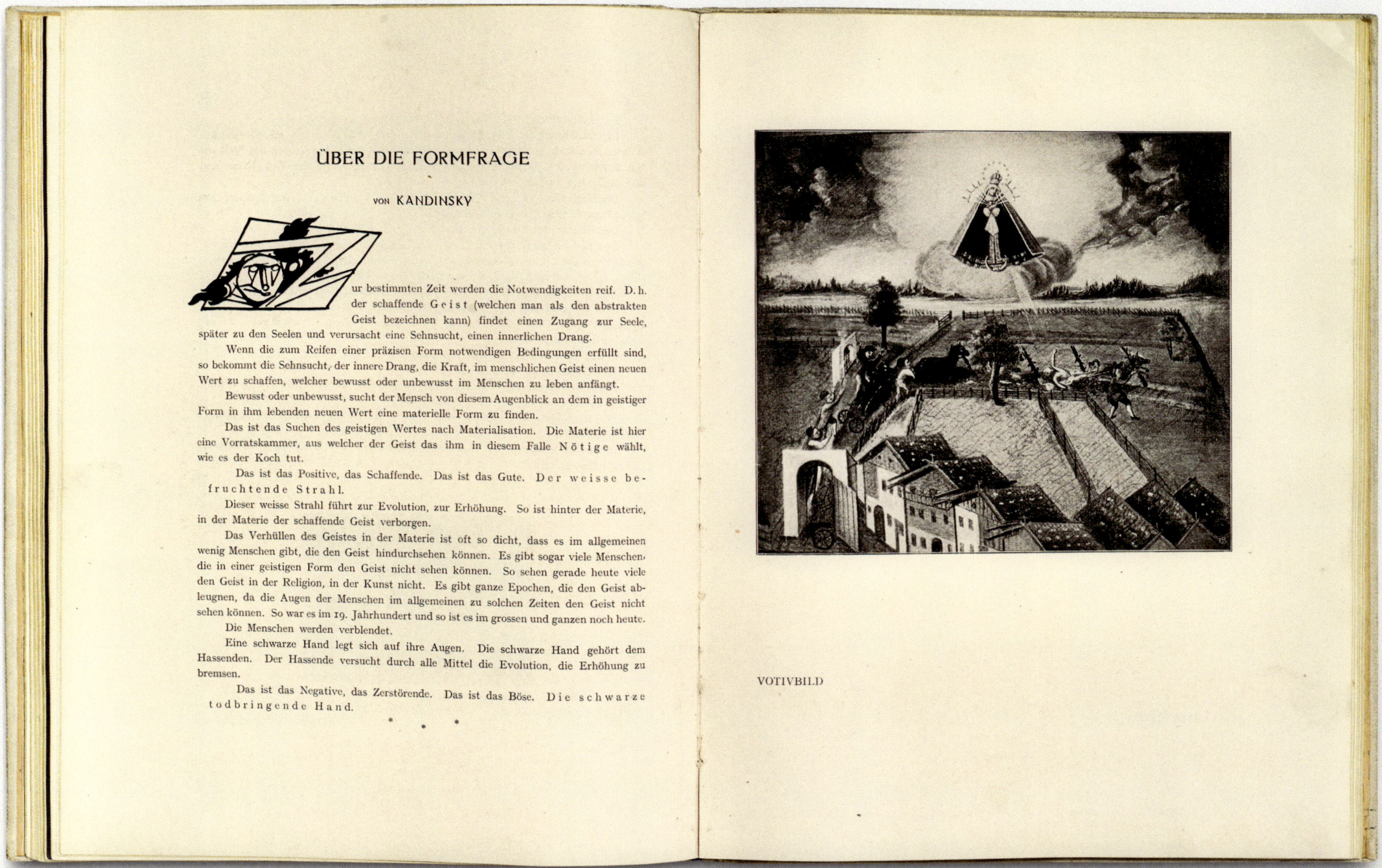

ÜBER DIE FORMFRAGE

VON KANDINSKY

ur bestimmten Zeit werden die Notwendigkeiten reif. D. h. der schaffende Geist (welchen man als den abstrakten Geist bezeichnen kann) findet einen Zugang zur Seele, später zu den Seelen und verursacht eine Sehnsucht, einen innerlichen Drang.

Wenn die zum Reifen einer präzisen Form notwendigen Bedingungen erfüllt sind, so bekommt die Sehnsucht, der innere Drang, die Kraft, im menschlichen Geist einen neuen Wert zu schaffen, welcher bewusst oder unbewusst im Menschen zu leben anfängt.

Bewusst oder unbewusst, sucht der Mensch von diesem Augenblick an dem in geistiger Form in ihm lebenden neuen Wert eine materielle Form zu finden.

Das ist das Suchen des geistigen Wertes nach Materialisation. Die Materie ist hier eine Vorratskammer, aus welcher der Geist das ihm in diesem Falle Nötige wählt, wie es der Koch tut.

Das ist das Positive, das Schaffende. Das ist das Gute. Der weisse befruchtende Strahl.

Dieser weisse Strahl führt zur Evolution, zur Erhöhung. So ist hinter der Materie, in der Materie der schaffende Geist verborgen.

Das Verhüllen des Geistes in der Materie ist oft so dicht, dass es im allgemeinen wenig Menschen gibt, die den Geist hindurchsehen können. Es gibt sogar viele Menschen, die in einer geistigen Form den Geist nicht sehen können. So sehen gerade heute viele den Geist in der Religion, in der Kunst nicht. Es gibt ganze Epochen, die den Geist ableugnen, da die Augen der Menschen im allgemeinen zu solchen Zeiten den Geist nicht sehen können. So war es im 19. Jahrhundert und so ist es im grossen und ganzen noch heute.

Die Menschen werden verblendet.

Eine schwarze Hand legt sich auf ihre Augen. Die schwarze Hand gehört dem Hassenden. Der Hassende versucht durch alle Mittel die Evolution, die Erhöhung zu bremsen.

Das ist das Negative, das Zerstörende. Das ist das Böse. Die schwarze todbringende Hand.

* * *

VOTIVBILD

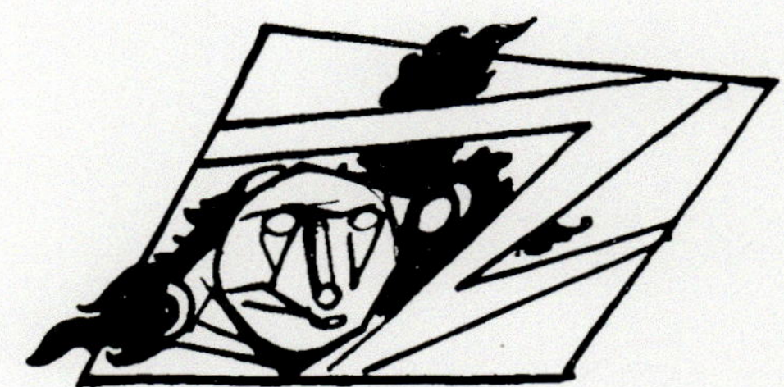

Both the votive image and the initial in Kandinsky's article "Über die Formfrage" (On the Question of Form) relate to the passage in which he describes the positive, the creative, and goodness in terms of the metaphor of the "white, fertilizing ray." Six of the fifteen texts in the almanac begin with a decorative initial that was specially designed for the publication. Hans Arp's lightning-bolt "Z" obviously relates to the white ray leading from the Virgin to the afflicted man in the votive image, producing its own connection between the levels of image and text.

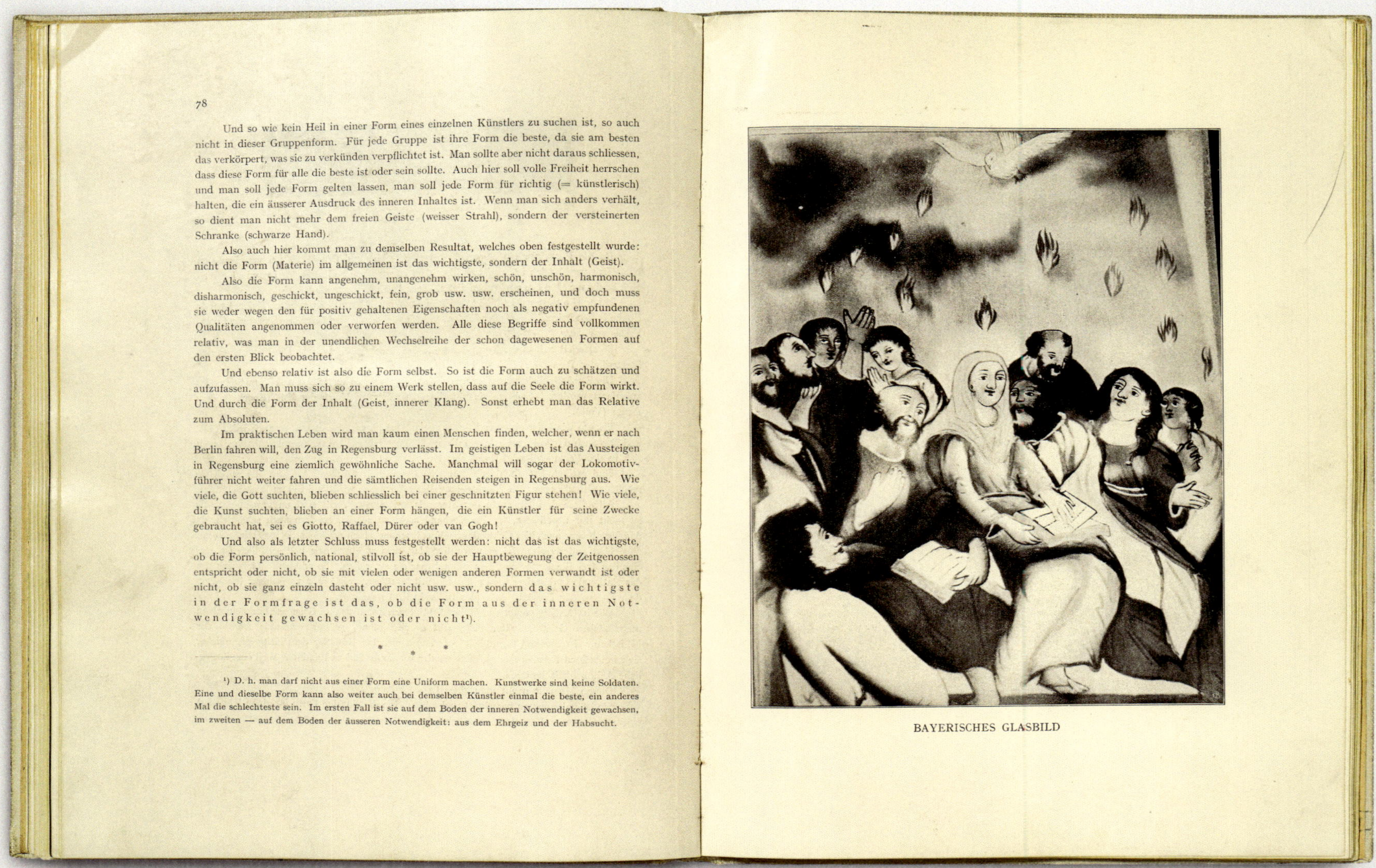

78

Und so wie kein Heil in einer Form eines einzelnen Künstlers zu suchen ist, so auch nicht in dieser Gruppenform. Für jede Gruppe ist ihre Form die beste, da sie am besten das verkörpert, was sie zu verkünden verpflichtet ist. Man sollte aber nicht daraus schliessen, dass diese Form für alle die beste ist oder sein sollte. Auch hier soll volle Freiheit herrschen und man soll jede Form gelten lassen, man soll jede Form für richtig (= künstlerisch) halten, die ein äusserer Ausdruck des inneren Inhaltes ist. Wenn man sich anders verhält, so dient man nicht mehr dem freien Geiste (weisser Strahl), sondern der versteinerten Schranke (schwarze Hand).

Also auch hier kommt man zu demselben Resultat, welches oben festgestellt wurde: nicht die Form (Materie) im allgemeinen ist das wichtigste, sondern der Inhalt (Geist).

Also die Form kann angenehm, unangenehm wirken, schön, unschön, harmonisch, disharmonisch, geschickt, ungeschickt, fein, grob usw. usw. erscheinen, und doch muss sie weder wegen den für positiv gehaltenen Eigenschaften noch als negativ empfundenen Qualitäten angenommen oder verworfen werden. Alle diese Begriffe sind vollkommen relativ, was man in der unendlichen Wechselreihe der schon dagewesenen Formen auf den ersten Blick beobachtet.

Und ebenso relativ ist also die Form selbst. So ist die Form auch zu schätzen und aufzufassen. Man muss sich so zu einem Werk stellen, dass auf die Seele die Form wirkt. Und durch die Form der Inhalt (Geist, innerer Klang). Sonst erhebt man das Relative zum Absoluten.

Im praktischen Leben wird man kaum einen Menschen finden, welcher, wenn er nach Berlin fahren will, den Zug in Regensburg verlässt. Im geistigen Leben ist das Aussteigen in Regensburg eine ziemlich gewöhnliche Sache. Manchmal will sogar der Lokomotivführer nicht weiter fahren und die sämtlichen Reisenden steigen in Regensburg aus. Wie viele, die Gott suchten, blieben schliesslich bei einer geschnitzten Figur stehen! Wie viele, die Kunst suchten, blieben an einer Form hängen, die ein Künstler für seine Zwecke gebraucht hat, sei es Giotto, Raffael, Dürer oder van Gogh!

Und also als letzter Schluss muss festgestellt werden: nicht das ist das wichtigste, ob die Form persönlich, national, stilvoll ist, ob sie der Hauptbewegung der Zeitgenossen entspricht oder nicht, ob sie mit vielen oder wenigen anderen Formen verwandt ist oder nicht, ob sie ganz einzeln dasteht oder nicht usw. usw., sondern das wichtigste in der Formfrage ist das, ob die Form aus der inneren Notwendigkeit gewachsen ist oder nicht[1]).

* * *

[1]) D. h. man darf nicht aus einer Form eine Uniform machen. Kunstwerke sind keine Soldaten. Eine und dieselbe Form kann also weiter auch bei demselben Künstler einmal die beste, ein anderes Mal die schlechteste sein. Im ersten Fall ist sie auf dem Boden der inneren Notwendigkeit gewachsen, im zweiten — auf dem Boden der äusseren Notwendigkeit: aus dem Ehrgeiz und der Habsucht.

BAYERISCHES GLASBILD

The Upper Bavarian glass painting with its depiction of the miracle of the Pentecost, the effusion of the Holy Spirit, might well be seen as an illustration of the adjacent statement in Kandinsky's "Über die Formfrage" (On the Question of Form): "it is not form (matter) that is generally most important but content (spirit)."

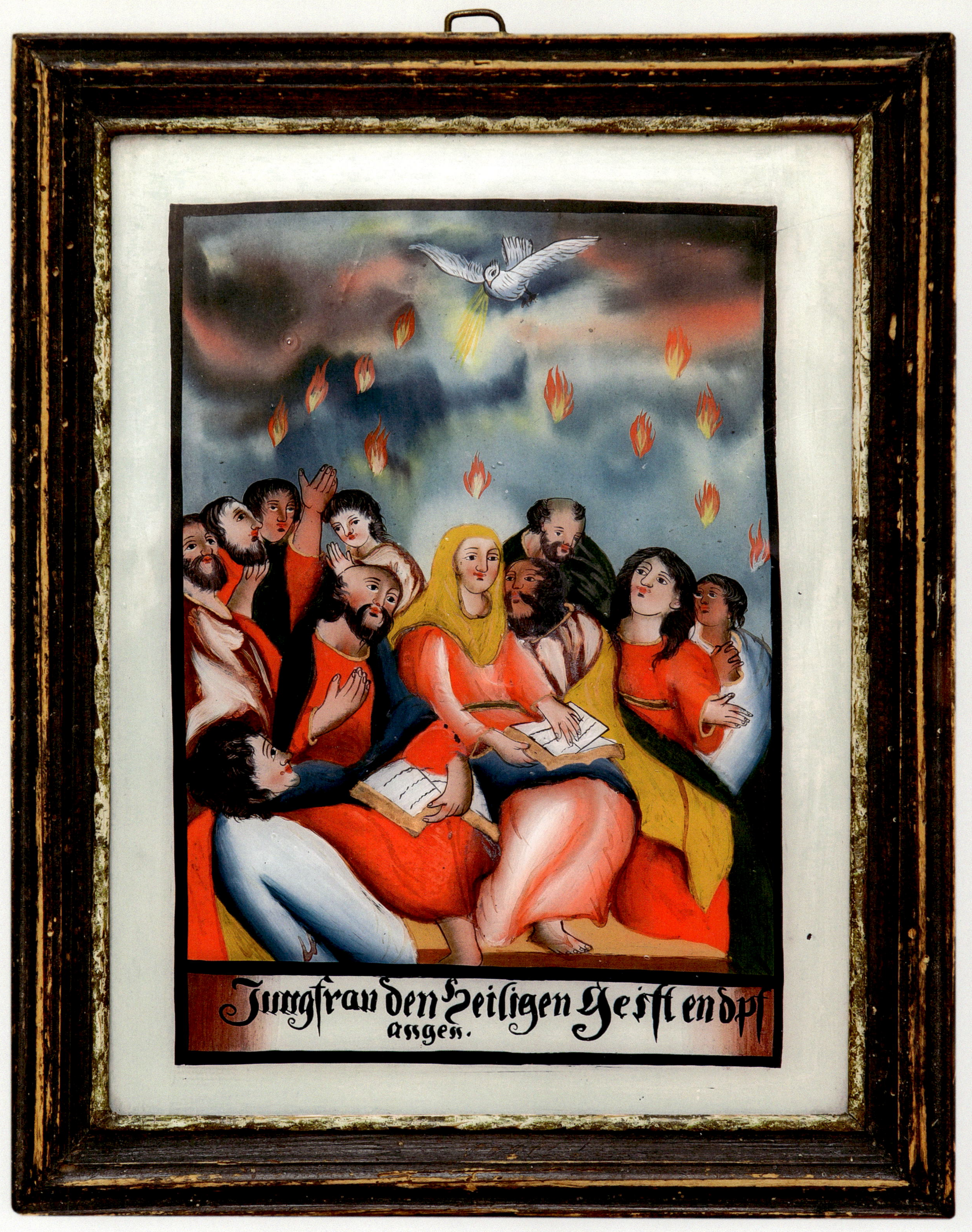

Descent of the Holy Ghost, Staffelsee region (Bavaria), 1800–50, reverse glass painting, 28.5 x 18.4 cm, Oberammergau Museum

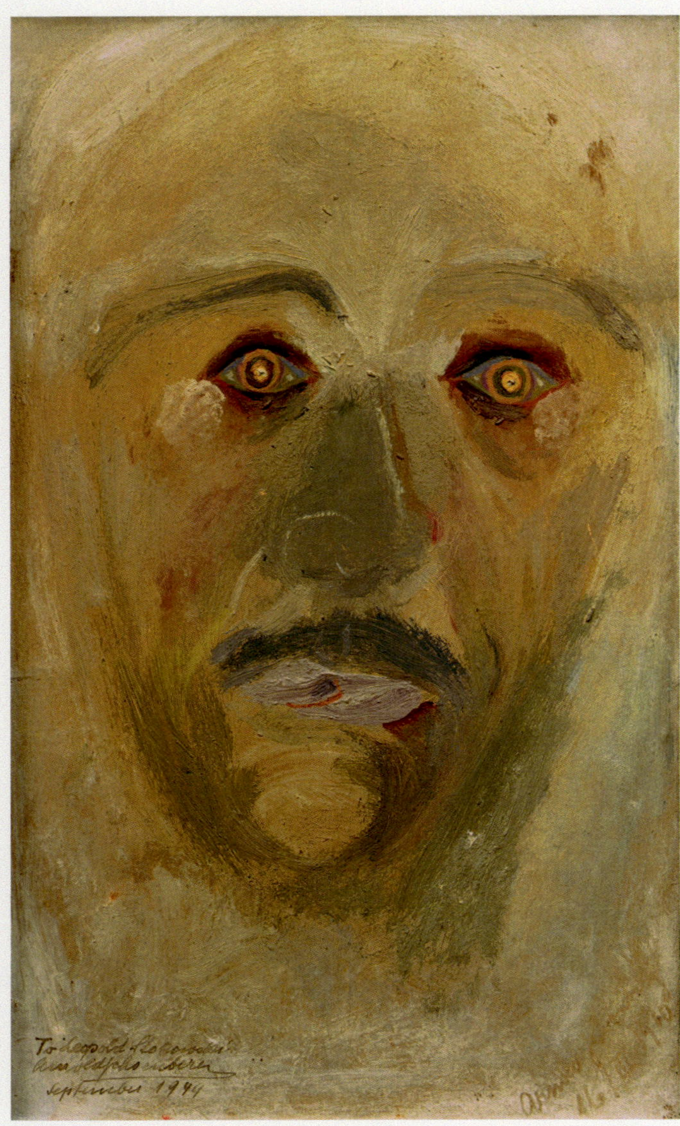

Arnold Schoenberg, *Vision (Self-Portrait)*, 1910, oil on cardboard, 32 x 20 cm, Music Division, Library of Congress, Washington, DC

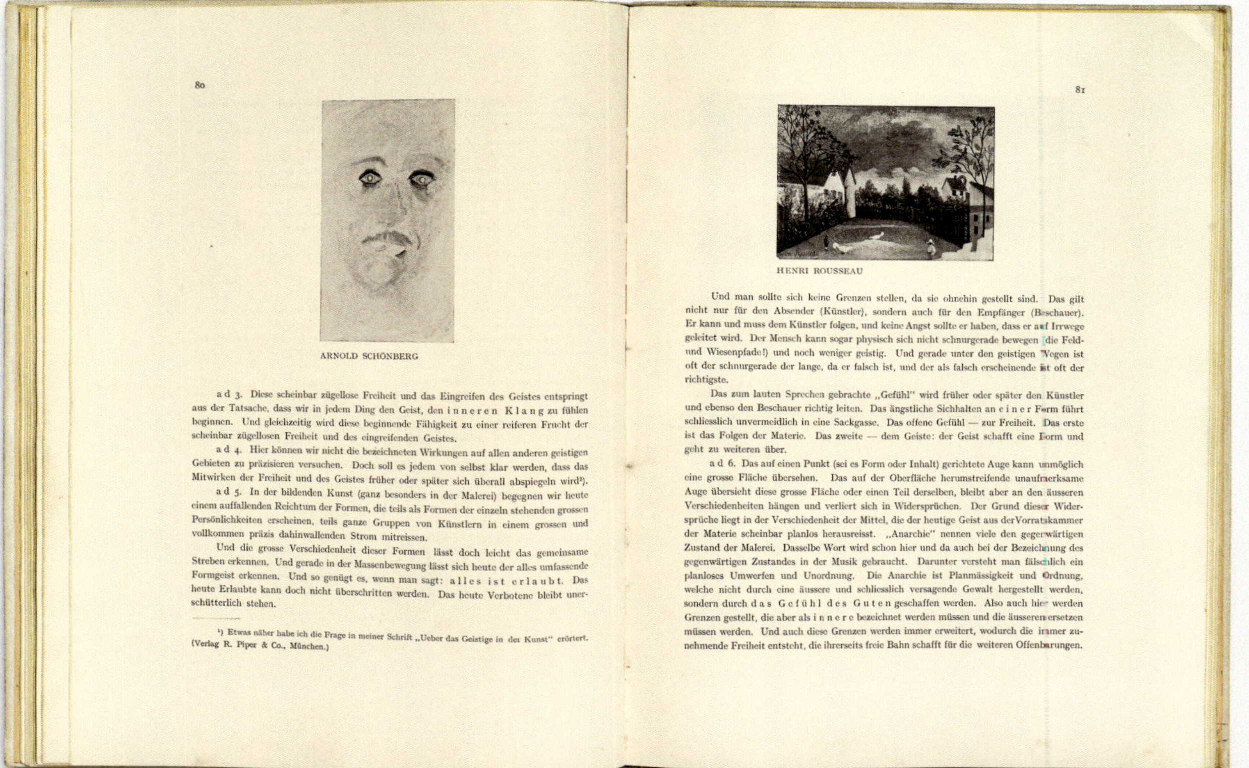

80

ARNOLD SCHÖNBERG

ad 3. Diese scheinbar zügellose Freiheit und das Eingreifen des Geistes entspringt aus der Tatsache, dass wir in jedem Ding den Geist, den inneren Klang zu fühlen beginnen. Und gleichzeitig wird diese beginnende Fähigkeit zu einer reiferen Frucht der scheinbar zügellosen Freiheit und des eingreifenden Geistes.

ad 4. Hier können wir nicht die bezeichneten Wirkungen auf allen anderen geistigen Gebieten zu präzisieren versuchen. Doch soll es jedem von selbst klar werden, dass das Mitwirken der Freiheit und des Geistes früher oder später sich überall abspiegeln wird[1]).

ad 5. In der bildenden Kunst (ganz besonders in der Malerei) begegnen wir heute einem auffallenden Reichtum der Formen, die teils als Formen der einzeln stehenden grossen Persönlichkeiten erscheinen, teils ganze Gruppen von Künstlern in einem grossen und vollkommen präzis dahinwallenden Strom mitreissen.

Und die grosse Verschiedenheit dieser Formen lässt doch leicht das gemeinsame Streben erkennen. Und gerade in der Massenbewegung lässt sich heute der alles umfassende Formgeist erkennen. Und so genügt es, wenn man sagt: alles ist erlaubt. Das heute Erlaubte kann doch nicht überschritten werden. Das heute Verbotene bleibt unerschütterlich stehen.

[1]) Etwas näher habe ich die Frage in meiner Schrift „Ueber das Geistige in der Kunst" erörtert. (Verlag R. Piper & Co., München.)

81

HENRI ROUSSEAU

Und man sollte sich keine Grenzen stellen, da sie ohnehin gestellt sind. Das gilt nicht nur für den Absender (Künstler), sondern auch für den Empfänger (Beschauer). Er kann und muss dem Künstler folgen, und keine Angst sollte er haben, dass er auf Irrwege geleitet wird. Der Mensch kann sogar physisch sich nicht schnurgerade bewegen (die Feld- und Wiesenpfade!) und noch weniger geistig. Und gerade unter den geistigen Wegen ist oft der schnurgerade der lange, da er falsch ist, und der als falsch erscheinende ist oft der richtigste.

Das zum lauten Sprechen gebrachte „Gefühl" wird früher oder später den Künstler und ebenso den Beschauer richtig leiten. Das ängstliche Sichhalten an einer Form führt schliesslich unvermeidlich in eine Sackgasse. Das offene Gefühl — zur Freiheit. Das erste ist das Folgen der Materie. Das zweite — dem Geiste: der Geist schafft eine Form und geht zu weiteren über.

ad 6. Das auf einen Punkt (sei es Form oder Inhalt) gerichtete Auge kann unmöglich eine grosse Fläche übersehen. Das auf der Oberfläche herumstreifende unaufmerksame Auge übersieht diese grosse Fläche oder einen Teil derselben, bleibt aber an den äusseren Verschiedenheiten hängen und verliert sich in Widersprüchen. Der Grund dieser Widersprüche liegt in der Verschiedenheit der Mittel, die der heutige Geist aus der Vorratskammer der Materie scheinbar planlos herausreisst. „Anarchie" nennen viele den gegenwärtigen Zustand der Malerei. Dasselbe Wort wird schon hier und da auch bei der Bezeichnung des gegenwärtigen Zustandes in der Musik gebraucht. Darunter versteht man fälschlich ein planloses Umwerfen und Unordnung. Die Anarchie ist Planmässigkeit und Ordnung, welche nicht durch eine äussere und schliesslich versagende Gewalt hergestellt werden, sondern durch das Gefühl des Guten geschaffen werden. Also auch hier werden Grenzen gestellt, die aber als innere bezeichnet werden müssen und die äusseren ersetzen müssen werden. Und auch diese Grenzen werden immer erweitert, wodurch die immer zunehmende Freiheit entsteht, die ihrerseits freie Bahn schafft für die weiteren Offenbarungen.

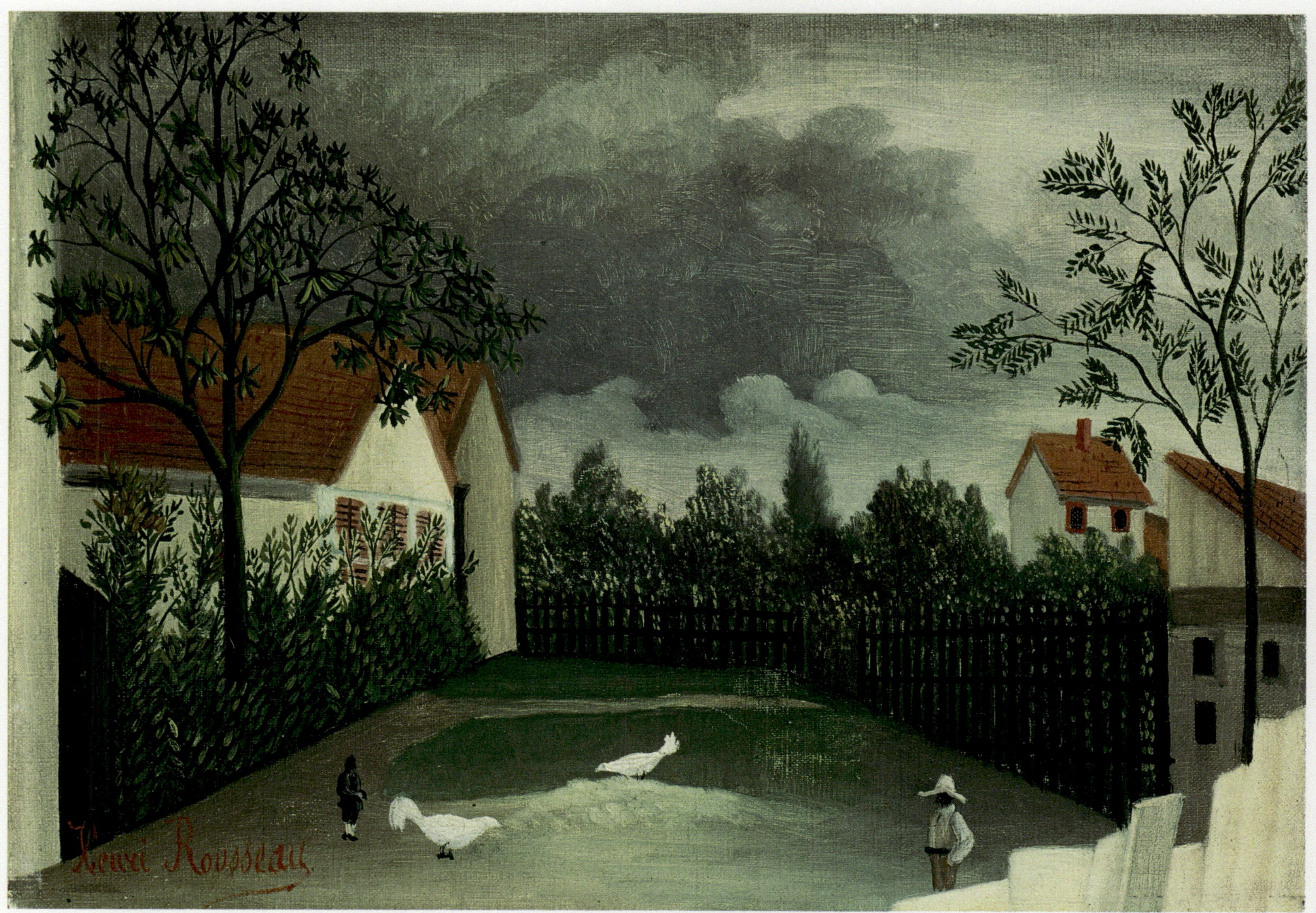

Henri Rousseau, *The Poultry Yard,* 1896–98, oil on canvas, 24.6 x 32.9 cm,
Musée national d'art moderne, Centre Pompidou, Paris, Bequest of Nina Kandinsky, 1981

A self-portrait by Arnold Schoenberg and a painting by Henri Rousseau, which Kandinsky had acquired from Rousseau's estate, appear opposite one another on a two-page spread. At first sight, the two images evince few points in common. Perhaps it was Schoenberg's idea of "pure vision" that found a correspondence in Rousseau's conscious simplicity. Yet there are textual links as well. Below Schoenberg's painting, the notion of "inner sound," so crucial to Kandinsky's art theory, is mentioned. His encounter with the Viennese composer's music at a concert in January 1911 in Munich was a key experience for Kandinsky. In his very first letter to Schoenberg, he wrote that he had discovered in his music exactly "what I too attempt to discover in painterly form," a "'new' harmony." Rousseau's painting *La Basse-Cour* (*The Poultry Yard*), had been shown in the first exhibition of the Blaue Reiter in December 1911, illustrated as no. 1 in the catalogue, and used in the publisher's advertising for the almanac. Kandinsky revered Rousseau, known as the *Douanier,* or customs official, as "the father of this [great] realism" in art. A full seven of his works are illustrated in the almanac. In this case, the work appears above a passage in which the viewer is recommended to faithfully follow the artist.

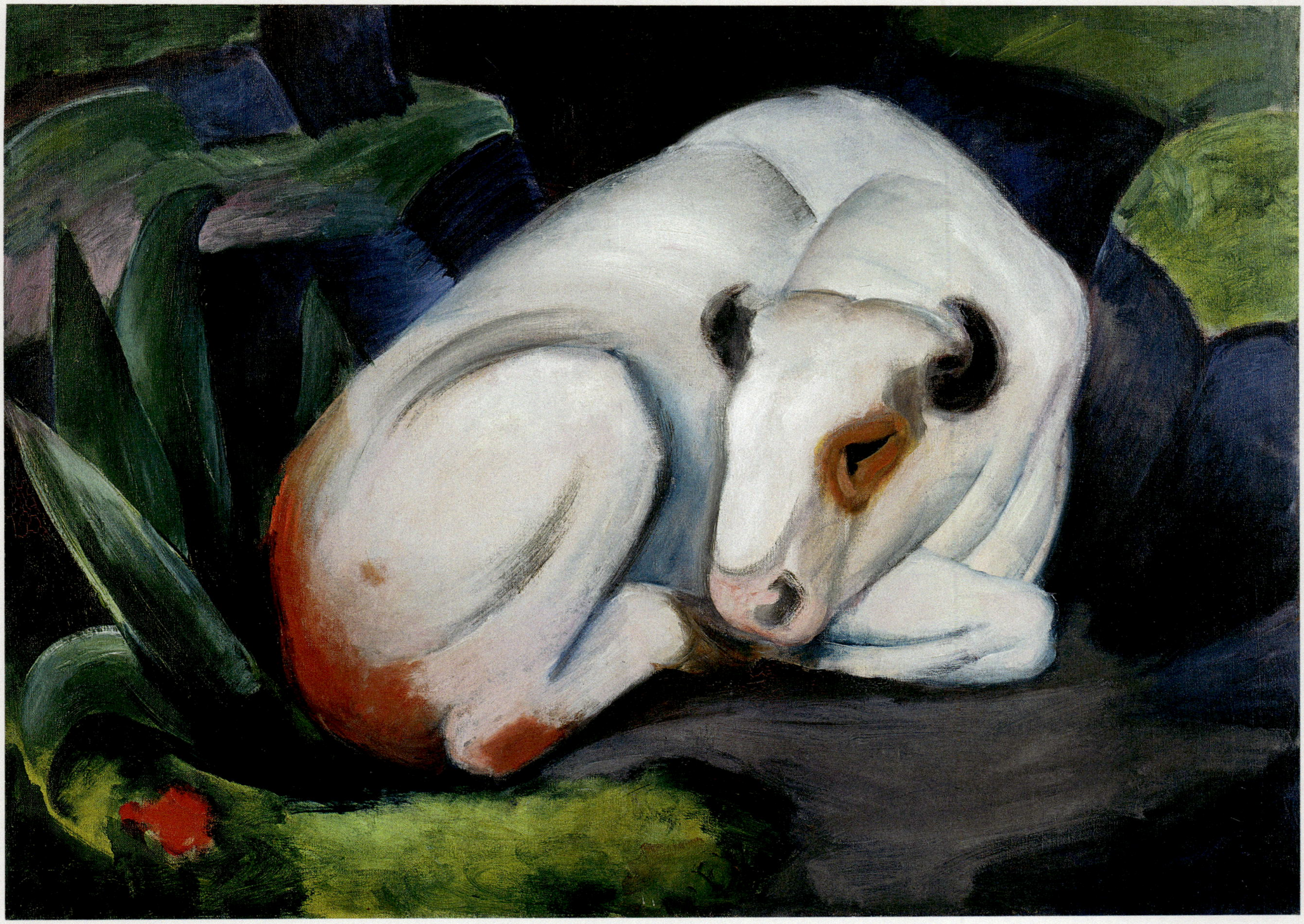

Franz Marc, *White Bull*, 1911, oil on canvas, 100 x 135.2 cm,
Solomon R. Guggenheim Museum, New York

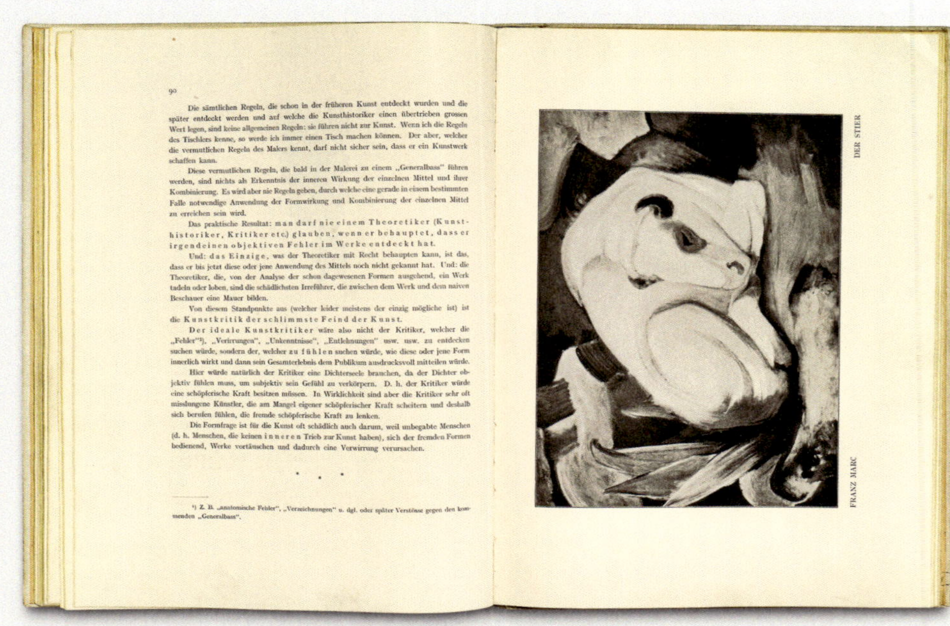

90

Die sämtlichen Regeln, die schon in der früheren Kunst entdeckt wurden und die später entdeckt werden und auf welche die Kunsthistoriker einen übertrieben grossen Wert legen, sind keine allgemeinen Regeln: sie führen nicht zur Kunst. Wenn ich die Regeln des Tischlers kenne, so werde ich immer einen Tisch machen können. Der aber, welcher die vermutlichen Regeln des Malers kennt, darf nicht sicher sein, dass er ein Kunstwerk schaffen kann.

Diese vermutlichen Regeln, die bald in der Malerei zu einem „Generalbass" führen werden, sind nichts als Erkenntnis der inneren Wirkung der einzelnen Mittel und ihrer Kombinierung. Es wird aber nie Regeln geben, durch welche eine gerade in einem bestimmten Falle notwendige Anwendung der Formwirkung und Kombinierung der einzelnen Mittel zu erreichen sein wird.

Das praktische Resultat: man darf nie einem Theoretiker (Kunsthistoriker, Kritiker etc.) glauben, wenn er behauptet, dass er irgendeinen objektiven Fehler im Werke entdeckt hat.

Und: das Einzige, was der Theoretiker mit Recht behaupten kann, ist das, dass er bis jetzt diese oder jene Anwendung des Mittels noch nicht gekannt hat. Und: die Theoretiker, die, von der Analyse der schon dagewesenen Formen ausgehend, ein Werk tadeln oder loben, sind die schädlichsten Irreführer, die zwischen dem Werk und dem naiven Beschauer eine Mauer bilden.

Von diesem Standpunkte aus (welcher leider meistens der einzig mögliche ist) ist die Kunstkritik der schlimmste Feind der Kunst.

Der ideale Kunstkritiker wäre also nicht der Kritiker, welcher die „Fehler"[1]), „Verirrungen", „Unkenntnisse", „Entlehnungen" usw. usw. zu entdecken suchen würde, sondern der, welcher zu fühlen suchen würde, wie diese oder jene Form innerlich wirkt und dann sein Gesamterlebnis dem Publikum ausdrucksvoll mitteilen würde.

Hier würde natürlich der Kritiker eine Dichterseele brauchen, da der Dichter objektiv fühlen muss, um subjektiv sein Gefühl zu verkörpern. D. h. der Kritiker würde eine schöpferische Kraft besitzen müssen. In Wirklichkeit sind aber die Kritiker sehr oft misslungene Künstler, die am Mangel eigener schöpferischer Kraft scheitern und deshalb sich berufen fühlen, die fremde schöpferische Kraft zu lenken.

Die Formfrage ist für die Kunst oft schädlich auch darum, weil unbegabte Menschen (d. h. Menschen, die keinen inneren Trieb zur Kunst haben), sich der fremden Formen bedienend, Werke vortäuschen und dadurch eine Verwirrung verursachen.

* * *

[1]) Z. B. „anatomische Fehler", „Verzeichnungen" u. dgl. oder später Verstösse gegen den kommenden „Generalbass".

DER STIER

FRANZ MARC

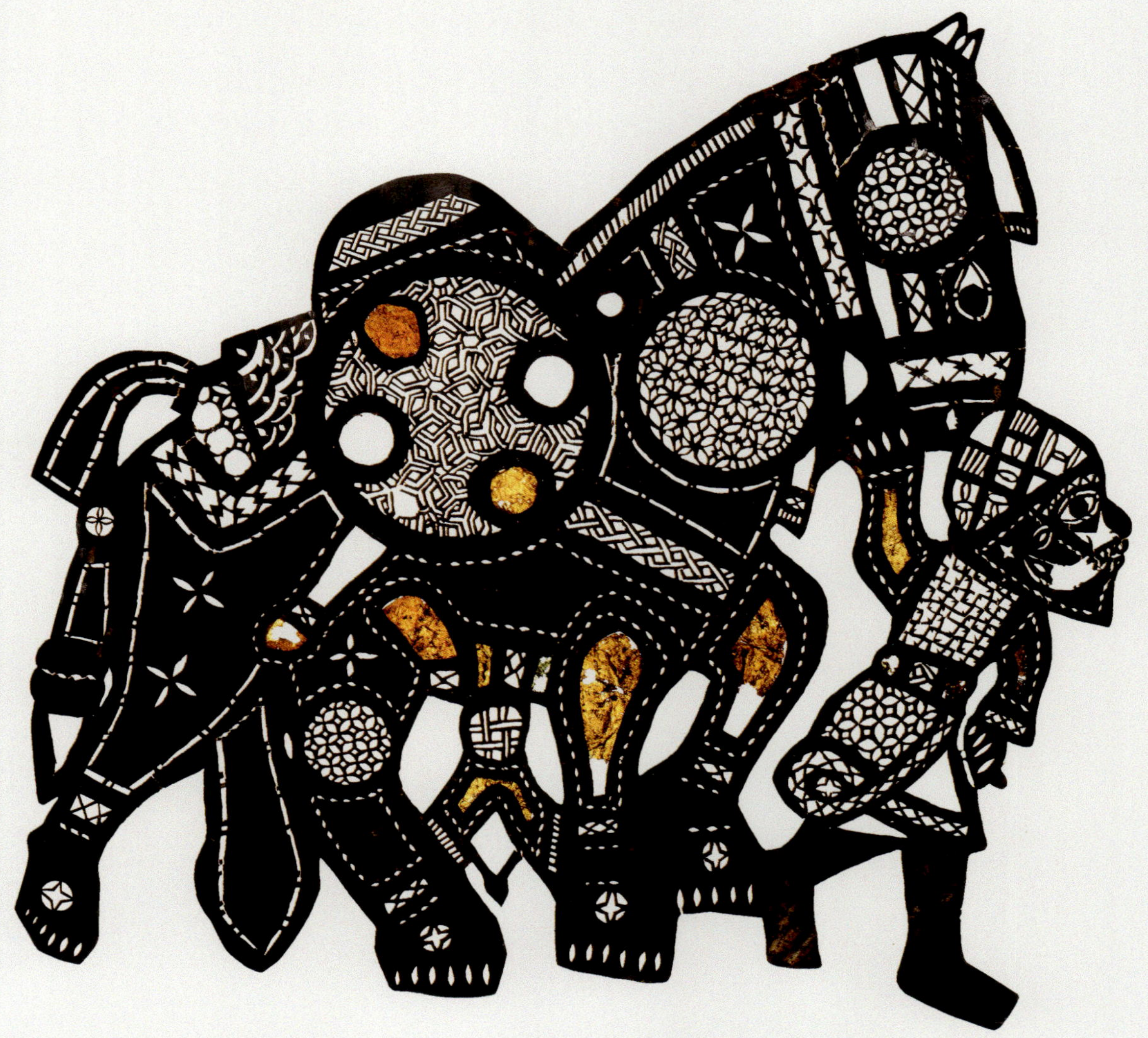

Horse with Groom, Egyptian shadow play, 14th–18th cent., vellum and colored fabric, 63 x 69.5 cm, Münchner Stadtmuseum, Collection Puppentheater/Schaustellerei

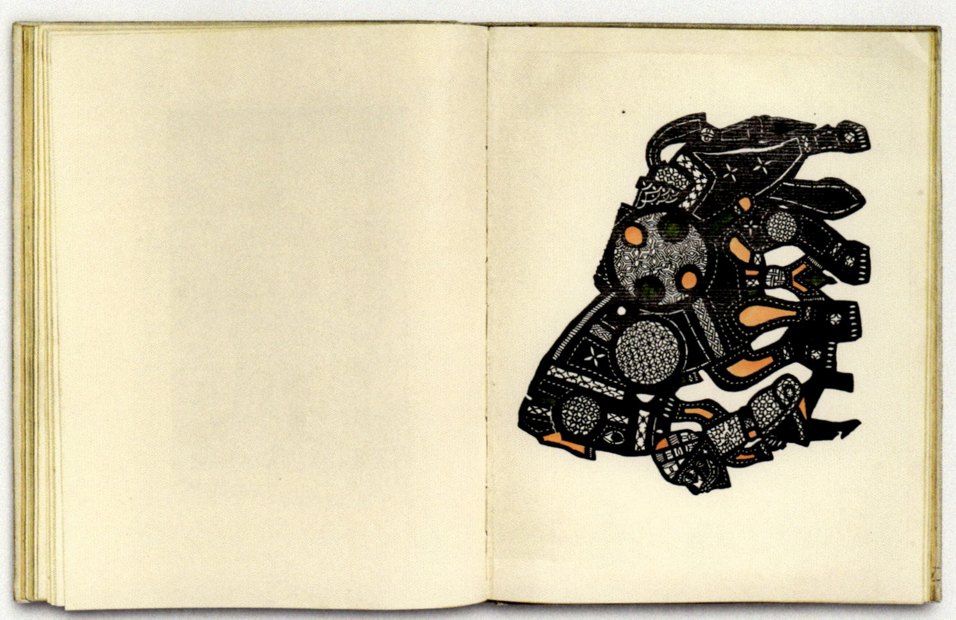

Kandinsky was intrigued by the ornamental form of Egyptian shadow play figures, which he had seen in a 1911 issue of the journal *Der Islam.* A total of nine such figures are illustrated in the almanac, one of them in color. They date from the fourteenth to the eighteenth century. The horse and groom are reproduced in reversed form.

It might have been the analogy between the position of the hand in Oskar Kokoschka's portrait of *Else Kupfer* and the ornament under the depiction of the kneeling Saint Francis receiving the stigmata that suggested their combination in the second edition of the almanac. In the first edition Kokoschka's portrait was placed facing Henri Rousseau's *Portrait de la seconde femme de l'artiste* (*Portrait of the Artist's Second Wife with a Lamp*). The two-page spread may be an example of the way formal similarities influenced the juxtaposition of images in the almanac.

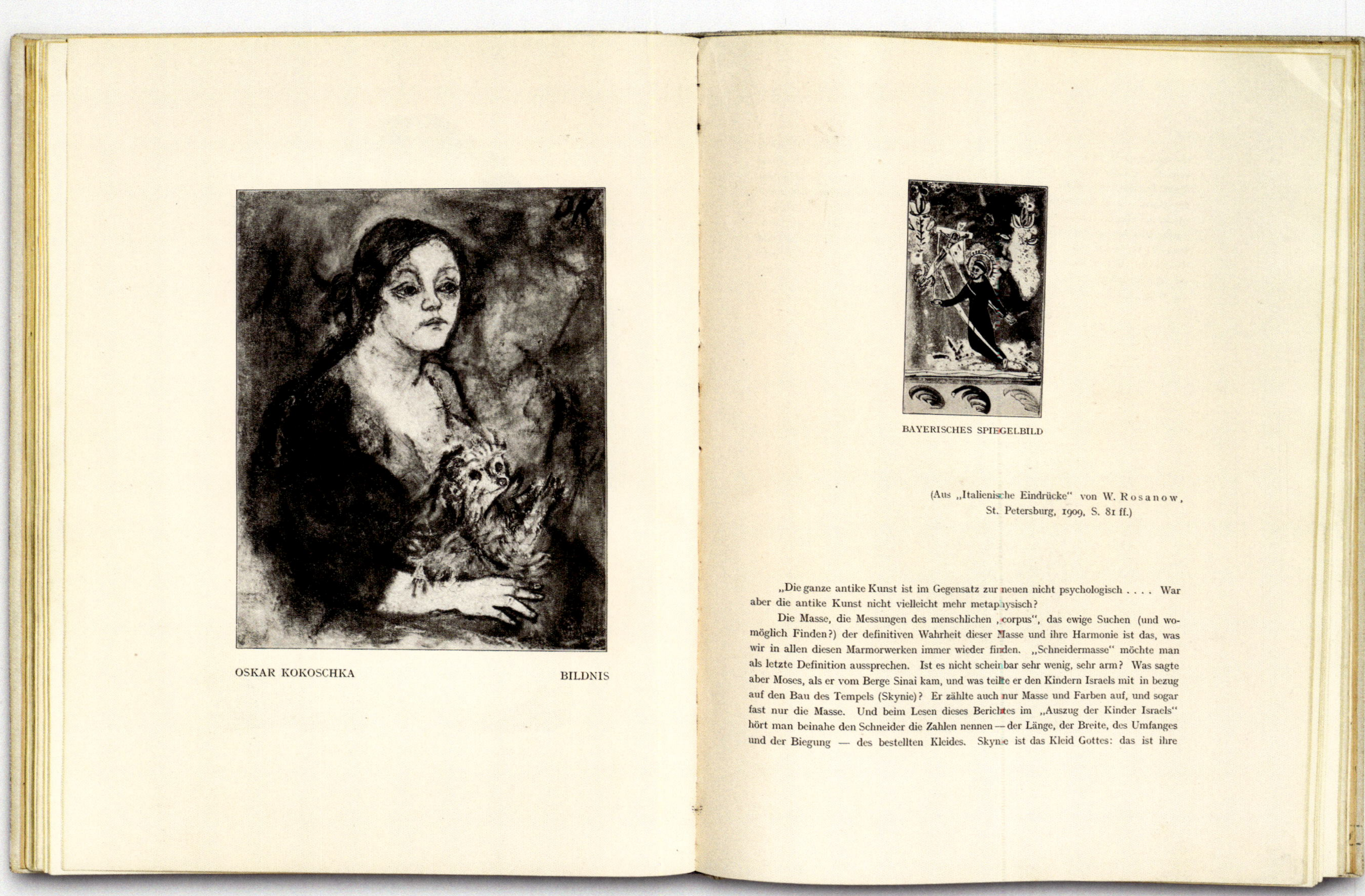

OSKAR KOKOSCHKA BILDNIS

BAYERISCHES SPIEGELBILD

(Aus „Italienische Eindrücke" von W. Rosanow, St. Petersburg, 1909, S. 81 ff.)

„Die ganze antike Kunst ist im Gegensatz zur neuen nicht psychologisch .... War aber die antike Kunst nicht vielleicht mehr metaphysisch?

Die Masse, die Messungen des menschlichen ‚corpus", das ewige Suchen (und womöglich Finden?) der definitiven Wahrheit dieser Masse und ihre Harmonie ist das, was wir in allen diesen Marmorwerken immer wieder finden. „Schneidermasse" möchte man als letzte Definition aussprechen. Ist es nicht scheinbar sehr wenig, sehr arm? Was sagte aber Moses, als er vom Berge Sinai kam, und was teilte er den Kindern Israels mit in bezug auf den Bau des Tempels (Skynie)? Er zählte auch nur Masse und Farben auf, und sogar fast nur die Masse. Und beim Lesen dieses Berichtes im „Auszug der Kinder Israels" hört man beinahe den Schneider die Zahlen nennen — der Länge, der Breite, des Umfanges und der Biegung — des bestellten Kleides. Skynie ist das Kleid Gottes: das ist ihre

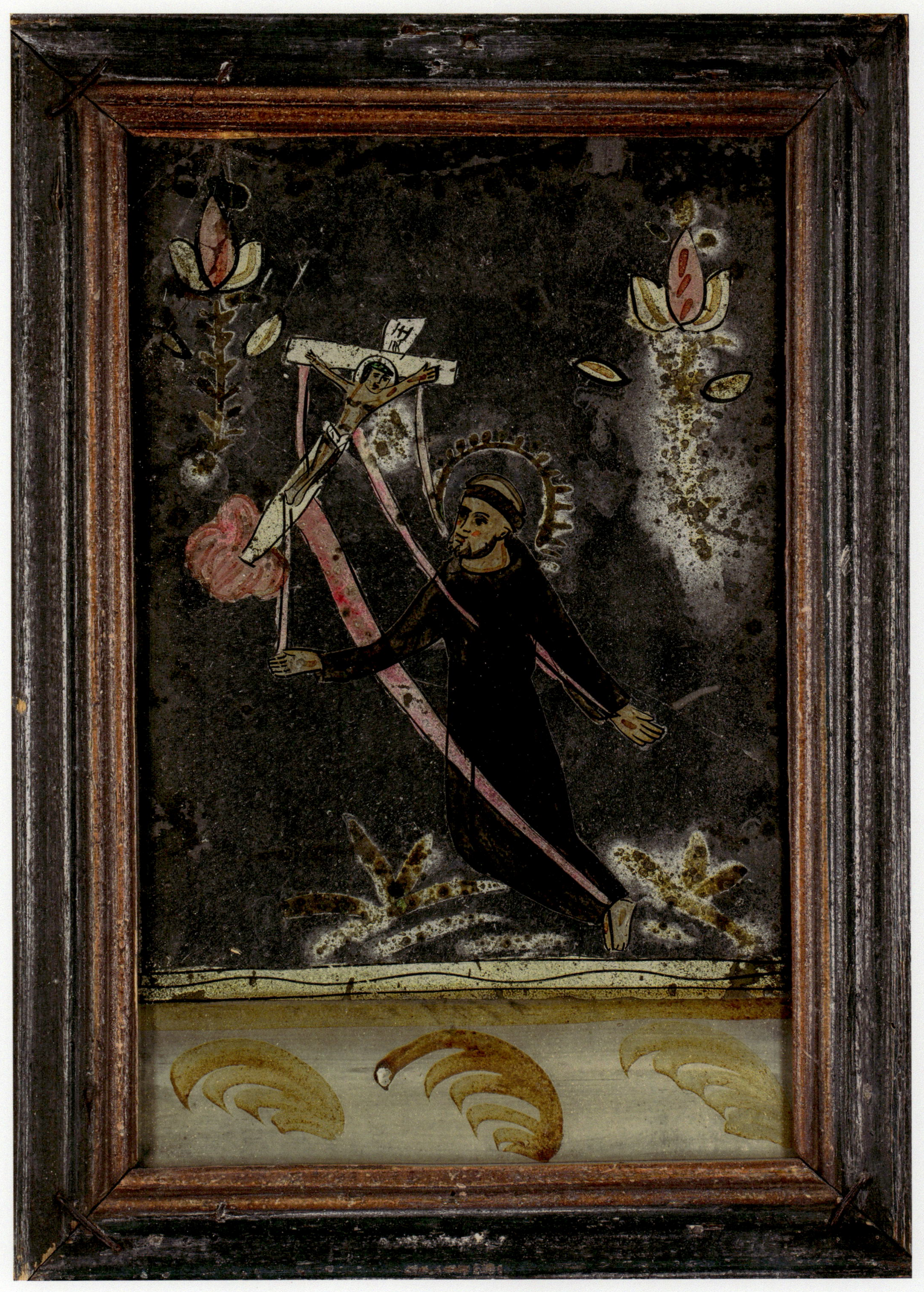

Stigmatization of Saint Francis of Assisi, Raimundsreut (Bavaria), 1775–1800, mirror painting, 32.4 x 22.5 cm, Oberammergau Museum

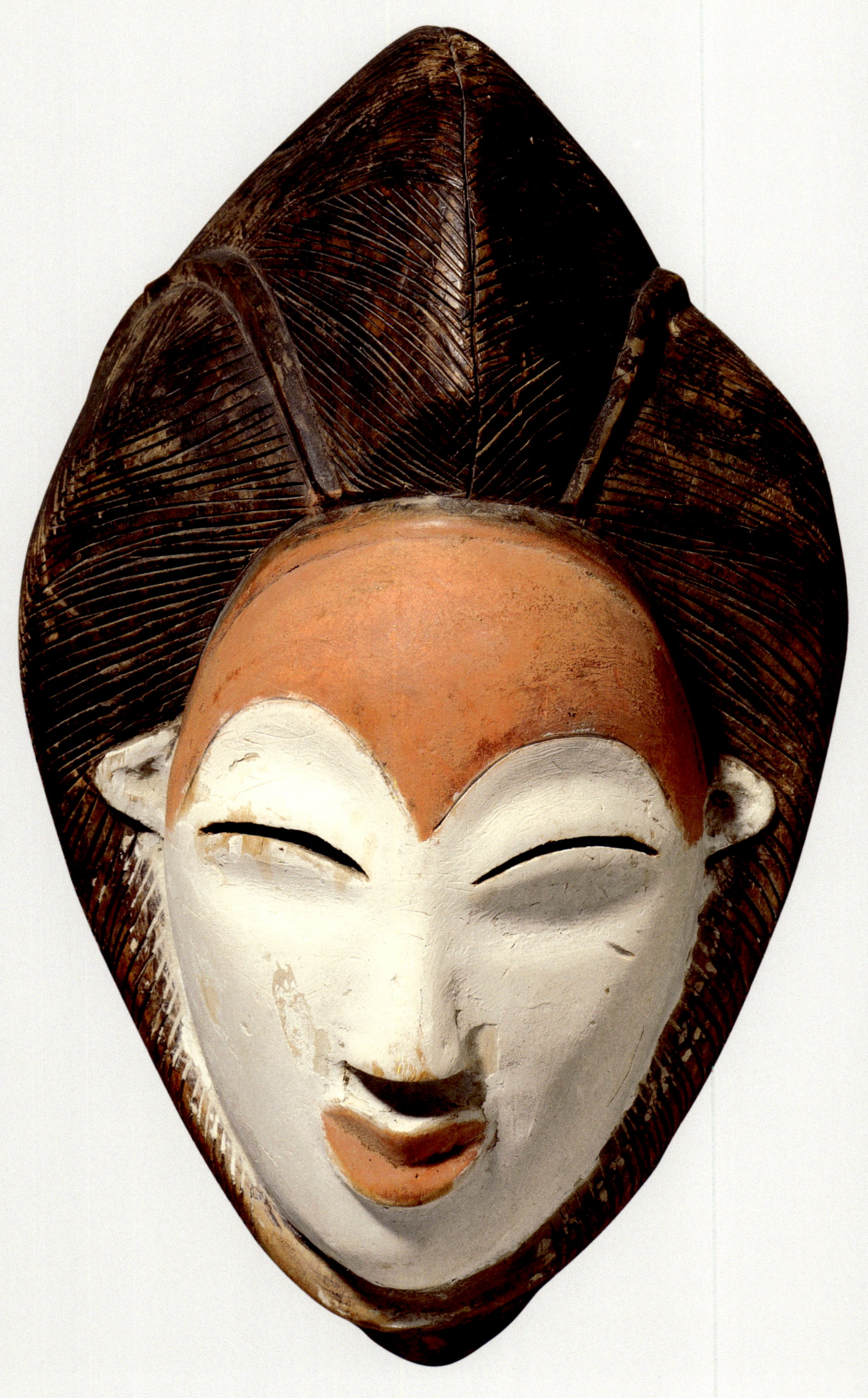

Face mask, *okuyi/mukuyi*, Punu region, Gabon, before 1889, painted wood, 34 x 21 x 16 cm, Bernisches Historisches Museum, Bern

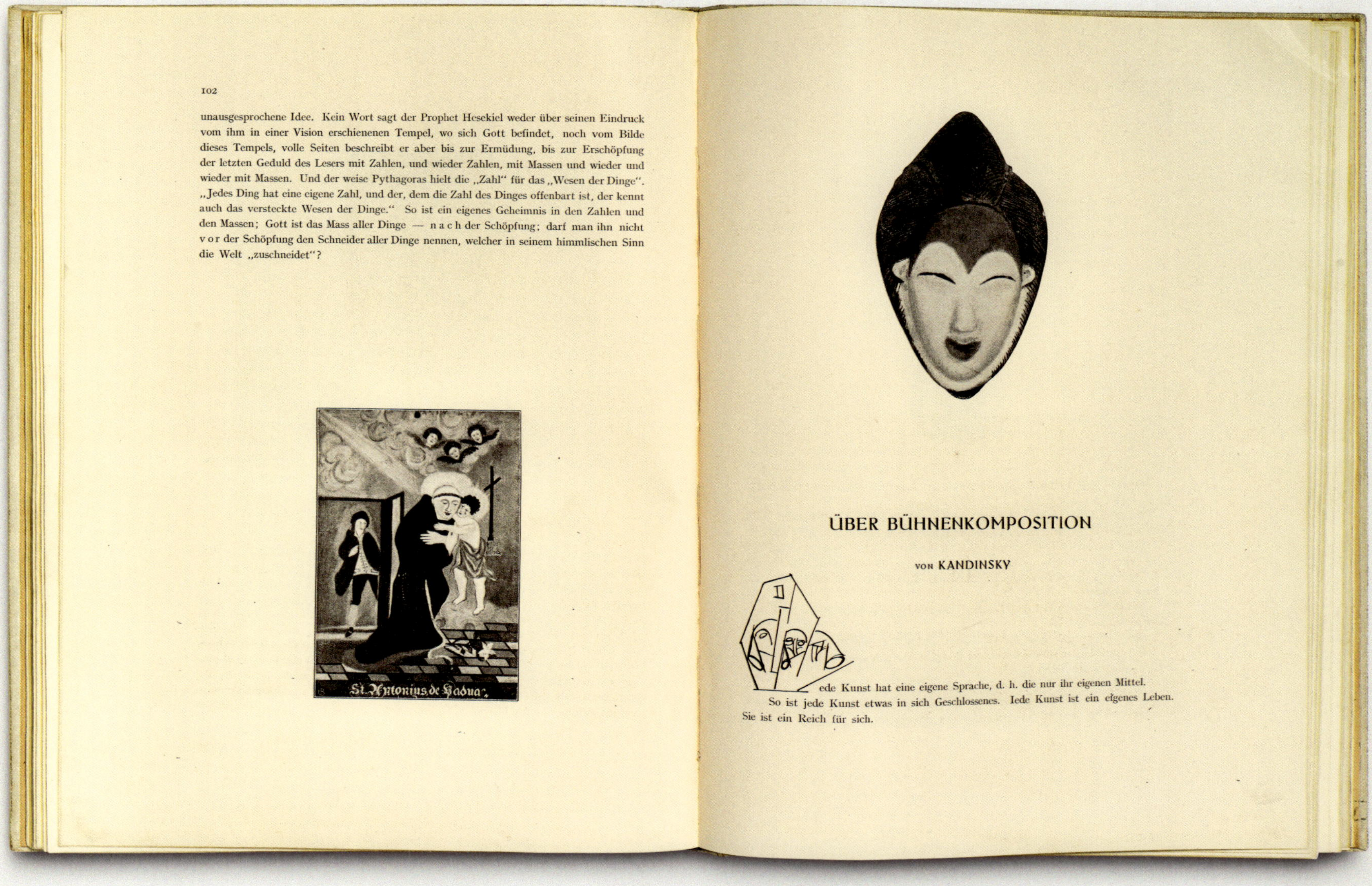

102

unausgesprochene Idee. Kein Wort sagt der Prophet Hesekiel weder über seinen Eindruck vom ihm in einer Vision erschienenen Tempel, wo sich Gott befindet, noch vom Bilde dieses Tempels, volle Seiten beschreibt er aber bis zur Ermüdung, bis zur Erschöpfung der letzten Geduld des Lesers mit Zahlen, und wieder Zahlen, mit Massen und wieder und wieder mit Massen. Und der weise Pythagoras hielt die „Zahl“ für das „Wesen der Dinge“. „Jedes Ding hat eine eigene Zahl, und der, dem die Zahl des Dinges offenbart ist, der kennt auch das versteckte Wesen der Dinge.“ So ist ein eigenes Geheimnis in den Zahlen und den Massen; Gott ist das Mass aller Dinge — n a c h der Schöpfung; darf man ihn nicht v o r der Schöpfung den Schneider aller Dinge nennen, welcher in seinem himmlischen Sinn die Welt „zuschneidet“?

St. Antonius de Padua

ÜBER BÜHNENKOMPOSITION

von KANDINSKY

ede Kunst hat eine eigene Sprache, d. h. die nur ihr eigenen Mittel.

So ist jede Kunst etwas in sich Geschlossenes. Iede Kunst ist ein eigenes Leben. Sie ist ein Reich für sich.

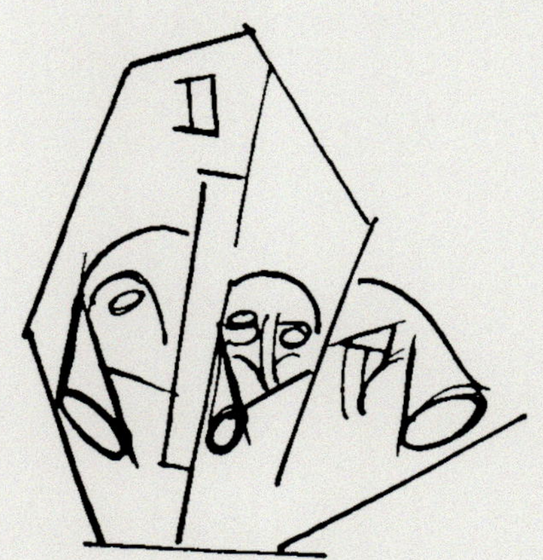

A formal harmony also determines the combination of illustrations here. The drawing of the face of Saint Anthony of Padua resembles the mask, whose Asian-looking facial features led Kandinsky to believe it was a Chinese theater mask and prompted him to place it at the beginning of his essay “Über Bühnenkomposition” (On Stage Composition). The initial “J,” by Hans Arp, takes up the mask theme addressed in Kandinsky’s article.

The editors' highly unconventional approach to formal analogies is reflectec in this pair of images. Vincent van Gogh's portrait of *Dr. Paul Gachet* is juxtaposed with an excerpt from a Japanese woodblock print from Marc's collection. Beyond the compositional echo, a substantial relationship appears to exist. As we read in Macke's almanac article, "Die Masken" (Masks), "does Van Gogh's portrait of Dr. Gachet not originate from a spiritual life similar to the amazed grimace of a Japanese juggler cut in a wood block?"

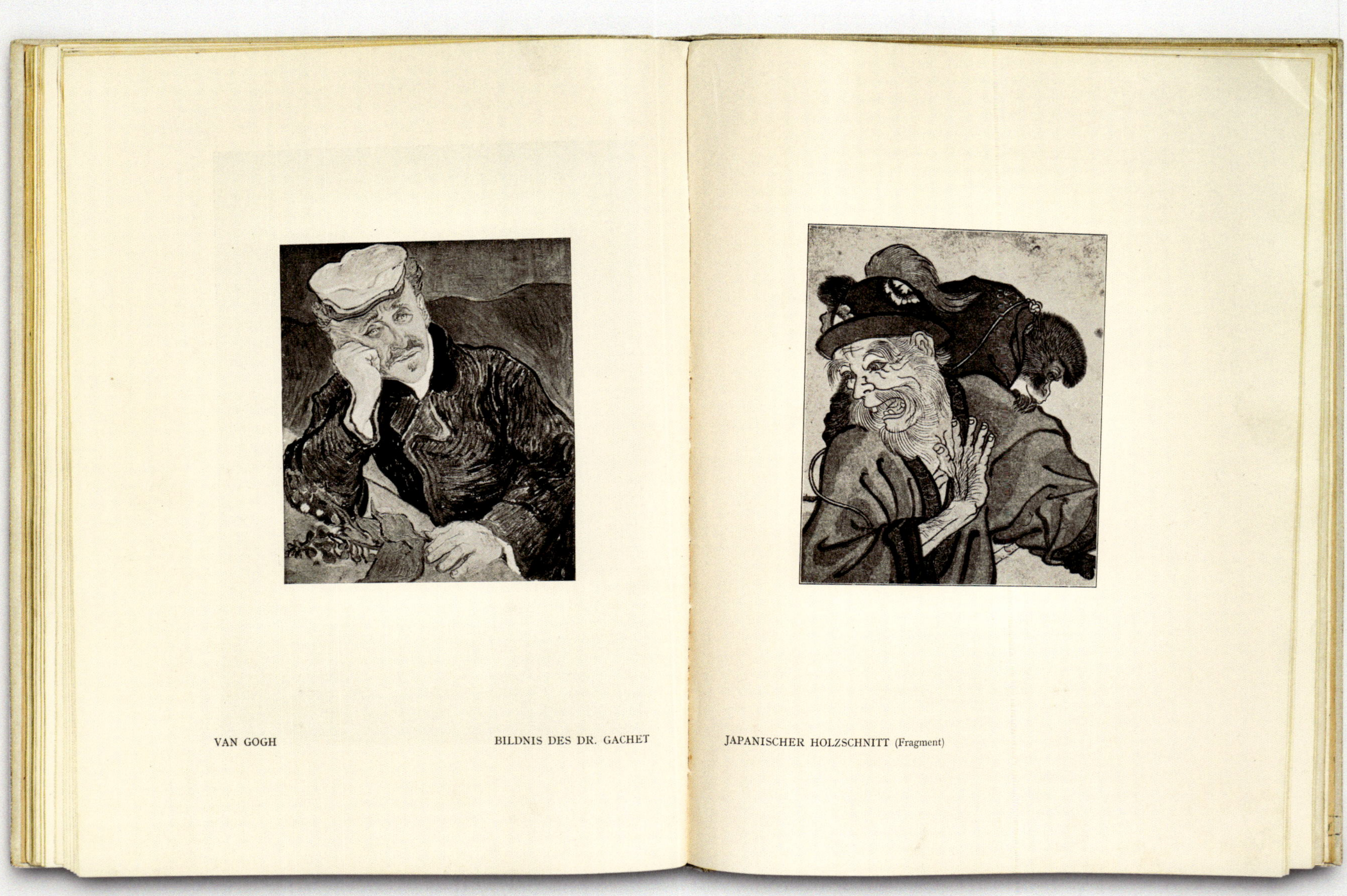

VAN GOGH BILDNIS DES DR. GACHET

JAPANISCHER HOLZSCHNITT (Fragment)

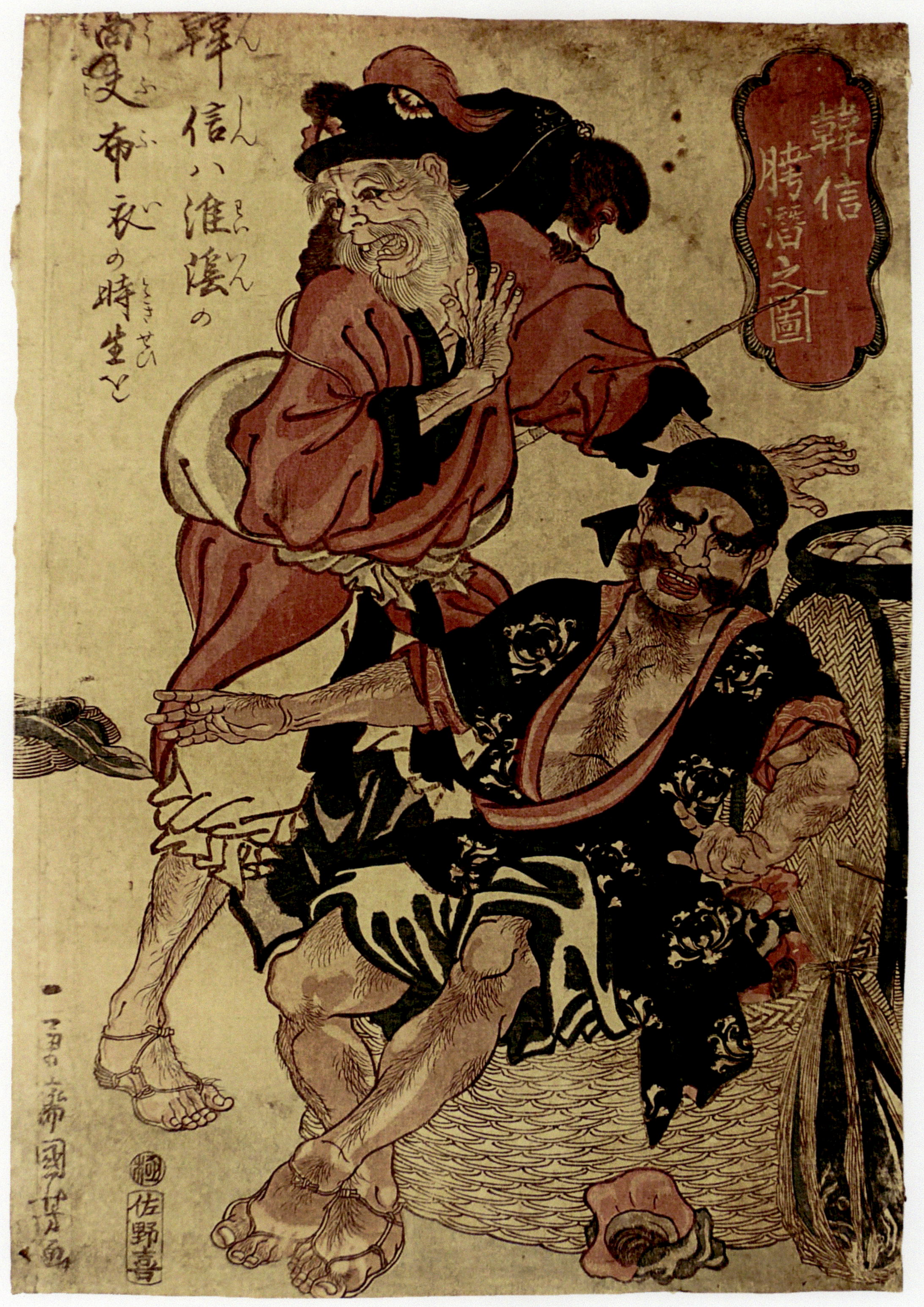

Utagawa Kuniyoshi, *Two Fishermen,* Japan, ca. 1835, detail from the triptych *The Humility of Kanshin*, color woodcut, 36.1 x 24.5 cm, Franz Marc Museum, Kochel am See, Franz Marc Stiftung, on permanent loan from the community of Maria Marc's heirs

MURNAU

In the first years of the twentieth century, the small, Upper Bavarian town of Murnau on Lake Staffel, located some seventy kilometers south of Munich in the foothills of the Alps, became a favorite destination for city dwellers. What they sought and found there was not so much the simple life as rural recreation. The picturesque architecture, graceful Baroque church, and view of the Alps made Murnau especially popular among artists. Along with the colorful house façades—a particularly charming feature, now as ever—is the light in summer and autumn, which makes the mountains glow in a deep blue and heightens color contrasts.

The artist Gabriele Münter, then Kandinsky's companion, described how the two of them came to Murnau in 1908 and worked alongside another artist couple, Marianne von Werefkin and Alexei von Jawlensky:

> *We had seen Murnau on an excursion and recommended it to Jawlensky and Werefkin—and they asked us to come there in the fall. We stayed at the Griesbräu [an inn that still exists today] & liked it very much. After a short period of agony I took a great leap forward, from copying nature—in a more or less Impressionist style—to feeling the content of things—abstracting—conveying an extract. . . . I particularly enjoyed showing my work to Jawlensky—who praised it lavishly and also explained a number of things to me—passed on what he had experienced and learned—talked about "synthesis." He's a good colleague. All 4 of us were keenly ambitious and each of us made progress.*[1]

In this context, "synthesis," or "Synthès," as Jawlensky pronounced it, means color synthesis. The Impressionist-influenced approach relied on closely juxtaposed dabs of different colors that came together in the eye to suggest forms. The type of painting Jawlensky and Münter aspired to translated this juxtaposition of colored dots into brightly colored areas that emphasized and simplified the natural model to the point of abstraction. In Jawlensky's work, for instance, a cloud might become a brilliant orange plane (cat. p. 81) or mountains be rendered pink (cat. p. 79). Yet one always has the impression of a faithful depiction of the foothills of the Bavarian Alps.

Münter succeeded wonderfully in capturing the atmosphere of the Murnau area by reducing colors and forms. She rendered swaths of the countryside dotted with bright red haystacks (cat. p. 74) or, as in *Garten in Murnau* (*Garden in Murnau*), set a light blue house in the midst of tropical greens (cat. p. 77). Feeling a great attraction to the area, she bought a house in Murnau in 1909, where she and Kandinsky would live until 1914, especially in the summer. Later she would return and spend the last years of her life there. This home, known as the Russian House, is an interdisciplinary work of art, containing decorations by Münter and Kandinsky, and is now one of the town's main tourist attractions.

Yet the two artist couples were inspired not just by the atmosphere and light there. Upper Bavarian folk art, the votive images in the church (cat. p. 44), and the glass paintings that are still produced in the region provided stimuli for their own approaches. Kandinsky (cat. p. 62) and Münter tried their own hand at glass painting, and the flatness of their oil paintings may have been influenced by it, since on glass it is much easier to set color areas next to one another than to blend fine gradations.

It is significant that Münter does not mention her companion Kandinsky in the passage cited above—he was much less involved in "copying nature—in a more or less Impressionist style," than she was. Kandinsky was always a storyteller—in the best sense of the word—whose encounter with the landscape around Murnau only briefly prompted him to become a "nature painter," albeit a highly convincing one. Before the Murnau phase, Kandinsky produced a great number of oil studies after nature that tended to be influenced by the Impressionist tradition; yet above all he was known for fairy-tale scenes suffused with symbolism and inspired by Russian folk art. His paintings of horses and riders give an idea of this approach (cat. pp. 62–65).

Nevertheless, Murnau brought about a transition for Kandinsky, too. His painting became more oriented on the natural model and became flatter. When he depicted the castle courtyard, however, it still resonated with the fairy-tale fantasy of his earlier style (cat. p. 71). Kandinsky had initially studied law and national economics, only deciding to become an artist at age thirty. As a university student he undertook sociological and anthropological studies of peasant communities in Vologda Province, northeast of Moscow. In other words, he had long been interested in rural culture, and was chiefly the one who turned to Upper Bavarian folk art. His pictures with blue mountains and simplified renderings of churches seem to have been influenced by votive images, and the motif of the rider can be associated with the folk depictions of riders, including Saint George, in Kandinsky's collection.[2]

Kandinsky's Murnau works differ from Münter's and Jawlensky's in terms of his ability to convey dynamism, as is clearly evident in the painting with the steam-spouting locomotive (cat. p. 73). A railway line still runs through the town today, not far from the Russian House—a constant of movement in the area, as it were. The picture shows swelling summer clouds in advance of a storm; the steam gushing from the engine's stack and spreading in the wind sets a sort of technological counterpoint to the natural events. Kandinsky's approximations to the configuration of the Murnau church likewise reflect his concern to lend dynamism to his compositions. The church stands as if blown awry by the wind. The fluffy clouds around it inadvertently evoke steam puffing from the "church-engine" (cat. p. 68).

One of Kandinsky's most important paintings from the early Murnau period is *Murnau—Kohlgruberstrasse* (cat. p. 67), from 1908. One has the impression that the artist has taken the sunlight falling on the street, a field, and trees, and associated it with certain, vibrant shades of color including yellow, red, and pink, and then superimposed these on his rendering of the street and landscape. An interesting element is the tree or mast to the left of center, whose broken appearance infuses the composition with movement. The free application of color and concomitant dynamic impulse are prerequisites for the increasingly intense degree of abstraction in Kandinsky's art.

[1] Gabriele Münter, "Tagebuchaufzeichnung" [1911 for 1908], in *Der Blaue Reiter: Eine Geschichte in Dokumenten*, ec. Andreas Hüneke (Stuttgart, 2011), p. 7; English trans.: diary entry of May 17, 1911 [retrospective account of 1908 events], quoted from: Annegret Hoberg, ed., *Wassily Kandinsky and Gabriele Münter: Letters and Reminiscences, 1902–1914* (Munich and New York, 1994), pp. 45–46.

[2] See the reproductions in *"Die Blaue Reiterei stürmt voran": Bildquellen für den Almanach Der Blaue Reiter: Die Sammlung von Wassily Kandinsky und Gabriele Münter,* ed. Helmut Friedel, Isabelle Jansen, and the Gabriele Münter- und Johannes Eichner-Stiftung, exh. cat. Münter-Haus, Murnau (Munich, 2012).

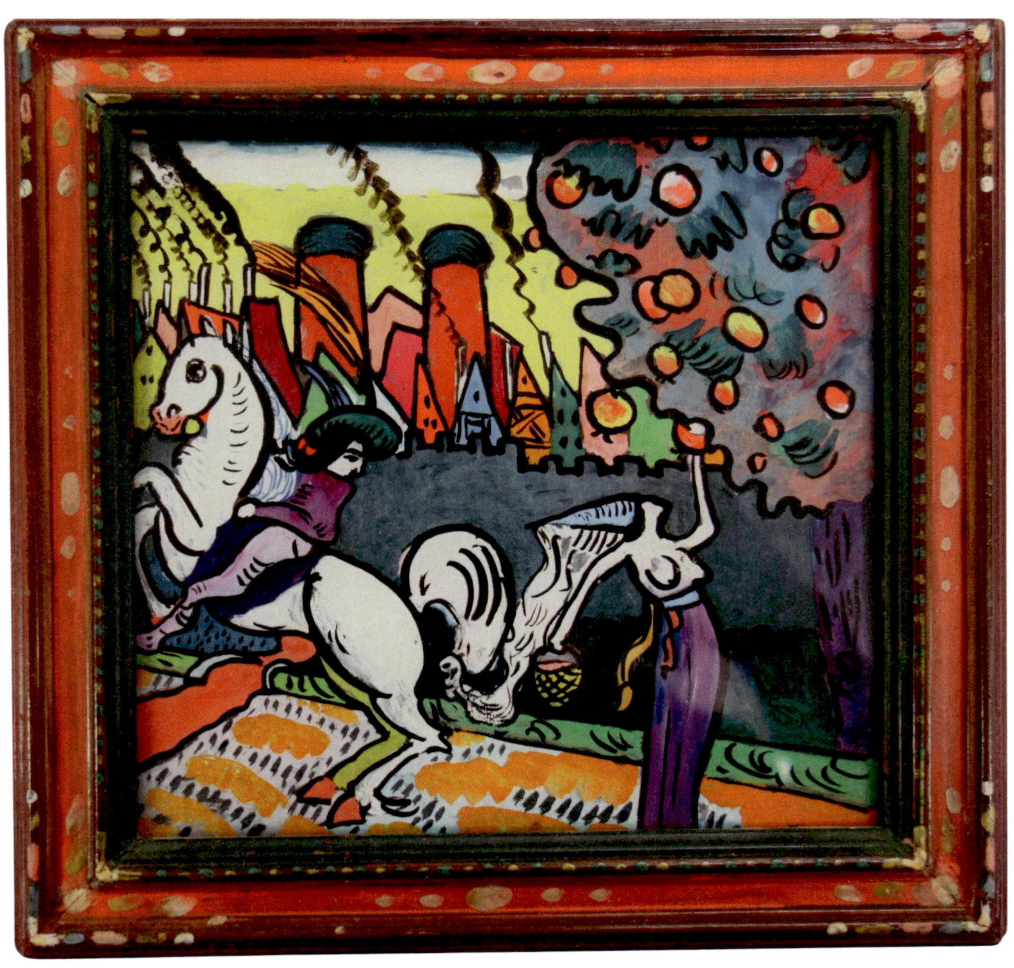

Wassily Kandinsky *Rider and Woman Picking Apples*, 1911
ahlers collection

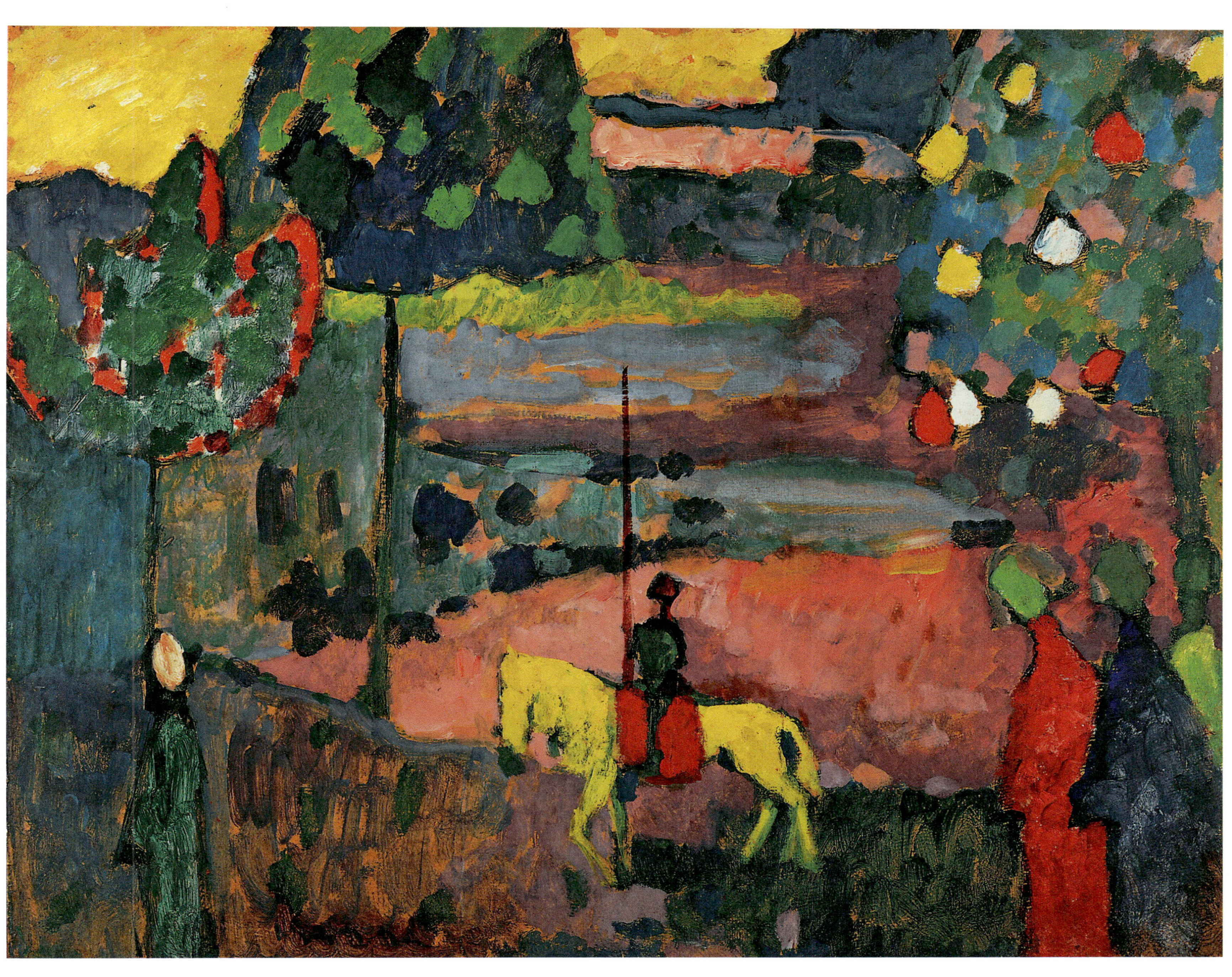

Wassily Kandinsky *Lancer in Landscape*, 1908
Merzbacher Kunststiftung

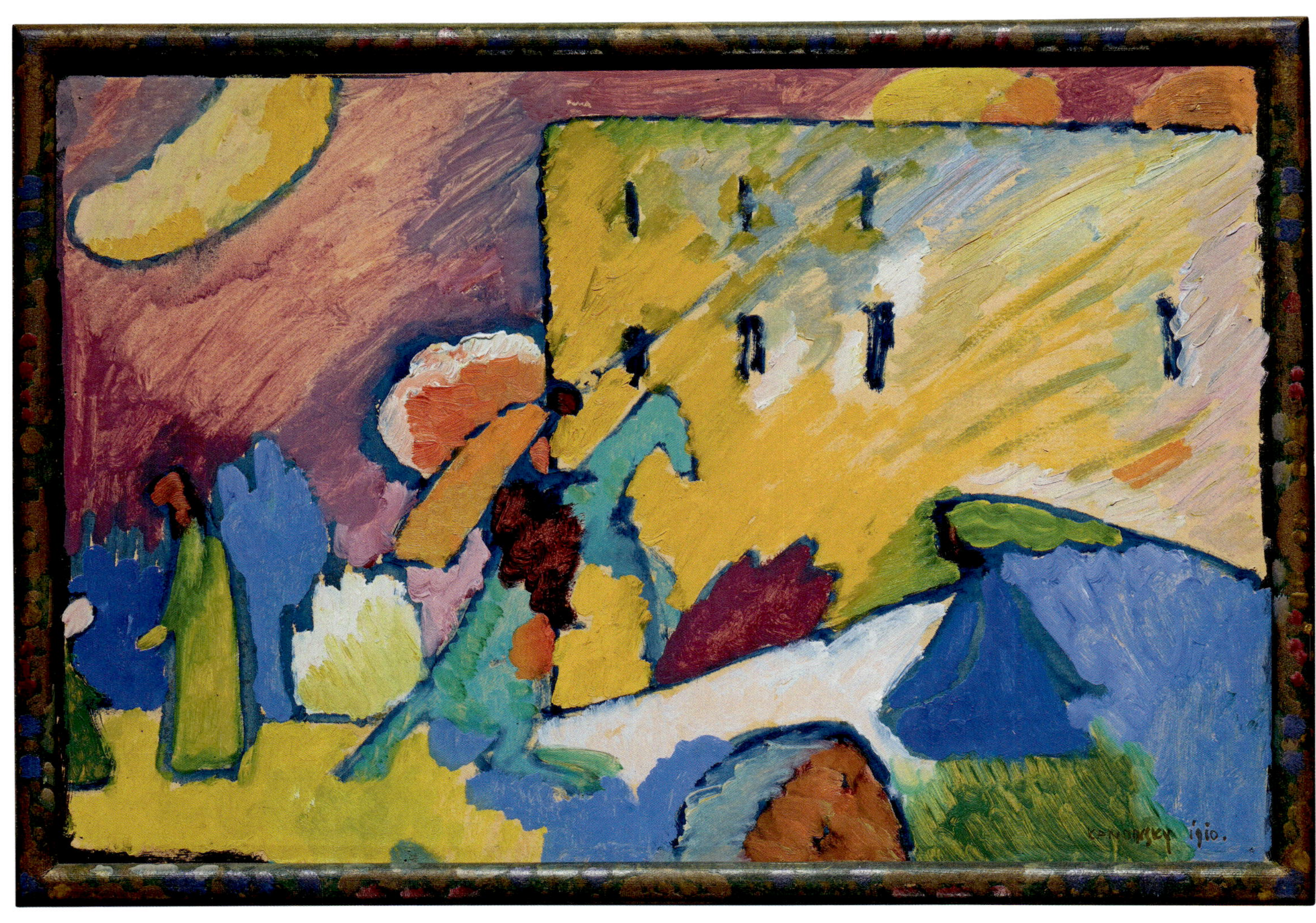

Wassily Kandinsky *Study for Improvisation 3*, 1909
Private collection

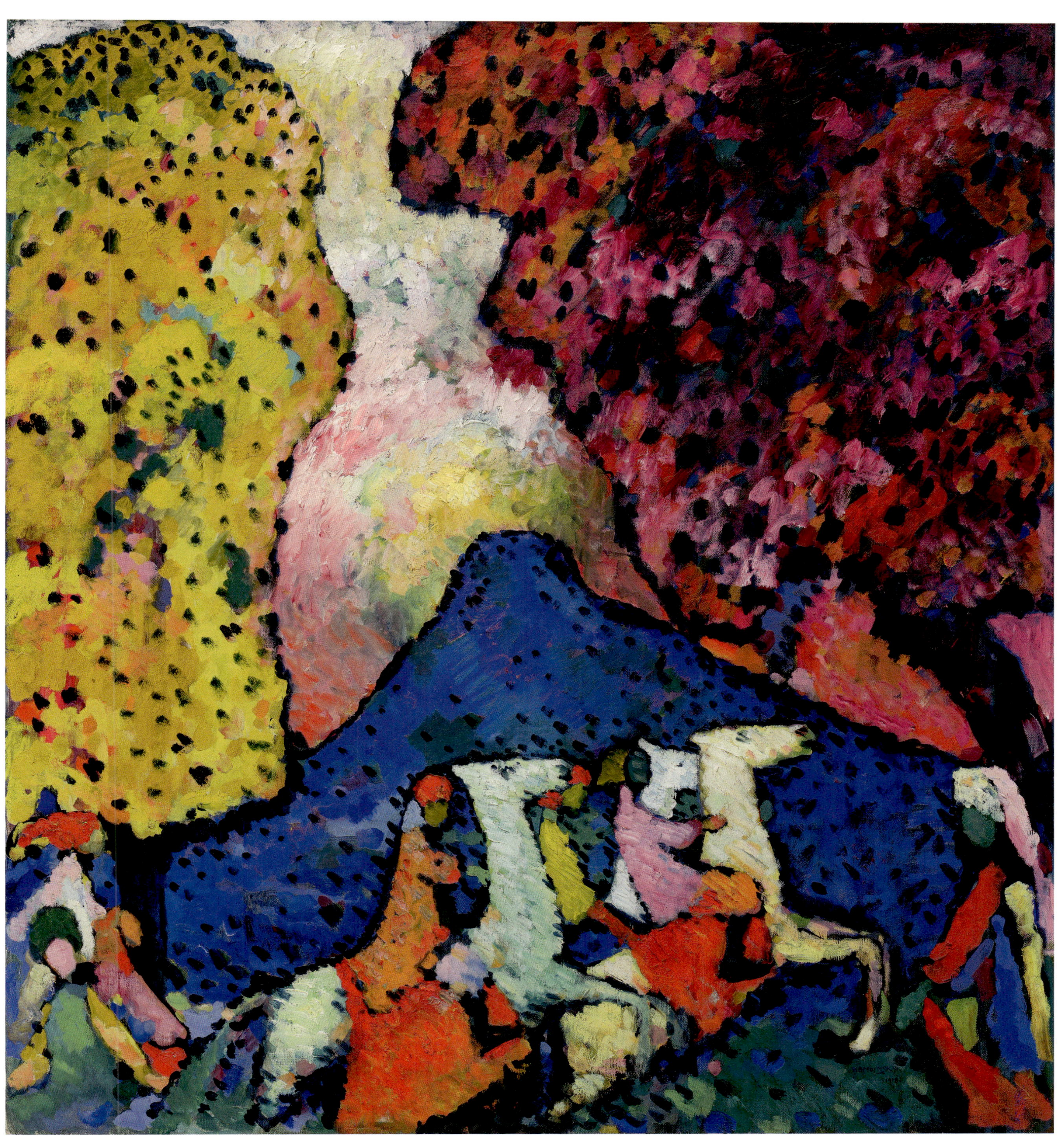

Wassily Kandinsky *Blue Mountain*, 1908–09
Solomon R. Guggenheim Museum, New York, Solomon R. Guggenheim Founding Collection, By gift

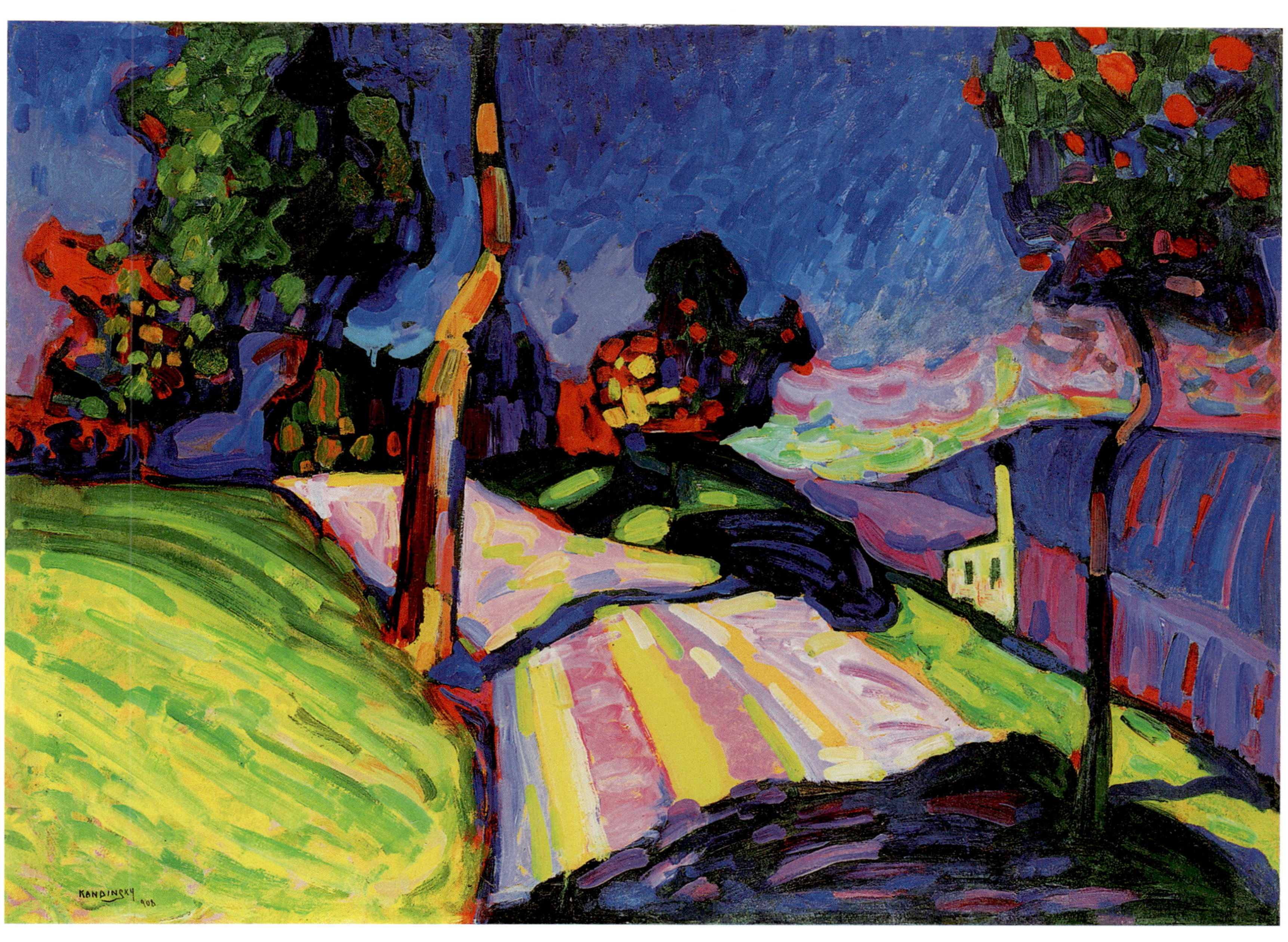

Wassily Kandinsky *Murnau—Kohlgruberstrasse,* 1908
Merzbacher Kunststiftung

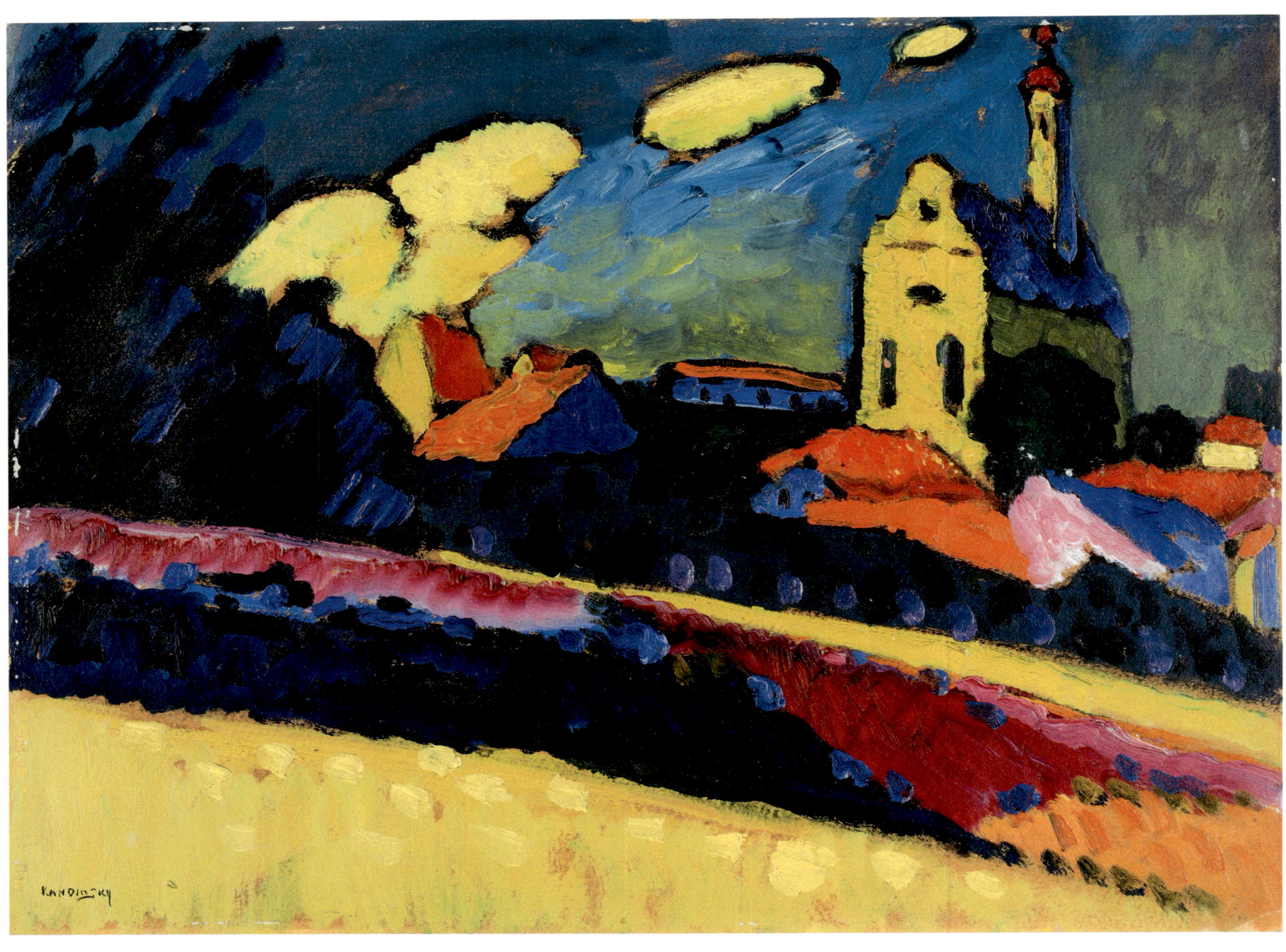

Wassily Kandinsky *Study for Murnau—Landscape with Church*, 1909
Stiftung Im Obersteg, on loan to the Kunstmuseum Basel

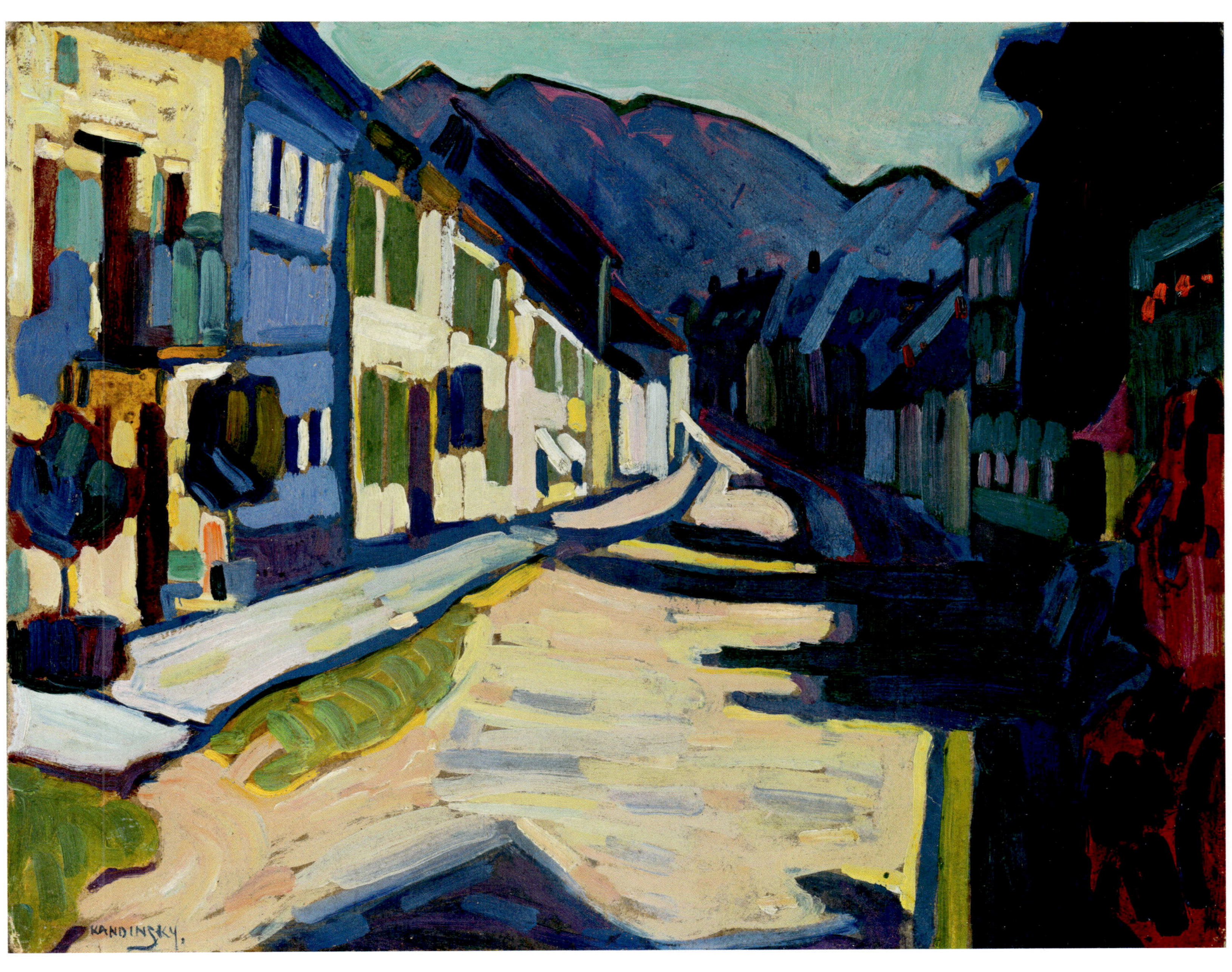

Wassily Kandinsky *Murnau—Obermarkt with Mountains*, 1908
Private collection

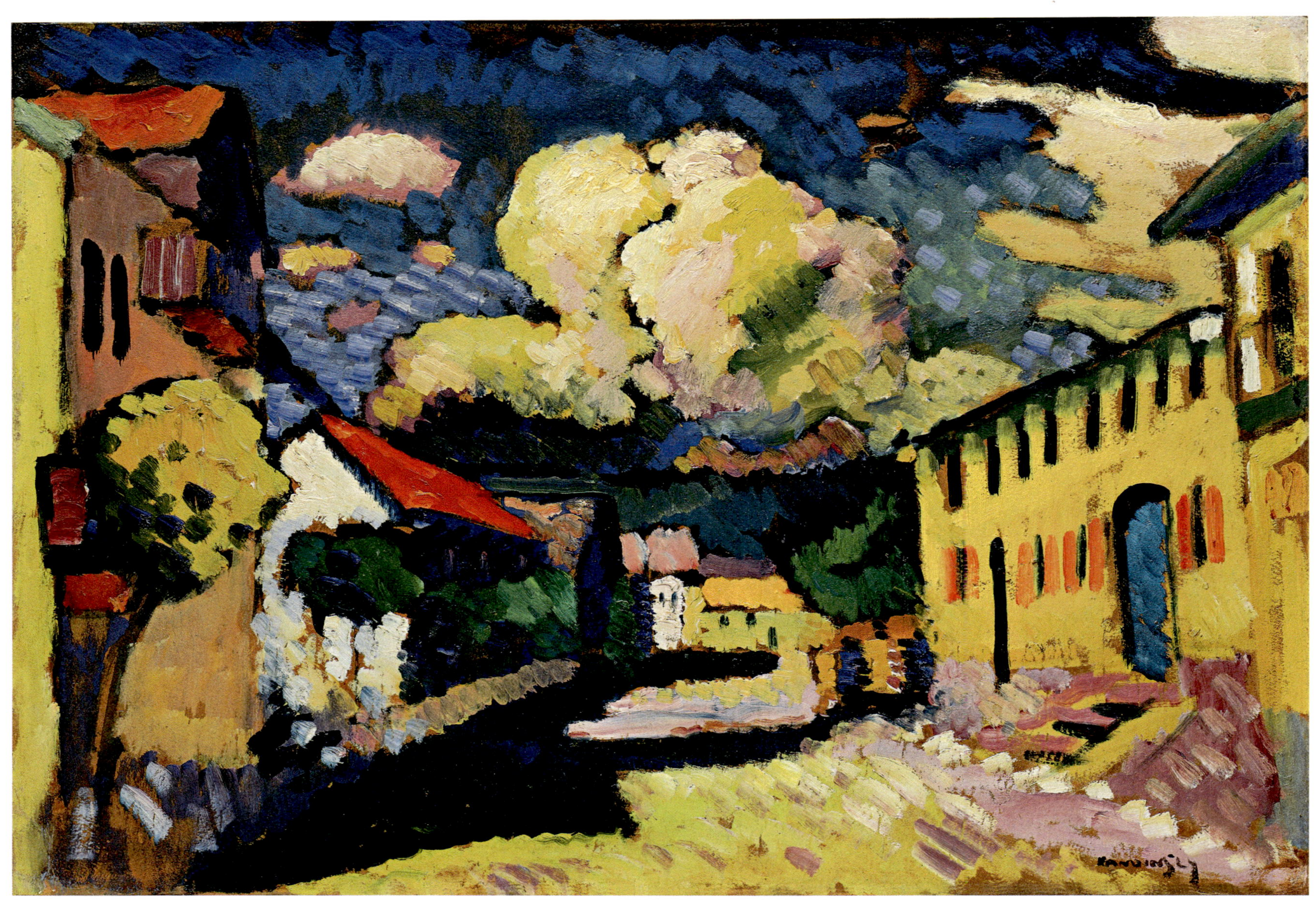

Wassily Kandinsky *Murnau—Village Street*, 1908
Merzbacher Kunststiftung

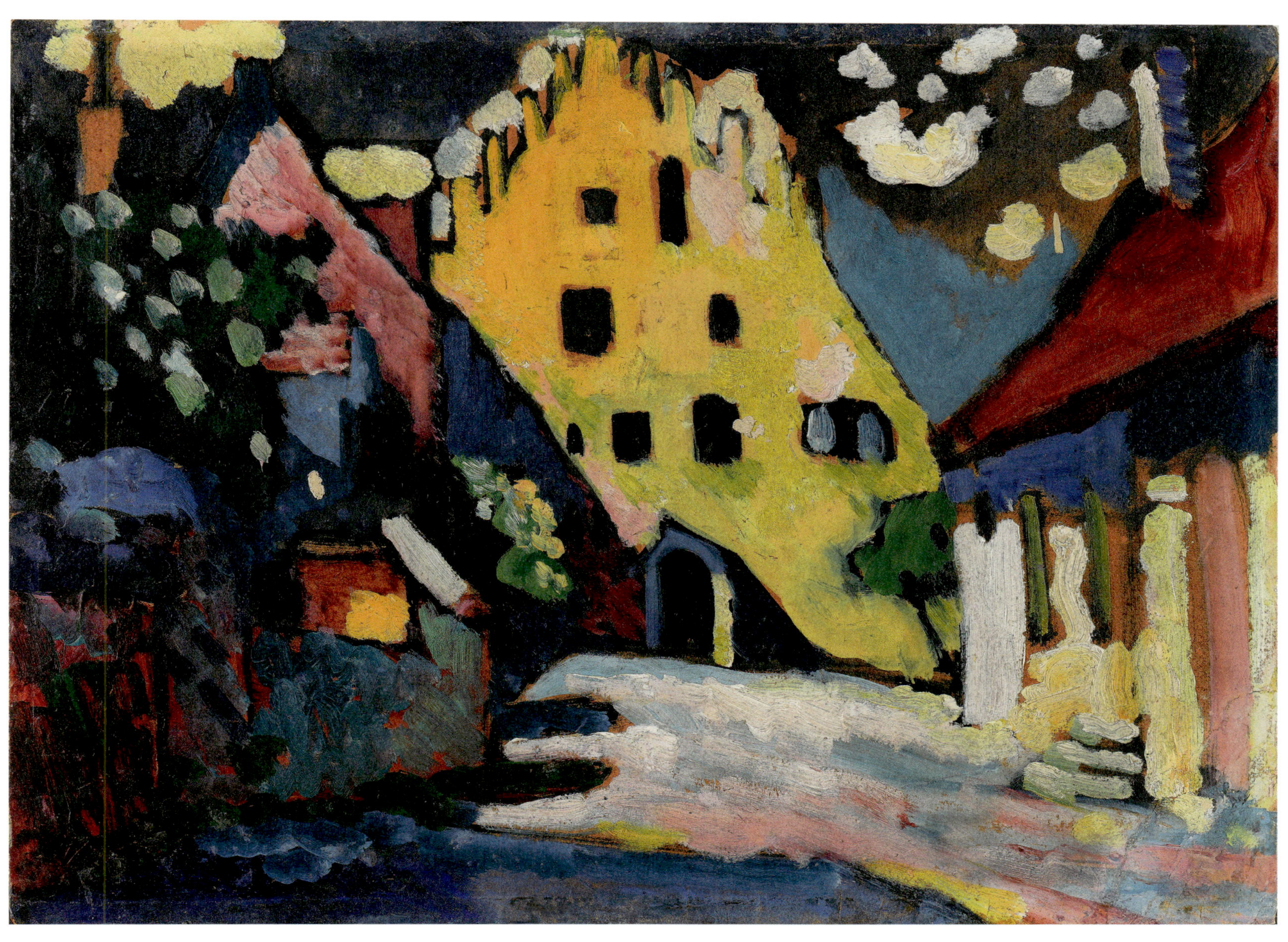

Wassily Kandinsky *Murnau—Castle Courtyard I*, 1908
The State Tretyakov Gallery, Moscow

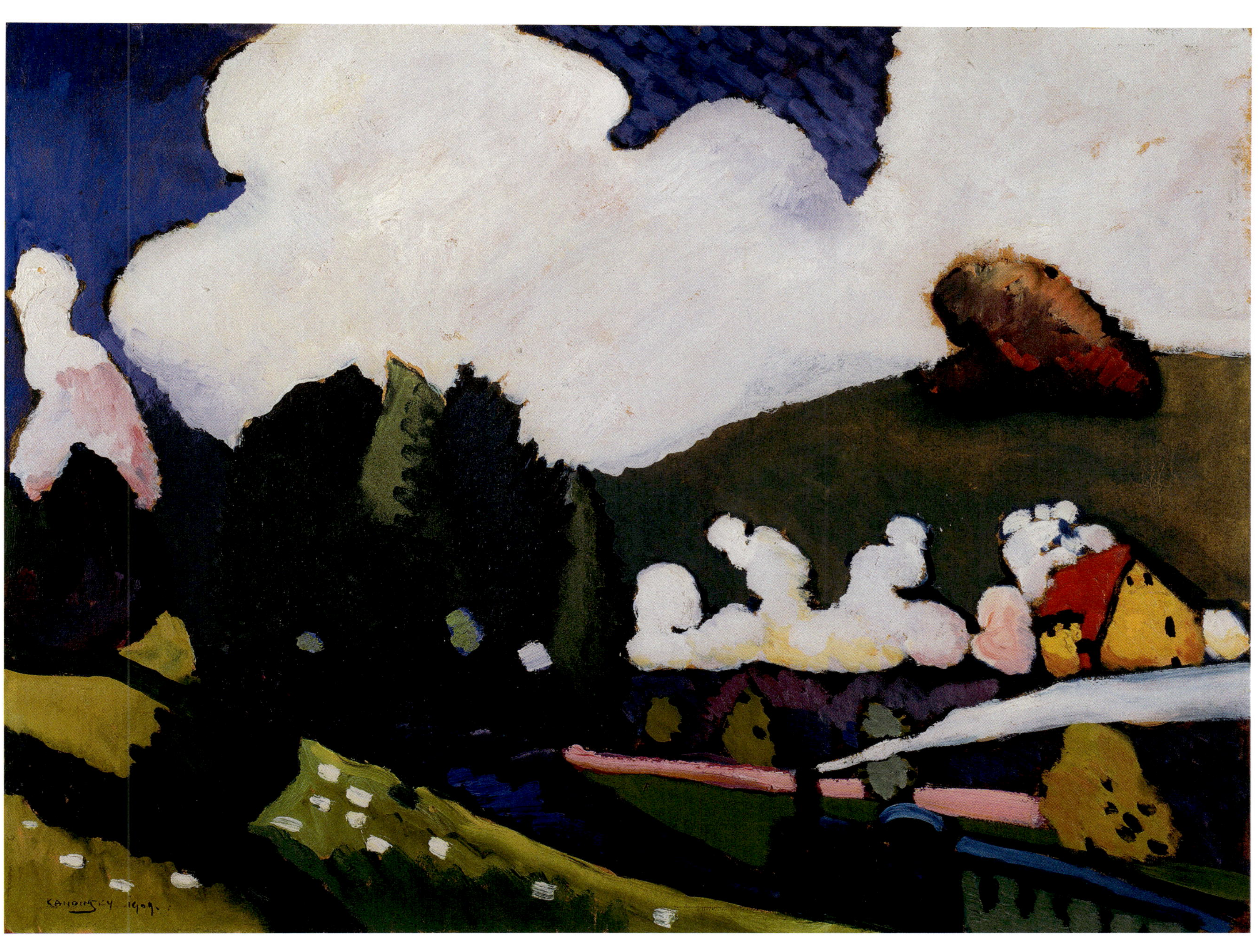

Wassily Kandinsky *Landscape near Murnau with Locomotive*, 1909
Solomon R. Guggenheim Museum, New York

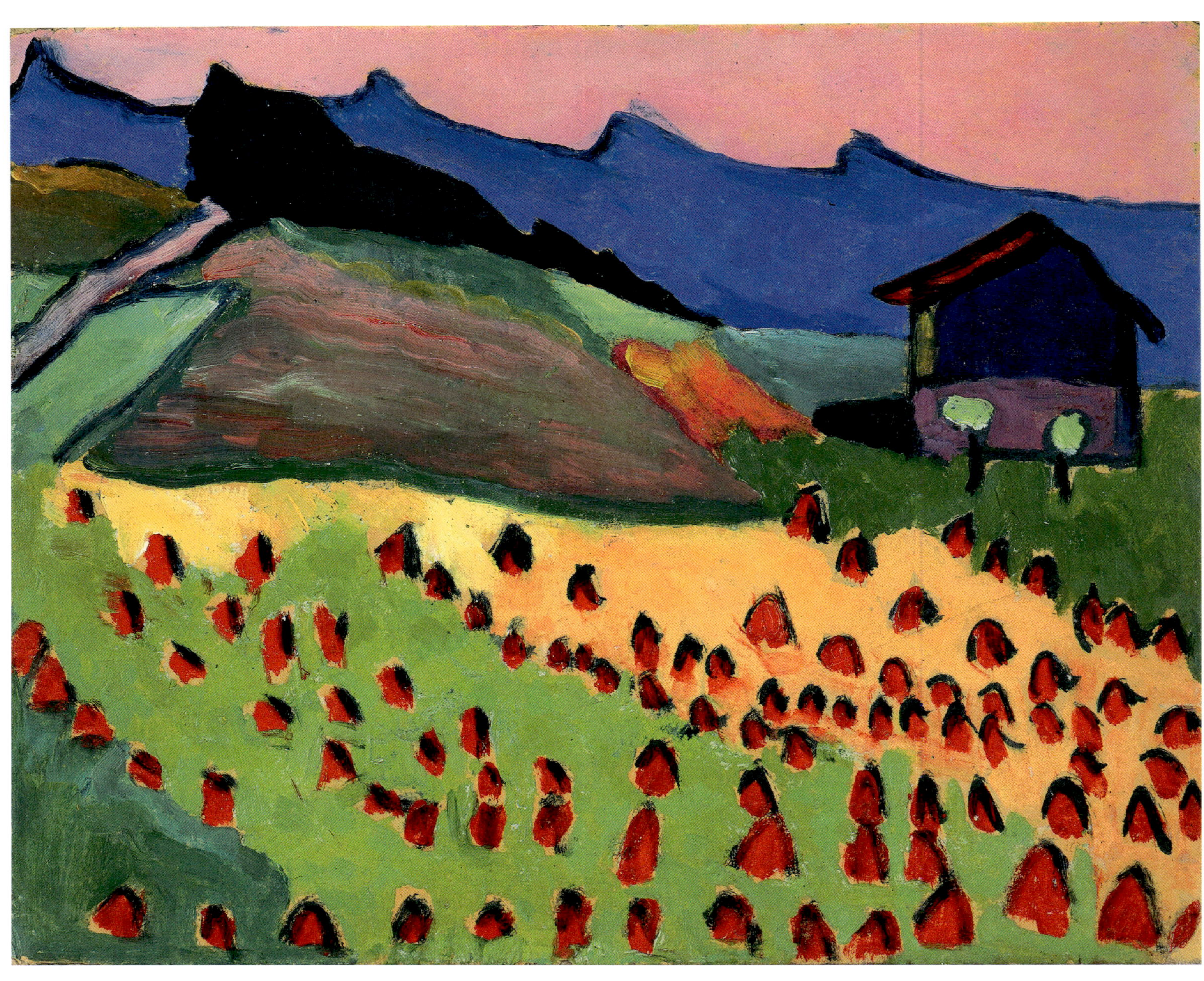

Gabriele Münter *Landscape with Cabin at Sunset,* 1908
Kunstsammlungen Chemnitz, Museum Gunzenhauser

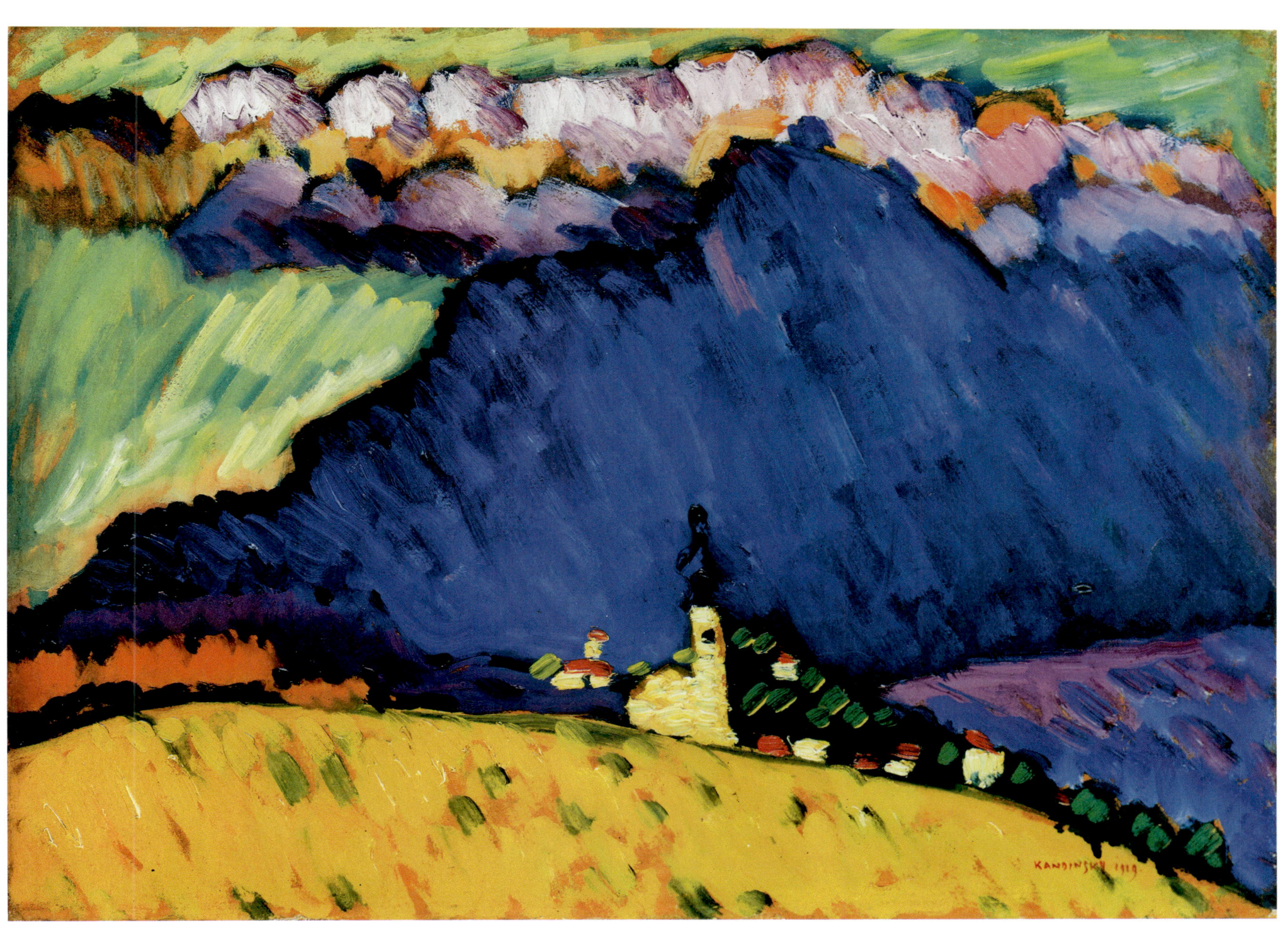

Wassily Kandinsky *Dünaberg*, 1909
Private collection

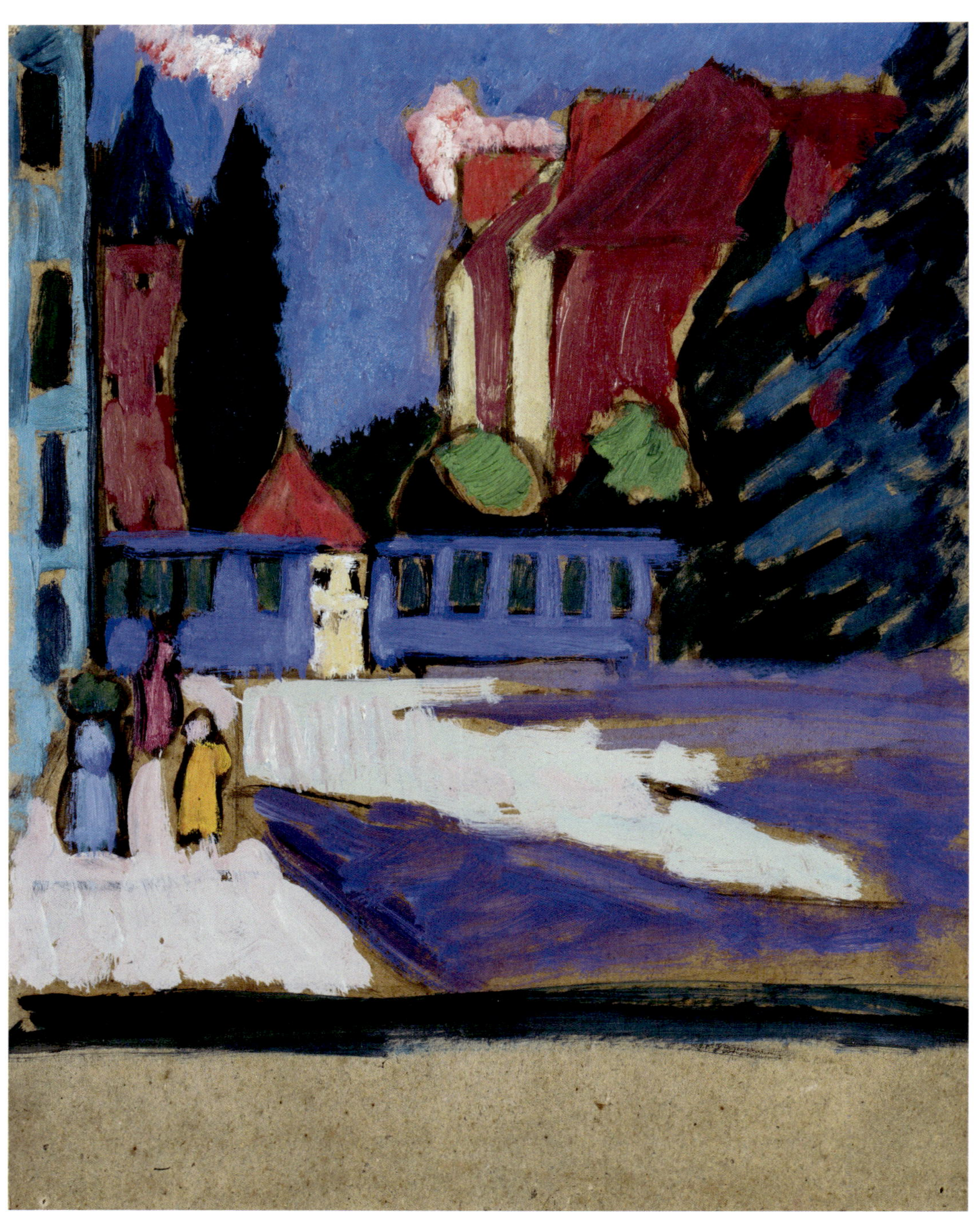

Gabriele Münter *Streetcar in Munich*, 1910–12
Private collection

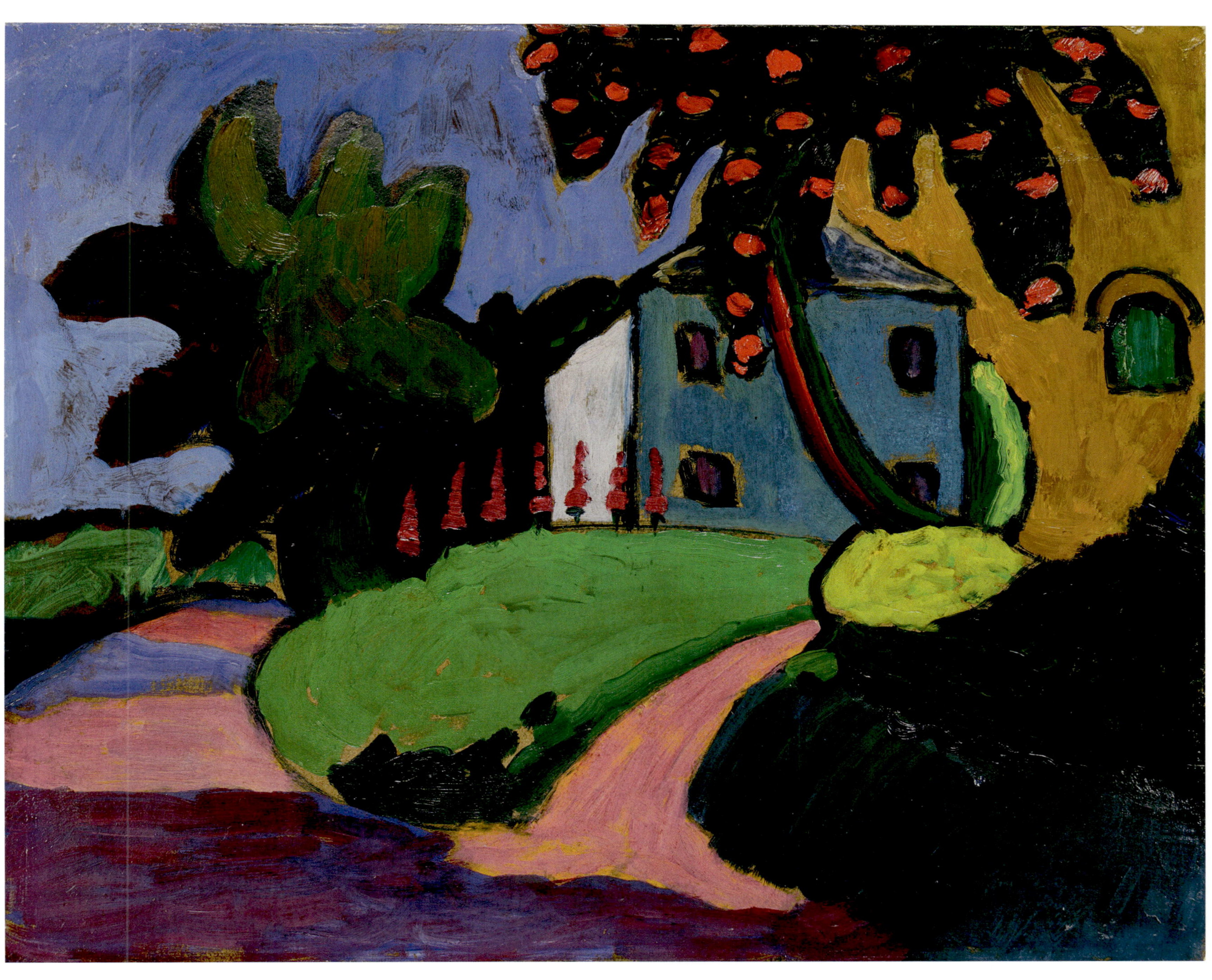

Gabriele Münter *Garden in Murnau*, 1910
Museum Wiesbaden, donated by M. and W. Rick, 2013

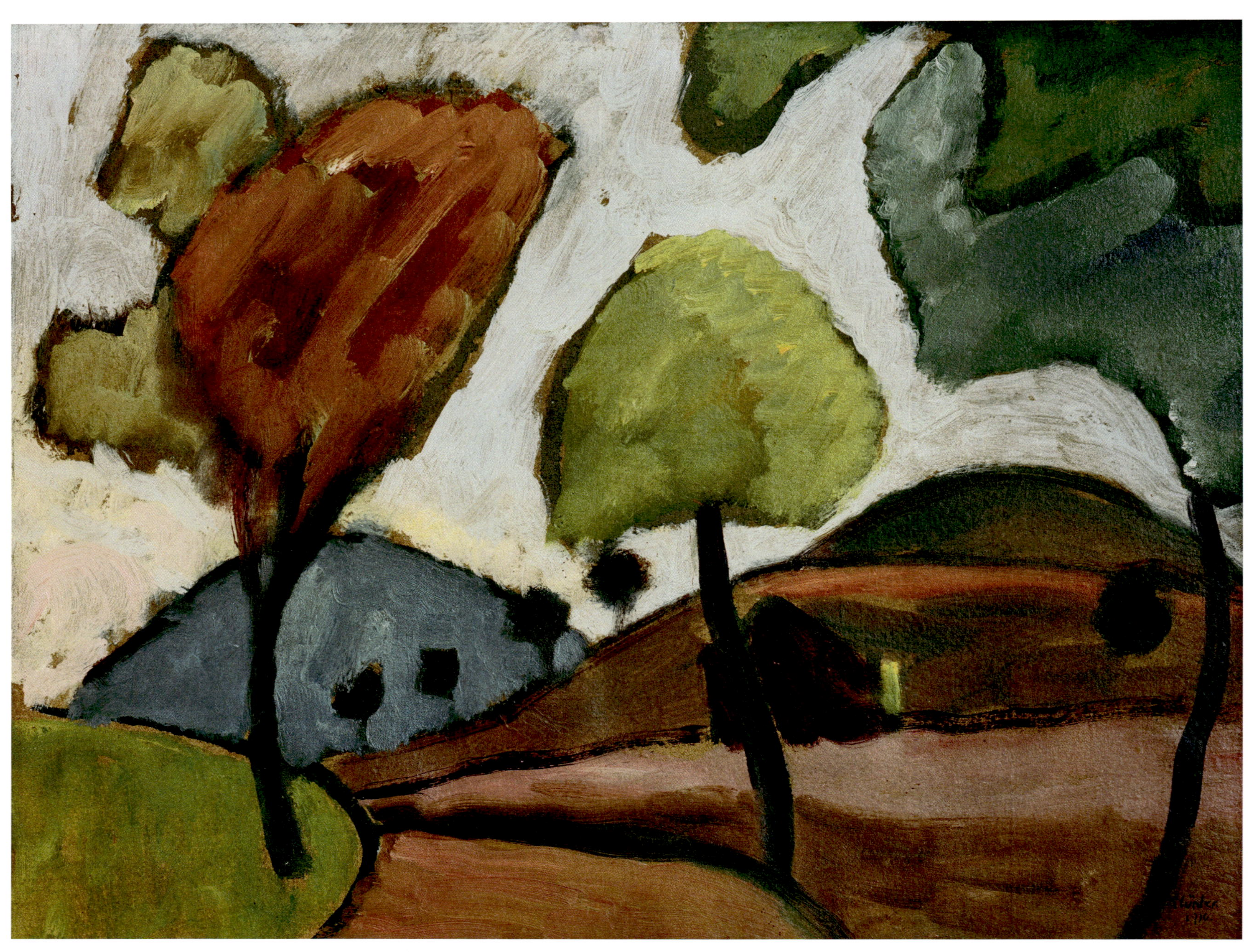

Gabriele Münter *Country Road in Autumn*, 1910
Private collection

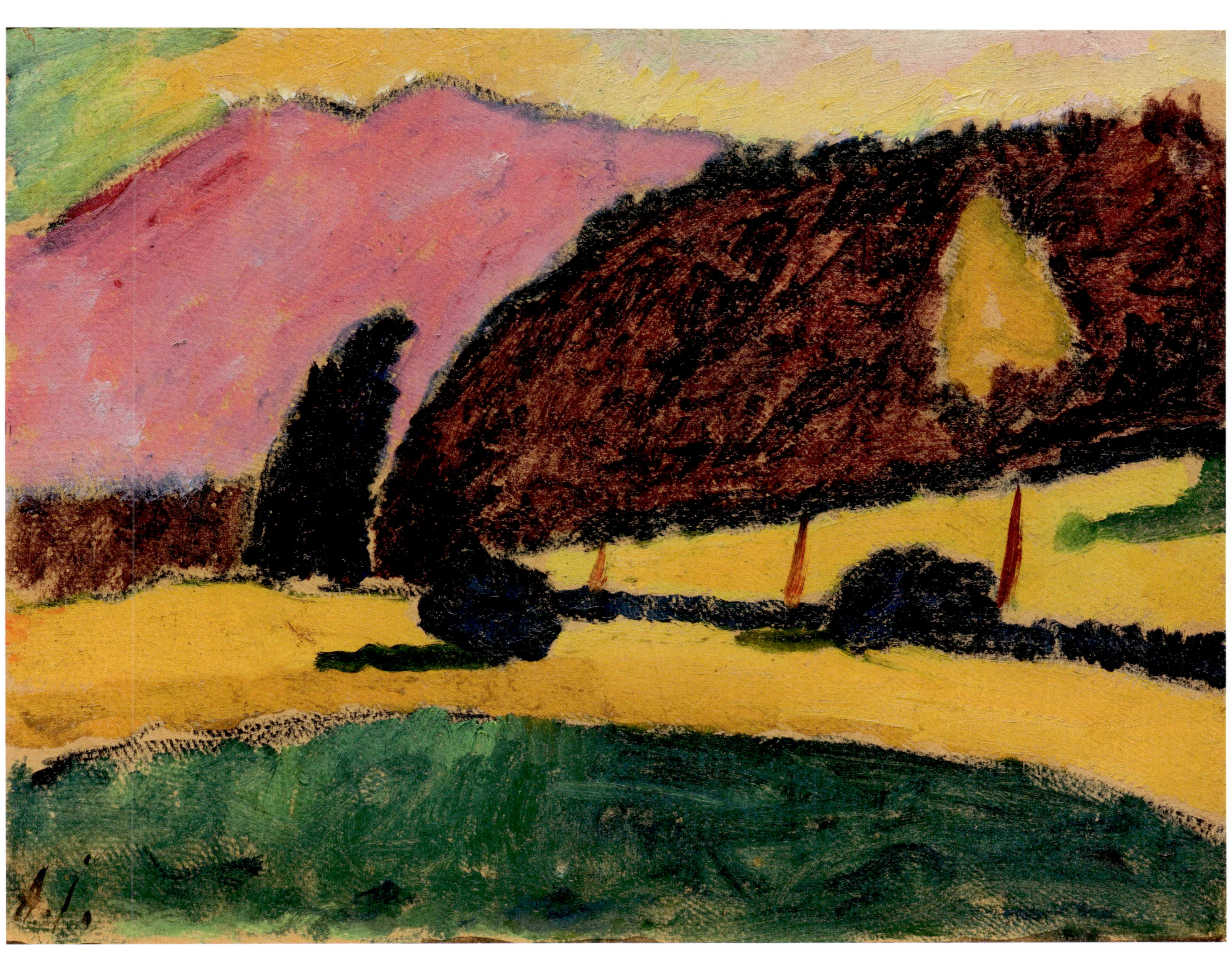

Alexei von Jawlensky *Autumn in Murnau*, 1909
Sprengel Museum Hannover

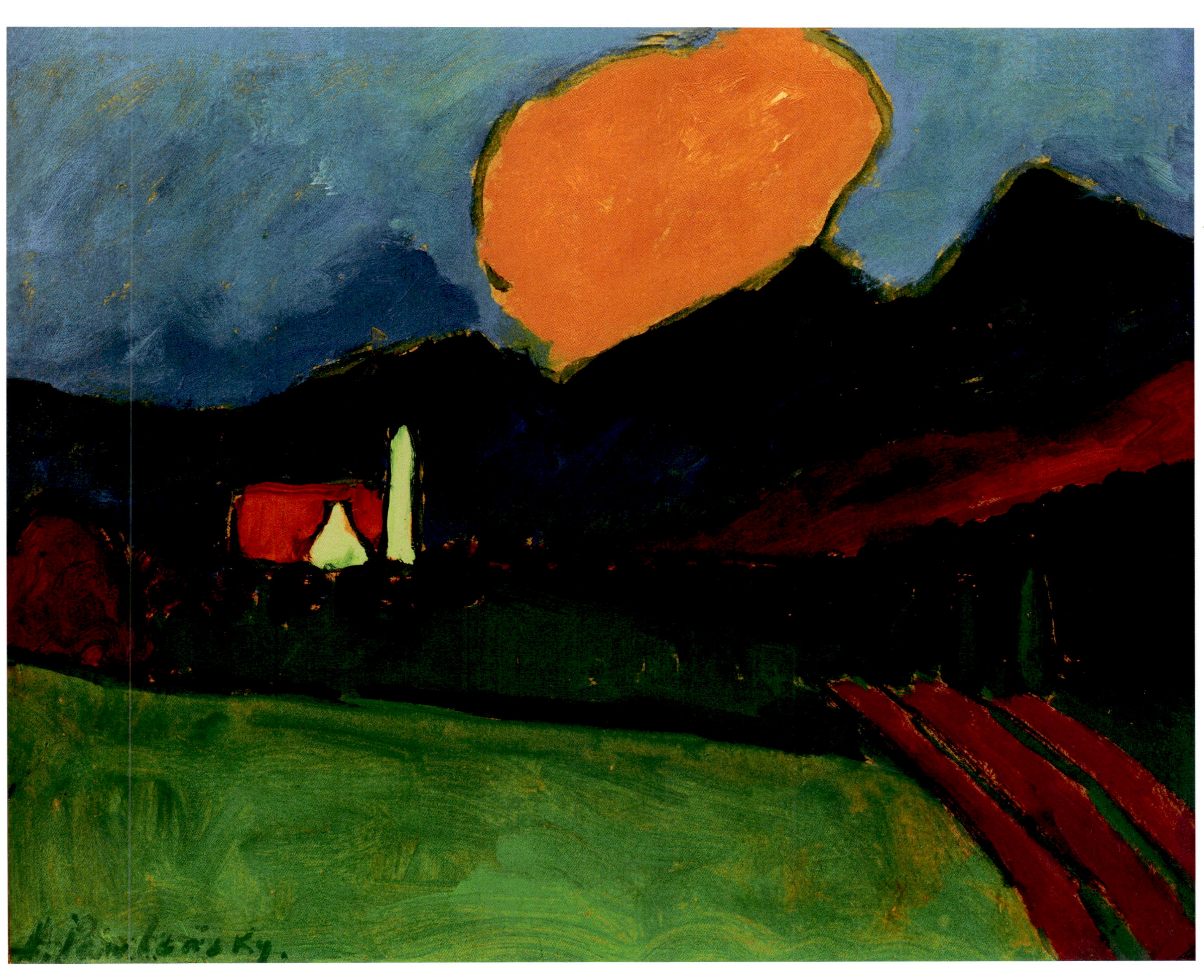

Alexei von Jawlensky *Murnau—Landscape, Orange Cloud,* ca. 1909
Private collection

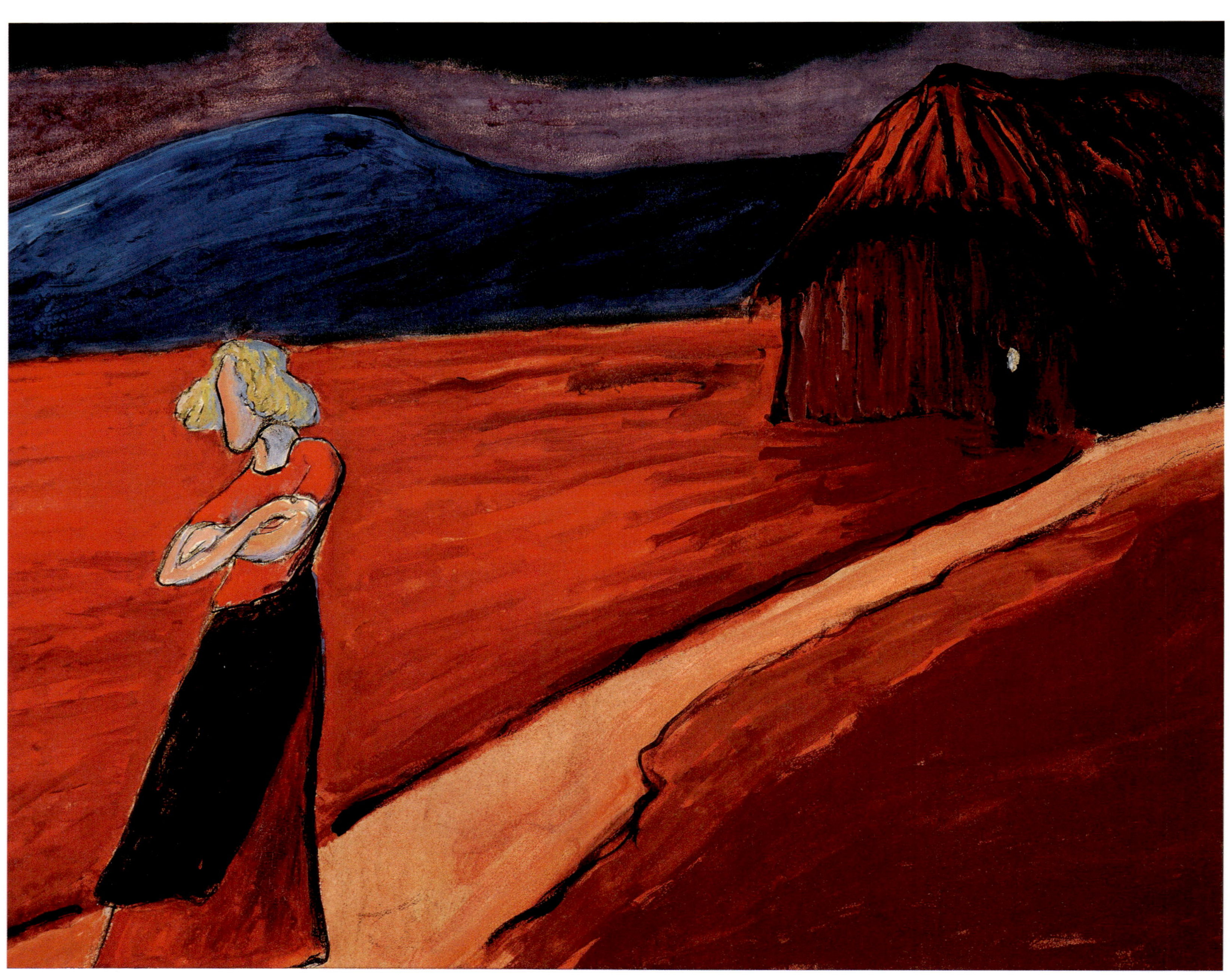

Marianne von Werefkin *Tragic Mood*, 1910
Museo Comunale d'Arte Moderna, Commune of Ascona

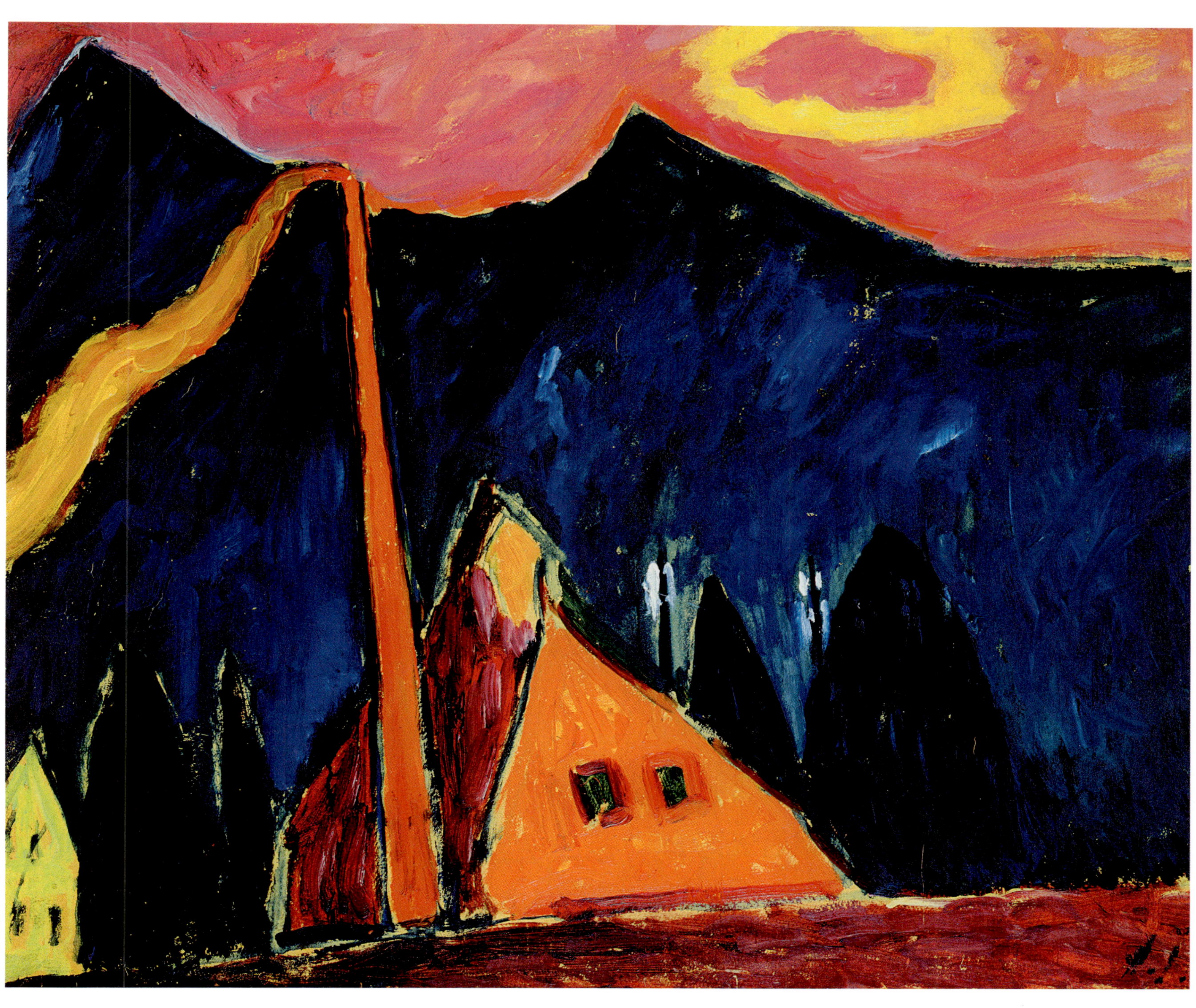

Alexei von Jawlensky *The Factory*, 1910
Private collection, Switzerland

WASSILY KANDINSKY IN 1910: FROM FIGURATION TO ABSTRACTION

The exhibition includes a series of works Kandinsky produced in 1910 that illustrates how he moved beyond figuration to embrace abstraction. Not that this development was absolutely linear, as becomes evident from the selection of works. Here, painting is an intellectual process. Anyone who paints an abstract picture is generally capable of working figuratively. The notion that abstract art is a step in the development beyond figurative art is a convention of modernism that was significantly defined by Kandinsky himself.

The horizontal format of *Murnau—Garten I* (*Murnau—The Garden I;* cat. p. 88) provides a view of Murnau as seen from the garden of the house where Münter and Kandinsky spent the summer months. It is an atmospheric rather than a topographical panorama, depicting the vitality of nature, the flourishing garden, and the town's striking buildings in the form of a semicircle that suggests a "hemisphere" and anticipates analogous compositions of the coming years. The following painting, *Murnau—Garten II* (*Murnau—The Garden II;* cat. p. 89), has a vertical format that emphasizes upward movement. The white and red shapes in the background might still be read as houses, and the yellowish-brown forms in the foreground as sunflowers. Ultimately, however, such attributions are now secondary. The point of the exercise is the rising wave of different colors, a free composition in color.

Yet the term "composition" is misleading when referring to Kandinsky. In connection with the garden paintings he would likely have spoken of "impressions," since in 1909 he began classifying his works in three categories. The first were *Impressions,* depicting the effects of "external nature," which were "expressed in linear-painterly form." His *Improvisations,* in contrast, were "chiefly unconscious, for the most part suddenly arising expressions of events of an inner character, hence impressions of 'internal nature.'" *Compositions,* finally, were "expressions of feelings that have been forming within me in a similar way (but over a very long period of time). . . . Here, reason, the conscious, the deliberate, and the purposeful play a preponderant role."[1]

Kandinsky's *Compositions,* and some of his *Improvisations,* might have been based on preliminary studies that themselves are autonomous images. The artist even sometimes painted the frames for them. Two such works are on view in the exhibition: *Studie zu Improvisation 3* (*Study for Improvisation 3;* cat. p. 64), from 1909, and *Fragment zu Komposition II* (*Fragment for Composition II;* cat. p. 87), from 1910. The preliminary study for *Komposition II* contains forms that recall a group of kneeling women, which, although defined by a contour line, cannot be associated with any particular activity. We as viewers confront a story that remains open-ended, which draws us into the picture.

Much the same is true of the larger-format *Improvisations* of 1910, although *Improvisation 10* (cat. p. 97) depends more strongly on the viewer's expectation of discovering suggestions of a story in the image than does *Improvisation 13* (cat. p. 95). Perhaps this is a result of the red shapes at the upper right, which recall the domes of Orthodox churches. The flat segments in the foreground play a leading role in *Improvisation 13;* on the whole, the work represents more of a close-up than *Improvisation 10,* whose round forms evoke more of an overview. The numerous circling lines there seem to vibrate, lending the image a tremendous sense of tension whose effect extends beyond the actual picture space.

1 Wassily Kandinsky, *Über das Geistige in der Kunst: insbesondere in der Malerei*, with an introduction by Max Bill and a foreword and annotation on the rev. new ed. by Jelena Hahl-Fontaine (Munich, 1912; 5th ed., Zurich, 2016), p. 146; English ed.: "On the Spiritual in Art," in *Kandinsky: Complete Writings on Art,* ed. Kenneth C. Lindsay and Peter Vergo (Boston, 1982; new, repr. ed., New York, 1994), p. 218.

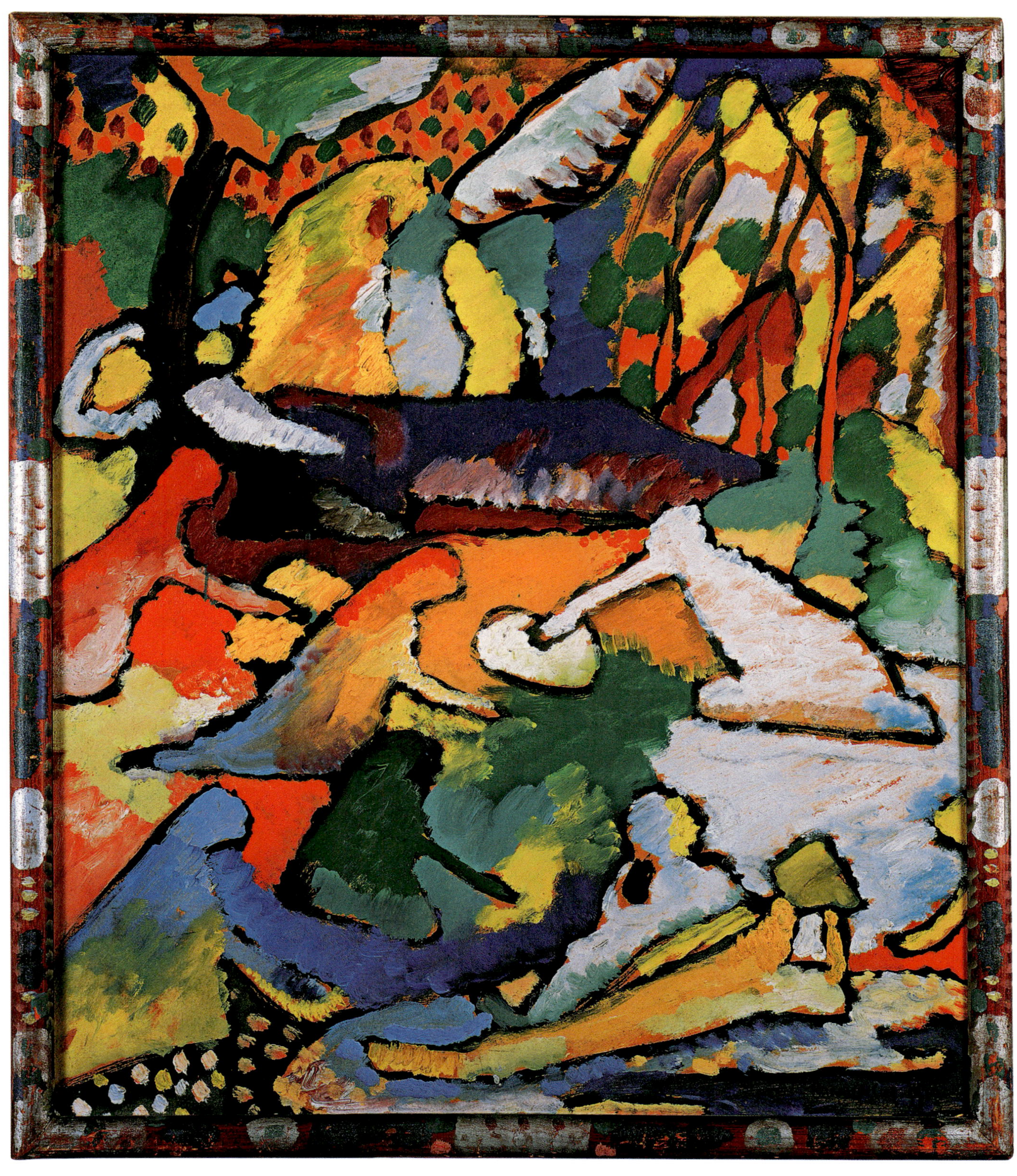

Wassily Kandinsky *Fragment for Composition II*, 1910
Merzbacher Kunststiftung

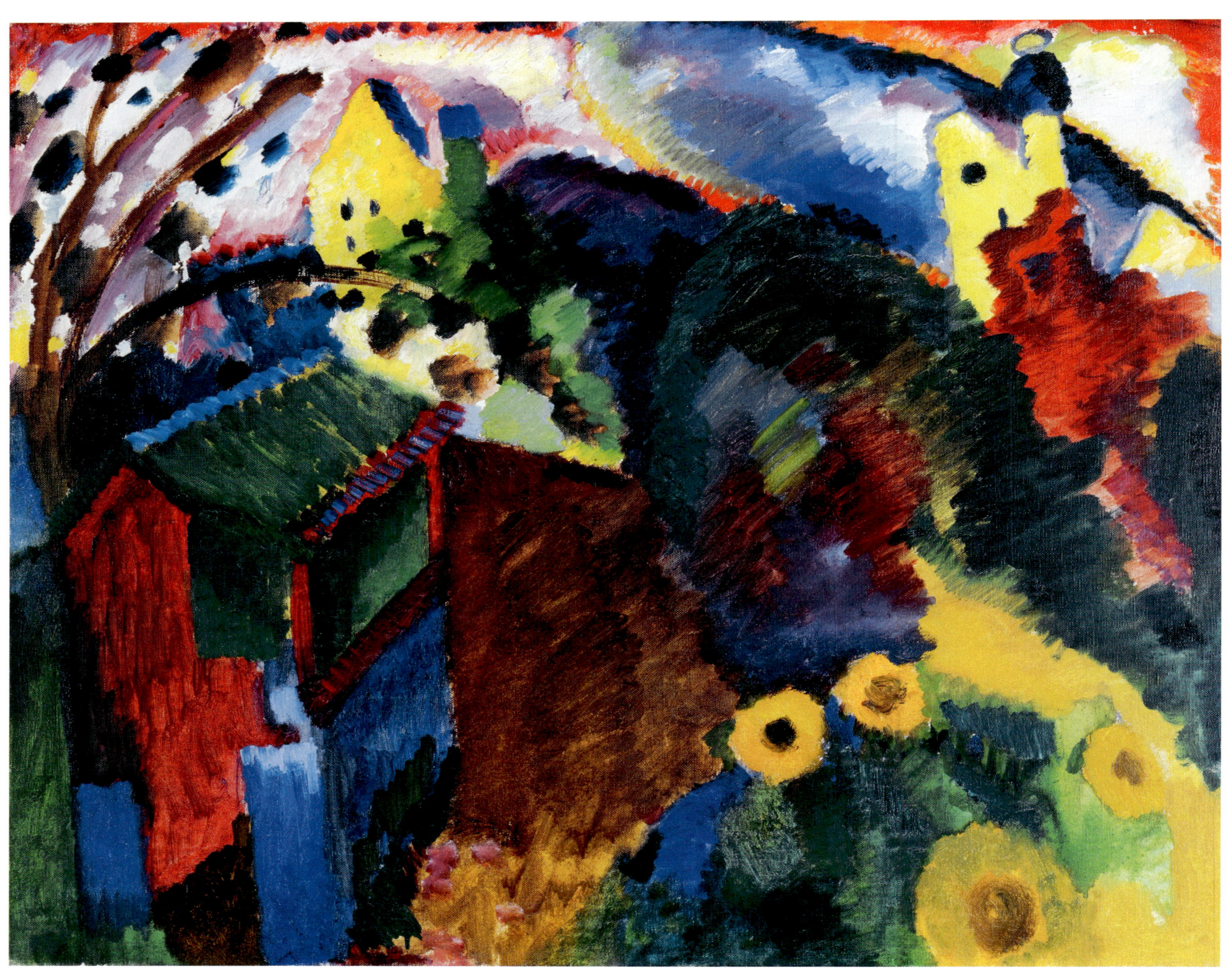

Wassily Kandinsky *Murnau—The Garden I*, 1910
Städtische Galerie im Lenbachhaus, Munich

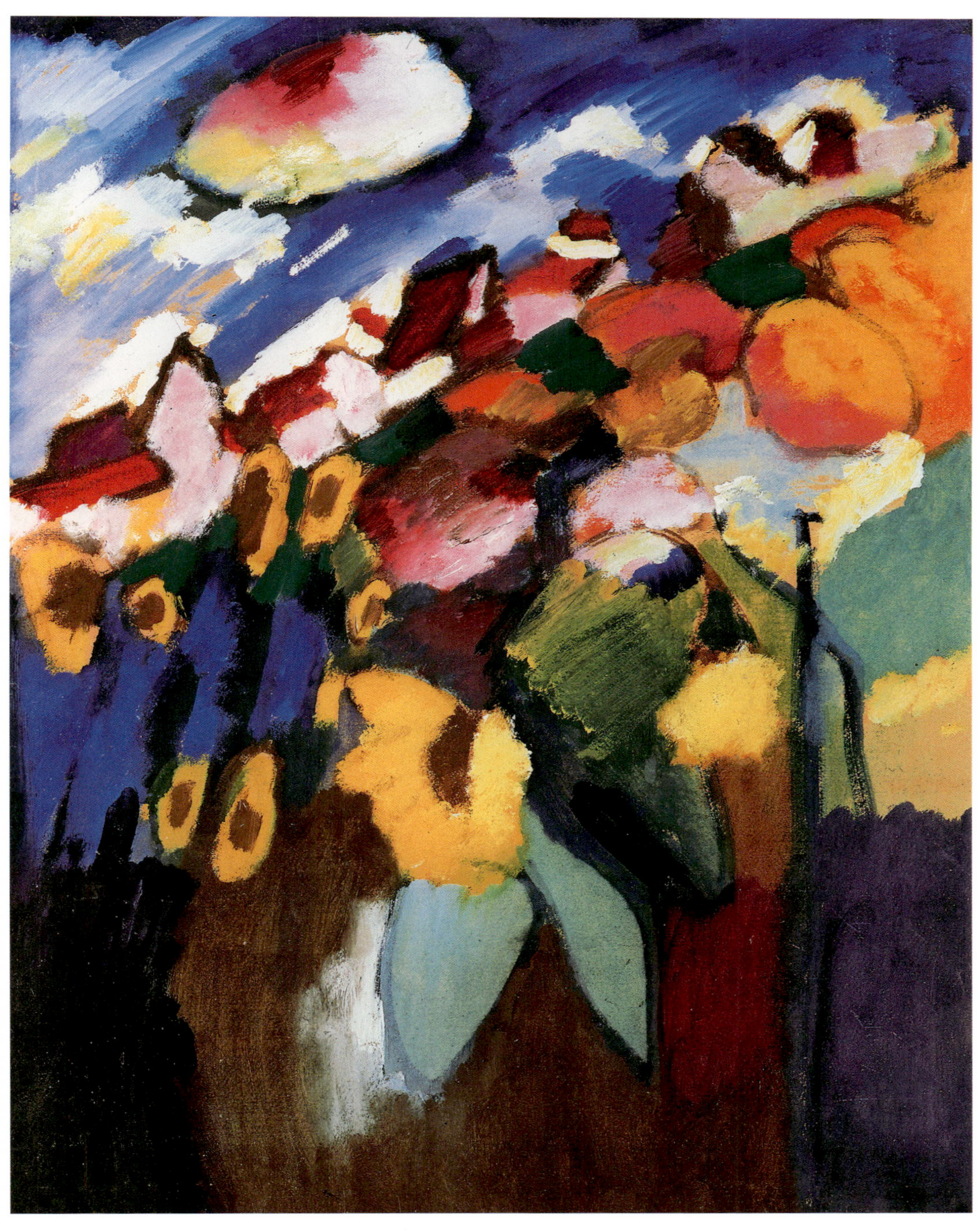

Wassily Kandinsky *Murnau—The Garden II,* 1910
Merzbacher Kunststiftung

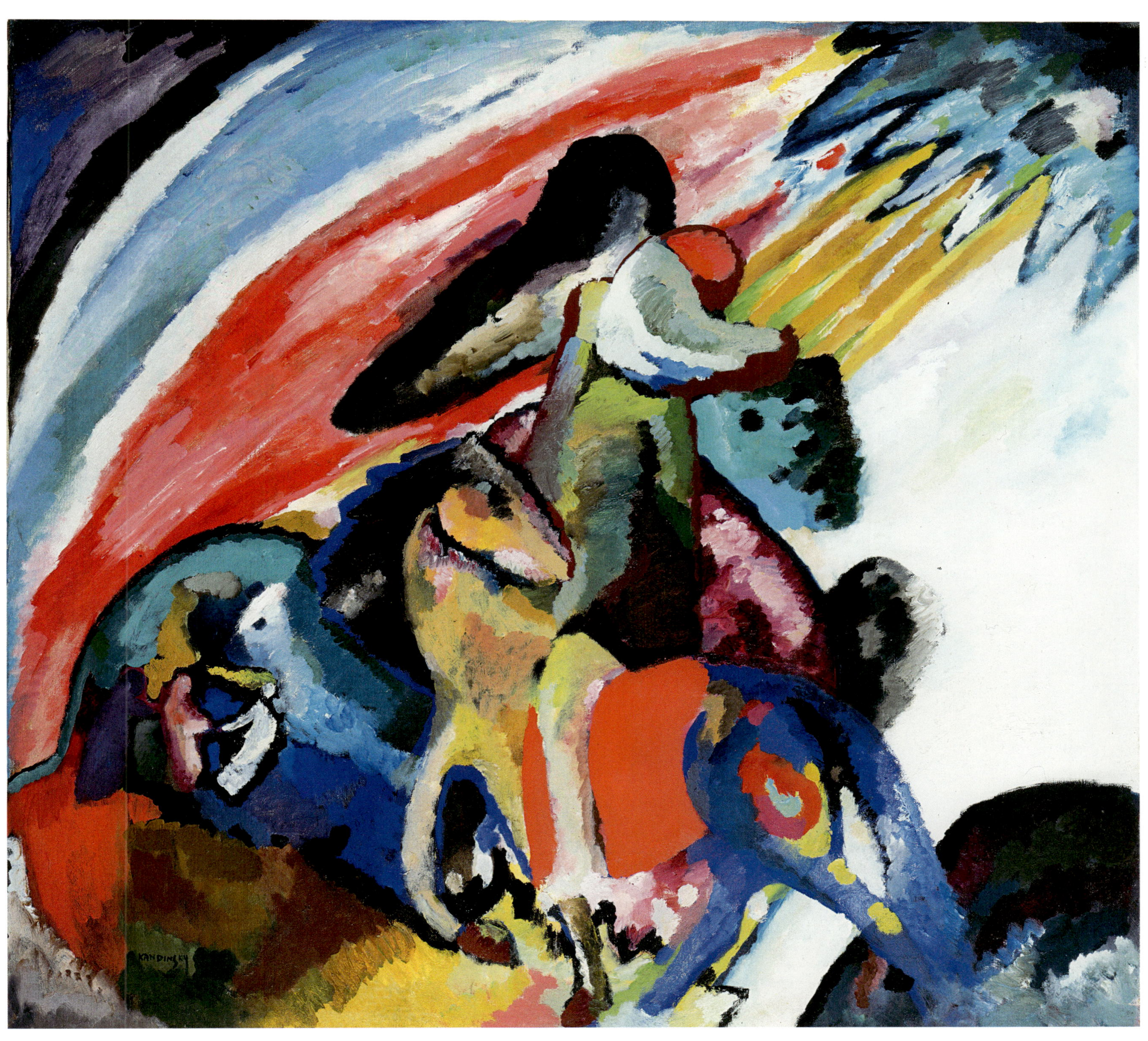

Wassily Kandinsky *Improvisation 12*, 1910
Bayerische Staatsgemäldesammlungen, Munich

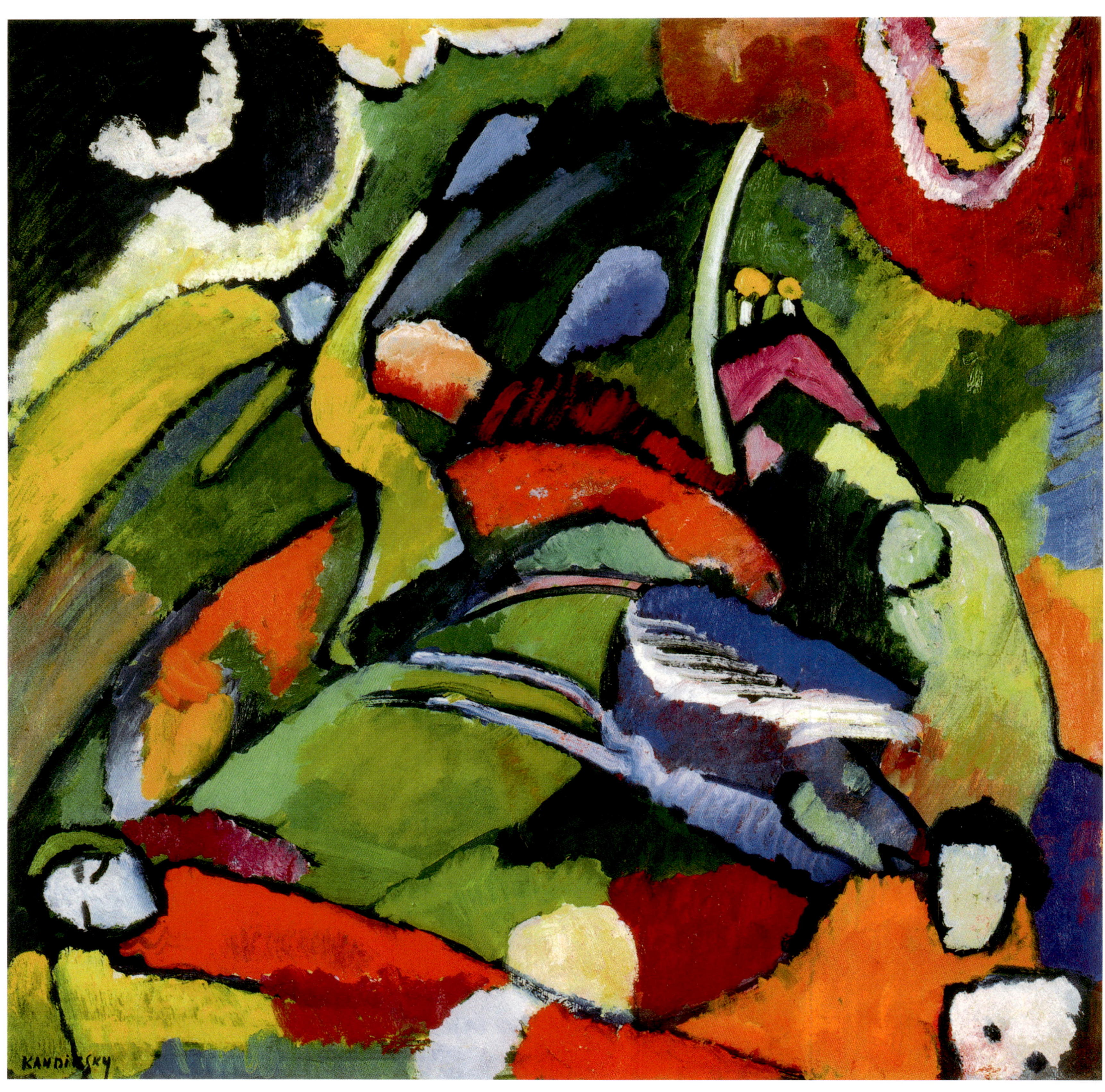

Wassily Kandinsky *Two Riders and Reclining Figure,* 1909–10
Merzbacher Kunststiftung

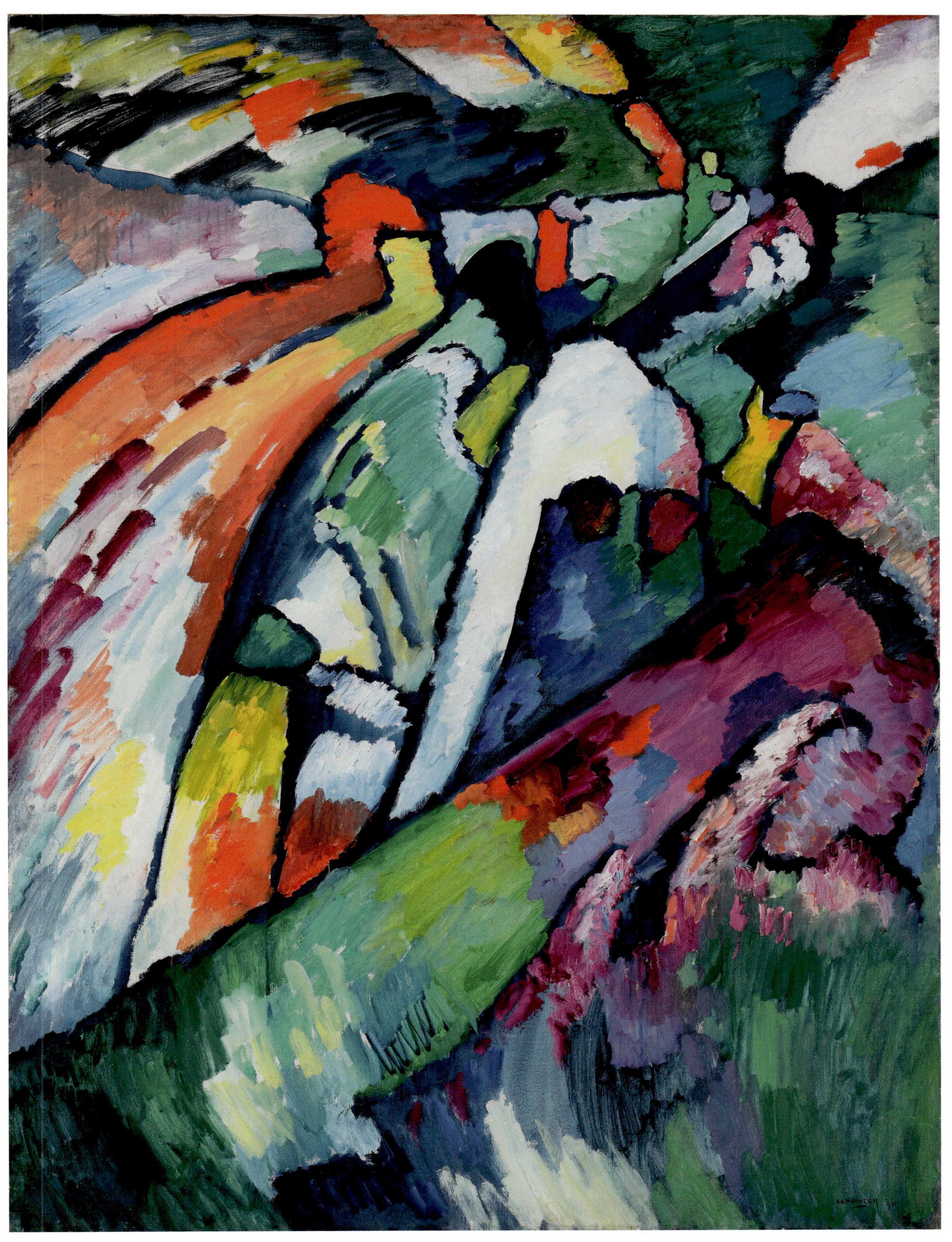

Wassily Kandinsky *Improvisation 7*, 1910
The State Tretyakov Gallery, Moscow

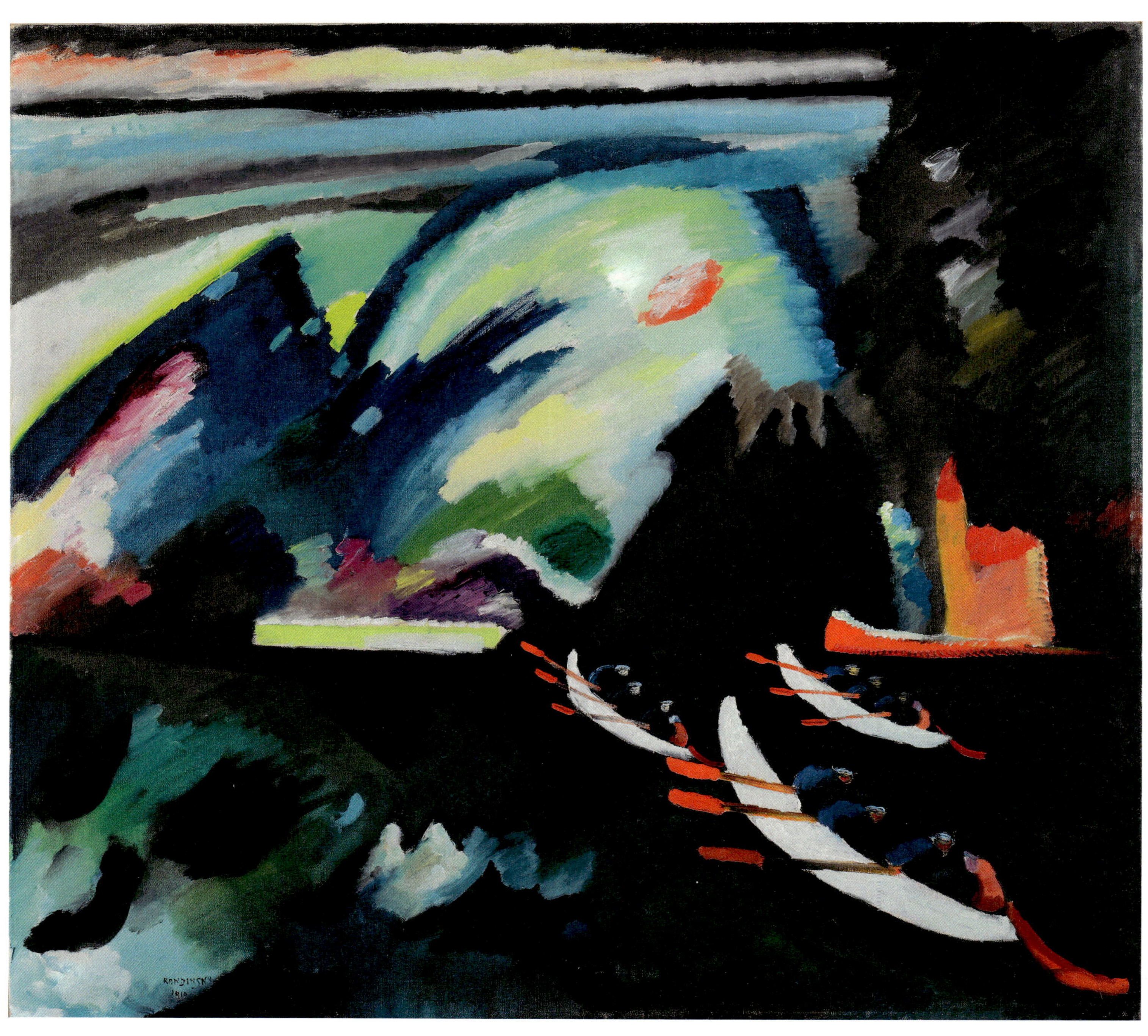

Wassily Kandinsky *Boat Trip,* 1910
The State Tretyakov Gallery, Moscow

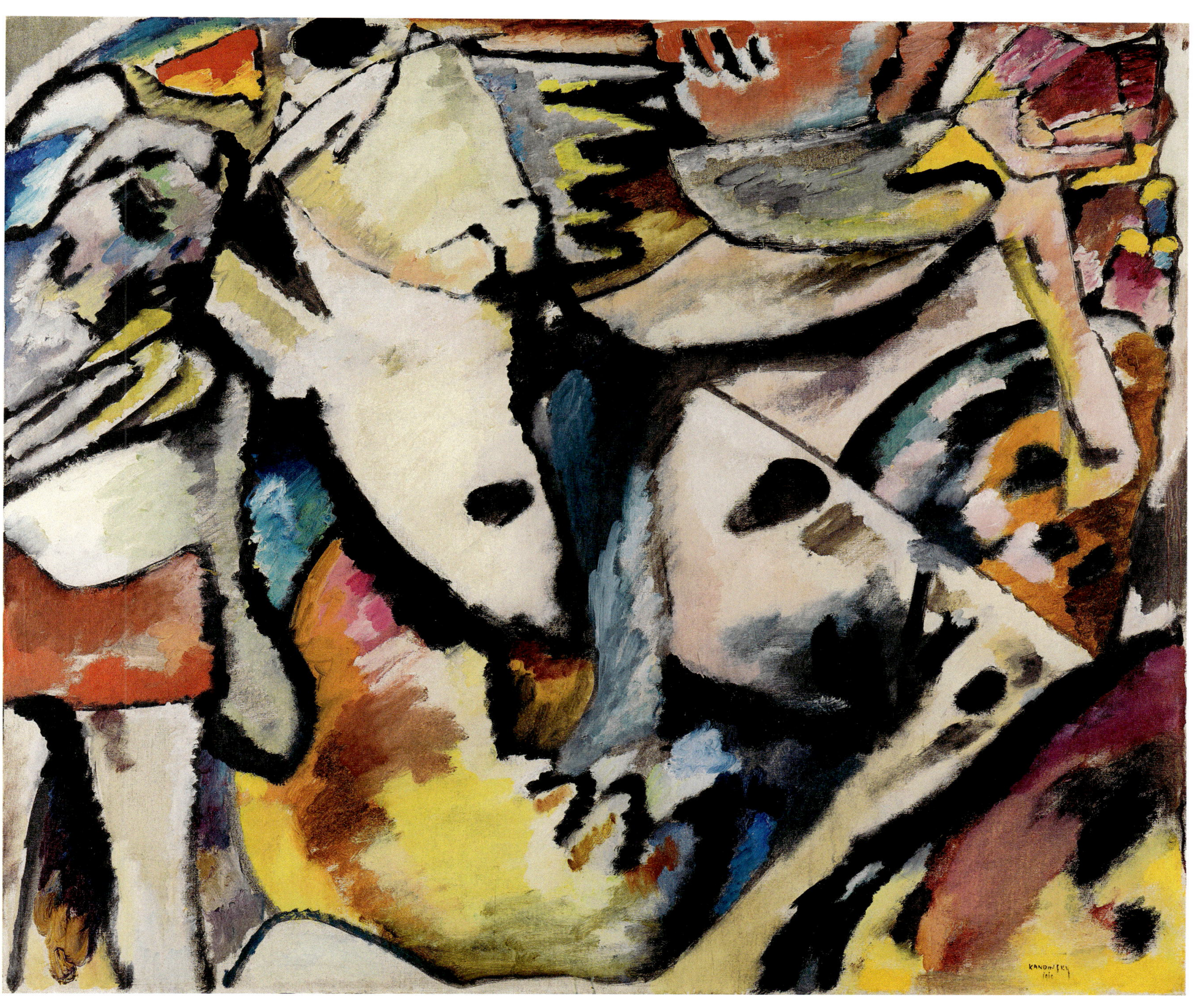

Wassily Kandinsky *Improvisation 13,* 1910
Staatliche Kunsthalle Karlsruhe

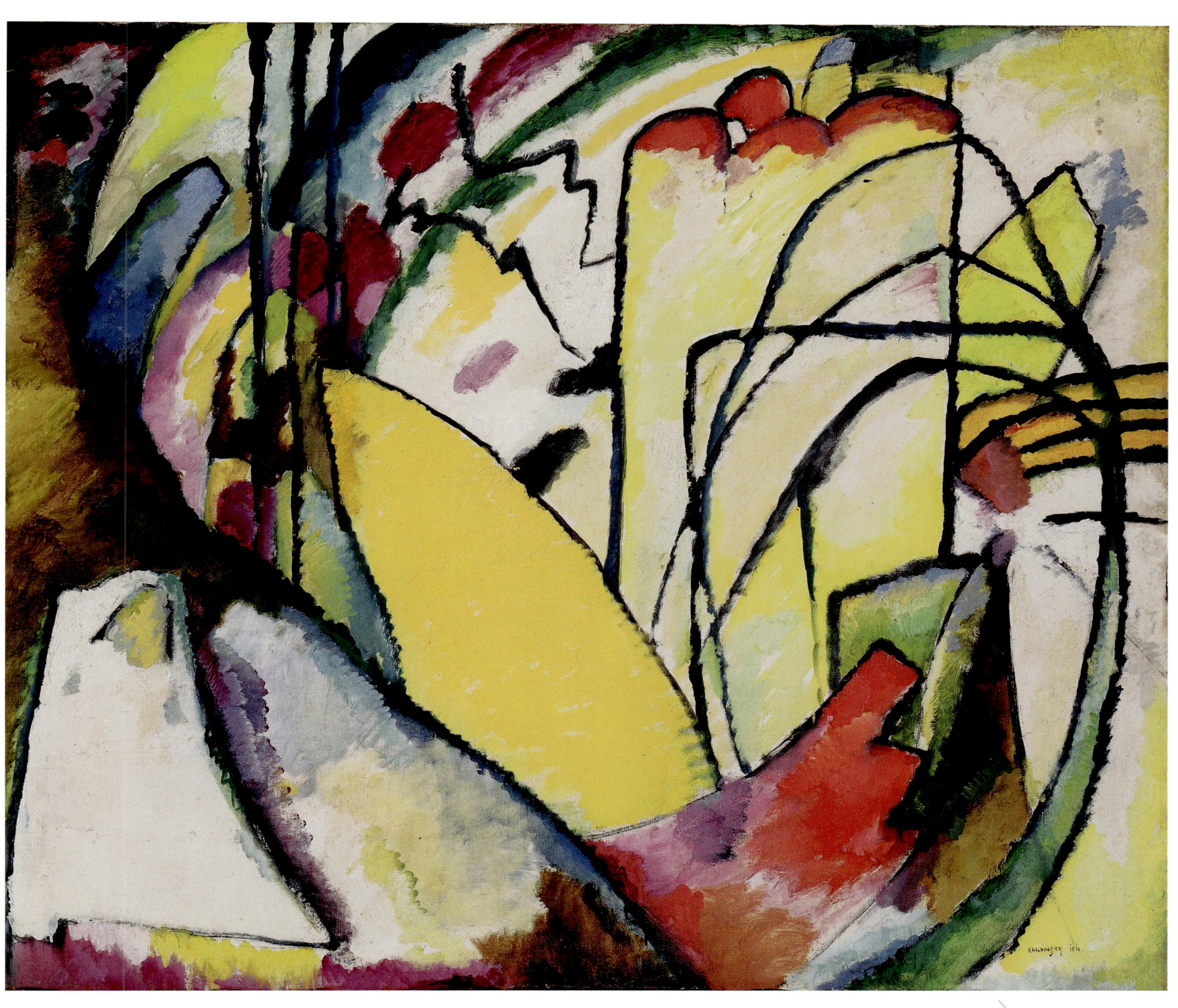

Wassily Kandinsky *Improvisation 10*, 1910
Fondation Beyeler, Riehen/Basel, Beyeler Collection

FRANZ MARC: HORSES AND PAINTING

Franz Marc and Wassily Kandinsky did not meet each other personally until early 1911. Prior to this time, Marc had written an enthusiastic review of a show of the Neue Künstlervereinigung München (New Artists' Association Munich), whose members included Kandinsky, Werefkin, Münter, and Jawlensky. Marc, too, joined the group, but left it again together with Kandinsky in December of that same year, due to a disagreement about its statutes. Kandinsky and he had different characters; furthermore, Kandinsky was fourteen years older than Marc. While the former pursued his aims purposefully, even dogmatically, Marc always endeavored to mediate among the almanac's contributors. The correspondence between the two editors of *Der Blaue Reiter* (*The Blaue Reiter Almanac*) is among the most interesting documents in modern art.

Marc died while engaged in mounted reconnaissance near Verdun on March 4, 1916. He was thirty-six years old. Stylized as a "hero's death" in the language of the day, his end and the fact that an artist famed for his depictions of horses died himself on horseback continue to fuel myths to this day.[1] His not particularly extensive oeuvre is extremely popular, especially in Germany. Under the Nazis Marc was defamed as a "degenerate artist."

After World War II, Marc's works helped to reconcile German audiences with modern art. This probably resulted from the fact that although his paintings, such as those of blue horses, were radically new in terms of color, they appeared comparatively intelligible. In addition, his depictions, especially those of animals from 1910 onward, have a sublimated, timeless character. After all, rather than being simply concerned with reproducing the look of an animal, Marc aimed at capturing its essence, as a token of an archaic, unsullied nature. Marc's paintings of horses emerged at a time when the centuries-long relationship between human beings and horses was radically changing as a result of the development of the automobile.[2] His celebration of the creature's soul should be seen against the backdrop of the incipient nature conservancy movement prior to World War I; it seems to represent an alternative world to that of technological progress, and hence to correspond to the ongoing tendency in to critique progress, particularly in German society.

It is striking that Marc's animals are frequently represented as sleeping (cat. pp. 50, 107–09) or resting in a group. He also depicted a horse that appears to survey the field across which it is about to gallop (cat. p. 101). Marc was evidently more interested in animals' potentials than in their actions, although an extreme counterexample exists in the form of *Die gelbe Kuh* (*Yellow Cow;* cat. pp. 110–11), from 1911. Yet, perhaps we should not reduce his imagery too exclusively to the representation of living beings. Wasn't his principal concern to express the potential and expressive power of color and painting? This may well be the sense in which the following passage from a letter to his future wife, Maria Franck, should be understood:

> *I would* never *paint a bush blue for the sake of decorative effect, but only in order to enhance the entire essence of the horse standing in front of it. But the means must always be* purely painterly*, and heightened to the utmost possible degree.*[3]

[1] As for instance the documentary film by Hedwig Schmutte, *Franz Marc: Der letzte Ritt des Blauen Reiters,* 52 min, produced by Tag/Traum Köln in Cologne, Germany, for ZDF/Arte in 2015, most recently broadcast on Arte, March 6, 2016.
[2] On this topic, see Ulrich Raulff, *Die alte Welt der Pferde,* Jacob Burckhardt-Gespräche auf Castelen 31 (Basel, 2016).
[3] Franz Marc, letter to Maria Franck, February 10, 1911, in *Der Blaue Reiter: Eine Geschichte in Dokumenten,* ed. Andreas Hüneke (Stuttgart, 2011), p. 31.

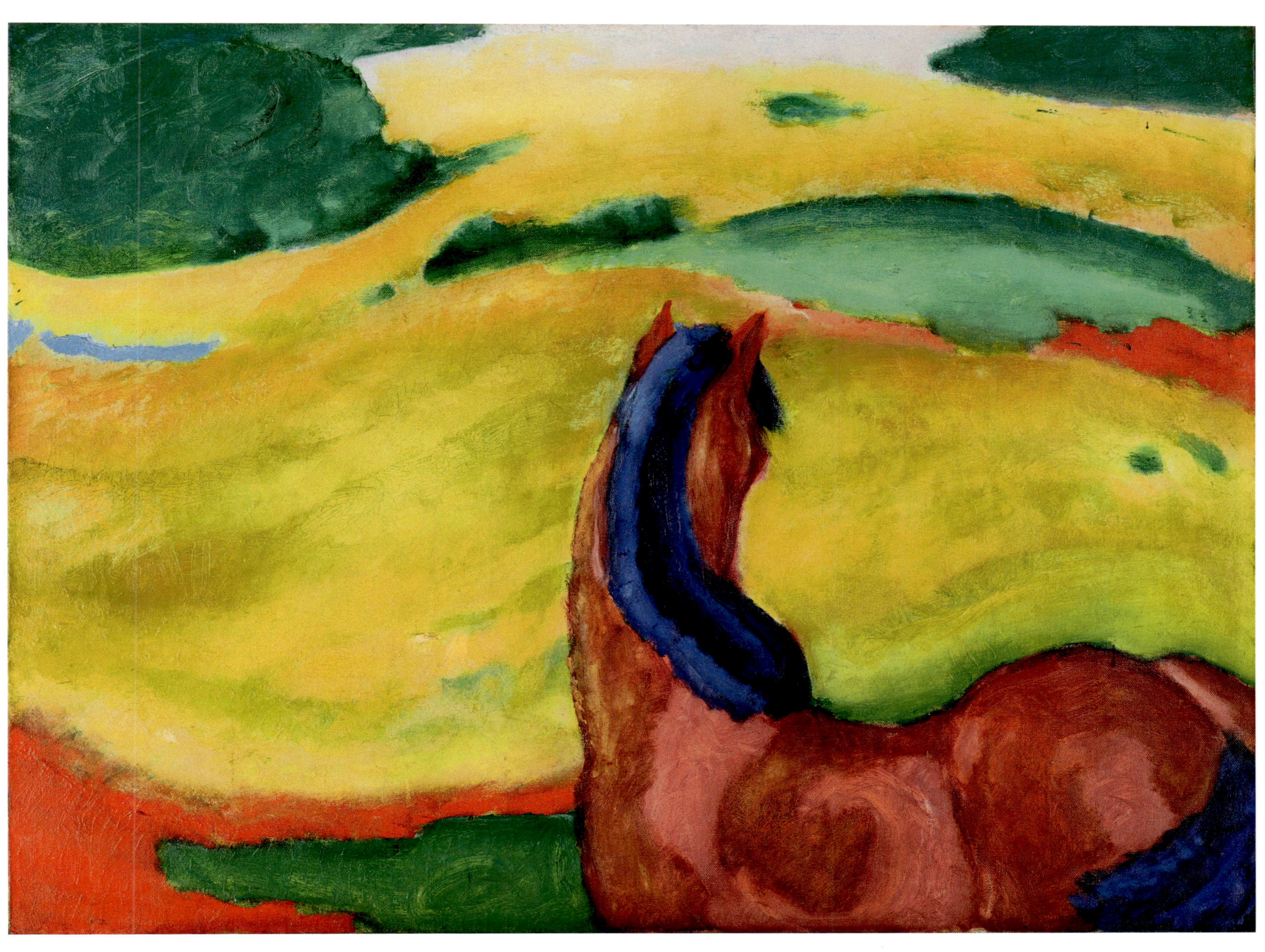

Franz Marc *Horse in a Landscape*, 1910
Museum Folkwang, Essen

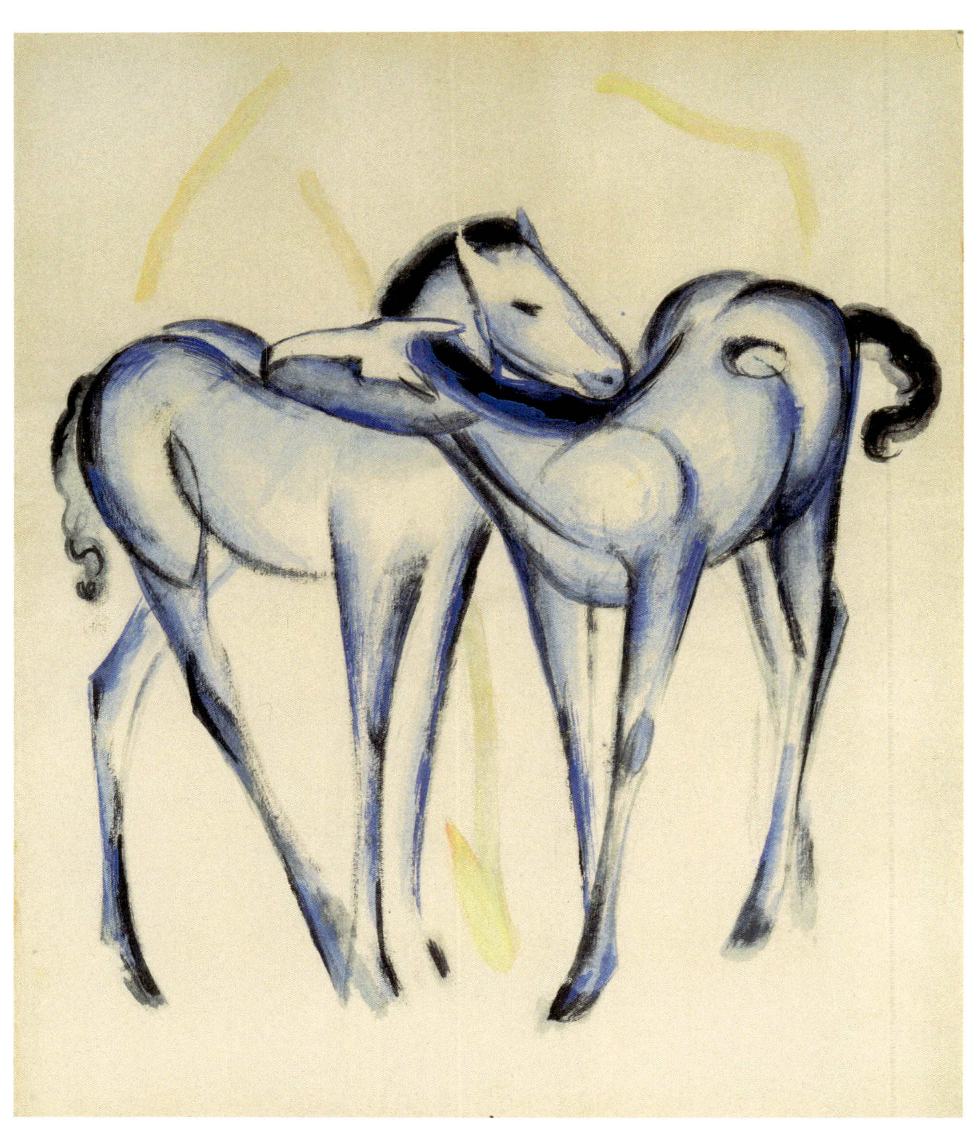

Franz Marc *Two Blue Foals*, 1911
Private collection

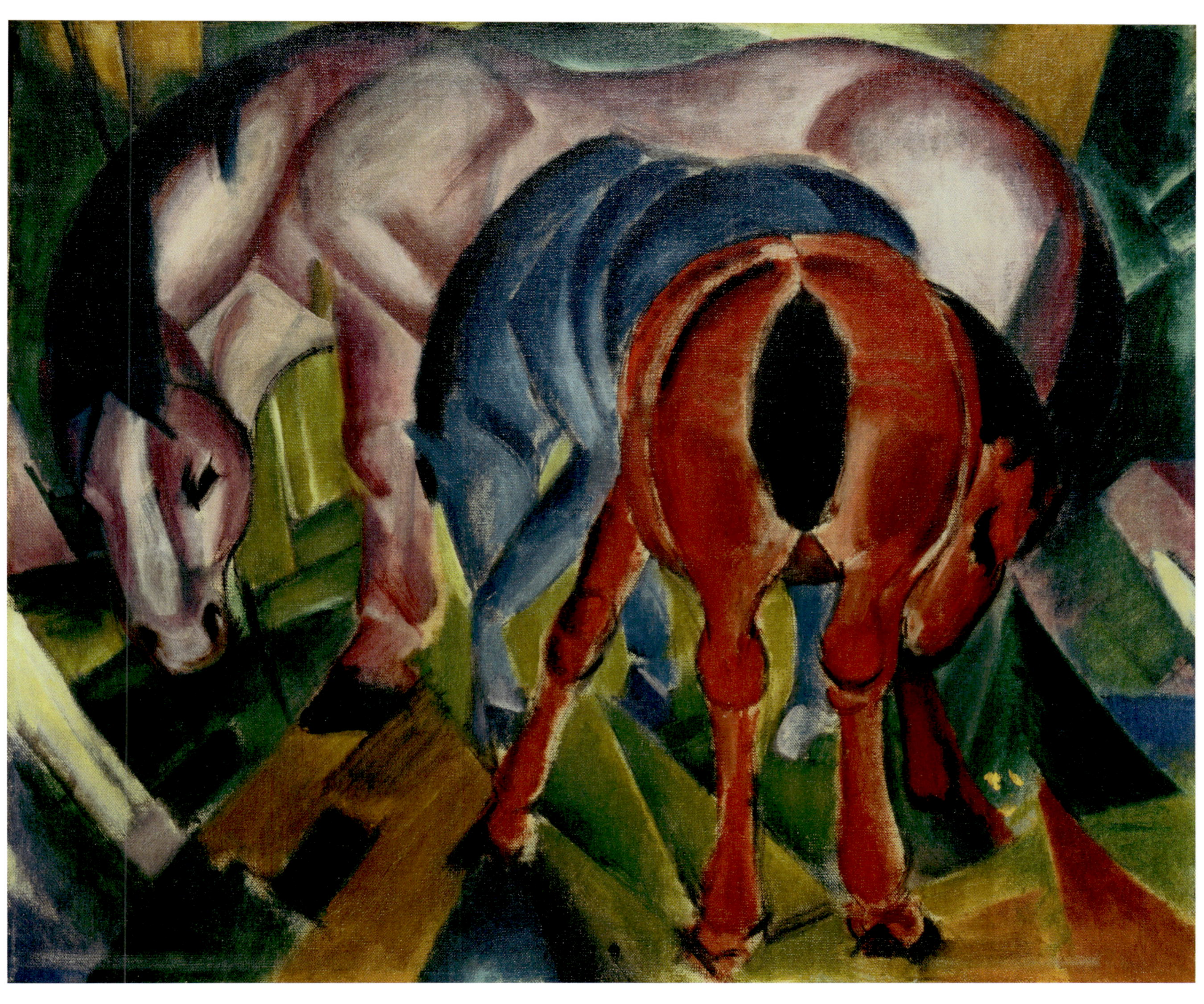

Franz Marc *Mare with Foals*, 1912
Private collection

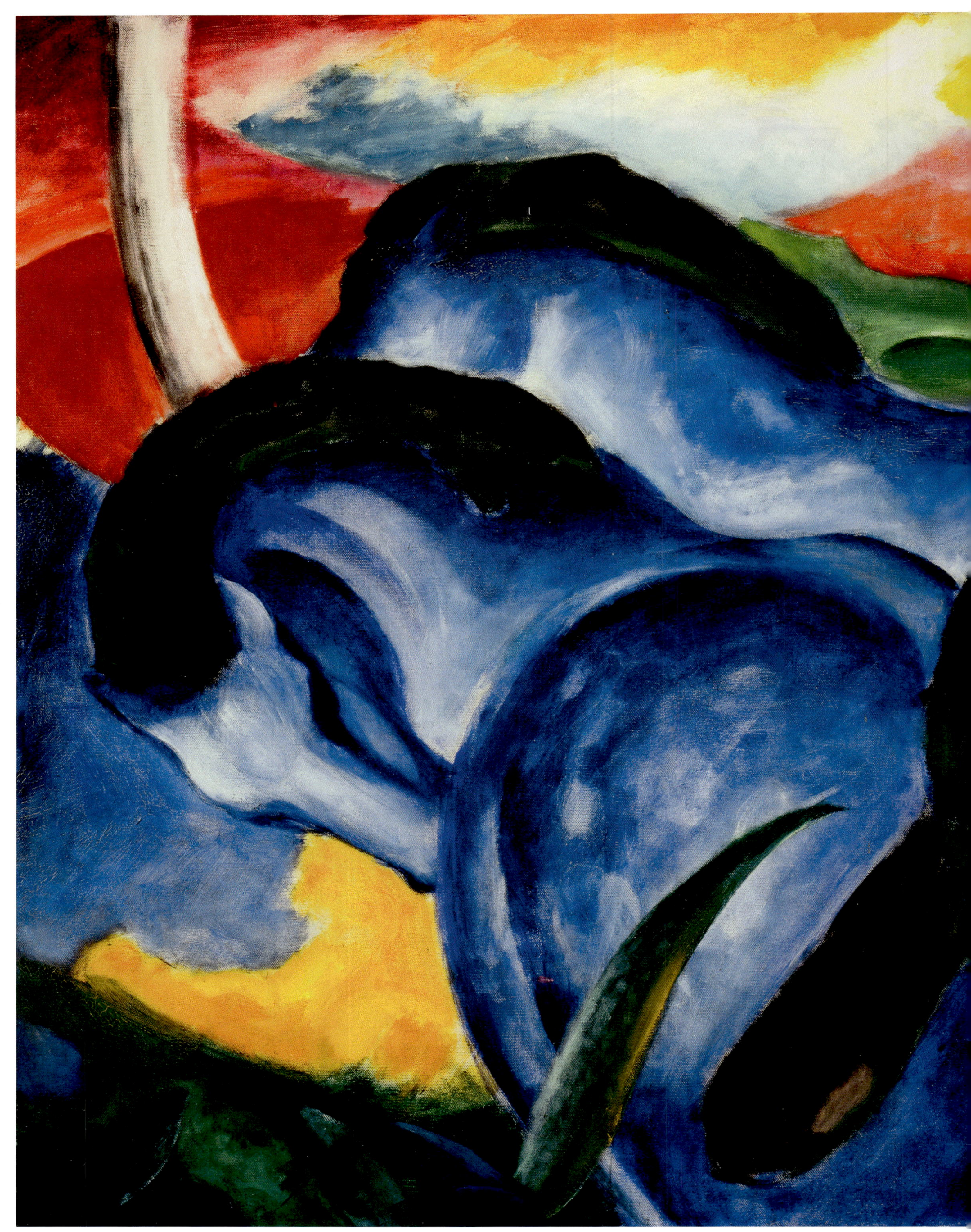

Franz Marc *The Large Blue Horses,* 1911
Collection Walker Art Center, Minneapolis, Gift of the T. B. Walker Foundation, Gilbert M. Walker Fund, 1942

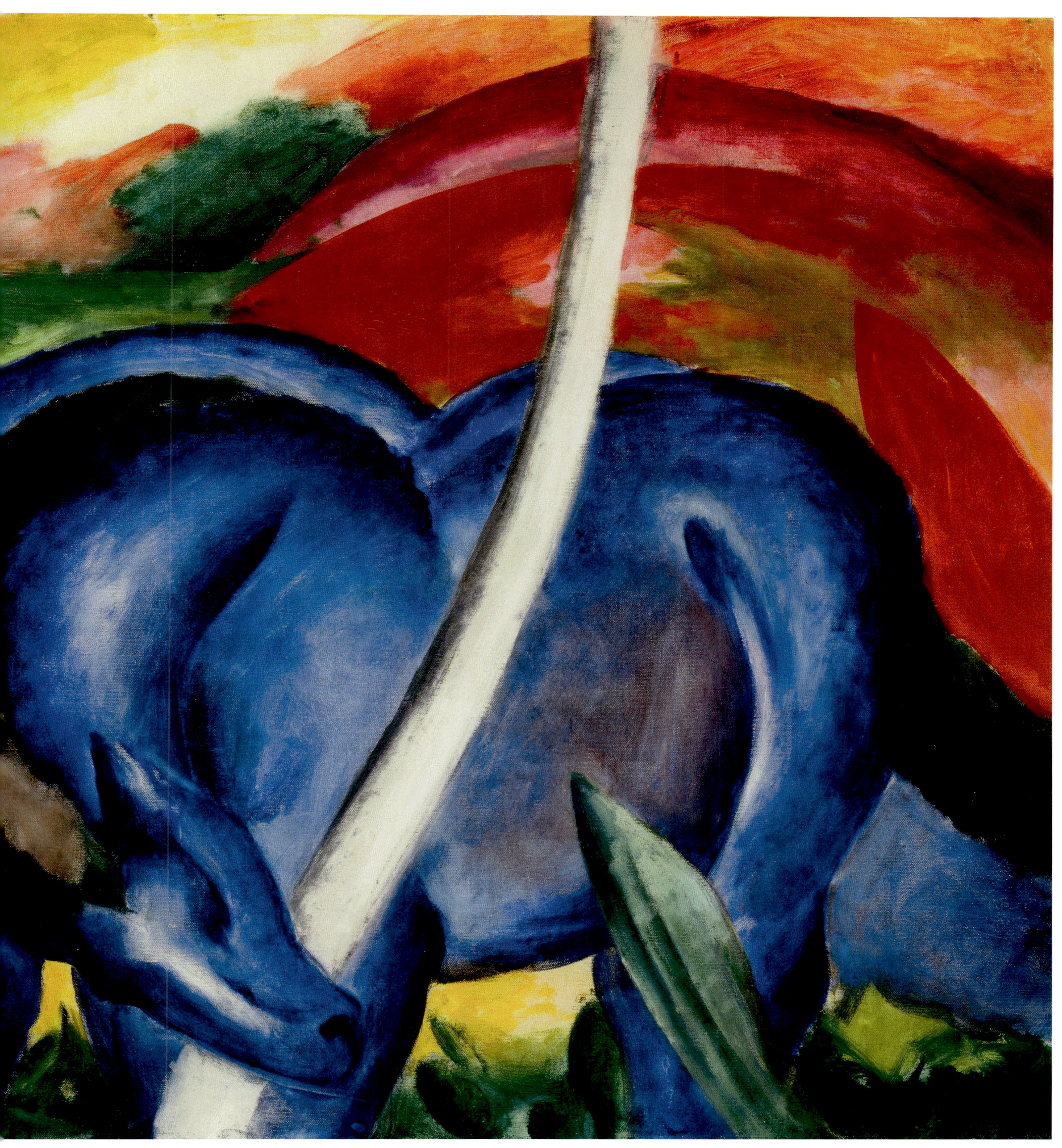

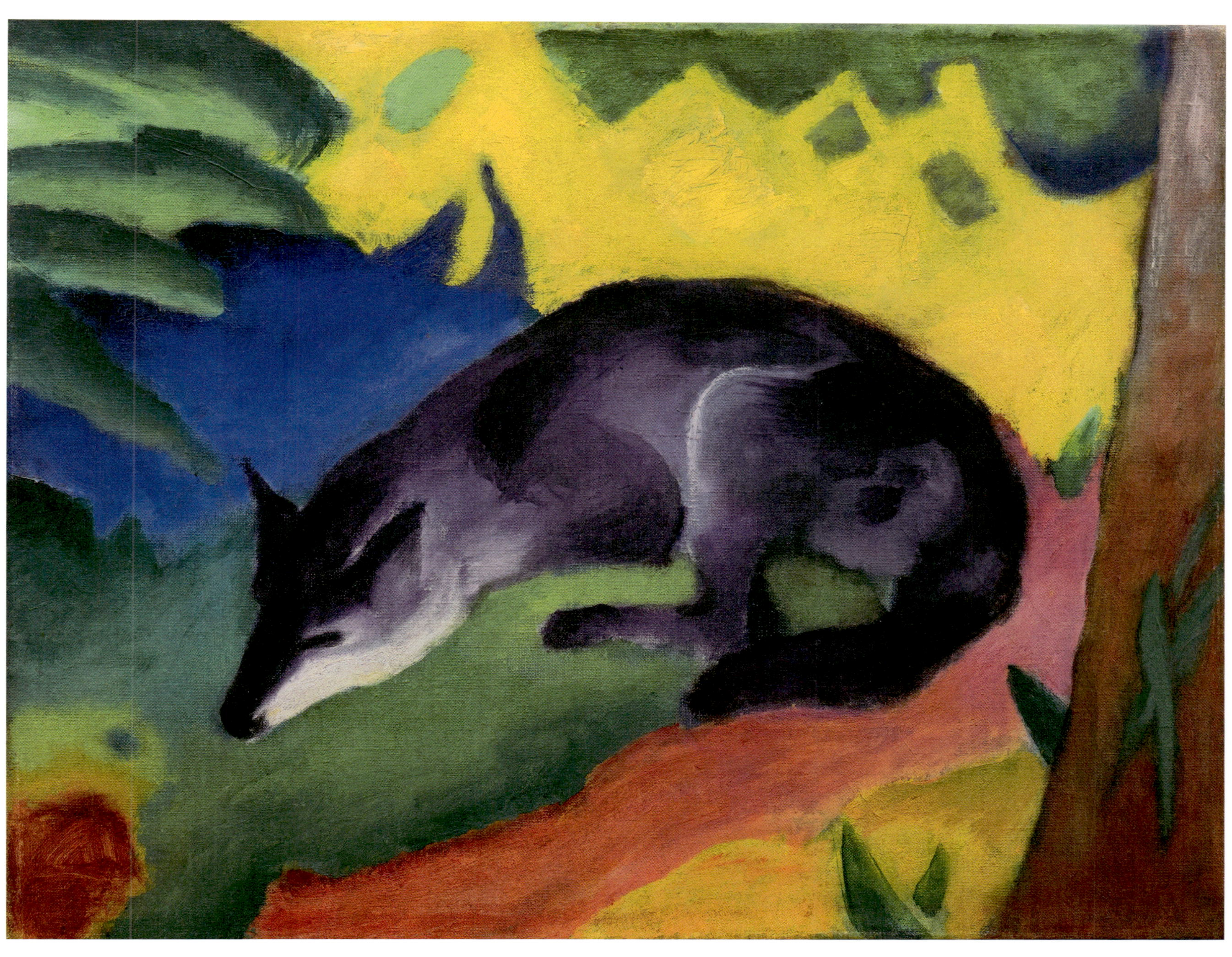

Franz Marc *Blue-Black Fox*, 1911
Von der Heydt-Museum Wuppertal

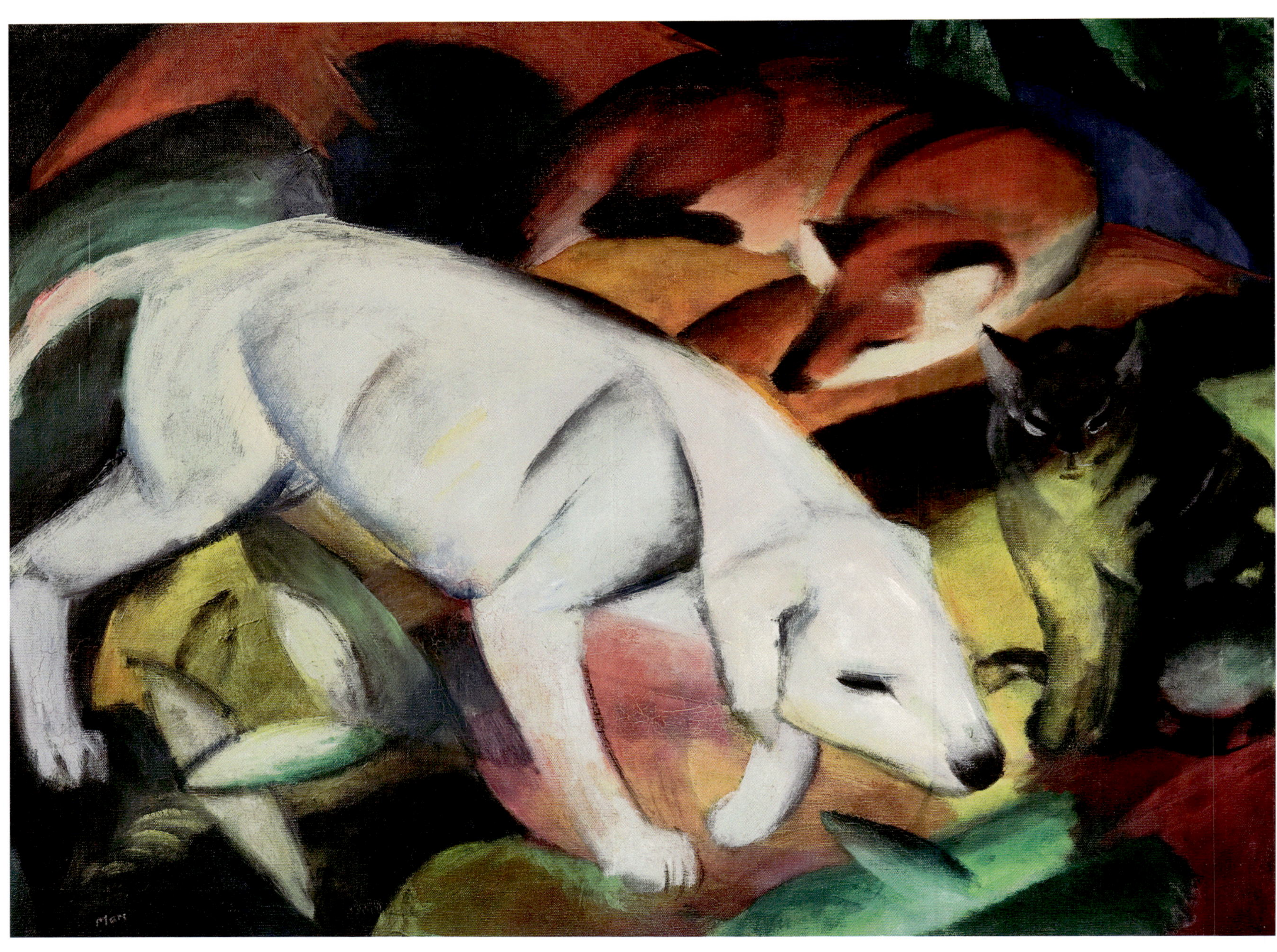

Franz Marc *Three Animals (Dog, Cat, and Fox)*, 1912
Kunsthalle Mannheim

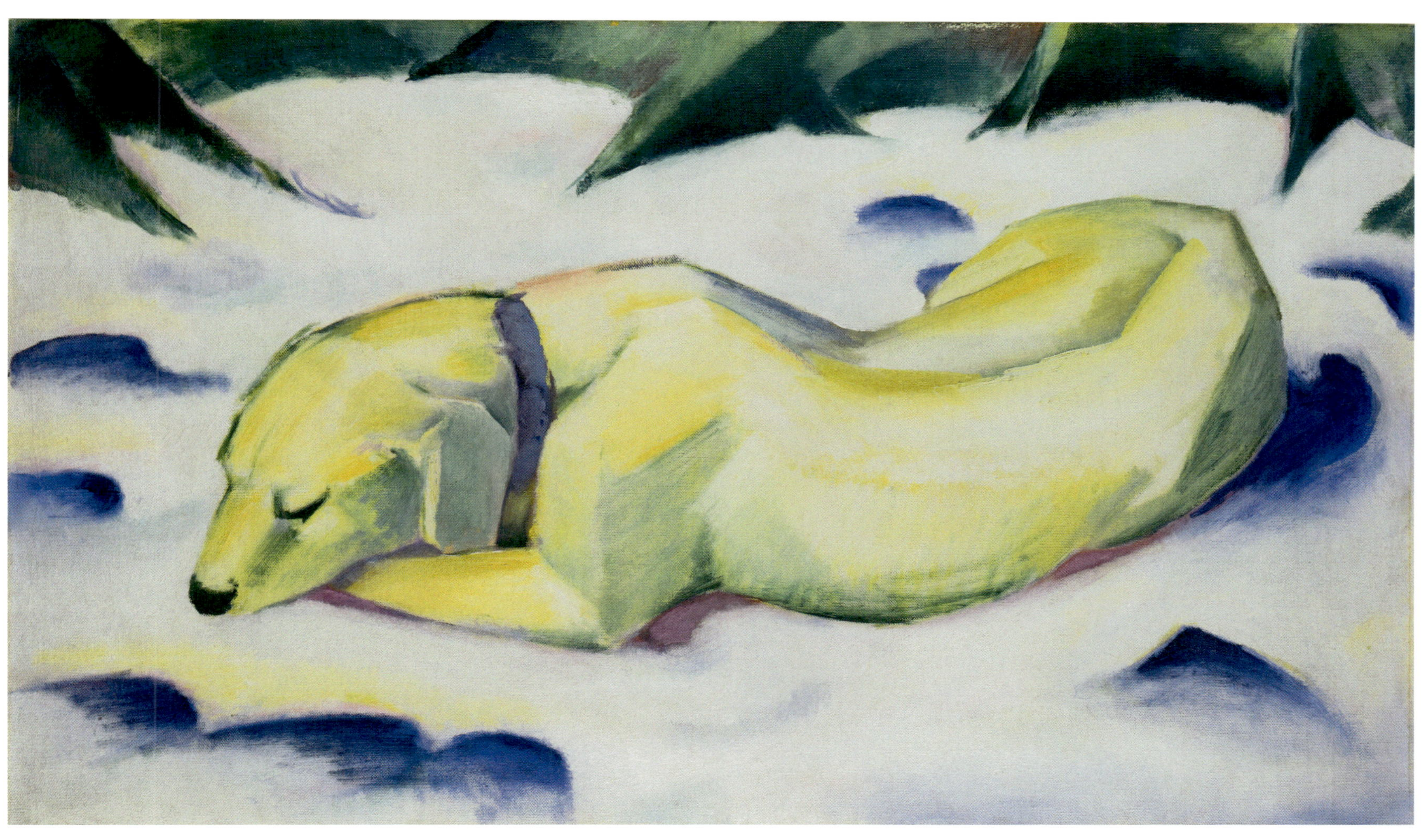

Franz Marc *Dog Lying in the Snow*, 1910–11
Städel Museum, Frankfurt am Main, property of the Städelscher Museums-Verein e. V.

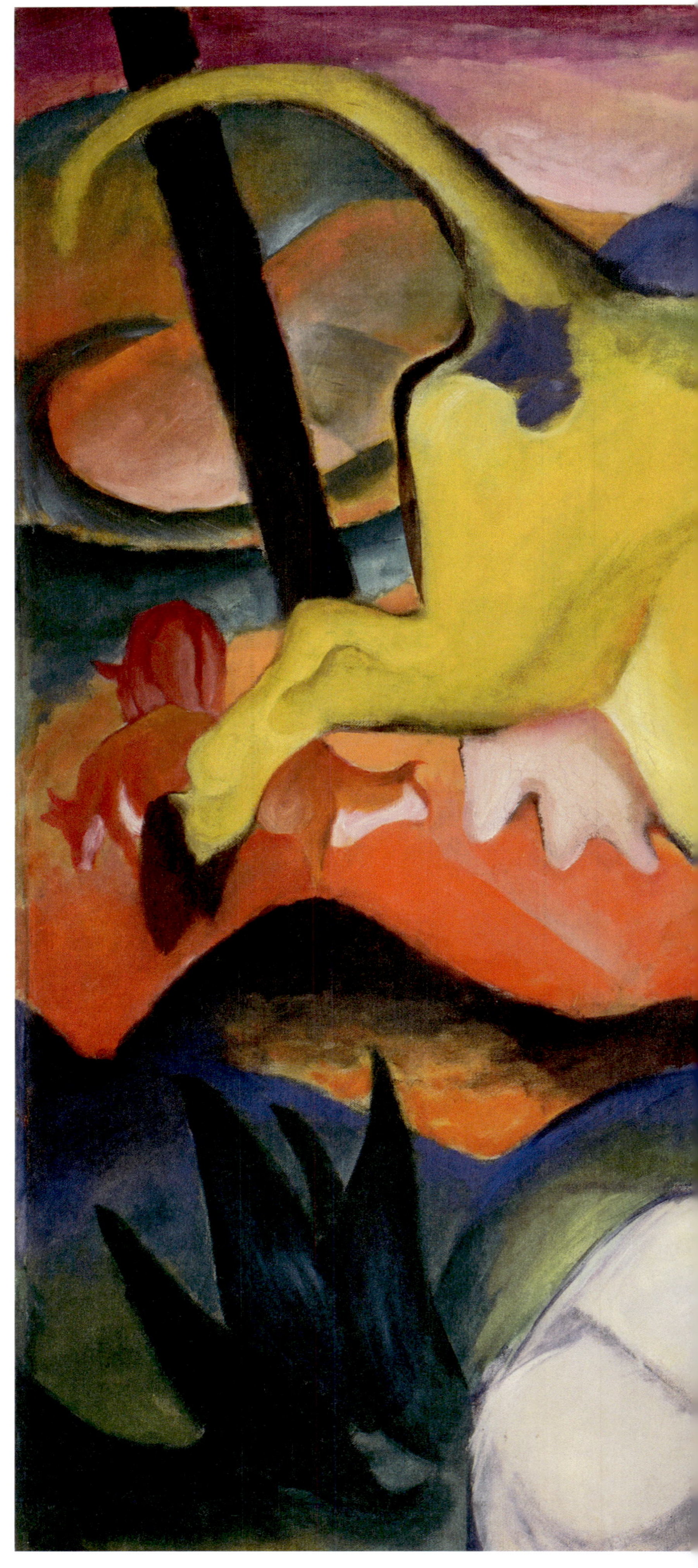

Franz Marc *Yellow Cow*, 1911
Solomon R. Guggenheim Museum, New York, Solomon R. Guggenheim Founding Collection

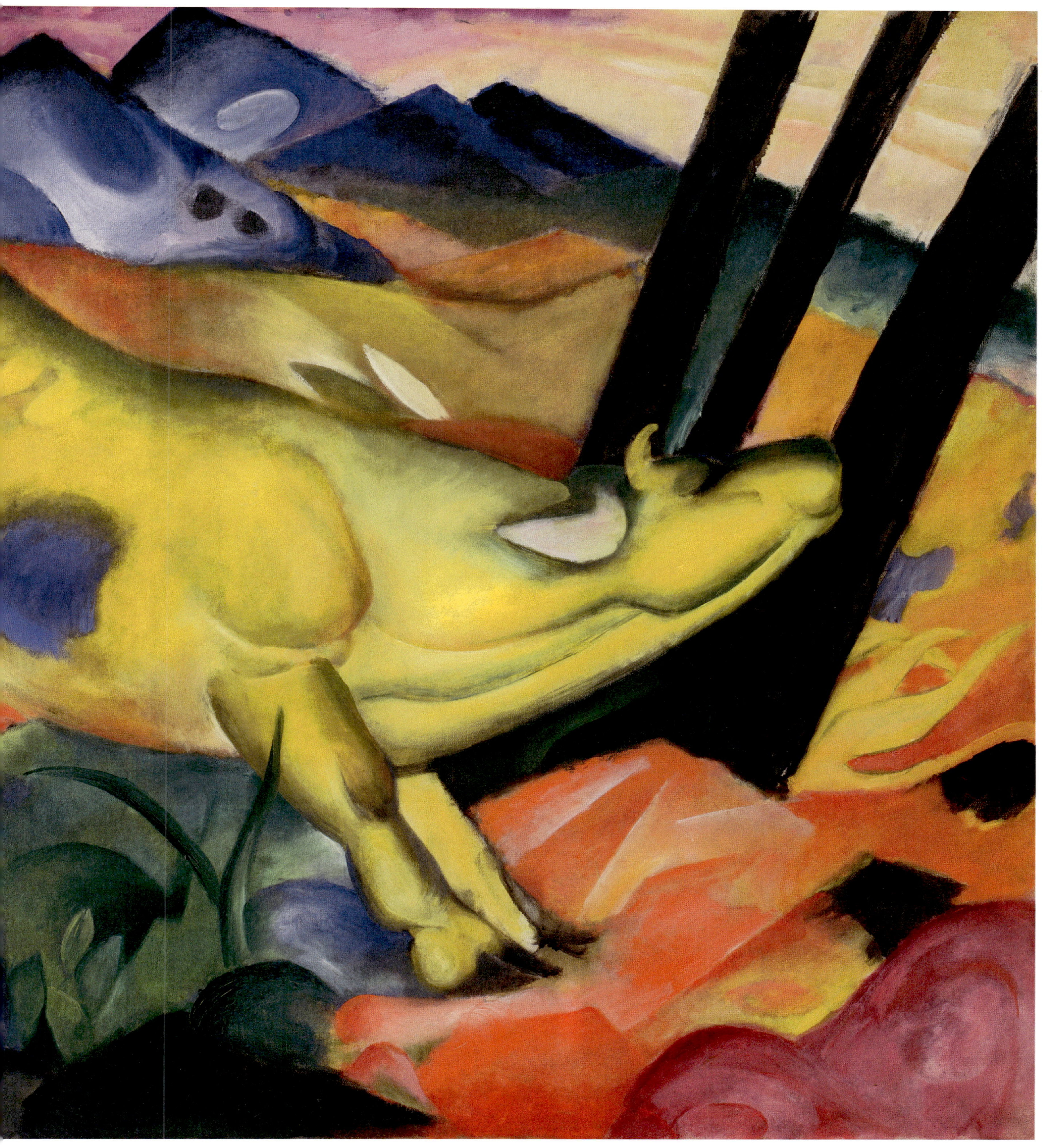

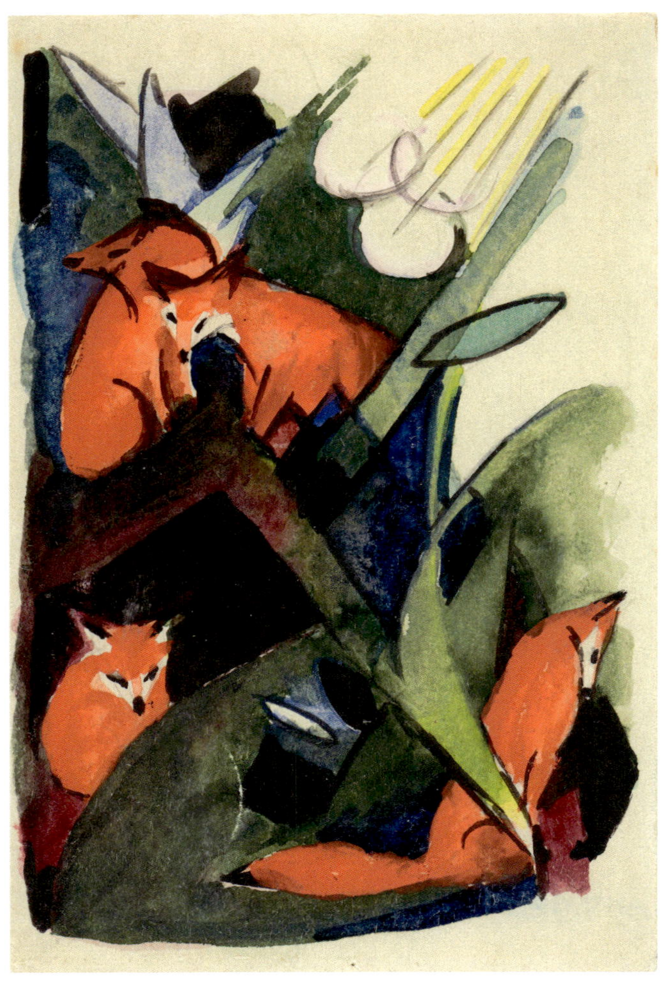

Franz Marc *Four Foxes* (postcard to Wassily Kandinsky), 1913
Städtische Galerie im Lenbachhaus, Munich

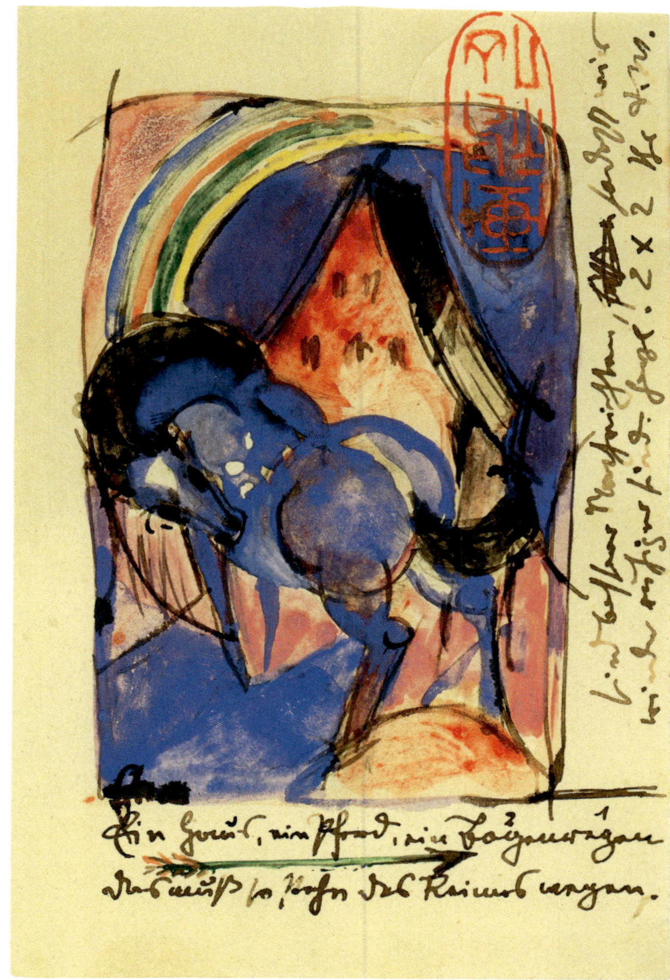

Franz Marc *Horse and House with Rainbow* (postcard to Paul Klee), 1913
ahlers collection

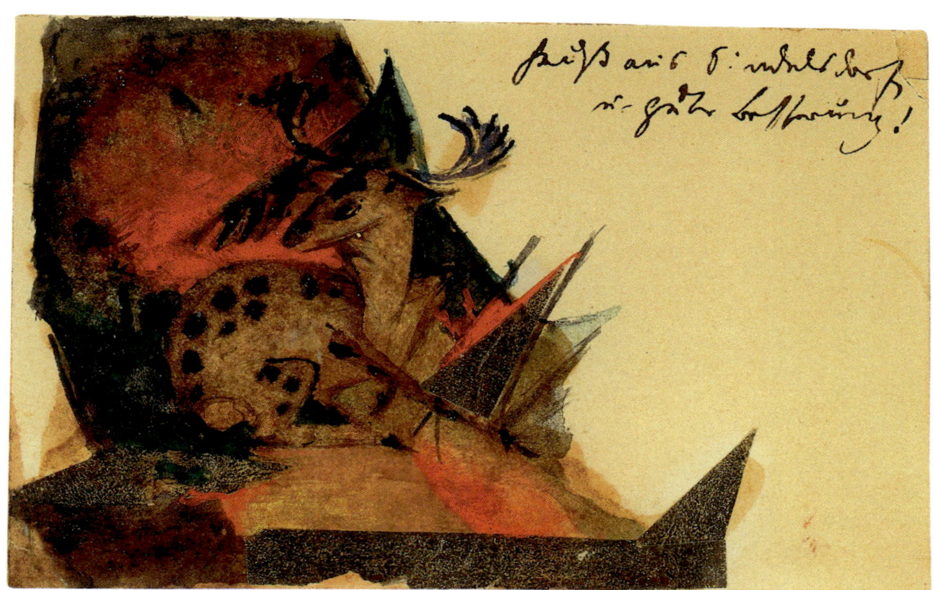

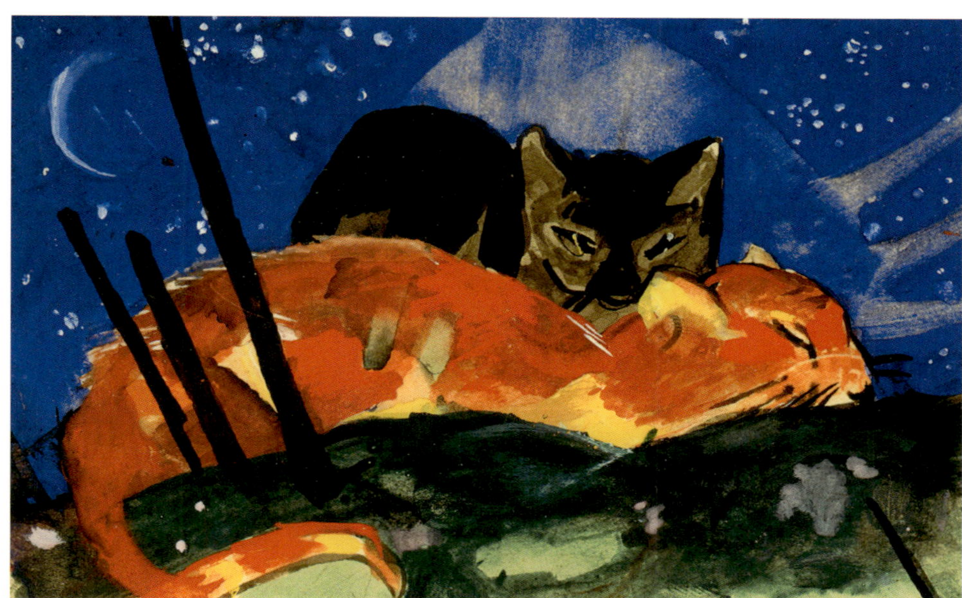

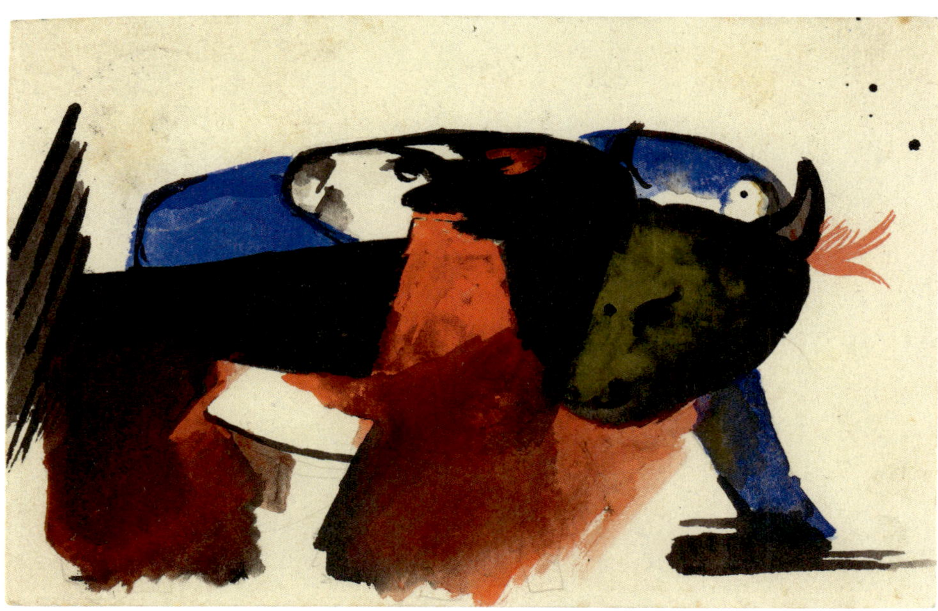

Franz Marc *Lying Stag* (postcard to Bernhard Koehler), 1913
ahlers collection

Franz Marc *Two Cats* (postcard to Lily Klee), 1913
ahlers collection

Franz Marc *Two Animals* (postcard to Wassily Kandinsky), 1913
Städtische Galerie im Lenbachhaus, Munich

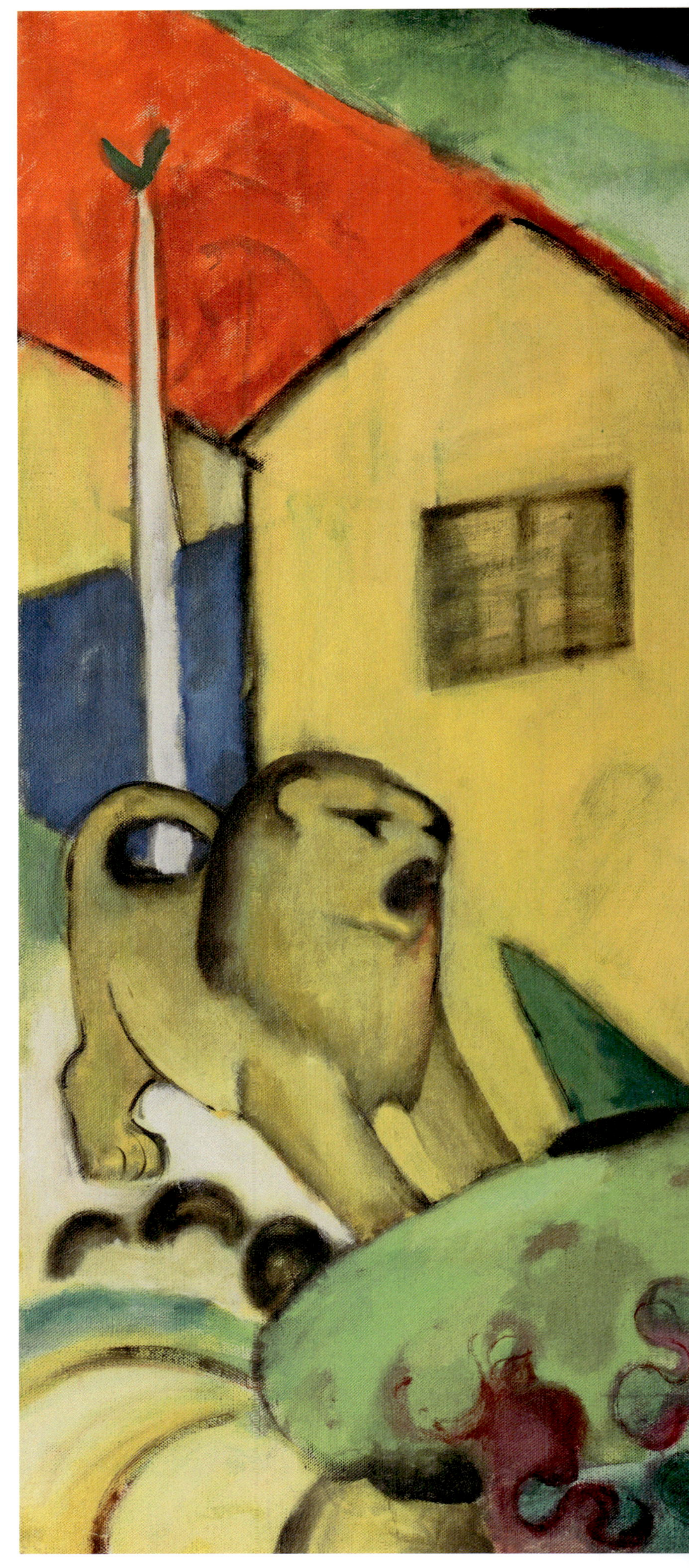

Franz Marc *The Dream*, 1912
Museo Thyssen-Bornemisza, Madrid

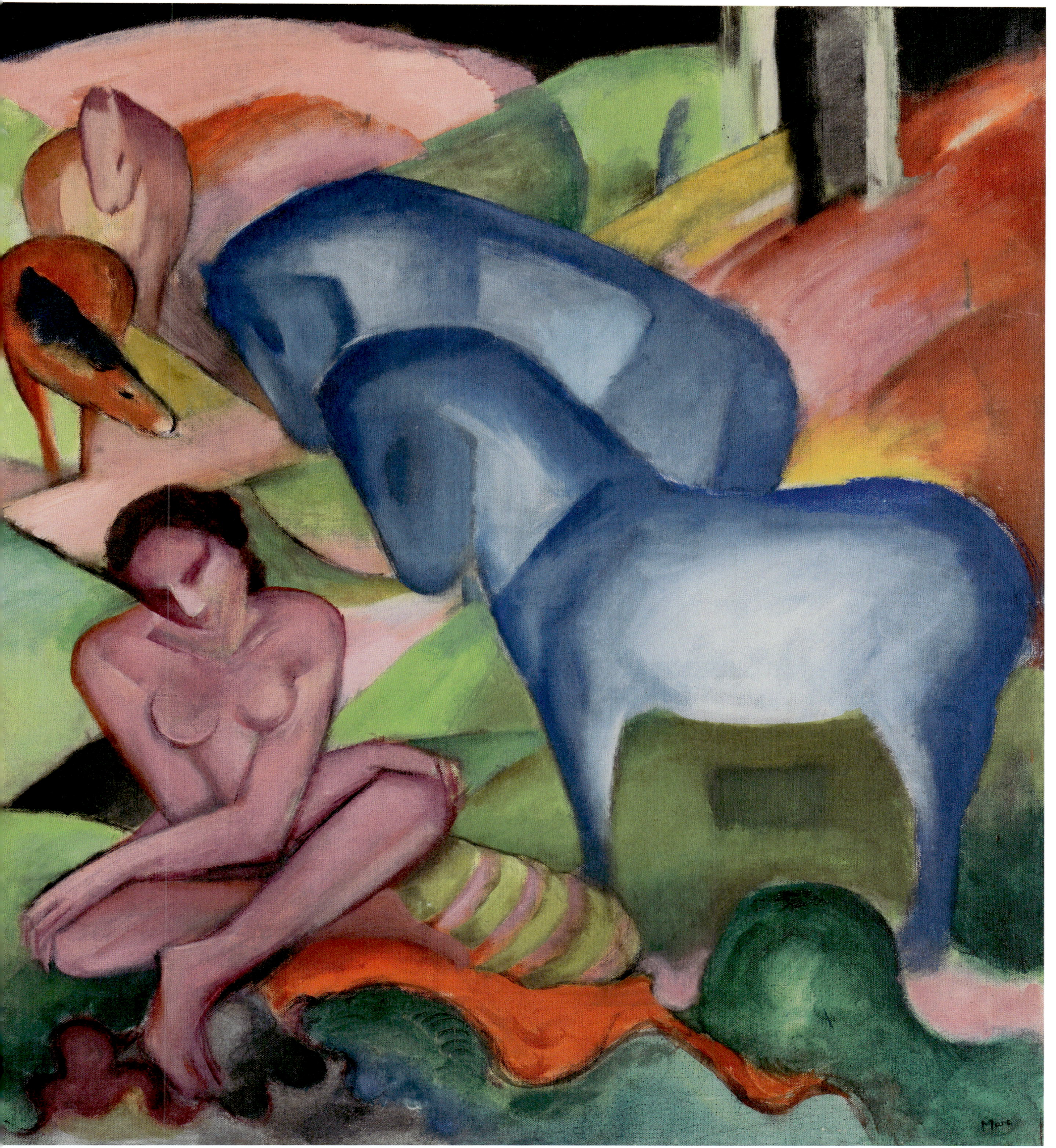
Marc

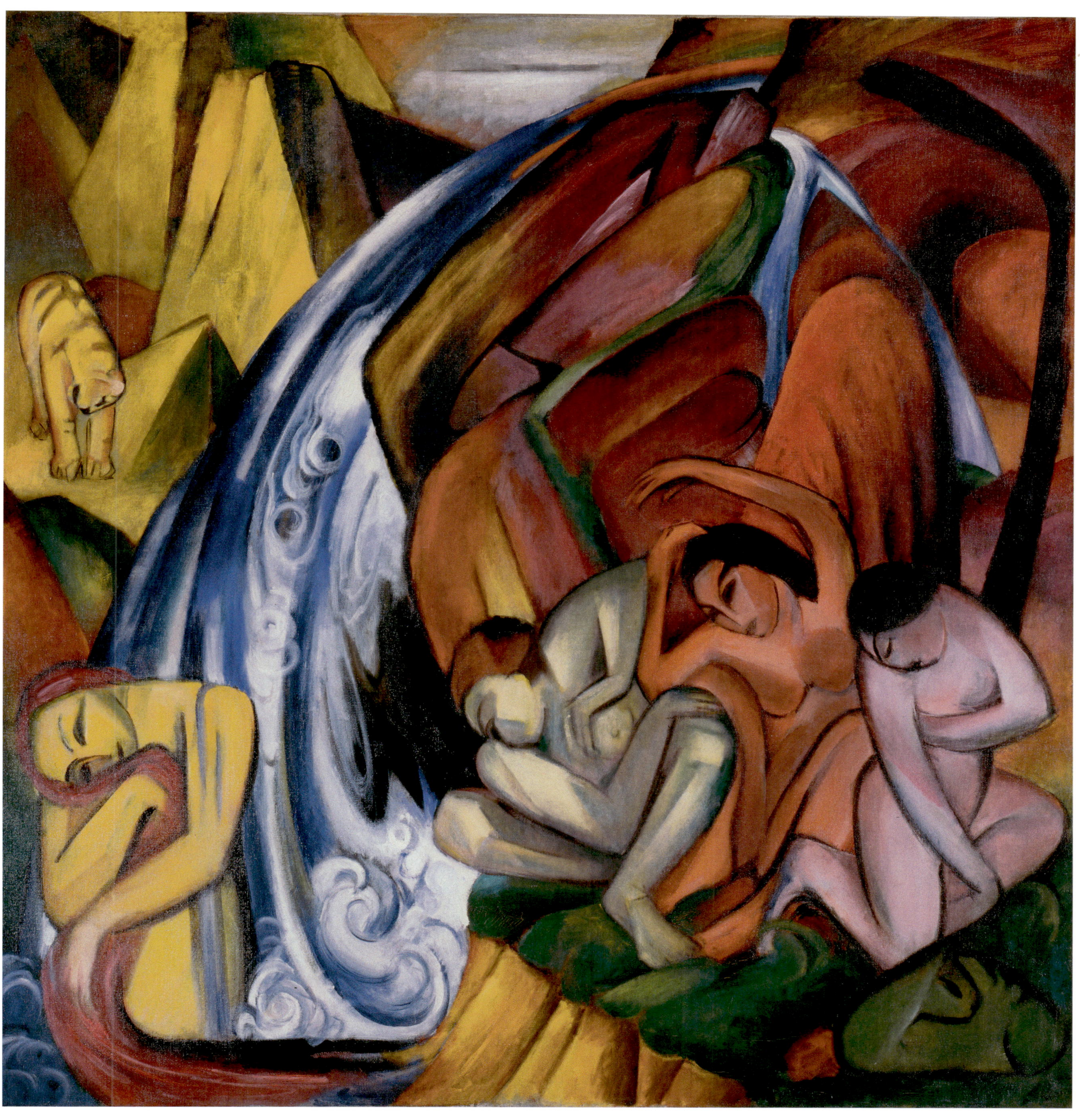

Franz Marc *The Waterfall (Women under a Waterfall)*, 1912
Private collection

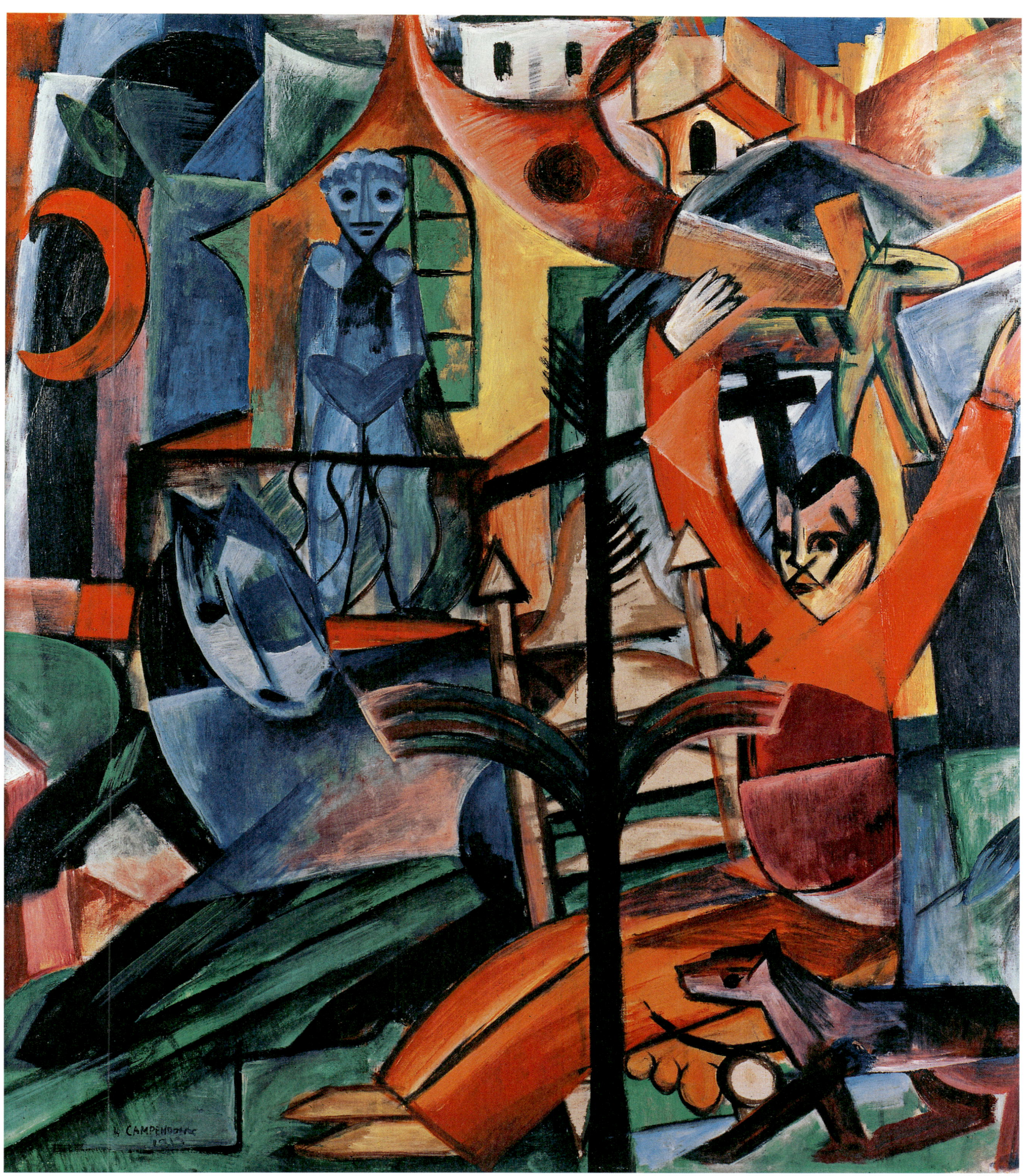

Heinrich Campendonk *The Balcony*, 1913
Merzbacher Kunststiftung

AUGUST MACKE

Like Marc, August Macke fell in World War I, already in 1914, at the age of just twenty-seven. Macke joined the Blaue Reiter at the recommendation of Marc, who recorded their first encounter in a letter to his future wife, Maria Franck, on January 6, 1910:

> *Now I must tell you about an experience today from which I expect many pleasant possibilities to arise. There was a knock on the door—outside the door stand three very young and elegant gentlemen. They ask for me. . . . The three gentlemen are painters & Cézanne is their god. And the father of one of them has a famous collection of Van Gogh, Cézanne, Maillol, etc. Also, the three make a more than affluent impression. . . . At any rate, a different wind blows in this small circle. But not a trace of bohemia—the opposite, tip-top.*[1]

As far as "pleasant possibilities" were concerned, Marc, troubled by financial difficulties, was quite right. The collector he mentioned was Bernhard Koehler, whose son, Bernhard Koehler Jr., together with August Macke and his cousin Helmuth, formed the trio. Over the following years, father and son Koehler, especially the father, were to become the most important collectors of Marc and other artists from the Blaue Reiter circle. In addition, Koehler served as the main financer of the almanac.

Macke and Marc were soon involved in an intensive artistic exchange, with Marc increasingly in the role of mediator between Macke and Kandinsky. Macke thought Kandinsky too dogmatic and rejected his abstract paintings, preferring Robert Delaunay and his Orphism with its strongly colored Cubist-influenced compositions. Moreover, Macke thought the paintings of Arnold Schoenberg, which Kandinsky championed, completely insignificant and was put out by the prominence given to Schoenberg in the almanac. This is understandable from his perspective, given that Schoenberg had been allotted two reproductions and he himself was represented by only one painting. Macke's attempts to ironically puncture Kandinsky's pathos are recorded in Gabriele Münter's photo of her young fellow artist on the balcony of the house at Ainmillerstrasse 36 (where Münter and Kandinsky lived in Munich), engaged in watering the "tiny plant of modern art." Just how subtle Macke's irony could be, is indicated by his painting *Walterchens Spielsachen* (*Little Walter's Toys;* cat. p. 122). This charming picture of his son Walter's world might be read as an ironic commentary on Marc's paintings of animals, in which rabbits are depicted in a quite similar way (cat. pp. 138–39). In addition, Macke's work takes on a (naturally involuntary) tragic aspect, because we as viewers are aware of the fact that young Walter's father would not be able to watch him grow up.

Even more than Marc's work, Macke's oeuvre conveys the sense of being unfinished, as if manifesting unfulfilled promise. His works seem to represent an attempt to combine abstract color composition and figuration. Unlike the other artists of the Blaue Reiter, Macke depicted scenes from modern everyday life, using Cubist faceting to lend them an appearance of multiple perspectives. Perhaps his intentions can best be understood by reading the essay "Die Masken" (Masks), which he wrote for the almanac, one of the finest and linguistically most polished contributions in the volume. Macke avoids the term "internal necessity" and refers to the "mystery" or "secret" on which all art and its forms are based.[2]

[1] Franz Marc, letter to Maria Franck, January 6, 1910, in *Der Blaue Reiter: Eine Geschichte in Dokumenten,* ed. Andreas Hüneke (Stuttgart, 2011), pp. 10–11.
[2] August Macke, "Die Masken," in *Der Blaue Reiter,* ed. Wassily Kandinsky and Franz Marc (Munich, 1912), pp. 21–26, here pp. 21–22; English ed.: "Masks," in *The Blaue Reiter Almanac,* ed. Wassily Kandinsky and Franz Marc, documentary edition, ed. and with an introduction by Klaus Lankheit, trans. Henning Falkenstein with assistance of Manug Terzian and Gertrude Hinderlie (New York, 1974; repr. Boston, 2005), pp. 83–89, here p. 85.

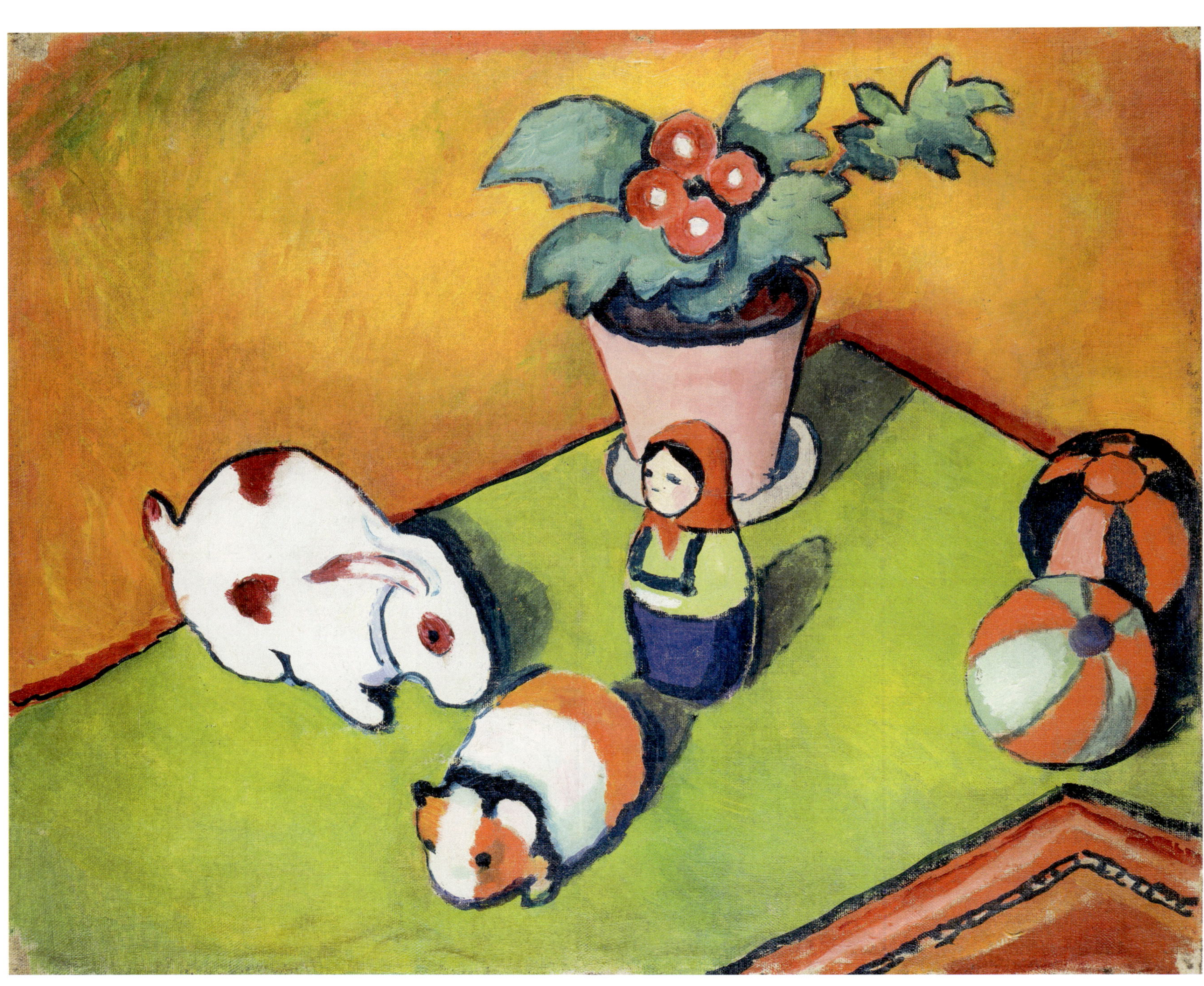

August Macke *Little Walter's Toys*, 1912
Städel Museum, Frankfurt am Main

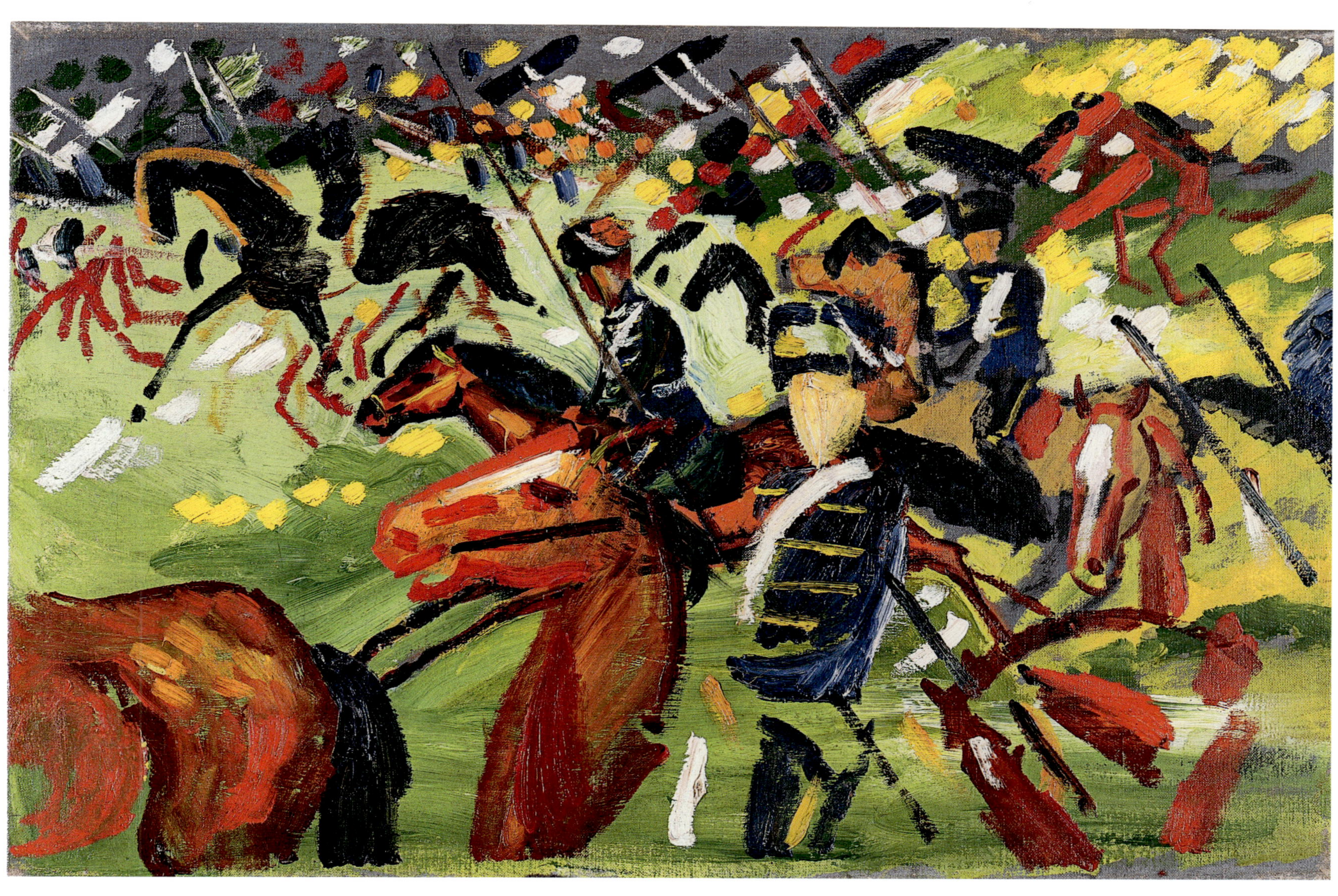

August Macke *Hussars on a Sortie*, 1913
Museo Thyssen-Bornemisza, Madrid

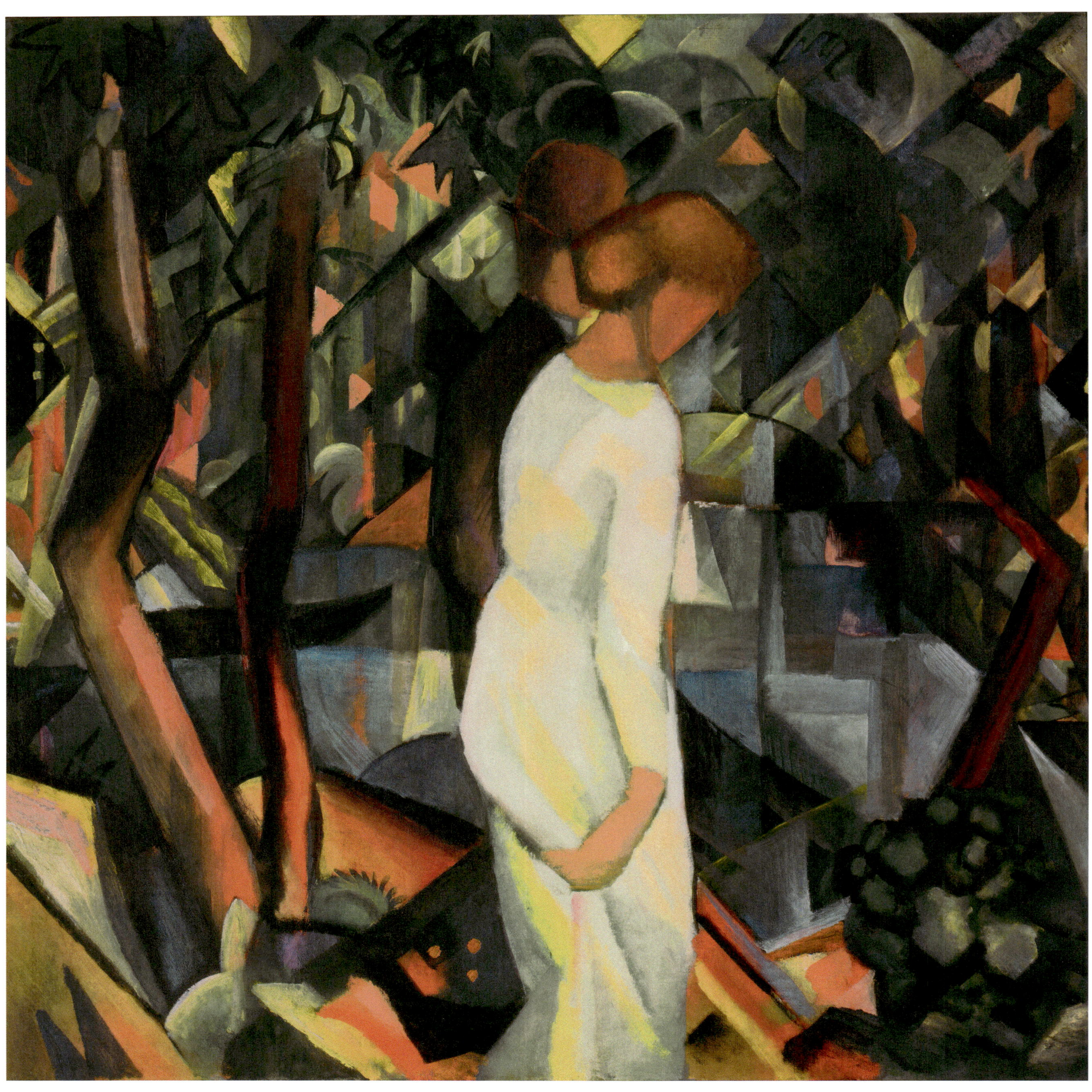

August Macke *Couple in the Forest*, 1912
Private collection

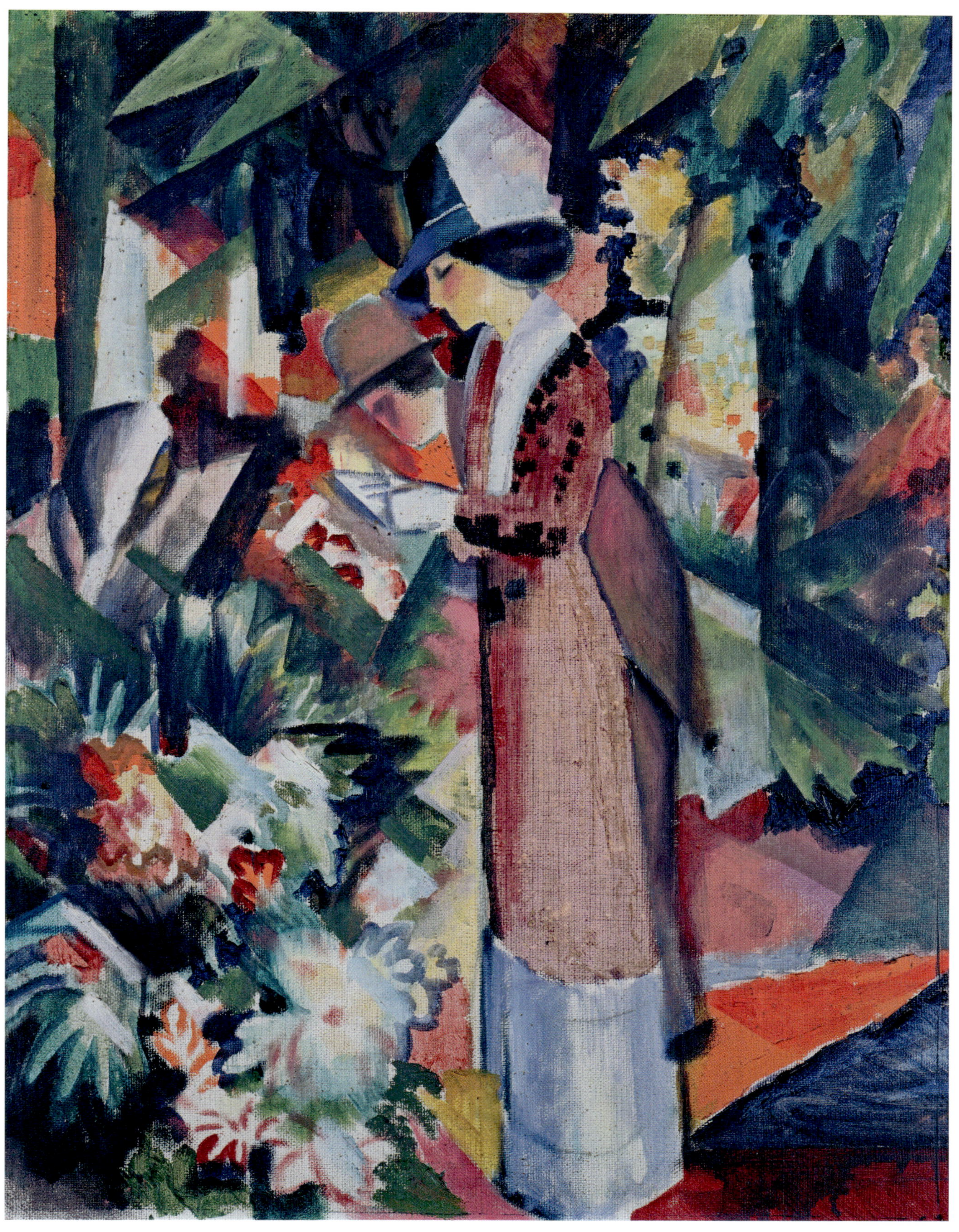

August Macke *Walk amongst Flowers*, 1912
Staatliche Museen zu Berlin, Nationalgalerie, acquired 1949 through the State of Berlin

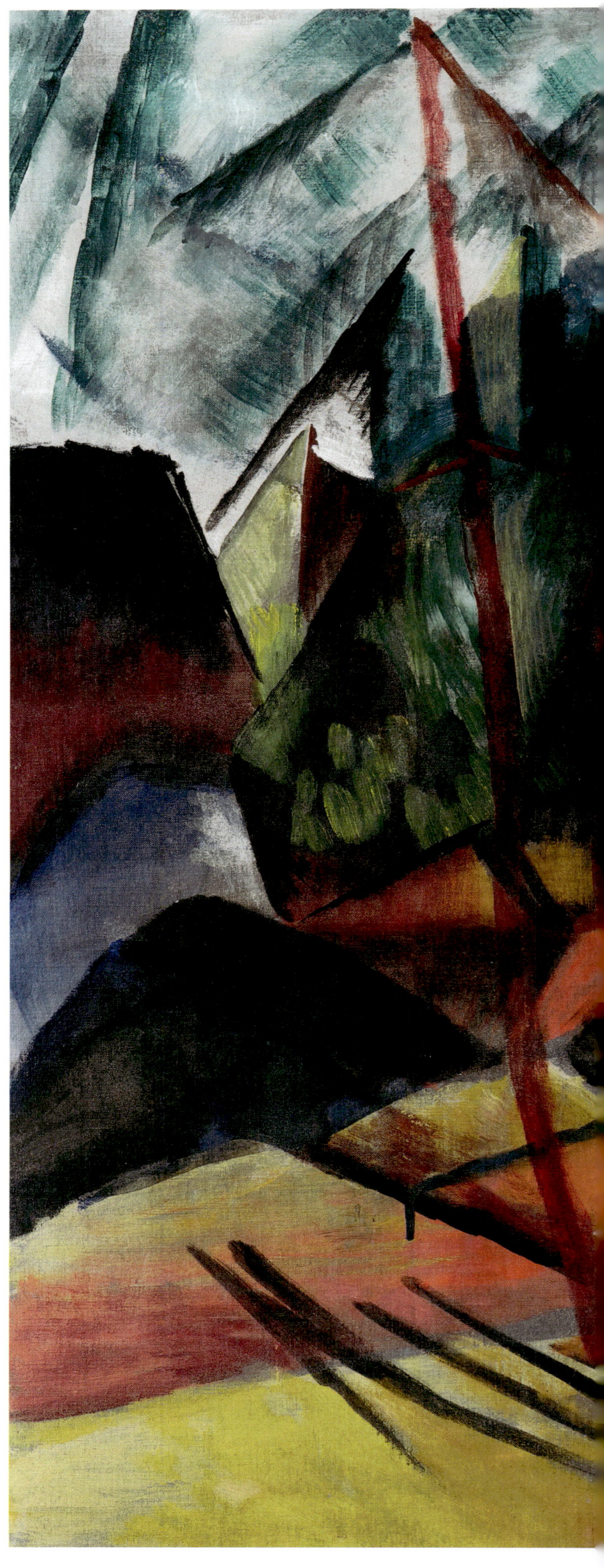

August Macke *Forest Walk*, 1913
Private collection

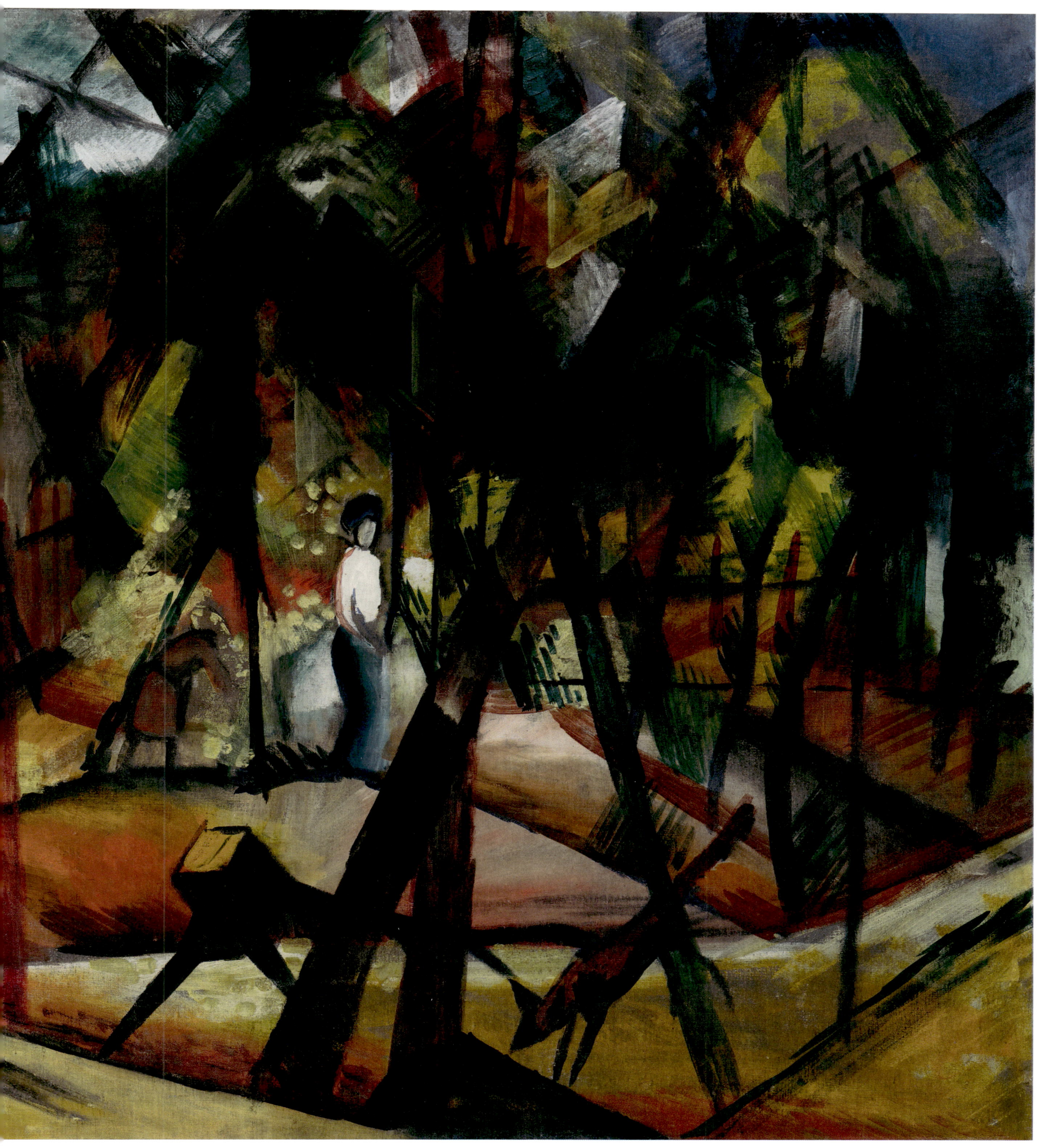

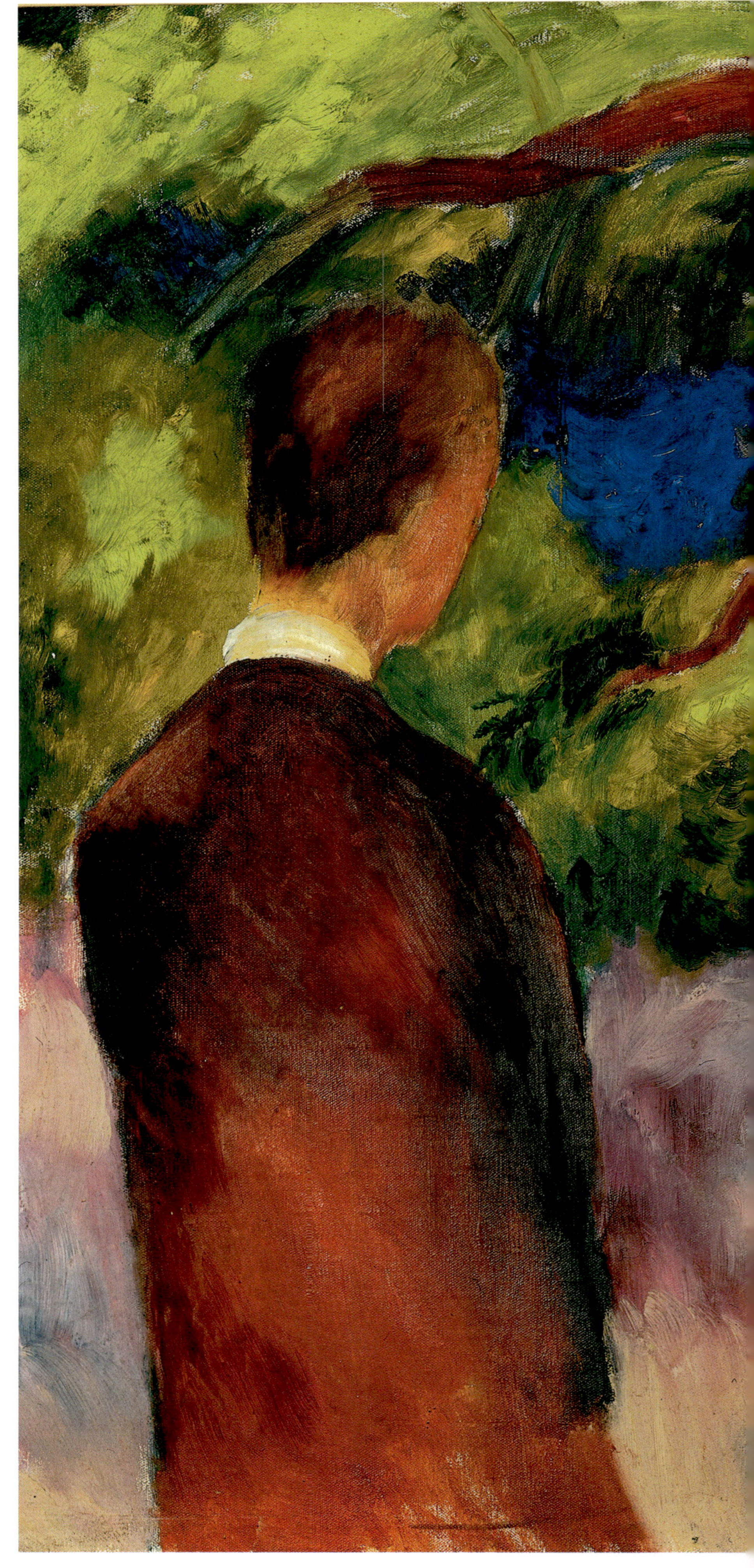

August Macke *Great Promenade: People in the Garden*, 1914
Franz Marc Museum, Kochel am See, loan from a private collection

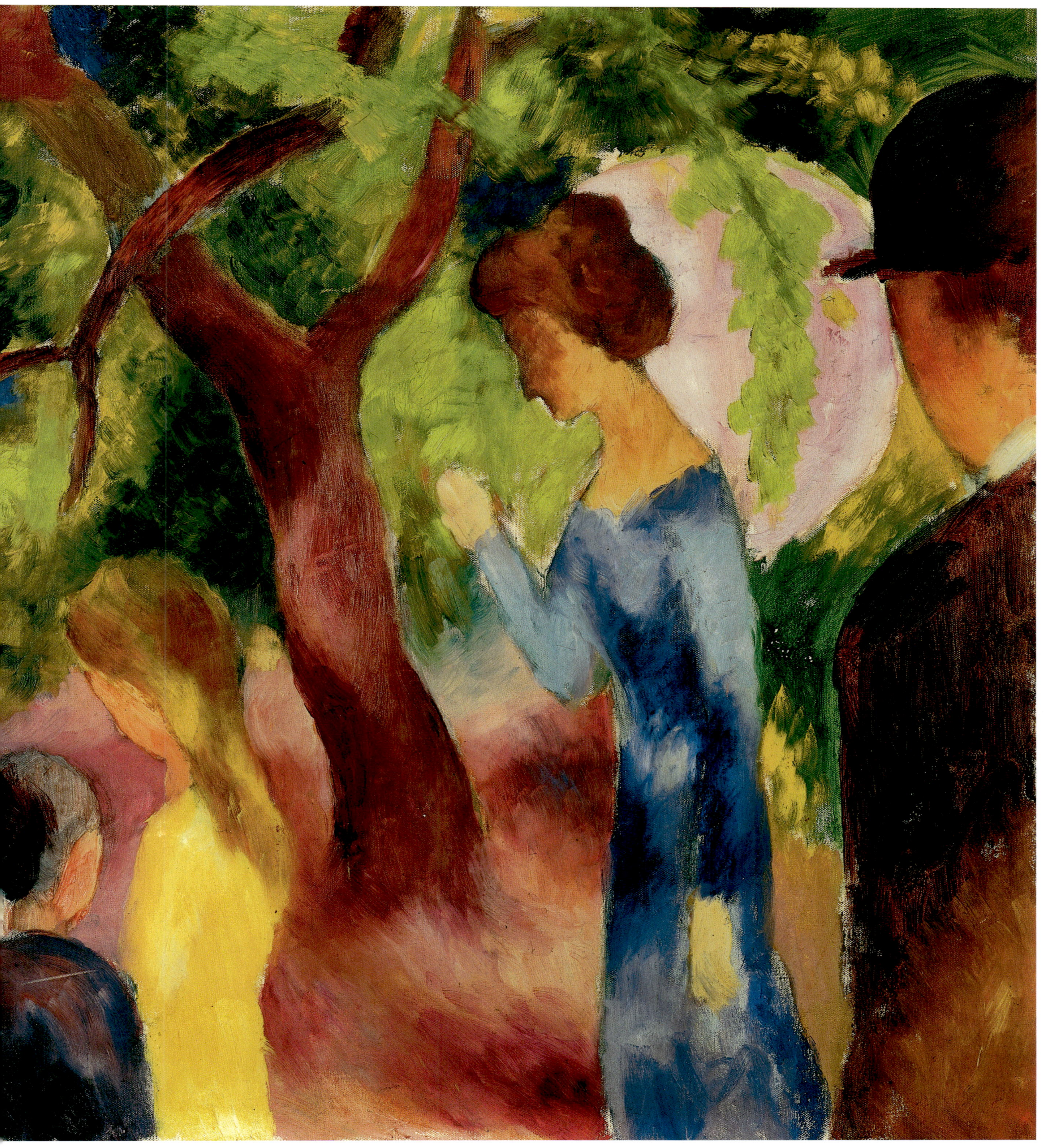

FRANZ MARC: DEMONS

Franz Marc's artistic development, too, tended to an ever greater degree of abstraction. His frieze-like painting *Stallungen* (*Stables;* cat. pp. 144–45), from 1913, conceals the horses' bodies behind a network of colored geometric crystals that seems to cover the entire chromatic spectrum. The influence of Delaunay is just as evident here as is the attempt to combine as many aspects of art as possible in a single picture: figuration, abstraction, two-dimensionality, and three-dimensional illusion.

Yet what strikes us in particular about the pictures Marc produced after 1912 is an idea that we do not necessarily associate with the painter of superbly graceful animals—a concern with the dark, demonic aspect of creatures, in oppressive imagery that even referred to current events, something that held much less interest for Kandinsky. We find not only emaciated horses (cat. p. 137) but also *Die Angst des Hasen* (*The Fear of the Hare;* cat. pp. 138–39), depicting a rabbit ducking into a furrow to escape being discovered by a dog. This picture can naturally be read as a direct commentary on a passage from a letter Marc wrote to Kandinsky on March 16, 1912, shortly before the publication of the almanac, in which he alludes to the criticism it was bound to prompt:

> *The hare will soon have escaped our caring hands. Then the beaters and hunters will come and hound it to death.*[1]

In the present exhibition, Marc's interest in the demonic aspect of animals culminates in the relatively large-format painting *Die Wölfe (Balkankrieg)* (*The Wolves [Balkan War]*; cat. pp. 134–35), which alludes to the political situation in the Balkans that led to the outbreak of World War I. Cowering wolves in various colors, with their hackles raised and eyes gleaming, creep up on sleeping animals, while beneath them, flowers appear to wilt—an apocalyptic landscape.

[1] Franz Marc, letter to Wassily Kandinsky, March 16, 1912, in Wassily Kandinsky and Franz Marc, *Briefwechsel: Mit Briefen von und an Gabriele Münter und Maria Marc*, ed., introduction, and annotation by Klaus Lankheit (Munich, 1983), pp. 140–43, here p. 142.

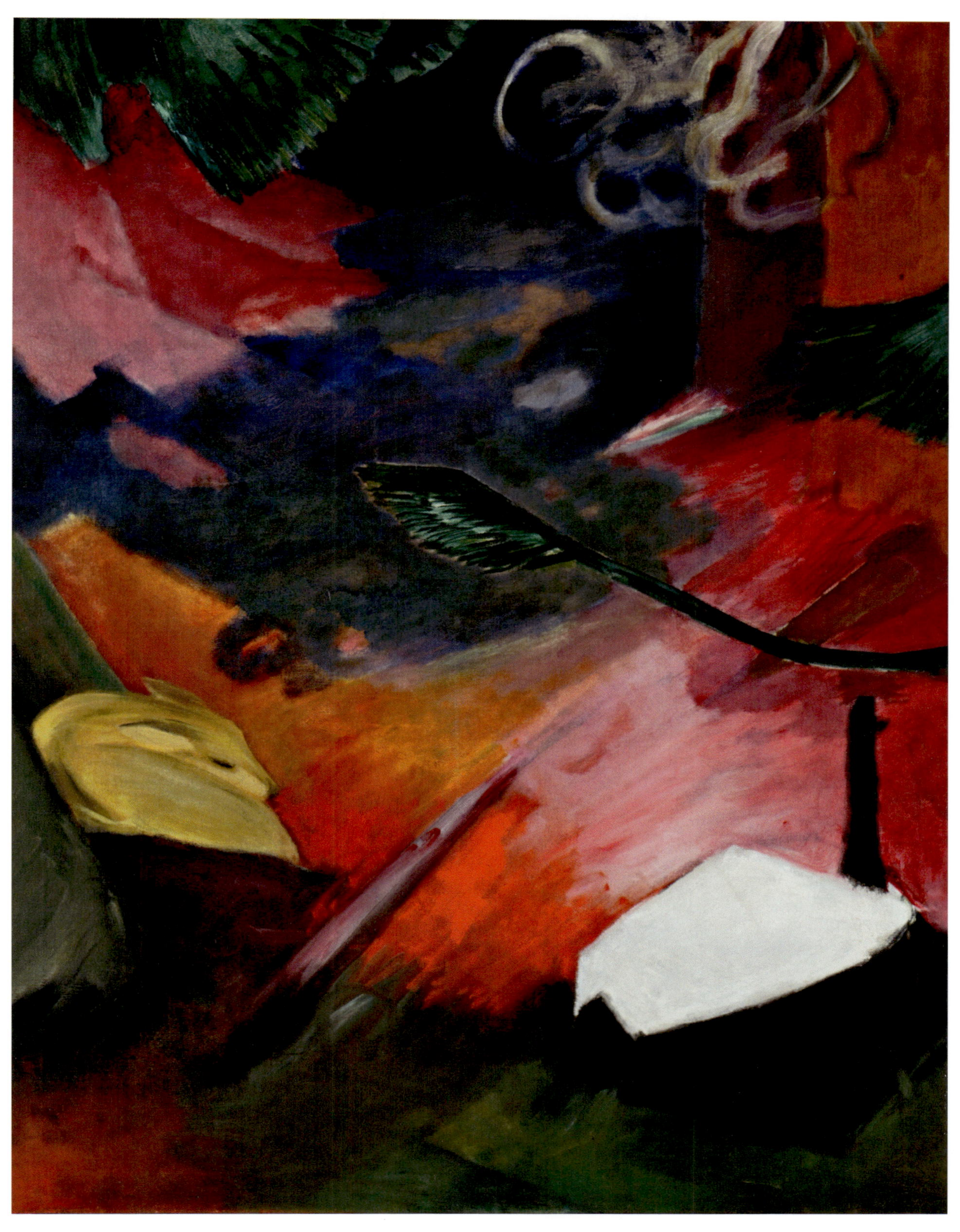

Franz Marc *Deer in the Woods I*, 1911
Private collection

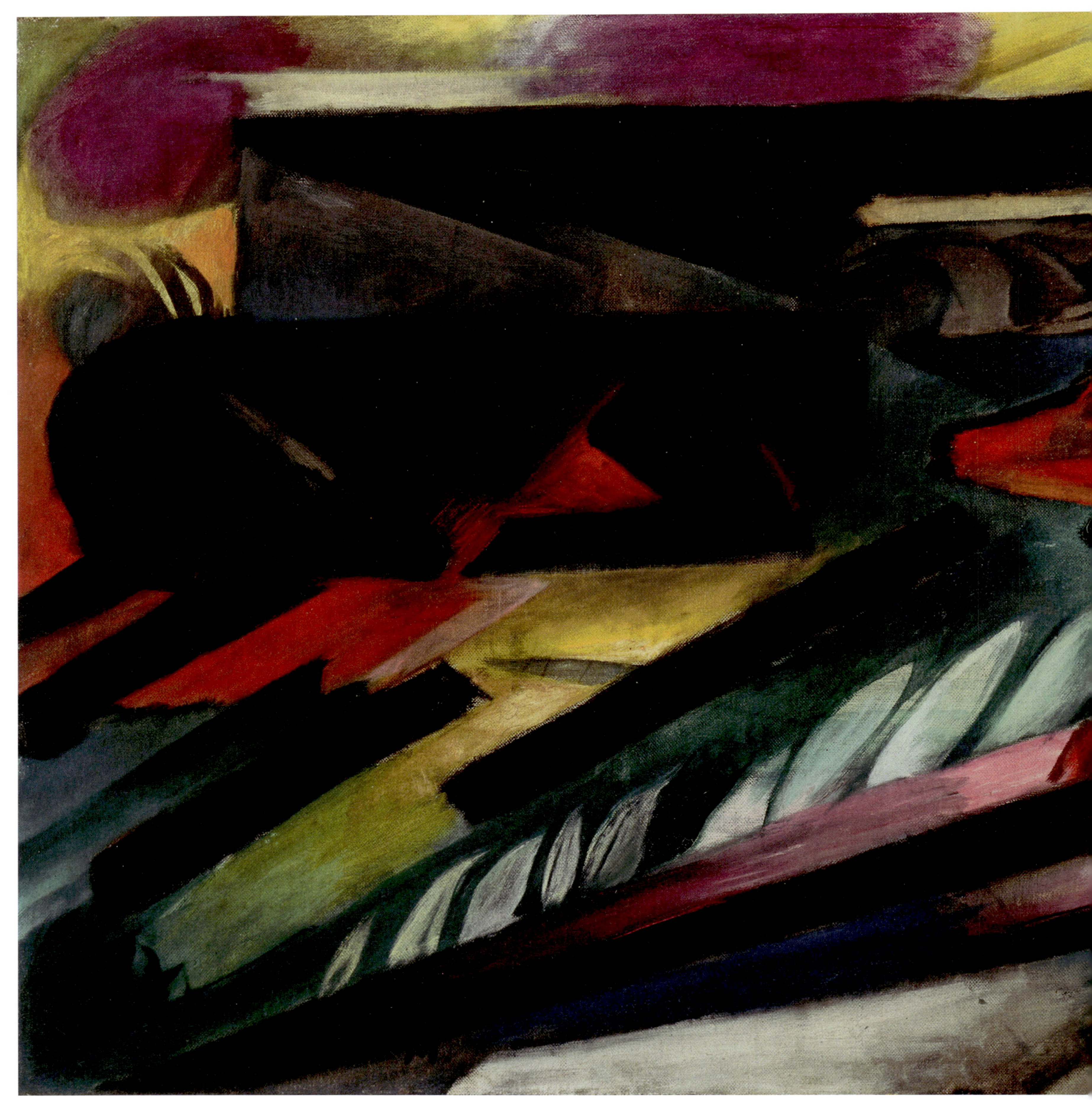

Franz Marc *The Wolves (Balkan War)*, 1913
Collection of the Albright-Knox Art Gallery, Buffalo, New York, Charles Clifton, James G. Forsyth, and George W. Goodyear Funds, 1951

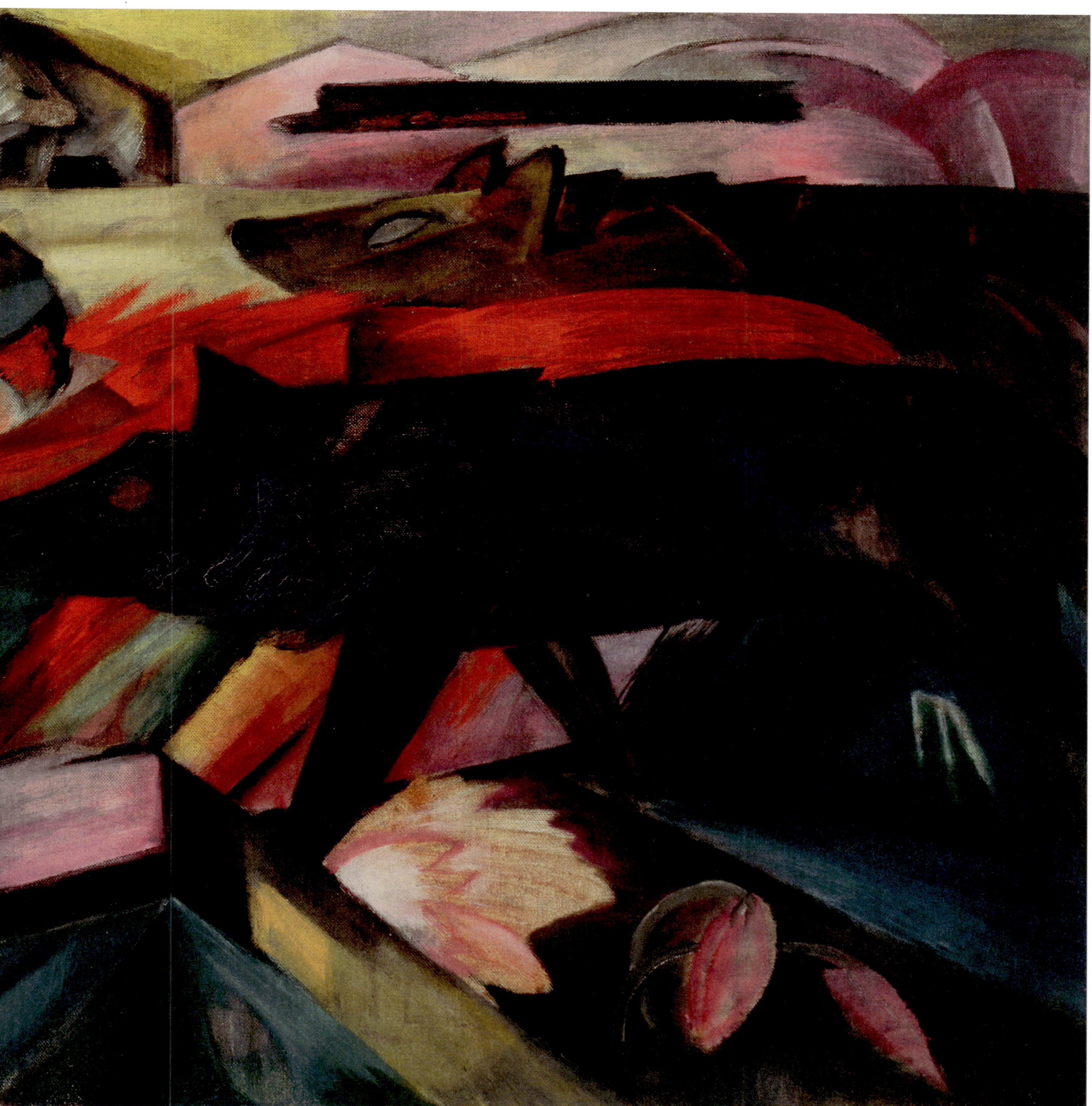

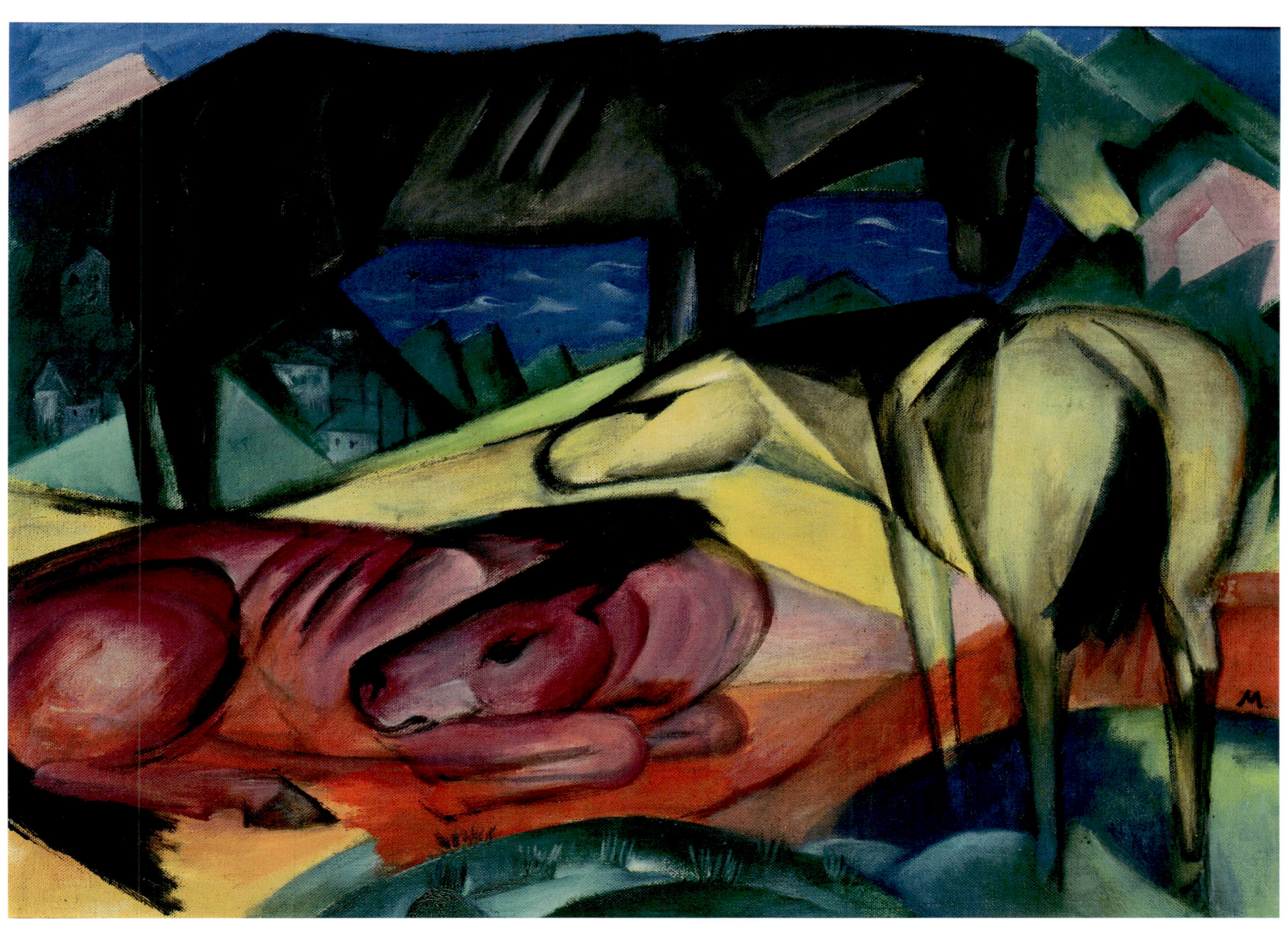

Franz Marc *Three Horses II*, 1913
Staatliche Kunstsammlungen Dresden, on permanent loan to the Galerie Neue Meister

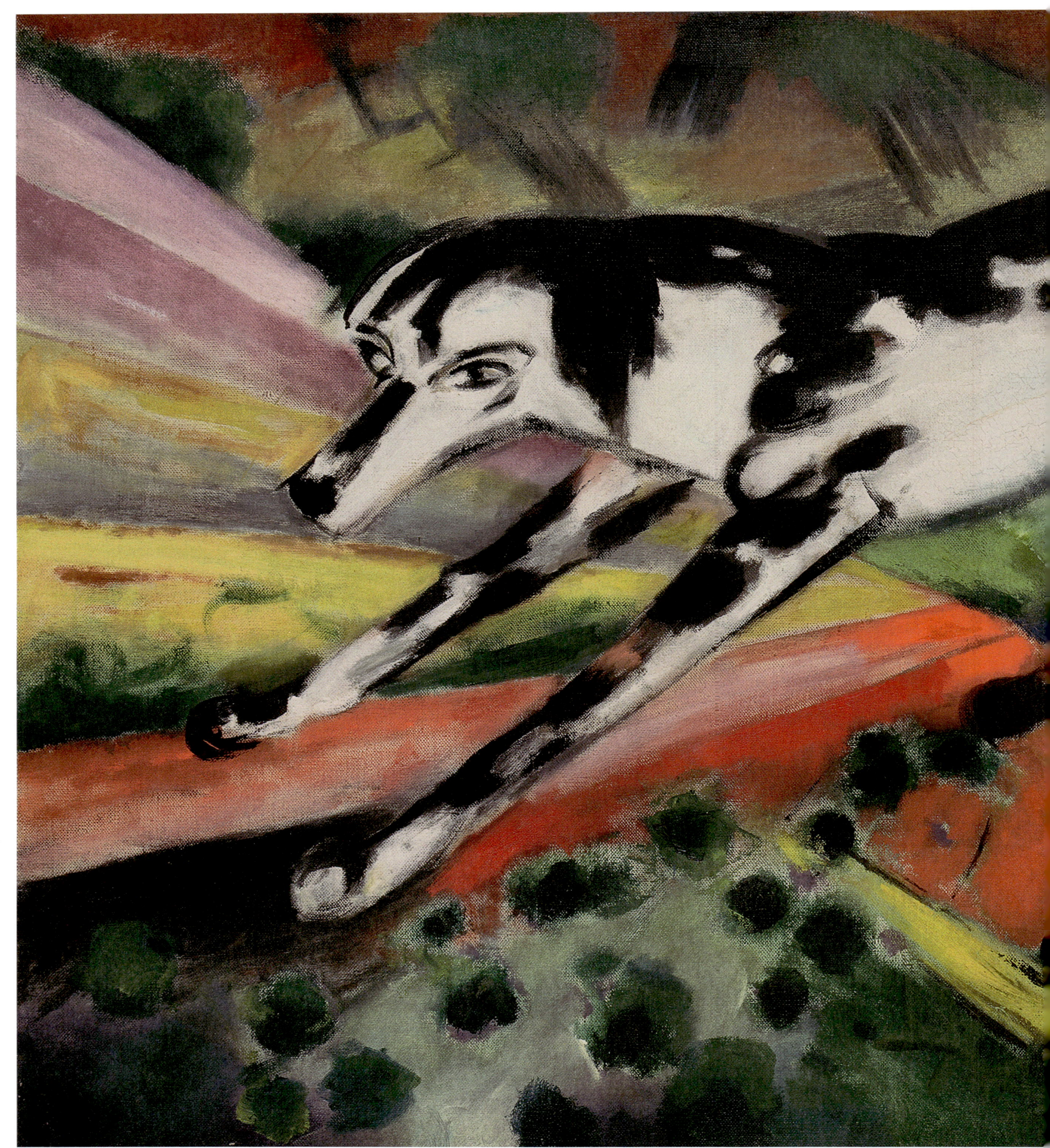

Franz Marc *The Fear of the Hare*, 1912
Private collection, Courtesy Peter Eltz GmbH, Salzburg

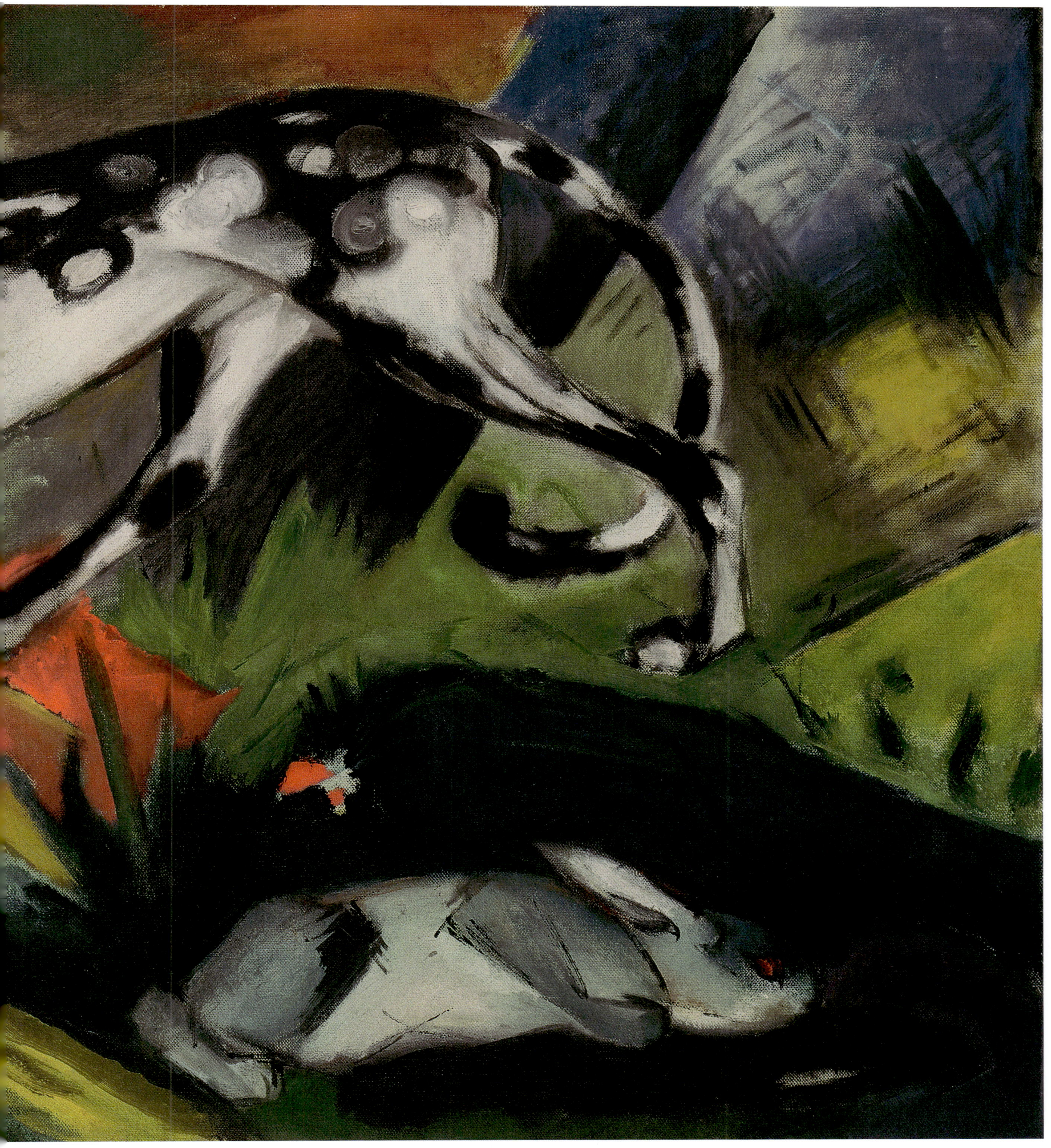

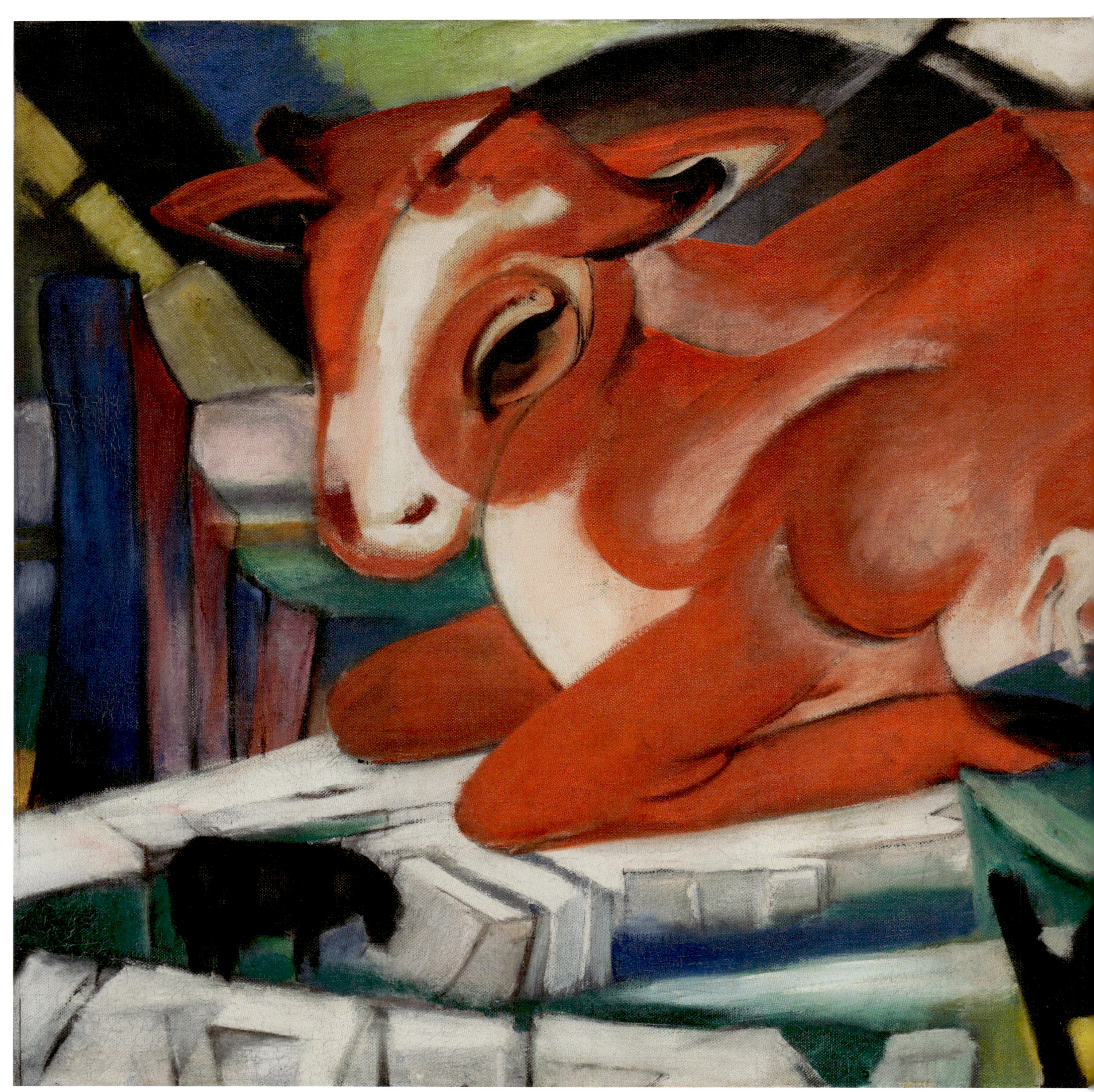

Franz Marc *The World Cow (Bos Orbis Mundi)*, 1913
The Museum of Modern Art, New York, Gift of Mr. and Mrs. Morton D. May, and Mr. and Mrs. Arnold H. Maremont (both by exchange), 1988

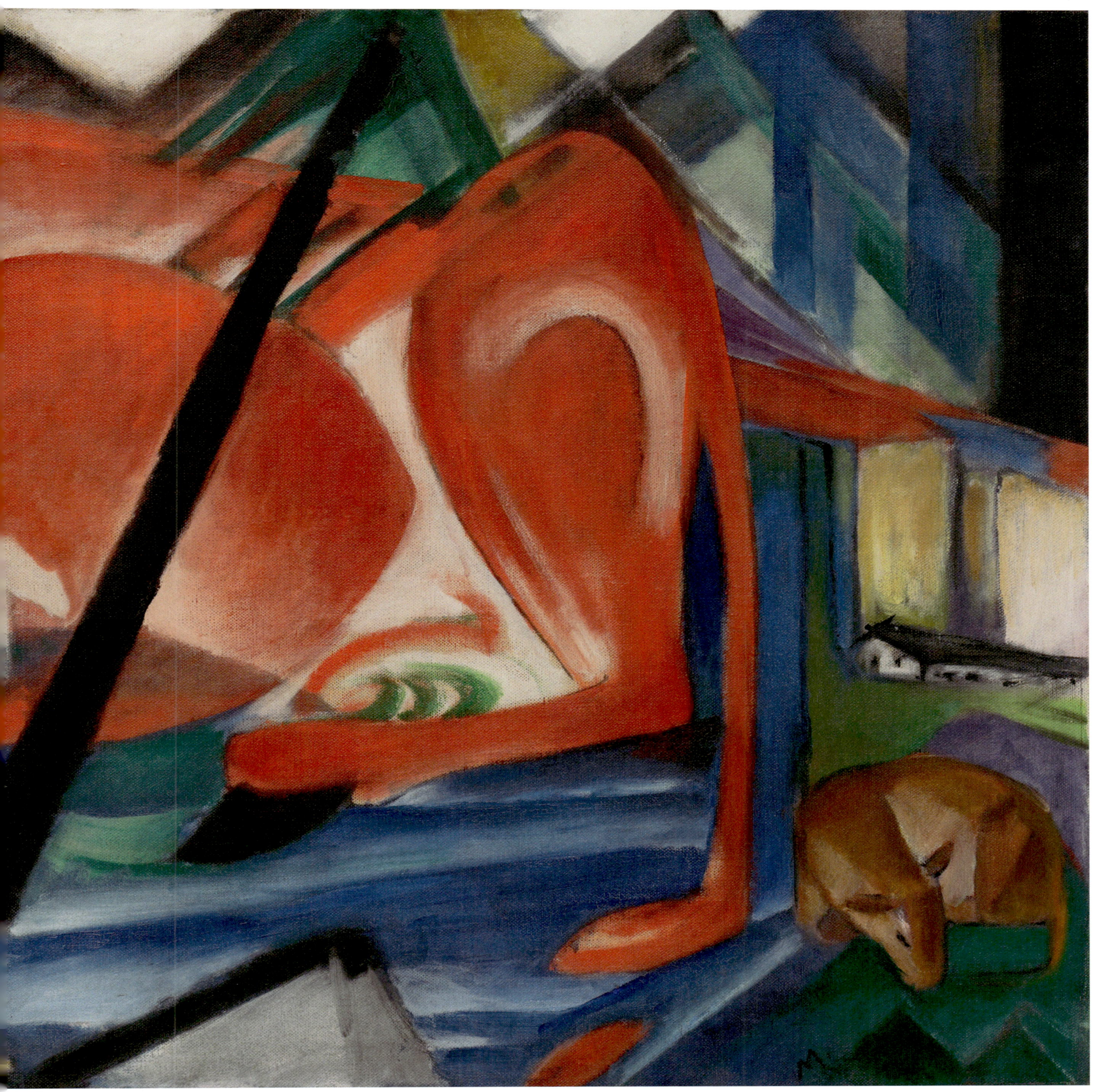

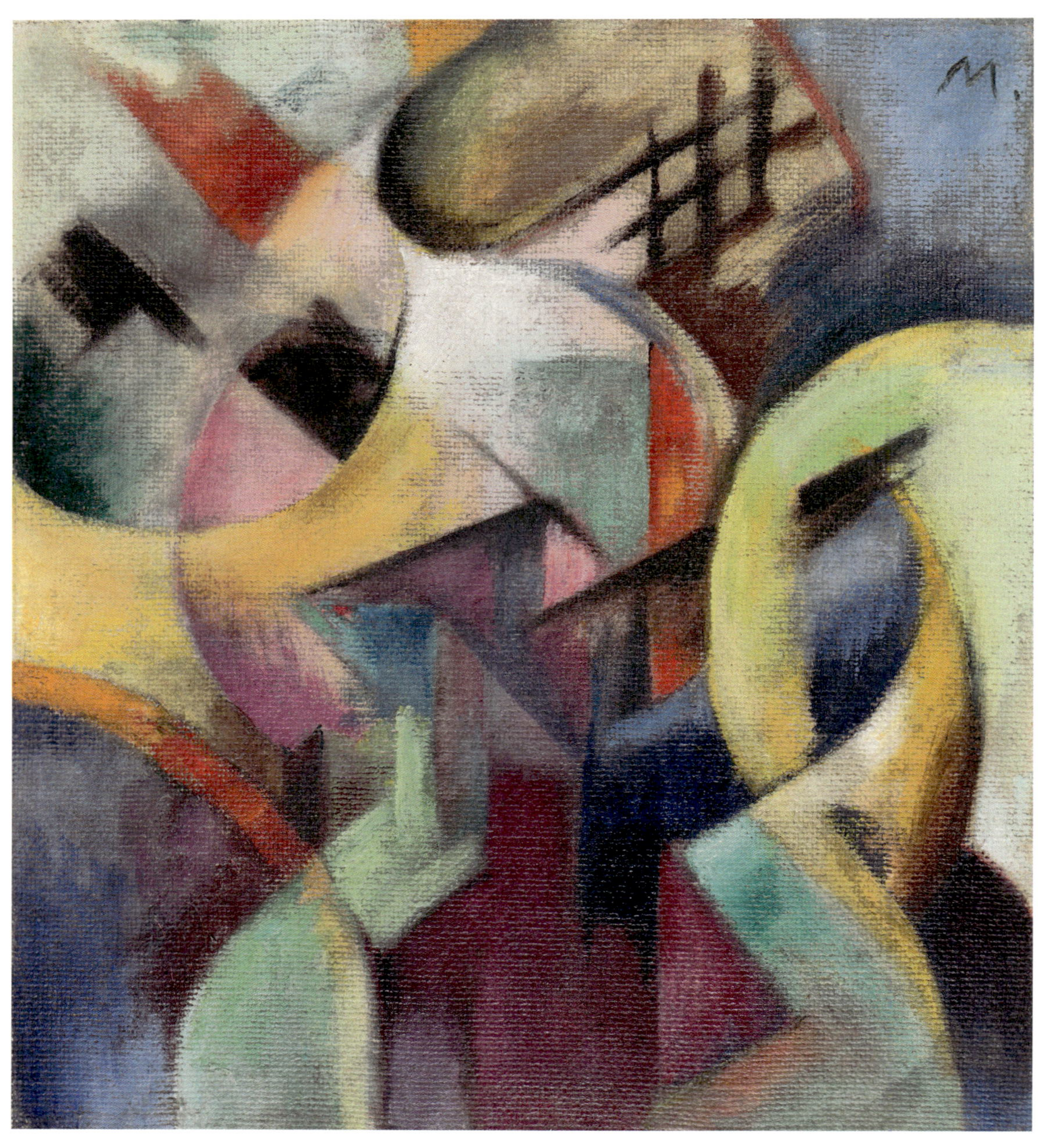

Franz Marc *Small Composition I*, 1913
Private collection, Switzerland, on permanent loan to the Zentrum Paul Klee, Bern

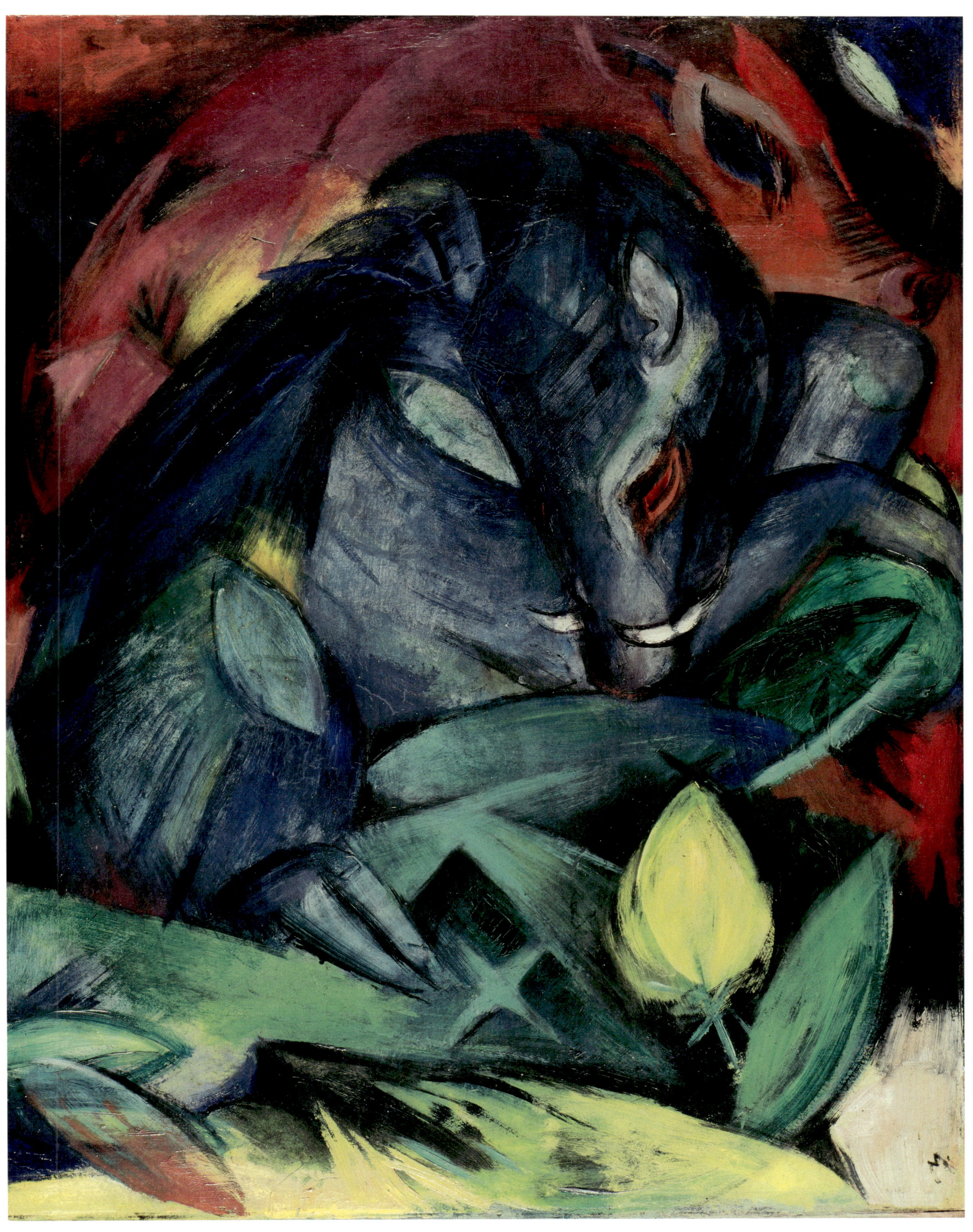

Franz Marc *Boar and Sow (Wild Boar)*, 1913
Museum Ludwig, Cologne

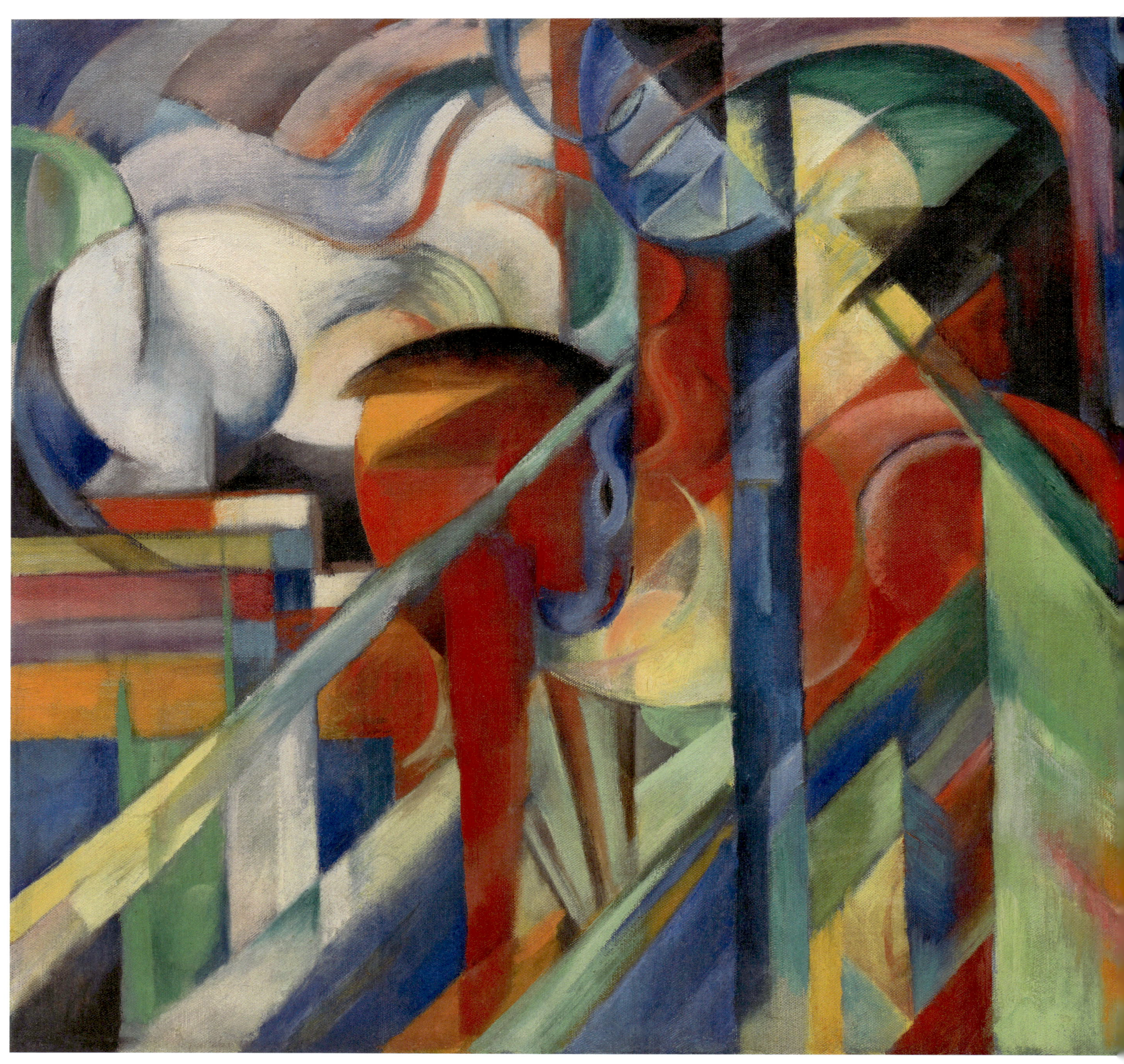

Franz Marc *Stables*, 1913
Solomon R. Guggenheim Museum, New York, Solomon R. Guggenheim Founding Collection

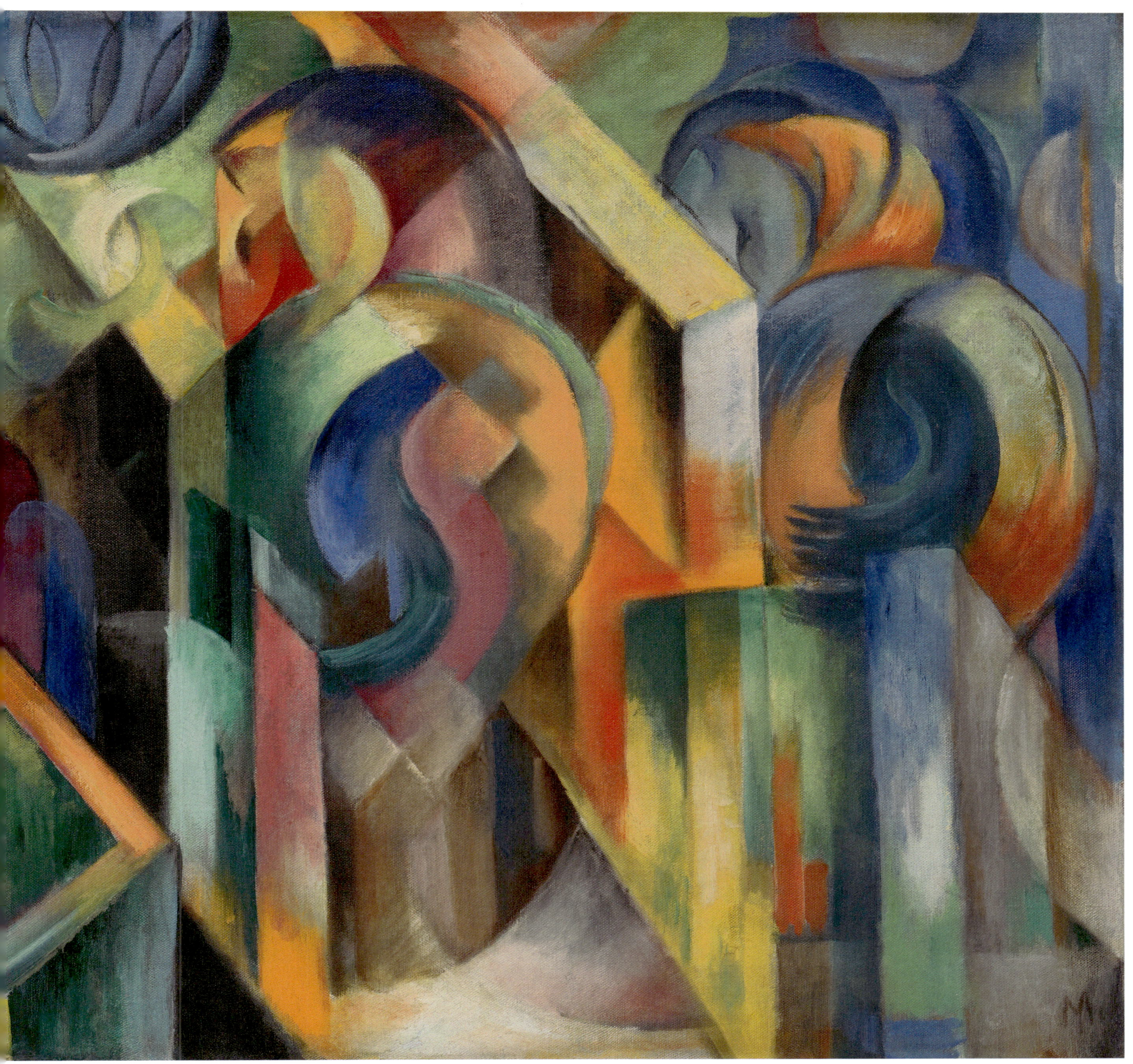

SYNAESTHESIA

One of the most important concerns of the Blaue Reiter artists lay in disseminating the idea that art was synaesthetic, that it transcended the boundaries to other forms of art. This concern was Kandinsky's above all, and the notion was central to his 1909 theater piece "Der gelbe Klang" (Yellow Sound), published in the almanac.[1]

The idea of synaesthesia is also reflected in everyday language. When we speak of a "composition," we may well be referring to a musical composition, though the term also applies to the structure of a work of visual art. Color can mean tonal color, and a tone can also be a color gradation. This should be kept in mind when viewing Kandinsky's large-format abstractions. But there is still another important element: rhythm, which emerges through the movements of the eye as it registers an image. Kandinsky's pictures are not the expression of painterly gestures. Yet ideally, the interaction between the viewer and the work gives rise to a rhythm of seeing that—just possibly—has a correspondence in music.

[1] Wassily Kandinsky, "Der gelbe Klang: Eine Bühnenkomposition," in *Der Blaue Reiter,* ed. Wassily Kandinsky and Franz Marc (Munich, 1912), pp. 115–39; English ed.: "Yellow Sound: A Stage Composition," in *Kandinsky: Complete Writings on Art,* ed. Kenneth C. Lindsay and Peter Vergo (Boston, 1982; new, repr. ed., New York, 1994), pp. 267–83.

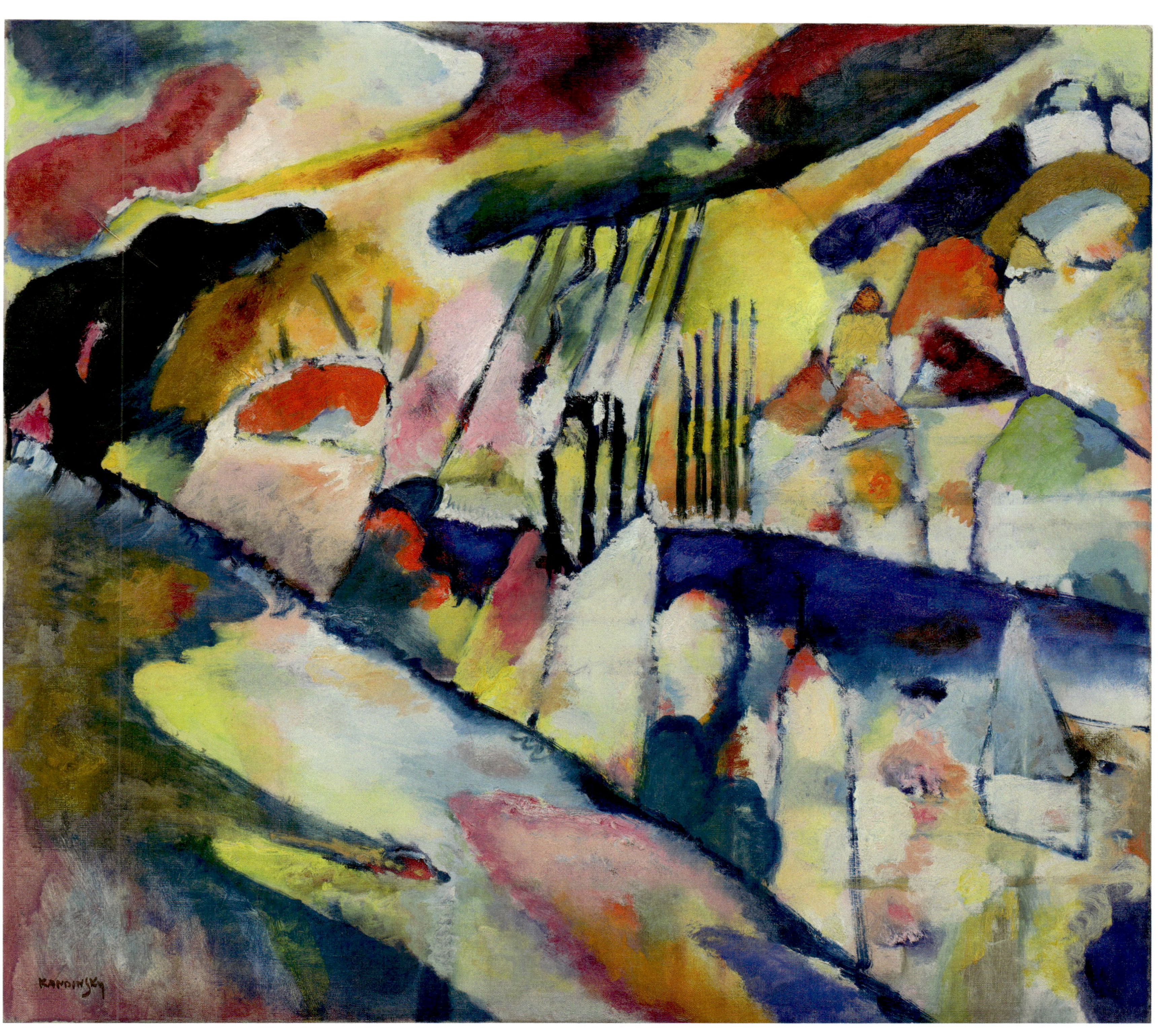

Wassily Kandinsky *Landscape with Rain*, 1913
Solomon R. Guggenheim Museum, New York, Solomon R. Guggenheim Founding Collection

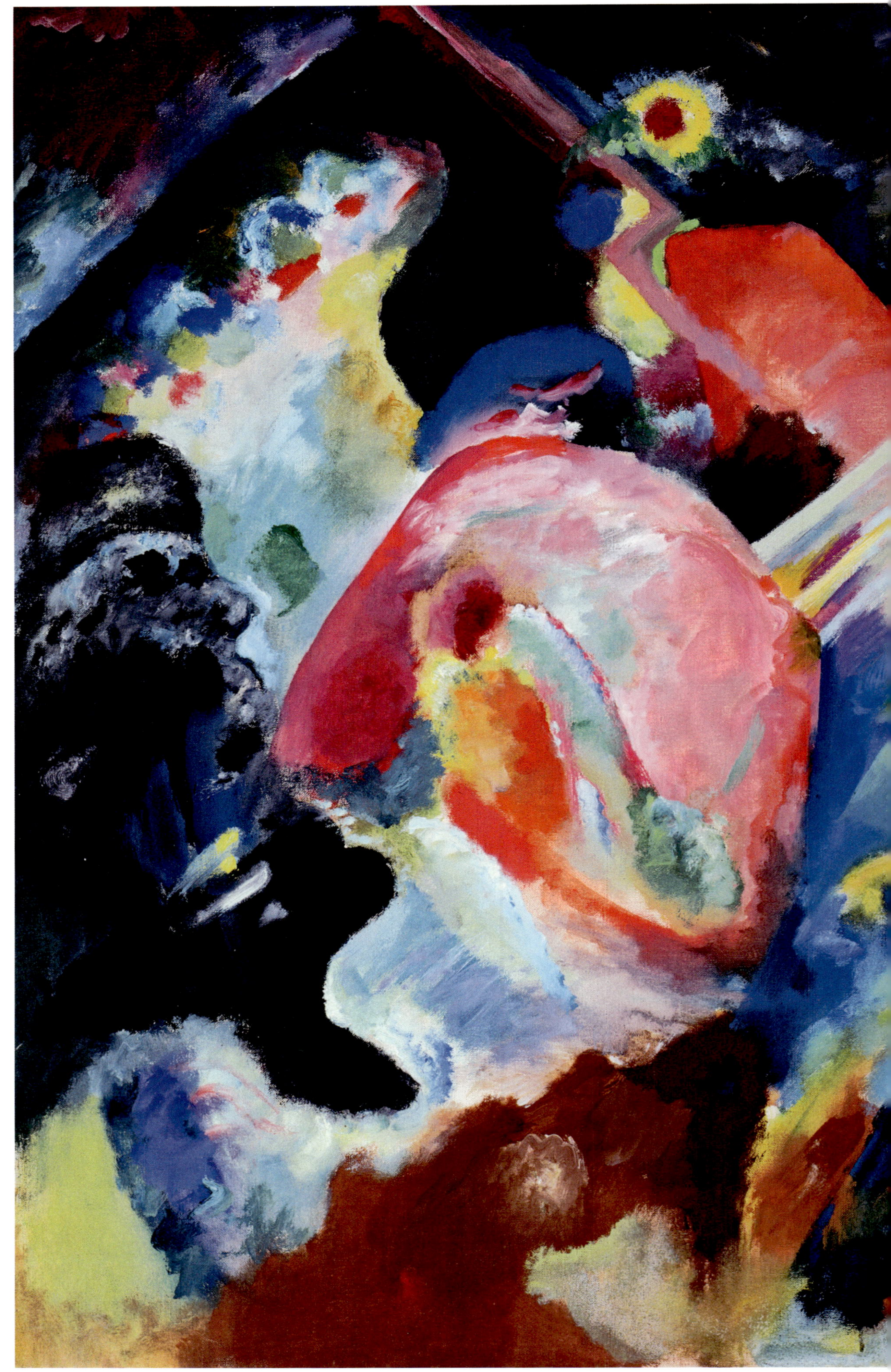

Wassily Kandinsky *Improvisation Deluge*, 1913
Städtische Galerie im Lenbachhaus, Munich

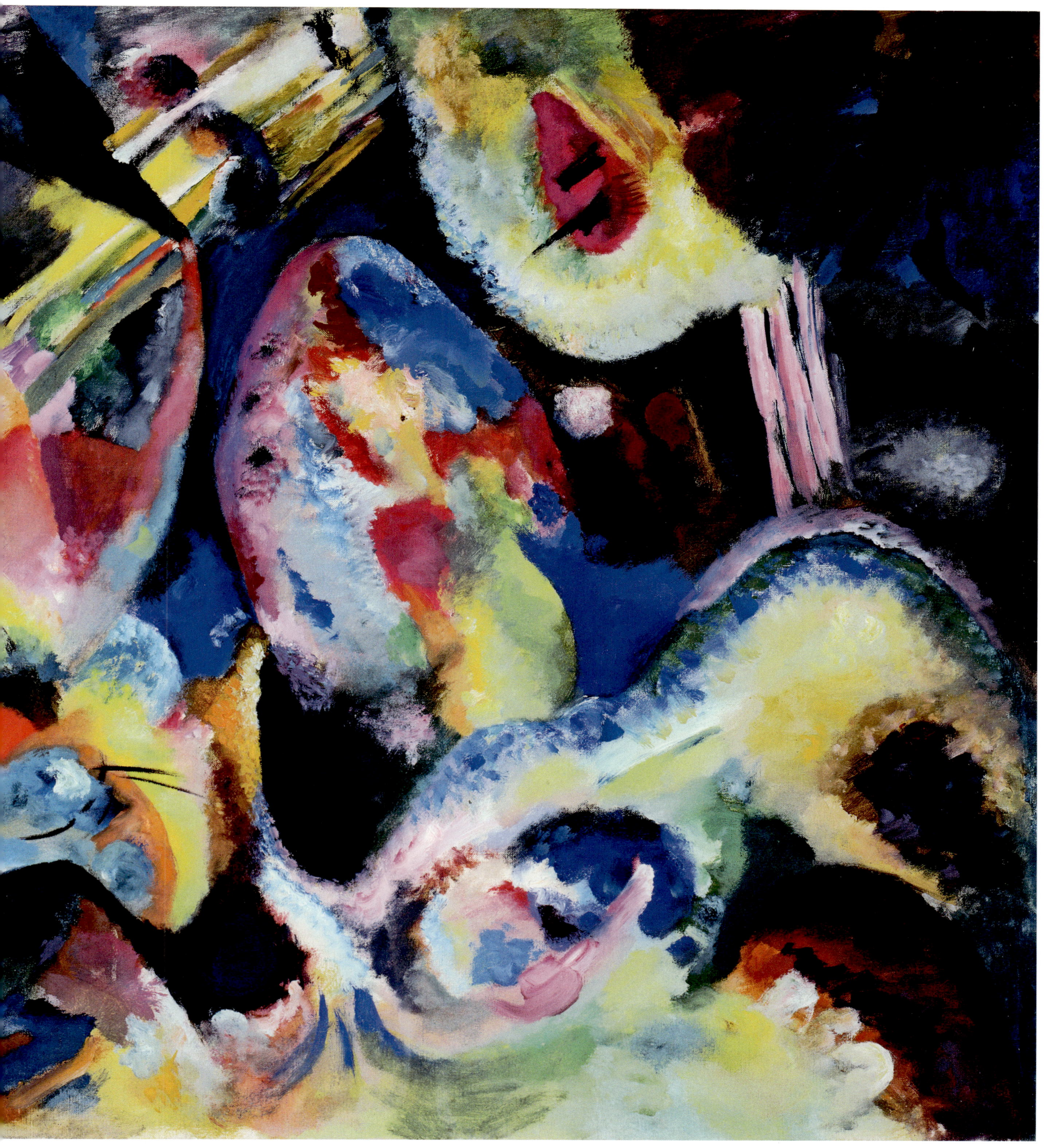

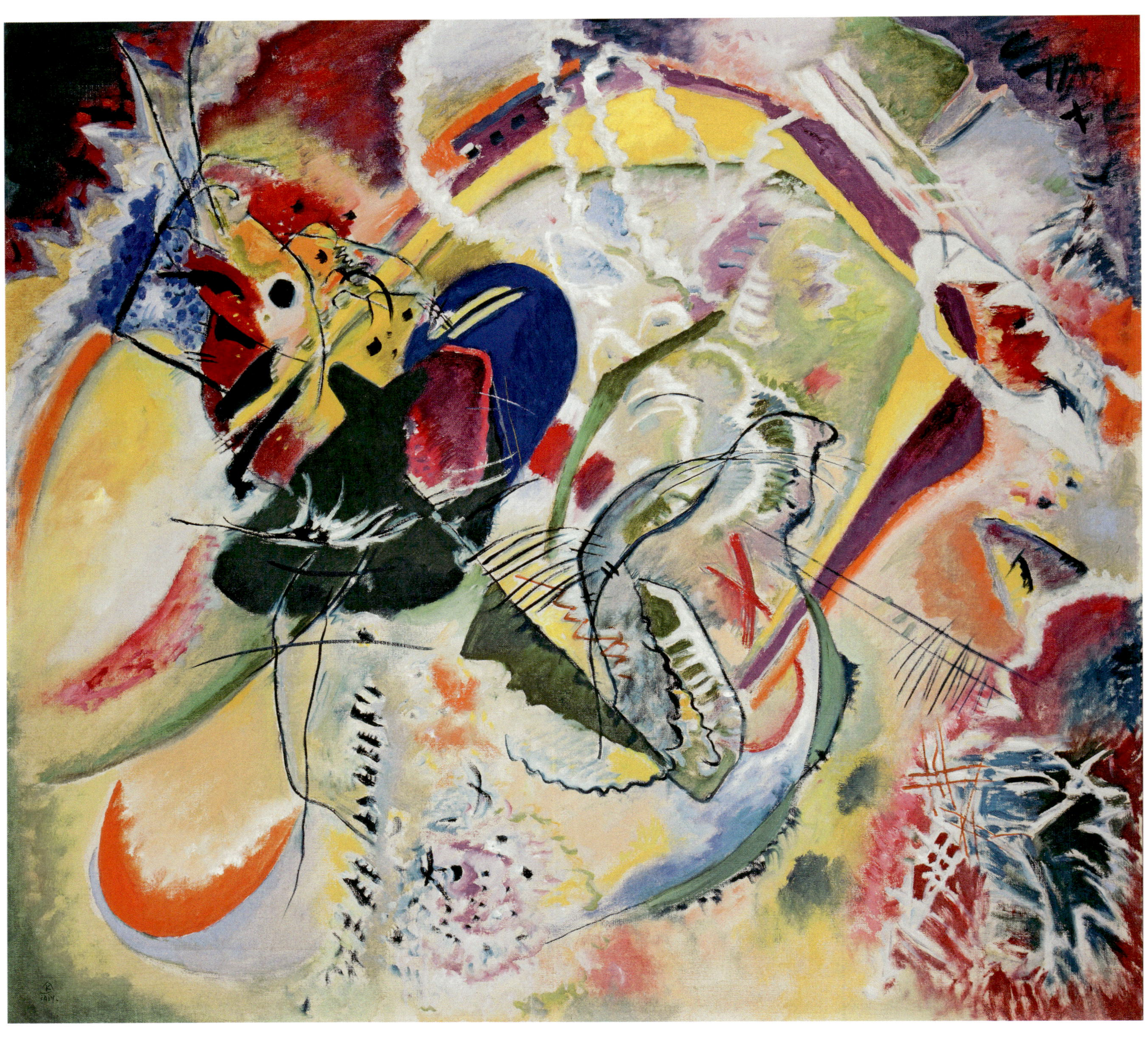

Wassily Kandinsky *Improvisation 35*, 1914
Kunstmuseum Basel, Gift of Hans Arp 1966

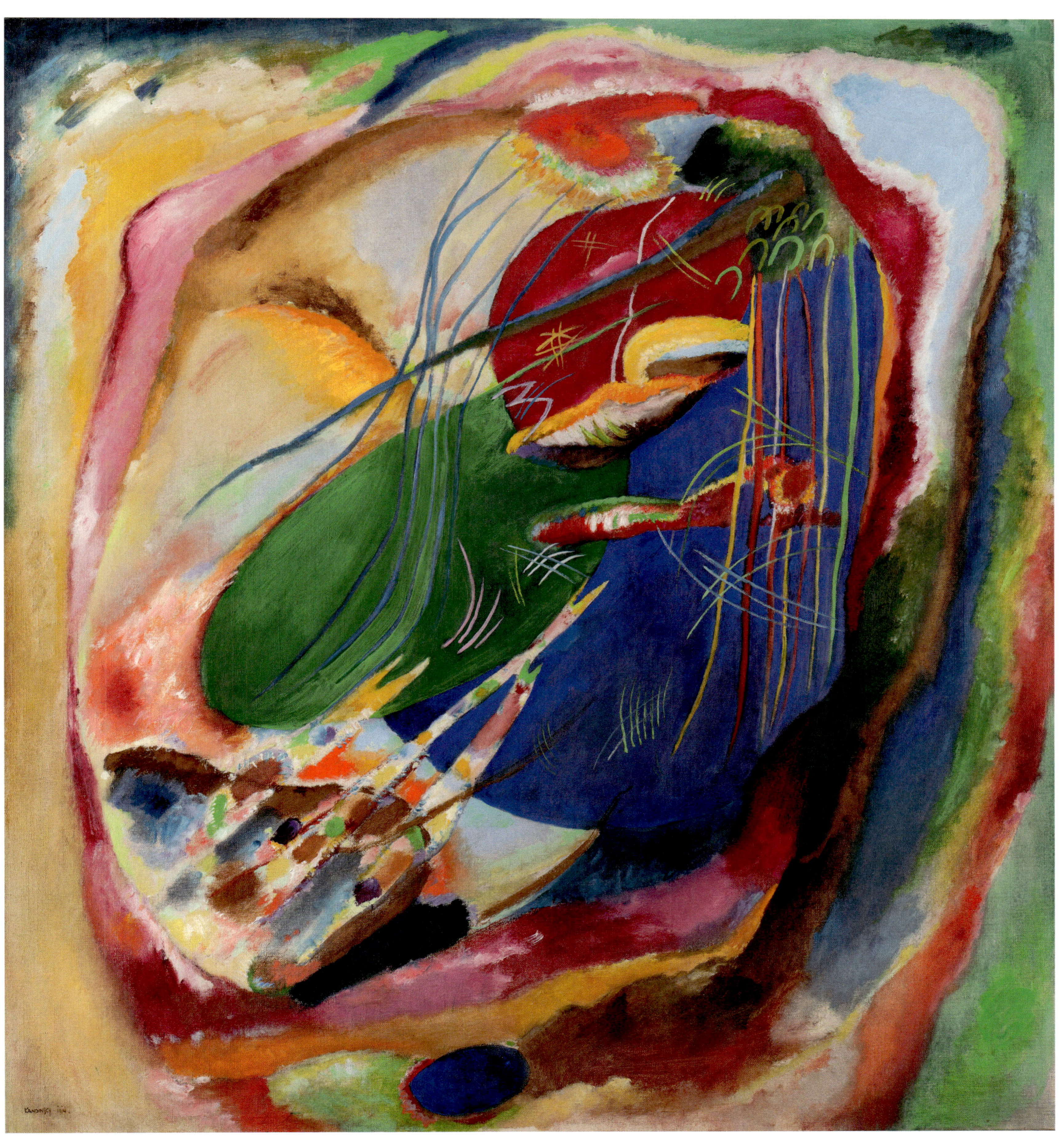

Wassily Kandinsky *Painting with Three Spots*, 1914
Museo Thyssen-Bornemisza, Madrid

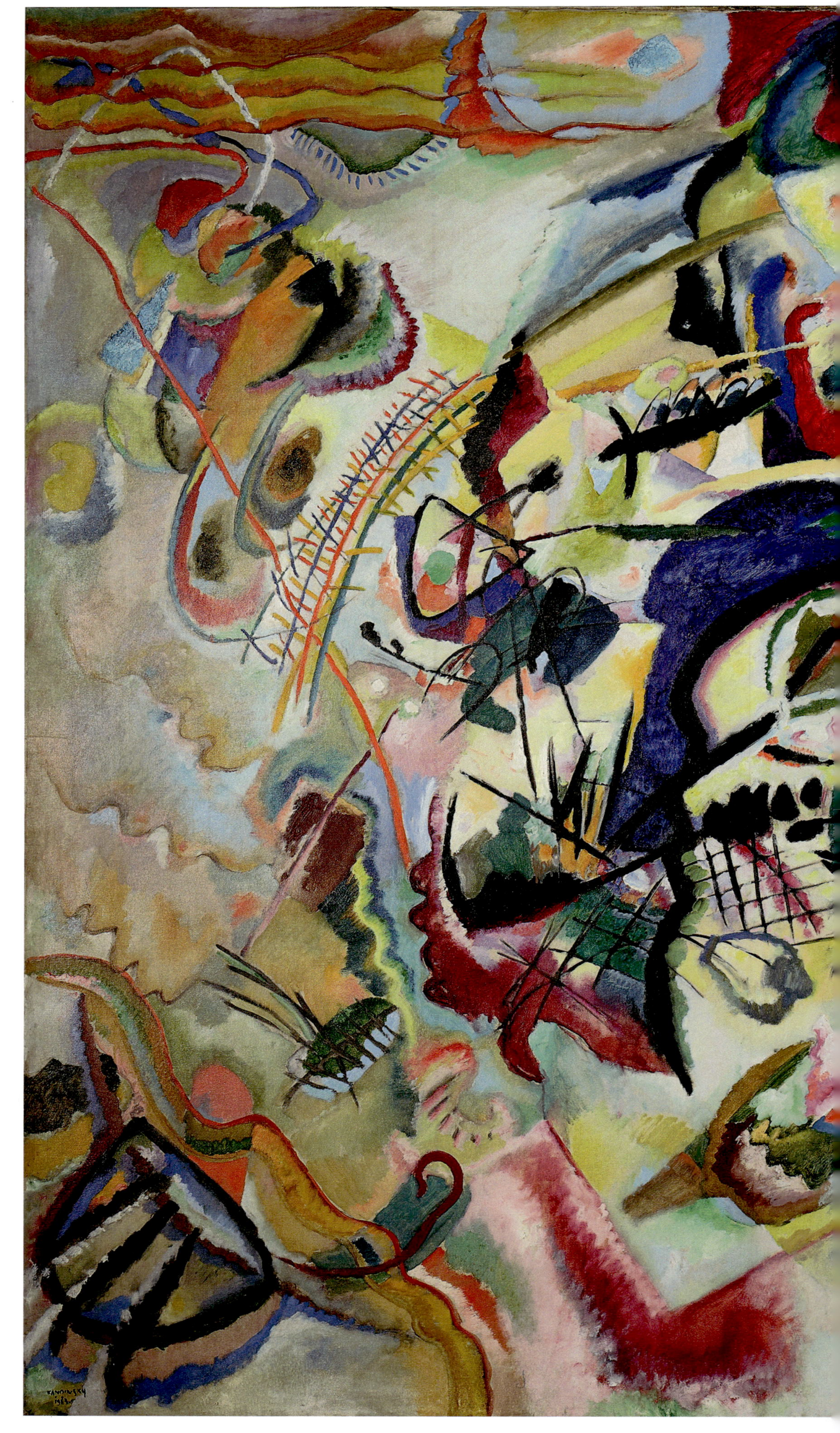

Wassily Kandinsky *Composition VII,* 1913
The State Tretyakov Gallery, Moscow

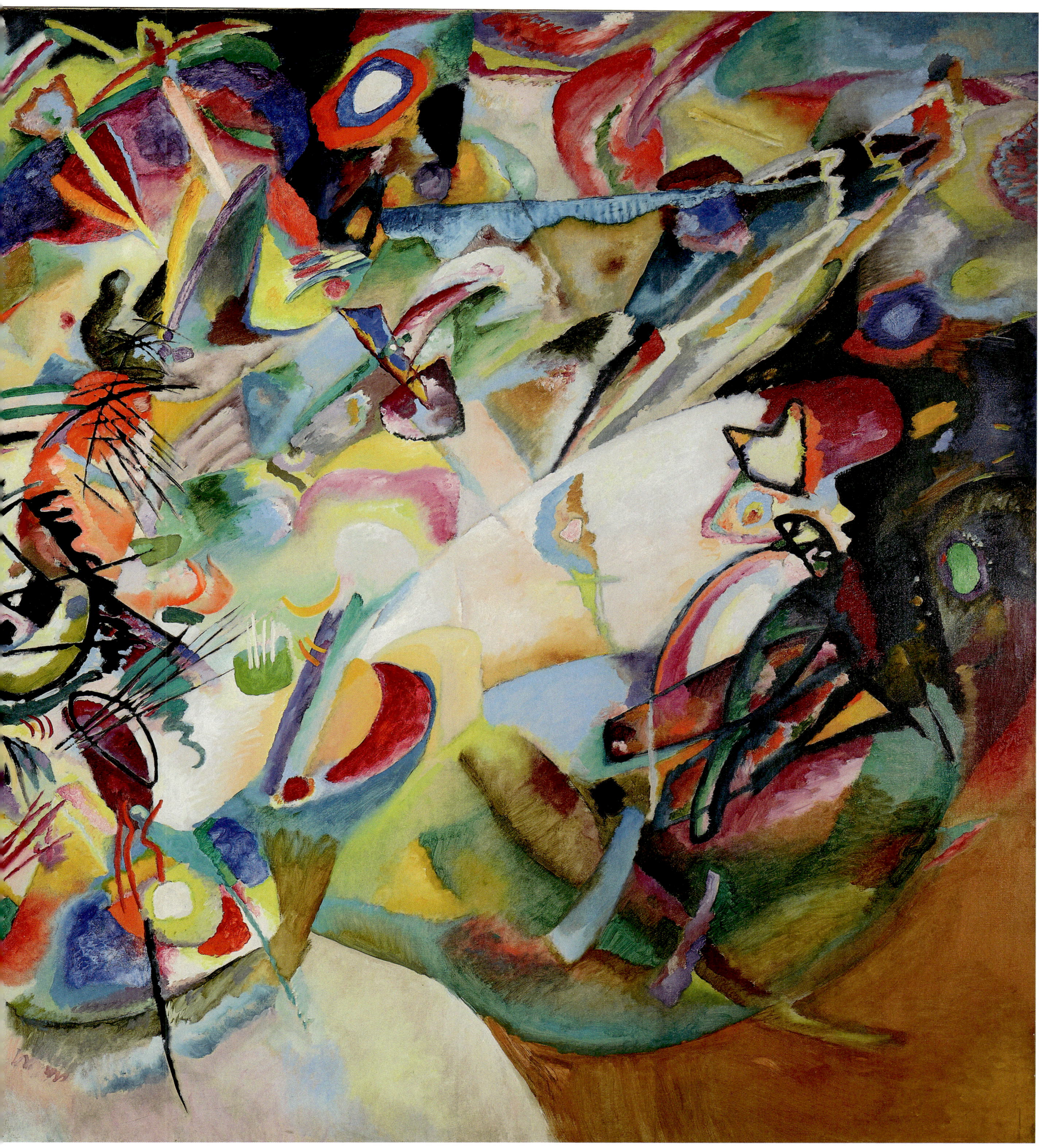

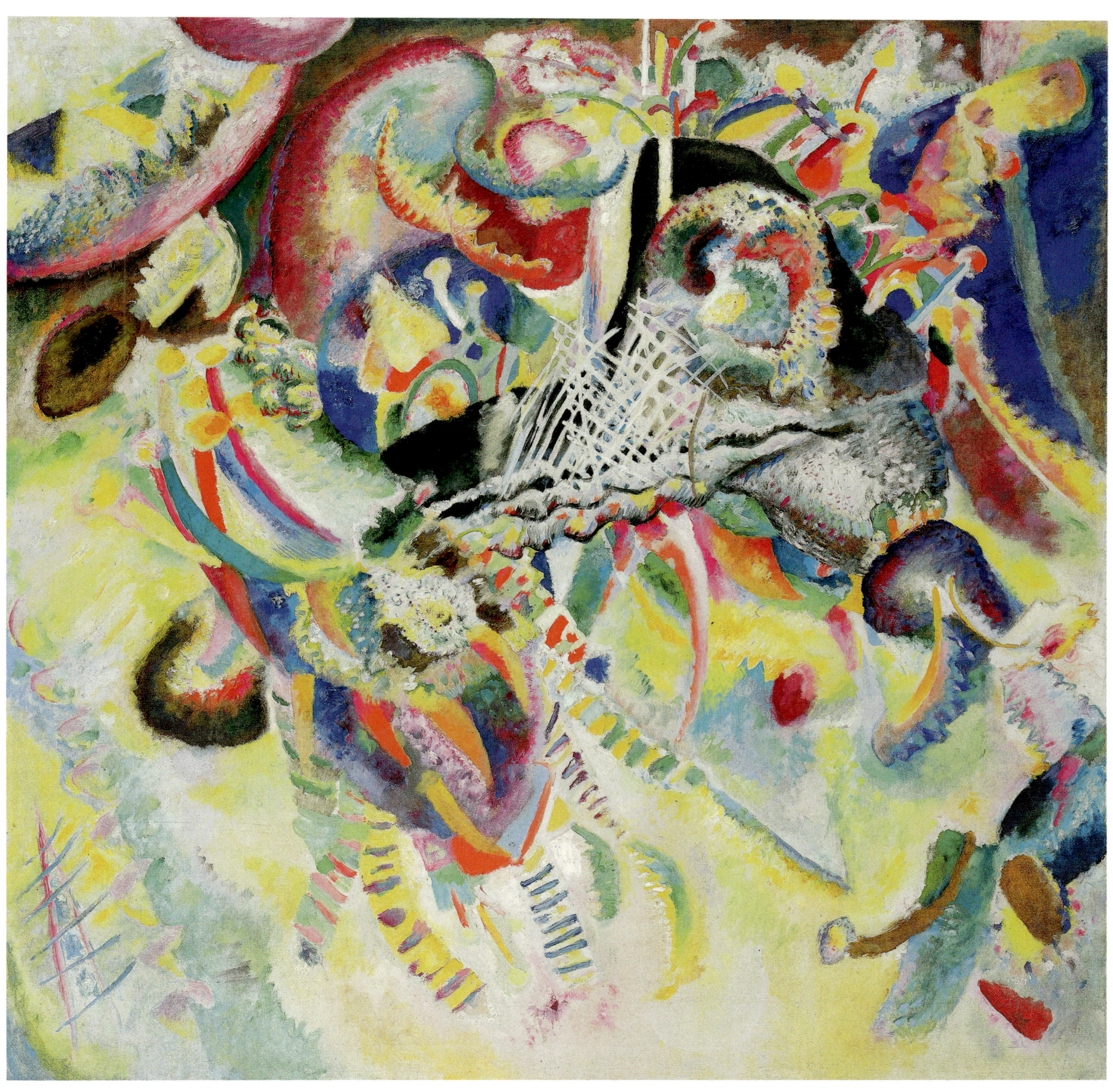

Wassily Kandinsky *Fugue,* 1914
Fondation Beyeler, Riehen/Basel, Beyeler Collection

THE RIDER AND THE DREAM: THE RELATIONSHIP BETWEEN FRANZ MARC AND WASSILY KANDINSKY THROUGH THE WORKS THEY EXCHANGED

MARTA RUIZ DEL ÁRBOL

It is terribly difficult to present one's contemporaries with spiritual gifts. Franz Marc, 1912[1]

Like many other artists before and after them, Wassily Kandinsky and Franz Marc sealed their friendship by exchanging their works. Along with paying tribute to each other in this way, they may have used their canvases to make a statement about the artistic aspirations that spurred them to create *Der Blaue Reiter* (*The Blaue Reiter Almanac*). To what extent did they take up their brushes to express their principles? Do their brushstrokes conceal underlying stories of common yearnings and dreams? Are these works anecdotes of competition or even rivalry? This essay sets out to analyze the context in which the editors of the almanac exchanged these works and attempts to ascertain how far the decision to present them as gifts made them particularly significant within their respective oeuvres and, in a sense, a declaration of intent for *Der Blaue Reiter*.

THE ORIGIN OF THE ALMANAC AND A RIDER FOR MARC

"Dear Kandinsky, your painting arrived safely, it came, was hung, and conquered. Many thanks!"[2] Marc informed his friend on a postcard dated July 31, 1911. Although the artists had known each other for just somewhat longer than half a year, the Russian painter sent his colleague a canvas at a time when the rapport between them had reached its height. Indeed, since they first met in January 1911, not only had Marc joined the Neue Künstlervereinigung München (New Artists' Association Munich)—of which Kandinsky was a founding member—but, in particular, Kandinsky had recently outlined the concept of the almanac.[3]

The work in question was *Improvisation 12* (cat. p. 91), of 1910, a canvas that Kandinsky had classified in accordance with the categories he had begun to establish for his oeuvre in 1909. The *Improvisations*—a name borrowed from musical terminology—stemmed from his wish for paintings to be "chiefly unconscious . . . expressions of events of an inner character, hence impressions of 'internal nature.'"[4] The work symbolized his desire to capture man's "internal nature" through an artistic process that shunned Western models of pictorial representation. Although certain elements of the composition are still recognizable, such as the horse and rider and the three small figures on the left, the scene is not set in a landscape. Instead, Kandinsky dispenses with any references to visible reality in order to situate the main figures in a sort of color storm. Emerging from the upper right corner, a burst of color looms above the horseman and spreads across the entire upper half of the canvas.

The fact that Kandinsky should have decided to give Marc a painting of a rider is highly significant, because when he sent it the almanac did not yet have a title. Indeed, the only name the Russian painter had suggested for the publication was "*Die Kette*" (The Chain), as he intended it to be "a link to the past as well as a ray to the future."[5] The gift not only further confirmed the importance he attached to this motif, but also heralded the prominence the figure of the rider would soon take on in his collaboration with Marc.[6] To what extent was *Improvisation 12* a determining influence in the final choice of the almanac's title *Der Blaue Reiter*?

In 1930, Kandinsky retrospectively explained that the final name arose one day over coffee at Marc's house: "We both loved blue, Marc liked horses, I riders. So the name came by itself."[7] This myth-destroying clarification has sparked much controversy among historians, since Kandinsky is considered to have consciously ignored the deep symbolism and many associations implicit in this choice.[8] Even so, it is likely that the Russian painter's account of the context is truthful, and that it was indeed during that hot summer of 1911 when, together in Sindelsdorf and gazing at Kandinsky's painting, they came up with the name of *Der Blaue Reiter,* which reflected their artistic longings so well.

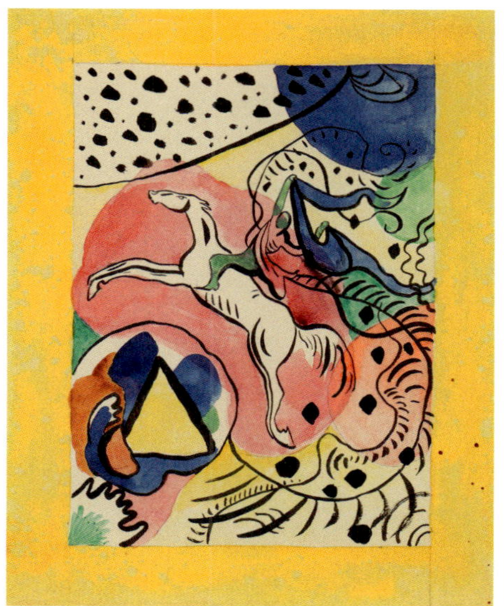

Fig. 1 Wassily Kandinsky, Study for the cover of *Der Blaue Reiter* almanac, 1911, watercolor, India ink, and pencil on paper, 27.7 x 21.9 cm, Städtische Galerie im Lenbachhaus, Munich

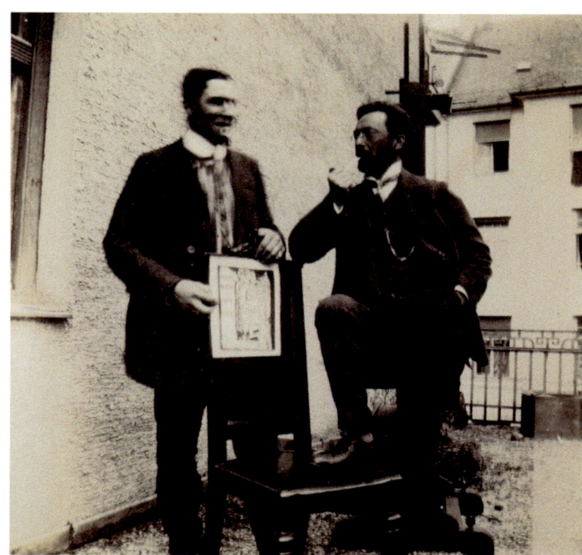

Fig. 2 Franz Marc and Wassily Kandinsky with the cover woodcut for *Der Blaue Reiter* almanac, Munich, 1911, photograph by Gabriele Münter, Gabriele Münter- und Johannes Eichner-Stiftung, Munich

By mid-September, the title for the almanac had been firmly decided upon and Kandinsky had prepared several cover designs to show the publisher Reinhard Piper.[9] Many of his sketches featured a figure on horseback moving upward across the composition (fig. 1). Although Kandinsky's vocabulary never allows for categorical statements or unilateral interpretations, these riders seem to hail from a legendary fairy-tale world that is present in many of his works from very early on (cat. pp. 62–65). Linked to an iconography related chiefly to his childhood and native Russia, the figures in these preparatory drawings are connected with the main motif in the work Kandinsky had given Marc not long before. The most anecdotal elements, such as the tiny figures—lingering remnants of narrative, still found in the 1910 canvas—have disappeared, and the figure on horseback has become a kind of ethical symbol of the triumphant power of the spirit over the materialism that had pervaded art since the nineteenth century.[10] Could a parallel be drawn between Kandinsky's gift to Marc and the initial idea the Russian artist explored for the cover of the almanac?

As is well known, the rider they finally adopted as the publication's emblem is far removed from the initial design recalling Kandinsky's gift and closer to the iconography of Saint George. The Christian knight slaying the dragon—a motif that gained prominence in the Russian painter's iconography around this time—thus took the place of the horseman (cat. pp. 28–29) in his early sketches, apparently at Marc's wishes (fig. 2).[11] The choice of the saint on horseback—an allegory of the triumph of good over evil—as the cover image for the almanac imbued the modern artist with the saint's virtues. In Marc's words, penned in his essay "Die 'Wilden' Deutschlands" (The "Savages" of Germany), his weapons were the "*new ideas*" that "kill better than steel and destroy what was thought to be indestructible."[12]

It should be pointed out that *Improvisation 12* was again specifically mentioned in the many letters the two artists exchanged during the autumn of 1911. Both painters, busy preparing the almanac, attached great importance to the illustrations that were to accompany the publication. During their discussions, Marc proposed including a reproduction of *Improvisation 12* to "complete the fantastical illustration."[13] This idea, which seems to have originally come from the German painter's then companion, Maria Franck, underlines the importance of the canvas and corroborates the fact that—at least for Marc and Maria Franck—it evoked a mythical iconography linked to fable. Kandinsky, however, was not entirely convinced, since he feared that it would encourage an overly fanciful interpretation of his work, and in the end the painting was not included.[14]

THE FIRST EXHIBITION AND A SLIGHT FORETASTE FOR KANDINSKY

The next gift came a few months later, at the end of 1911, following a busy autumn devoted to preparing the almanac as well as the discussions among members of the Neue Künstlervereinigung München, which prompted both Kandinsky and Marc to leave the group in early December. "If I may hope to offer you a token of Christmas joy, please accept the small portrait of Rousseau I made—I wish I had something better to give you at the moment" (fig. 3), Marc wrote in a letter of December 23, 1911.[15] He felt indebted to Kandinsky for the gift of *Improvisation 12* and offered his colleague his interpretation of the French artist Henri Rousseau's self-portrait *Portrait de l'artiste à la lampe* (*Portrait of the Artist with a Lamp*), of 1900–03. Yet Marc went on to explain in the letter that he would have liked "to have something better to give you," as he did not consider it a fitting exchange compared to Kandinsky's work. The "something better" finally came halfway through the following year.

Nevertheless, Marc's *Bildnis Henri Rousseau* (*Portrait of Henri Rousseau*) illustrated another of the decisive moments in his relationship with his colleague. It coincided precisely with the first *Der Blaue Reiter* exhibition at the Galerie Thannhauser, which ran from December 18, 1911 to January 3, 1912. In fact, this glass painting hung in

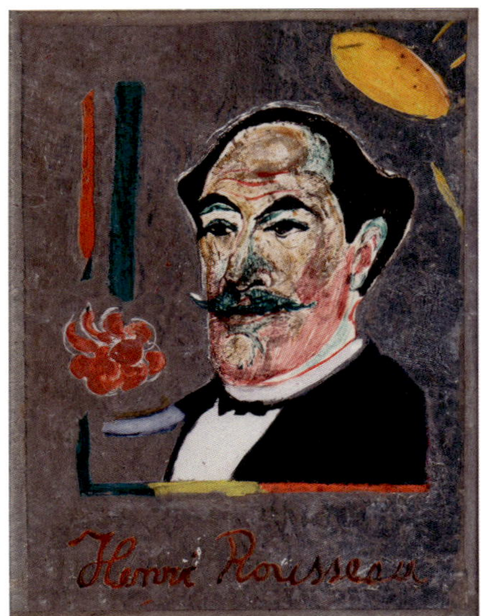

Fig. 3 Franz Marc, *Bildnis Henri Rousseau* (*Portrait of Henri Rousseau*), 1911, oil on glass, partly glazed, underlaid with tin foil, 15.3 x 11.4 cm, Städtische Galerie im Lenbachhaus, Munich

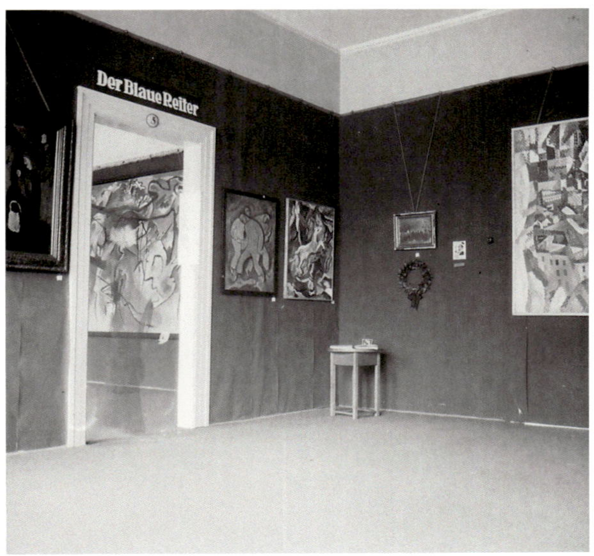

Fig. 4 *Die Erste Ausstellung der Redaktion Der Blaue Reiter* (*First Exhibition of the Editors of Der Blaue Reiter*), Galerie Thannhauser, Munich, 1911–12, first room with works by Münter, Kandinsky, Albert Bloch, Heinrich Campendonk, Rousseau (*La Basse-Cour* [*The Poultry Yard*]), Marc (*Portrait of Henri Rousseau*), Robert Delaunay; photograph by Gabriele Münter, Gabriele Münter- und Johannes Eichner-Stiftung, Munich

pride of place in the landmark exhibition, although it was not included in the catalogue's list of works. Marc is documented as having given Kandinsky the portrait on December 23, 1911—that is, after the opening of the first *Blaue Reiter* exhibition. The description of the work in the correspondence and its presence in Gabriele Münter's photos of the exhibition (fig. 4) also confirm that it is indeed his copy of Henri Rousseau's portrait. These circumstances raise the question of whether Marc's work was only featured in the exhibition during the first days of the show. Or, alternatively, did Kandinsky decide to include it after receiving it from his friend?

The painting was the expression of what was perhaps the greatest discovery for Marc and Kandinsky during the months prior to the publication of the almanac. Although Kandinsky had seen Rousseau's work during his trip to Paris in 1906–07, he did not become aware of its significance until 1911, when he read the French artist's first monograph.[16] Published that year by Wilhelm Uhde,[17] it marked a veritable revelation for the editors of *Der Blaue Reiter,* who immediately decided to include the French painter's work in the almanac and sought out images to illustrate it.

In his essay "Über die Formfrage" (On the Question of Form) in the almanac, Kandinsky, who divided art into "Great Abstraction" and "Great Realism," responded to Uhde's text by referring to Rousseau as the epitome of the second type.[18] *Le Douanier* perfectly exemplified the Russian painter's theory that form ought to conform solely to each artist's "internal necessity." This made it not only possible but also necessary for many different and equally valid forms of representation to coexist: from Rousseau's jungle scenes to children's drawings, along with African sculptures and his own nonfigurative compositions.

Marc reacted to the discovery of Rousseau by setting about copying the French artist's self-portrait reproduced in the monograph. His use of the Bavarian technique of glass painting (*Hinterglasmalerei*)—which Gabriele Münter and Kandinsky had first employed in Murnau—imbued the tribute to Henri Rousseau with a specifically German flavor. With a certain amount of irony, Marc painted a halo over the head of this newly discovered father of modernity, transforming him into a modern-day equivalent of the saints who populated the works on glass in Bavarian folk art.[19]

THE PUBLICATION OF THE ALMANAC AND A DREAM CONVERTED INTO A CANVAS FOR KANDINSKY

"The overall effect of the book is marvelous. What a delight to see it completed before me. I am sure of one thing: many silent readers and young people full of energy will secretly be grateful to us, will be fired by enthusiasm for this book and will judge the world in accordance with it," Marc wrote in May 1912.[20] The almanac at last saw the light of day at a time when, according to Klaus Lankheit, the artist was painting *Der Traum* (*The Dream;* cat. pp. 114–15).[21] This was the canvas with which Marc finally settled his outstanding debt to Kandinsky, as it was a worthy exchange for the *Improvisation 12*[22] the Russian had sent him nearly a year earlier.

Unlike Kandinsky's present, which he had selected from among the pictures he had painted before he and Marc had met, Marc set about painting this one after he and Kandinsky had been working together intensely for months. Whereas the first gift marked the start of *Der Blaue Reiter,* this one seemed to celebrate the end of a lengthy collaborative effort that resulted in the almanac. Did Marc intend this work to sum up in the ideas they had discussed during the previous months? To what extent does it reflect their shared yearning for a new, spiritual art?

In the center of the composition, a nude woman sits with her legs crossed and eyes closed. Nearby, several animals—a lion and four horses—gaze at her, stressing her importance. This enigmatic painting is one of the few compositions featuring human figures that Marc

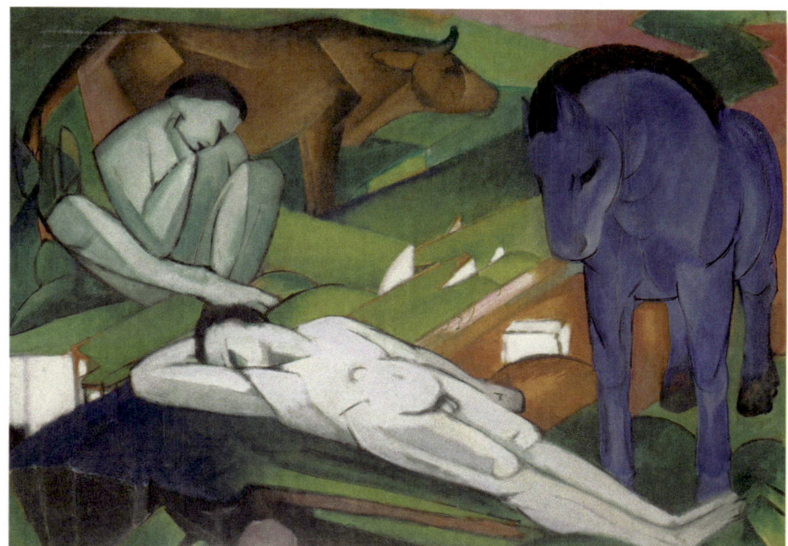

Fig. 5 Franz Marc, *Die Hirten* (*The Shepherds*), 1912, oil on canvas, 100 x 135 cm, Bayerische Staatsgemäldesammlungen, Pinakothek der Moderne, Munich

produced during his mature period. The German artist, known for his very early preference for animals as the main subjects of his works, decided to give Kandinsky a canvas that was unusual in his output. This rare inclusion of a human in the animal world so predominant in his oeuvre raises the question of whether his choice was somehow influenced by the intended use of the work and the recent publication of the almanac. According to Klaus Lankheit, the fact that it "was given to his friend cannot have been a coincidence" and signaled the possibility that it was a type of Orphic rhapsody—an allegorical transcription of the ideas that sparked the almanac's genesis.[23]

Despite the inclusion of the female figure, the work exudes the Arcadian spirit that Marc sought to achieve in his painting and described in what is held to be his first theoretic text, entitled "Über das Tier in der Kunst" (On the animal in art, 1910). In it the artist confessed that he was trying to achieve a heightened "awareness of the organic rhythm of all things, a pantheistic identification with the trembling and flowing of the blood of nature, in the trees, the animals, the air."[24] The female figure appears to be part of this primeval world, which in Marc's view belonged solely to animals, as humans had been banished from it. The work seems to embody his aspiration to "create a new paradisiacal realm in which man could achieve perfect harmony with nature."[25] What has enabled the woman in *Der Traum* to enter this territory that is the exclusive preserve of untainted beings? The key may lie in the title of the canvas.

Sleep and dreams are a recurring subject in Franz Marc's artistic production. We find sleeping beings in many of his works, such as *Liegender Hund im Schnee* (*Dog Lying in the Snow*), of 1910–11 (cat. p. 109), and *Der Stier* (*White Bull*), of 1911 (cat. p. 50). In these scenes, the earth welcomes and protects the placid animal. Indeed, unlike other artists, Marc does not associate sleep with nightmares. For him, slumber is the moment when we glimpse the most authentic side of things, the most intimate reality. These scenes thus represent moments of a purity and at-oneness with nature that are almost paradisiacal.[26] Like Kandinsky, Marc seeks the spiritual regeneration of society through art, and seems to present this moment as a remnant of what can be regenerated in human beings. In *Der Traum,* nature shelters not only animals but also humans, albeit sleeping. It is a Garden of Earthly Delights, a recoverable Arcadia. There is still hope.

This painting Marc gave Kandinsky was not his only work to include a human figure. It is usually related to another two paintings, also dated to that spring of 1912: *Der Wasserfall (Frauen unter einem Wasserfall)* (*The Waterfall [Women under a Waterfall];* cat. p. 117) and *Die Hirten* (*The Shepherds;* fig. 5). Similar in format to *Der Traum,* they evoke the pastoral tradition and the iconography of the Garden of Earthly Delights. This theme, which also interested Kandinsky,[27] is conveyed by men and women—always accompanied by animals—who are not ashamed of their nakedness. Portrayed before the Fall, the figures' bodies are folded in on themselves and adapt to the structure of the composition in order to accentuate, also formally, the sensation of their communion with nature. They are beings who sleep or are at least in a state of self-engrossment that isolates them from their surroundings. The solitary woman in *Der Traum* stands out among all the figures, as she seems to be meditating rather than sleeping or dreaming.

Marc showed an interest in non-European cultures from a very early age. He was not only familiar with the ethnological museums in Munich and Berlin but also collected small Asian art objects and prints.[28] This concern with the artistic expressions of other continents is reflected chiefly in his sketchbooks, which provide insight into the extent to which foreign sources influenced his own painting. The position of the woman in *Der Traum,* for instance, is probably inspired by Buddhist works. Two earlier drawings bear this out. As early as 1907–08, Marc made a quick sketch of what appears to be a female

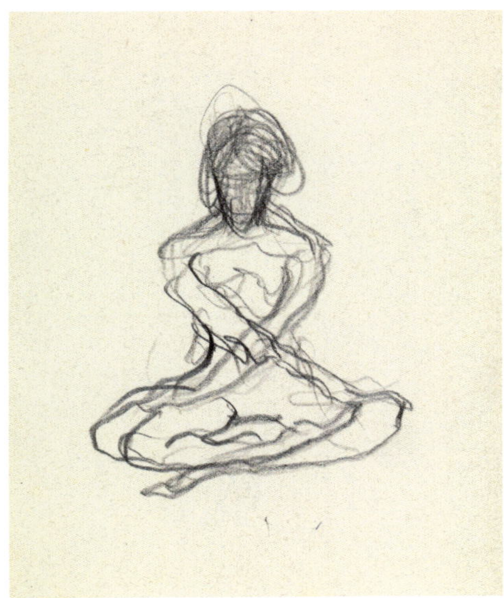

Fig. 6 Franz Marc, Nude, seated crossed-legged on the ground with arms crossed, 1907–08, pencil on paper, 19.8 x 13.5 cm, Germanisches Nationalmuseum, Nuremberg

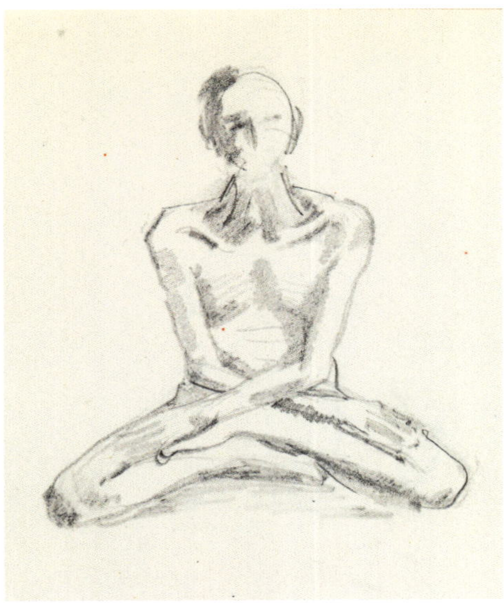

Fig. 7 Franz Marc, Male nude in a Buddha pose, 1910, pencil and chalk on paper, 20.9 x 16.7 cm, Germanisches Nationalmuseum, Nuremberg

figure (fig. 6). Two years later, he drew a male figure, which, according to the work's title in the catalogue raisonné, adopts "the position of a Buddha" (fig. 7).[29] Could, correspondingly, the figure in the canvas he exchanged with Kandinsky be an allusion to Buddhism?

Isabelle Jansen, who has analyzed the references to non-Western art in Marc's painting, argues in her study that his interest in Buddhist art was not limited to merely imitating formal aspects. He owned German translations of various Buddhist publications in his library,[30] whose influence probably supplemented the impulses he received from Kandinsky. Although some of his drawings of Buddha were made at an earlier date (fig. 8), it was precisely during the height of intensity in the relationship between the two artists, starting in 1912, that the German painter developed a greater interest in this religion. The close communication between the two artists must have brought Marc into contact with the heavily Eastern-influenced theosophical ideas that greatly concerned the Russian.[31] The wish to add a spiritual component to art, via the association with Buddhist iconography, conveyed the transcendental meaning Marc desired for the gift that was to symbolize his friendship with Kandinsky.[32]

As is often the case with Marc, however, we are not dealing with a literal transcription of his source of inspiration. Marc did not reproduce an orthodox position in *Der Traum,* but freely interpreted the representations of Buddha with which he was familiar[33] (fig. 9), rendering them first in his sketchbooks and later on canvas. In the final painting, he made a few alterations to the previously drawn versions. The woman's head is tilted slightly to the right and her torso leans slightly forward, so that her crossed arms rest on her knees. The result is a huddled figure of a woman who appears to be embracing herself. The dream would make it possible to again see the world through the untainted gaze of animals. But humans could only achieve the innocent and pleasurable rest of beasts through a conscious exercise such as meditation.

"Art is but the expression of a dream—the closer we come to it, the more we devote ourselves to the inner truth of things," Marc wrote in 1907 to Maria Franck, the woman who would become his second wife.[34] In that early letter, the German artist likened life to a parody that concealed the real truth—which for him was the moment of the dream. The role of art was to evoke this other reality, which emerged during the act of sleeping, when all of one's barriers were down. Years later—specifically in May 1912—the painter returned to this concept to explain the stage he was at in his art to Kandinsky. This time he used it to compare the creative process with a memory that lingers on in our minds after we awaken. "We are tortured by an enormously precise idea," he commented, "but we do not know what it is . . . (as in a dream: it is perfectly sensed on awakening, but we don't know how to tell it)."[35] The creative process is therefore similar to a dreamlike state in which reason does not dominate the mind; rather, it is a trance in which the soul is liberated and achieves a new vibration that is not limited to the artist himself, but designed to appeal to those who view the work. Artistic expressions capable of illustrating what Kandinsky called an "internal necessity" return humans to this primeval state, which is represented allegorically by the subject of *Der Traum,* the canvas Marc gave the Russian painter.[36]

EPILOGUE

In 1916, after Franz Marc died in the Great War, his widow wished to organize an exhibition in his honor. She contacted Gabriele Münter, who had been looking after Kandinsky's possessions since he departed for Russia.[37] After the exhibition ended, Maria Marc kept *Der Traum* for at least four years and displayed it in her home at Ried alongside *Improvisation 12,* the painting Kandinsky had given to Marc. This is the first time since then—a century later—that these two works, silent witnesses to one of the most influential artistic initiatives of the twentieth century, have been exhibited together.

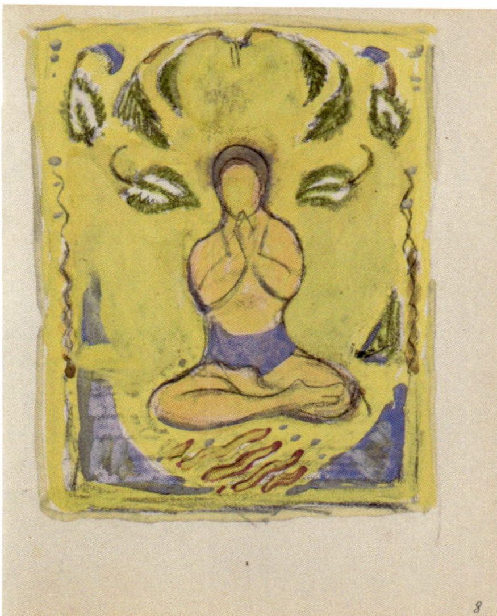

Fig. 8 Franz Marc, Composition sketch: exotic figure seated like a Buddha, 1909, gouache and pencil on paper, 13 x 10.5 cm, Germanisches Nationalmuseum, Nuremberg

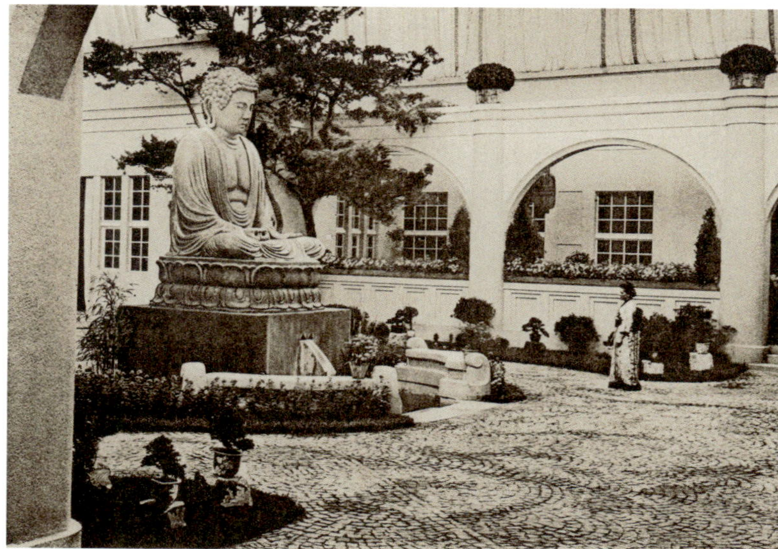

Fig. 9 Buddha courtyard at the *Japan und Ostasien in der Kunst* (*Japan and East Asia in Art*) exhibition, Munich, 1909, Postkartensammlung, Stadtarchiv München

1 Franz Marc, "Geistige Güter," in *Der Blaue Reiter,* ed. Wassily Kandinsky and Franz Marc (Munich, 1912), p. 1. English ed.: "Spiritual Treasures," in *The Blaue Reiter Almanac,* ed. Wassily Kandinsky and Franz Marc, documentary edition, ed. and with an introduction by Klaus Lankheit, trans. Henning Falkenstein with the assistance of Manug Terzian and Gertrude Hinderlie (London, 1974; repr., Boston, 2005), p. 55.
2 Franz Marc, postcard to Wassily Kandinsky, July 31, 1911, in Wassily Kandinsky and Franz Marc, *Briefwechsel: Mit Briefen von und an Gabriele Münter und Maria Marc,* ed., introduction, and annotation by Klaus Lankheit (Munich, 1983), pp. 48–49, here p. 48.
3 Wassily Kandinsky, letter to Franz Marc, June 19, 1911. Ibid., pp. 39–41.
4 Wassily Kandinsky, *Über das Geistige in der Kunst: insbesondere in der Malerei,* with an introduction by Max Bill and a foreword and annotation on the rev. new ed. by Jelena Hahl-Fontaine (Munich, 1912; 5th ed. Zurich, 2016), p. 146. English ed.: "On the Spiritual in Art," in *Kandinsky: Complete Writings on Art,* ed. Kenneth C. Lindsay and Peter Vergo (Boston, 1982; new, repr. ed., New York, 1994), p. 218.
5 Wassily Kandinsky, letter to Franz Marc, June 19, 1911. In Kandinsky and Marc 1983 (see note 2), p. 40. English trans. in Klaus Lankheit, "A History of the Almanac," in Kandinsky and Marc 2005 (see note 1), pp. 15–16.
6 On the importance of the rider in Kandinsky's oeuvre and the almanac, see for example Kenneth Lindsay, "The Genesis and Meaning of the Cover Design for the First 'Blaue Reiter' Exhibition Catalogue," *The Art Bulletin* 35, no. 1 (March 1953), pp. 47–52; Johannes Langner, "Improvisation 13: Zur Funktion des Gegenstandes in Kandinskys Abstraktion," in *Jahrbuch der Staatlichen Kunstsammlungen in Baden-Württemberg* (Berlin and Munich, 1977), no. 14, pp. 115–46; Eberhard Roters, "Wassily Kandinsky und die Gestalt des Blauen Reiters," *Jahrbuch der Berliner Museen* 5 (1963), pp. 201–26; and Peg Weiss, "Kandinsky und München: Begegnungen und Wandlungen," in *Kandinsky und München: Begegnungen und Wandlungen, 1896–1914,* ed. Armin Zweite, exh. cat. Städtische Galerie im Lenbachhaus, Munich (Munich, 1982), pp. 29–83.
7 Wassily Kandinsky, "'Der Blaue Reiter' (Rückblick)," *Das Kunstblatt* 14 (1930), p. 59. English trans. in Lankheit 2005 (see note 5), p. 18.
8 In particular, associations with the concept of the blue flower (*Blaue Blume*) of Romanticism. See for example, Peter-Klaus Schuster, "Vom Tier zum Tod: Zur Ideologie des Geistigen bei Franz Marc," in *Franz Marc: Kräfte der Natur: Werke 1912–1915,* ed. Erich Franz, exh. cat. Staatsgalerie moderner Kunst, Munich; Westfälisches Landesmuseum, Münster (Ostfildern, 1993), p. 183.
9 Wassily Kandinsky, letter to Franz Marc, September 18, 1911, in Kandinsky and Marc 1983 (see note 2), p. 59.
10 Langner 1977 (see note 6), pp. 130–31.
11 Schuster 1993 (see note 8), p. 183.
12 Franz Marc, "Die 'Wilden' Deutschlands," in Kandinsky and Marc 1912 (see note 1), p. 5; English ed.: "The 'Savages' of Germany," in Kandinsky and Marc 2005 (see note 1), p. 61.
13 Franz Marc, postcard to Wassily Kandinsky, November 10, 1911, in Kandinsky and Marc 1983 (see note 2), p. 76.
14 Wassily Kandinsky, letter to Franz Marc, n.d., in ibid, pp. 76–77.
15 Franz Marc, letter to Wassily Kandinsky, December 23, 1911, in ibid., p. 88.
16 Katherine Kuenzli, "Grenzerweiterung der modernen Kunst: Der 'Blaue Reiter,' die Pariser Moderne und Henri Rousseau," in *Expressionismus in Deutschland und Frankreich: Von Matisse zum Blauen Reiter,* exh. cat., Kunsthaus Zürich; Los Angeles County Museum of Art; Musée des Beaux-Arts de Montréal (Munich, 2014), p. 98.
17 Wilhelm Uhde, *Henri Rousseau* (Paris, 1911).
18 Wassily Kandinsky, "Über die Formfrage," in Kandinsky and Marc 1912 (see note 1), pp. 82, 94 and note 1. English ed.: "On the Question of Form," in Lindsay and Vergo 1994 (see note 4), pp. 242, 252, and note.
19 See the analysis in Angela Lampe, "Realistik = Abstraktion oder Kandinskys 'Neuer Realismus,'" in *Der Grosse Widerspruch: Franz Marc zwischen Delaunay und Rousseau,* ed. Cathrin Klingsöhr-Leroy and Franz Marc Museumsgesellschaft, exh. cat. Franz Marc Museum, Kochel am See (Berlin and Munich, 2009), pp. 42–45.
20 Franz Marc, letter to Wassily Kandinsky, May 11, 1912, in Kandinsky and Marc 1983 (see note 2), p. 169. English trans. in Annette Vezin and Luc Vezin, *Kandinsky and the Blue Rider* (Paris, 1992), p. 150.
21 Klaus Lankheit, *Franz Marc: Sein Leben und seine Kunst* (Cologne, 1976), p. 84.
22 Unlike the other gifts, the arrival of this one is not recorded in the correspondence. It is nonetheless reflected in Kandinsky's hand-written lists and also featured in all the catalogues raisonnés. See Klaus Lankheit, *Franz Marc: Katalog der Werke* (Cologne, 1970), no. 172, p. 60; Annegret Hoberg and Isabelle Jansen, *Franz Marc: The Complete Works,* 3 vols. (London, 2004–11), vol. I, no. 175, p. 196; Hans K. Roethel and Jean K. Benjamin, *Kandinsky: Catalogue Raisonné of the Oil-Paintings,* 2 vols. (London, 1982–84), vol. 1, no. 354, p. 332.
23 Lankheit 1976 (see note 21), p. 84.
24 This text is taken from Franz Marc, letter to the publisher Reinhard Piper, April 20, 1910; Piper then published it as *Das Tier in der Kunst* (Munich, 1910), p. 190. Reproduced in Klaus Lankheit, ed., *Franz Marc: Schriften* (Cologne, 1978), p. 98. English trans. in Vezin and Vezin 1992 (see note 20), p. 101.
25 Paloma Alarcó, *Museo Thyssen-Bornemisza: Pintura Moderna* (Madrid, 2009), p. 188.
26 See Mark Rosenthal, *Franz Marc* (Munich, 1989), p. 28; and Volker Adolphs, "Seeing the World and Seeing through the World," in *August Macke and Franz Marc: An Artist Friendship,* ed. by Volker Adolphs and Annegret Hoberg, exh. cat. Kunstmuseum Bonn; Städtische Galerie im Lenbachhaus and Kunstbau, Munich (Ostfildern, 2014), p. 13.
27 Peter Vergo, *Twentieth-century German Painting: The Thyssen-Bornemisza Collection* (London, 1992), p. 264.
28 Isabelle Jansen, "The Yearning of an Unspoilt World," in *Franz Marc: The Retrospective,* ed. Annegret Hoberg and Helmut Friedel, exh. cat. Städtische Galerie im Lenbachhaus and Kunstbau, Munich (Munich, 2005), p. 86.
29 The first of the drawings is found in sketchbook VI, 1907–08, p. 1a, and reproduced in Hoberg and Jansen 2004–11 (see note 22), vol. III, with the title "Sitzender Akt mit gekreuzten Armen und Beinen" (Nude, seated crossed-legged on the ground with arms crossed), p. 57. The second is found in sketchbook XIX, 1910, p. 8, and reproduced in Hoberg and Jansen 2004–11 (see note 22), vol. III, with the title "Männlicher Akt in der Haltung eines Buddhas" (Male nude in a Buddha pose), p. 153.
30 Jansen 2005 (see note 28), p. 86, lists the books on Buddhist themes in Marc's library. It should be stressed that the full bibliography mentioned by Jansen was published in 1911. It is likewise interesting to note that Reinhard Piper, the publisher of the almanac, also published a translation of Buddhist texts.
31 Ibid., pp. 86–87.
32 In a lecture on Franz Marc's *Der Traum,* Guillermo Solana established a possible link between the iconography of this work and Buddhist art and the lotus position. Guillermo Solana, "Franz Marc: El sueño," lecture in Spanish delivered on November 14, 2013, at the Museo Thyssen-Bornemisza auditorium, Madrid; http://www.museothyssen.org/thyssen/videoplayer/156 (accessed March 1, 2016).
33 The large Buddha that greeted visitors to the exhibition *Japan und Ostasien in der Kunst* (*Japan and East Asia in Art*), Munich, 1909, may have been one of his sources of inspiration. Although it is not known for certain that Marc visited the show, it is highly likely he did, given his interest in the subject. Whichever the case, it is a good example of the prevailing atmosphere in the Bavarian capital during the period and the host of initiatives aimed at promoting knowledge of Asian art. See Weiss 1982 (see note 6), p. 65.
34 Franz Marc, letter to Maria Franck, May 10,1907, in Alois J. Schardt, *Franz Marc* (Berlin, 1936), p. 28.
35 Franz Marc, letter to Wassily Kandinsky, n.d. [May 11, 1912], in Kandinsky and Marc 1983 (see note 2), May 11, 1912, p. 169.
36 Franz Marc, subscription prospectus for the almanac, mid-January 1912, in Kandinsky and Marc 2005 (see note 1), p. 252.
37 Maria Marc, letter to Gabriele Münter, July 15, 1916. In Kandinsky and Marc 1983 (see note 2), pp. 280–83.

FRENCH JOIE DE VIVRE AND GERMAN PROFUNDITY: AUGUST MACKE, FRANZ MARC, AND THEIR RELATIONSHIP TO FRENCH PAINTING

CATHRIN KLINGSÖHR-LEROY

"It was probably the most harmonious, happy period we spent together and that brought us so close to each other that we could hardly believe how incredibly rich we were. . . ."[1] Whether idealized recollection or experienced reality, these words of Elisabeth Macke's evoke the joie de vivre conveyed by the paintings created by August Macke in autumn 1913 and spring 1914. During these last months before World War I, Macke retreated with his family to Lake Thun.[2] There he executed pictures that are now spontaneously associated with his art—of pedestrians in the city, people enjoying sunny parks, zoo visitors, and carefree shoppers. These figures embodied the joy of a luminous moment in which time seemed to stand still. A characteristic example is *Grosse Promenade: Leute im Garten (Predigtamtskandidat)* (*Great Promenade: People in the Garden;* cat. pp. 128–29). The artist brings the painting's five protagonists—two men, a woman, and two children—close up to the beholder, depicting them in a three-quarter view from the back. The schematically rendered faces are shown in half profile. Their slight turn into the picture space invites the viewer along, into a world of forms and colors. The blue of the sky shimmers through dense green foliage; the beginning summer day lies before them like a promise.

On November 30, 1913, Macke wrote from the Swiss town of Hilterfingen to his friend and patron Bernhard Koehler, his wife Elisabeth's uncle: "I am glad Fénéon liked my pictures."[3] The couple knew the gallery owner Félix Fénéon from a trip to Paris that Macke, his then fiancée, Elisabeth Gerhardt, and Koehler made in 1908. The most important result of the trip was a reorientation of Koehler's collection, which until then had focused on German art of the late nineteenth century and exponents of the realist group Die Scholle (The Soil). Macke, for whom Koehler had already enabled a four-week stay in Paris in 1907, expanded his patron's collection by adding French Impressionists, giving it a direction that made it receptive to modernism. Even at that time, the choice was not limited to works by first-generation Impressionists—Claude Monet, Pierre-Auguste Renoir, Édouard Manet—but included pieces by Paul Cézanne, Vincent van Gogh, and the Pointillist Paul Signac, who together with Georges Seurat was a key pioneer of abstraction.[4] Seurat was represented by the Galerie Bernheim-Jeune, run by Fénéon. Elisabeth Gerhardt, Macke, and Koehler visited the gallery and even had an opportunity to see Fénéon's private collection in his apartment. Elisabeth Macke recalled this visit to Fénéon, who was a great admirer of Seurat and made his work public at an early date[5]: "An old-fashioned bourgeois dining room in which wonderful Seurats hung, especially a large picture with numerous people outdoors, the women in little capot hats and big sunshades and *queues* [bustles] of the kind they used to wear back then, everything in the strangely prickly way of applying the colors."[6] Seurat's drawings—Koehler acquired one at the time (fig. 1), along with two small oils—reduce the figures depicted to shadowy silhouettes. Due to a special, rough-textured paper on which the artist drew with hatching strokes of black chalk or crayon, the figures give the impression of blurred configurations emerging out of darkness, their surfaces softly reflecting the light. They are rendered as disembodied ghosts and hardly defined by interior articulation or details; their faces, too, remain unspecific. This leads to a semi-abstract effect, since identifiable figures and shapes are still included but remain without individual features. They have the appearance of relatives and early precursors of the dreamlike figures that would populate Macke's art in 1913–14.[7] So it comes as no surprise that Fénéon liked the paintings in Koehler's collection, and that Macke enjoyed this recognition.[8]

Macke would not reactivate the strong impression he received from Seurat's drawings and paintings until a few years after his Paris trip (fig. 2).[9] In the pictures he painted in Hilterfingen on Lake Thun this memory was combined with a further formative experience, his visit to Robert Delaunay's studio in autumn 1912.[10] Macke made this

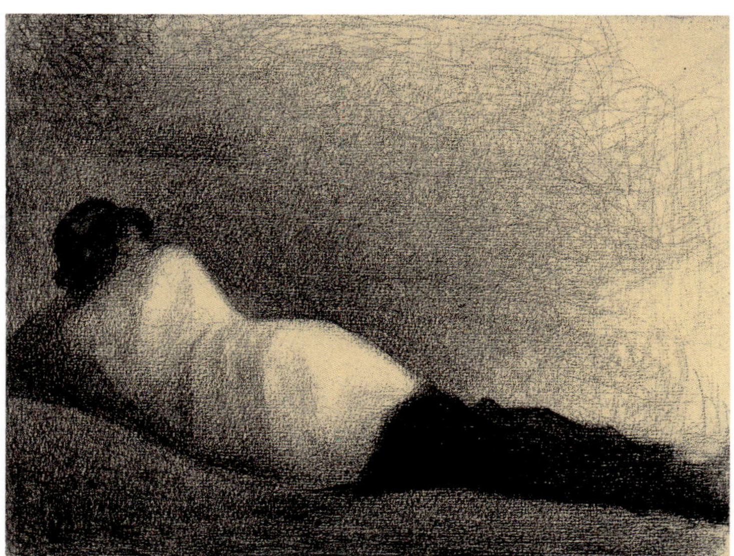

Fig. 1 Georges Seurat, *L'Homme couché* (*Reclining Man*), study for *Une Baignade, Asnières* (*Bathing Place, Asnières*), 1883–84, Conté crayon on paper, 24.5 × 31.5 cm, Fondation Beyeler, Riehen / Basel, Beyeler Collection

third trip to Paris together with Franz and Maria Marc, Hans Arp, and Bernhard Koehler Jr. The visitors enthused over the series of window views they saw in their French colleague's studio:

> *Reflecting windowpanes, through which one sees the city and the Eiffel Tower on a sunny day, the deep violet reflections, on the left this terrific orange, below, the pale blue buildings, from which, overlain by the sharply defined shine of the window, the green tower rises again and again into the azure blue sky. This is the external, basically very simple process. But what harmonies he distills from this simple motif. You should really see the way the colors assume a wonderful depth when you step farther back.*[11] (fig. 3)

In 1913–14 Macke would translate this perception of Delaunay's art into his own work. The complementary color contrasts he describes in his letter would suffuse his paintings, too, with brilliant effects of light and color. Just as the schematic Eiffel Tower in Delaunay's pictures stands for the dynamics and incessant rhythm of the metropolis as a symbol of modernity, the pedestrians in Macke's stand in for us viewers, inviting us to join them in celebrating the sun-drenched contemporary day.

Delaunay was also highly admired by Paul Klee and Wassily Kandinsky, and he was closely allied with the Blaue Reiter project from the outset.[12] This was in both Delaunay's interest, who—especially via the Galerie Der Sturm—wanted to obtain a foothold in the German art market, and in the interest of the Blaue Reiter artists, who were receptive to the international avant-garde. Their first show, at Galerie Thannhauser, included several works by Delaunay, one of them *Tour Eiffel* (*Eiffel Tower*, 1911), which Koehler acquired at Macke's suggestion.[13]

Delaunay's revolutionary way of visualizing reality fascinated Macke and Marc. It had a direct and profound impact on their own painting, because through Delaunay they gained access to the formal language of Cubism. Moreover, their engagement with Delaunay's compositions and art theory made it clear that Macke and Marc represented two opposing approaches, something that at the start of their friendship was obscured by their common striving to establish a "New Painting."[14] In his last letter to Macke, Marc expressed this difference in earthy terms:

> *What else can I say but that this painting business is now getting more difficult with every step you take, and I don't believe we two are taking the same path. I am a German and can only dig in my own field; what concern of mine is the* peinture *of the Orphists? We just can't do these things as beautifully as the French, or let's say, the Romanics, you know.*[15]

The fact that the Orphists' *peinture* concerned Marc despite all his theoretical objections is reflected in the significance that Delaunay's art had for his own. Ever since the encounter in Paris, he followed the Frenchman's work, down to the *Formes circulaires* (*Circular Forms*, 1913; figs. 4 and 5), thirteen examples of which were exhibited at the Berlin Autumn Salon in 1913. Initially Marc oriented himself on Delaunay's window pictures, a focus that helped him produce compositions in which the link between the central animal motif and the landscape background is so intimate that the contours of the animal's body dissolve and are interwoven with the surroundings. Like Macke, Marc too succeeded in employing the new method of complimentary contrast to achieve the intense effect of unmixed, prismatic colors that came to define his oeuvre. Depictions such as *Gazellen* (*Gazelles;* fig. 6) and *Rehe im Walde II* (*Deer in the Forest II*) clearly evince a new structure and the heightened coloration of his compositions. Even so, rather than applying this coloration to

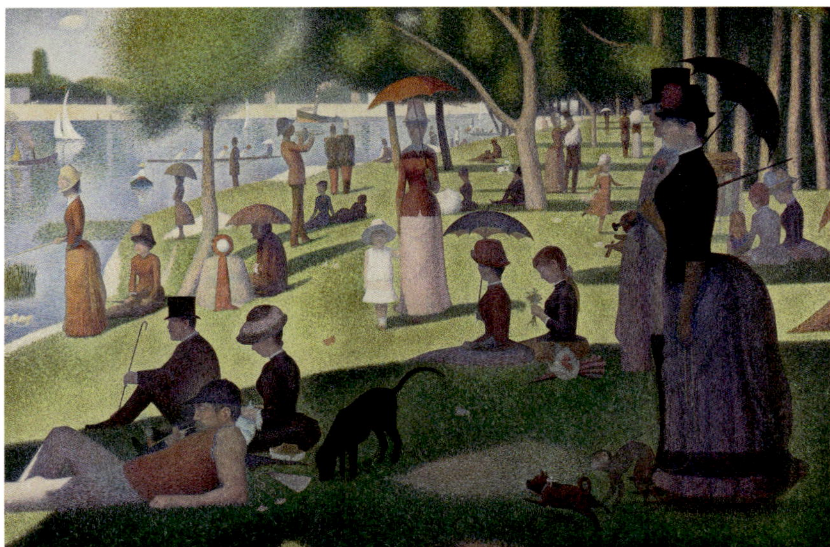

Fig. 2 Georges Seurat, *Un Dimanche à l'île de la Grande Jatte* (*A Sunday on La Grande Jatte—1884*), 1884–86, oil on canvas, 207.5 x 308.1 cm, The Art Institute of Chicago

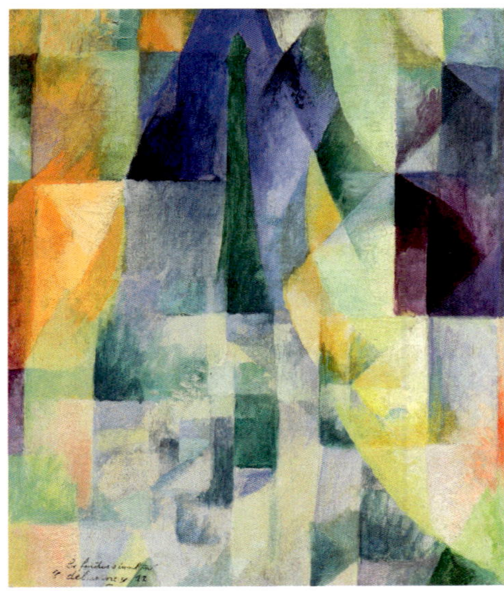

Fig. 3 Robert Delaunay, *Les Fenêtres simultanées sur la ville, 2e motif, 1er partie* (*Simultaneous Windows, 2nd motif, 1st part*), 1912, oil on canvas, 55.2 x 46.3 cm, Solomon R. Guggenheim Museum, New York, Solomon R. Guggenheim Founding Collection, By gift

straightforward renderings of a sun-drenched world like Macke, Marc emphasized the integration of animals in an endless rhythm that underlies all of life. His pictures stand for a utopia in which both animals and man are reunited with the cosmos, a vision that resulted from his critique of civilization and skepticism toward modernity. It was this conception that formed the background of Marc's critical reception of Delaunay.

In late 1912 Delaunay sent Marc his programmatic essay "La Lumière" (Light), which Marc then forwarded on to Klee, who had agreed to translate it into German. "Ueber das Licht" was published in the journal *Der Sturm* in January 1913.[16] In a letter to Delaunay, Marc responded to the passage in which Delaunay speaks of a visual sensibility ("sensibilité visuelle") by means of which light and movement are perceived. Light and movement find expression in the "movement of colors" and this movement ("mouvement synchrone [simultanéité] de la lumière") makes reality perceptible in a new way.[17] "Don't be angry with me," wrote Marc,

> *when I frankly admit that the way you attempt to approach the mysterious principles of art does not seem very fruitful to me. . . . You're turning yourself into a juggler of empty words. "Light affects you by way of sensibility." Why wouldn't sensibility affect you by way of light? . . . "The life itself of visual rhythm." What is that? Don't hold it against me, maybe I'm too stupid for this. All I know is pictures, the work, and the effort and the mysterious imagination of art. I'm crazy about forms, about colors, but I don't look for their schoolmasterly explanation.*[18]

With this polemical criticism of Delaunay's theory Marc turned to ideas he had developed in two articles for the art journal *Pan* in spring 1912.[19] Here he discussed a "New Painting" whose relationship to nature would not lead to the familiar mirroring of the actual motif but would reveal the "inner" laws of nature. "Under the veil of appearances we look today for hidden things in nature that seem more important to us than the discoveries of the Impressionists," wrote Marc, emphasizing that the thrust of his own art was counter to that of Impressionism. The present

> *movement, as far as it can be historically described today, takes a direction counter to all earlier ones in which impetus and skill strived for an ever-greater fidelity to the external natural image, whose bright daylight banishes the mysterious and abstract ideas of the inner life. In contrast, the new movement strives by a different path back to the images of the inner life, unknown to the demands of the scientifically understandable world.*[20]

Delaunay's conception of simultaneous color contrasts, on the other hand, was based on the color theory with which the Impressionists worked, whose "superficial" description of nature Marc rejected. His reaction to "La Lumière," however, toyed with terms and concepts without really clarifying the basic difference between his approach and Delaunay's. Delaunay saw this very clearly, writing to Marc:

> *You entirely lack clarity. "Crazy for drawing." Craziness is a pathological case, which is not my thing. . . . My only science is the choice of impressions which the light of the universe makes on my artistic consciousness, which I attempt to boil down, into an order, an art, a corresponding representative (visual) life. . . . These considerations lead neither to mathematical formulas nor to symbols of the Kabbala; they simply and naturally orient themselves to the painterly realities: colors and lines.*[21]

Delaunay's "superficiality," which Marc found dubious, appealed more to Macke, although he never offered his opinion on the French art-

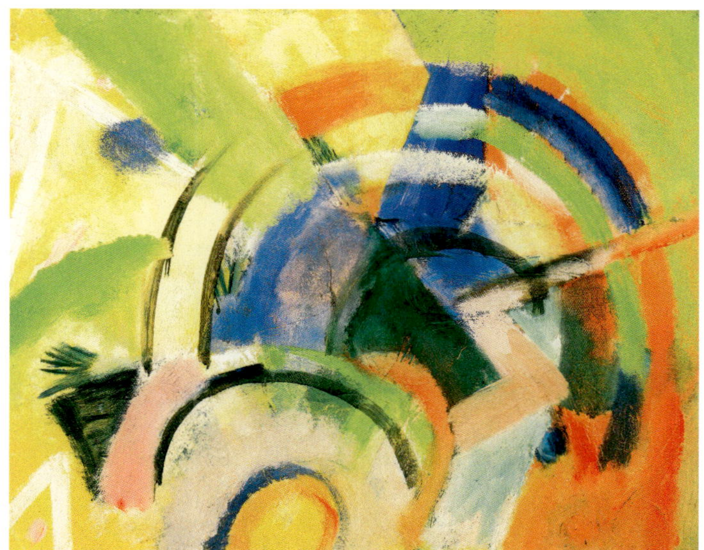

Fig. 4 Franz Marc, *Kleine Komposition IV* (*Small Composition IV*), 1914, oil on canvas, 39 x 49 cm, Franz Marc Museum, Kochel am See, Franz Marc Stiftung

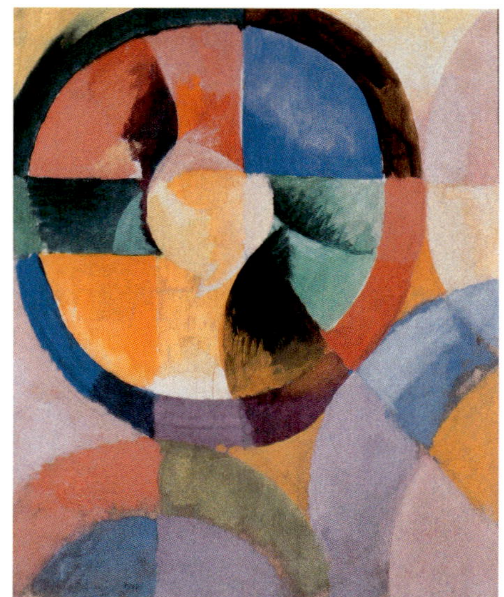

Fig. 5 Robert Delaunay, *Formes circulaires, Soleil no. 1* (*Circular Forms, Sun no. 1*), 1913, oil on canvas, 100 x 81 cm, Collection Wilhelm-Hack-Museum, Ludwigshafen am Rhein

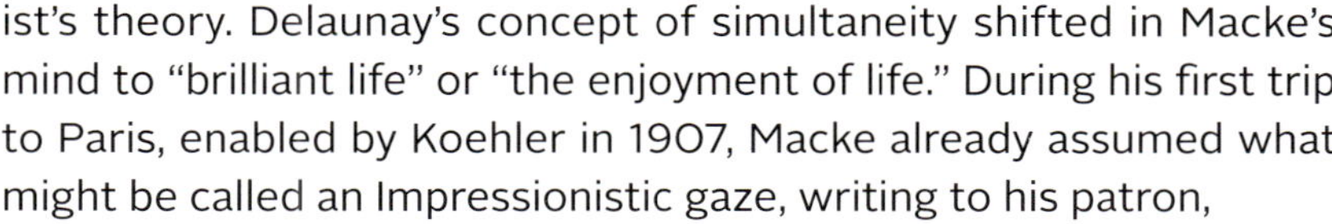

ist's theory. Delaunay's concept of simultaneity shifted in Macke's mind to "brilliant life" or "the enjoyment of life." During his first trip to Paris, enabled by Koehler in 1907, Macke already assumed what might be called an Impressionistic gaze, writing to his patron,

> *in the hot midday hours, I sit here in a park on one of the big round plazas with the big basins in the middle and the high fountains that glitter so marvelously in the sun. I have come to love fountains like this in the sun here. It is like life itself: sparkling and glittering, living. It doesn't know why. It just shoots up, foaming, jubilating into the light, into the sun. It doesn't ask why.*[22]

Macke's painting *Mädchen vor dem Springbrunnen* (*Girls at the Fountain,* 1914; fig. 7) shows two girls in front of a fountain in a park. As in a kaleidoscope, the forms splinter in the rising water, creating an almost Cubist, abstract structure that extends across the entire composition. At the time Macke created the painting, his visit to Delaunay's studio and discovery of his French colleague's window pictures lay in the past. When Delaunay's series of paintings was shown at the Gereonsclub (an avant-garde artists' association) in Cologne in March 1913, Macke tried to convince Koehler to acquire one of the window pictures by describing the special way in which it appropriated reality, writing, "that these pictures, more than any others, are capable of deluging you in a veritably heavenly joy in the sun and in life—they are not abstract at all, they are the highest reality, as I see quite clearly. . . ."[23] In his display window paintings, Macke translated this "heavenly joy in the sun and in life" into his own approach. The display in the hat shop (fig. 8), admired by a woman in red and green and a small child, seems to dissolve into a multi-colored mosaic behind the reflecting glass, a play of abstract colored shapes. The glass reflecting colored light is a picture within the picture; its interplay of abstract colored elements goes back to the compositional structure of Delaunay's window pictures. The French artist's neutral, rational conception of interpreting the depths of the universe in terms of the simultaneous effects of colors on the retina—thus provoking the perception at which his art aimed—is expanded by Macke by adding an aspect of emotion. This is linked with the stereotypical pedestrians who populate his "Sunday world," and the effect of his imagery is not limited to the perception of a luminous colored mosaic. Rather, Macke's color harmonies evoke the beauty and cheerfulness of a sunny day.

While Macke pursued the leitmotif of joie de vivre, formulated in Paris in 1907, with corresponding Impressionist consequences for his art, Marc revised his opinion of Impressionism, which, during his first trip to Paris in 1903, had struck him as "decisive for my art."[24] During his second visit to Paris in 1907, responding to paintings by Alfred Sisley, Monet, and Renoir, he wrote, "I always keenly felt the specific French aspect, which one must energetically exclude if one wishes to think of these things as models. . . . They never explode space and the soul. . . ."[25] This view already anticipates the unconditional rejection of Impressionism that Marc would express in 1912.[26] As his turn away from Impressionism and criticism of Delaunay's theory indicate, his attitude toward recent French art was characterized by a categorization in which he viewed it primarily as being dedicated to light-flooded surfaces, whereas German art possessed spatial and mental depth.

In other words, Marc continued to adhere to the distinction between French and German mentalities that had been current in Germany since before World War I. Thomas Mann was not alone in contrasting French "civilization" with German "culture."[27] Julius Meier-Graefe, in the introduction to his *Entwicklungsgeschichte der modernen Kunst* (*Modern Art: Being a Contribution to a New System of Aesthetics*), stated:

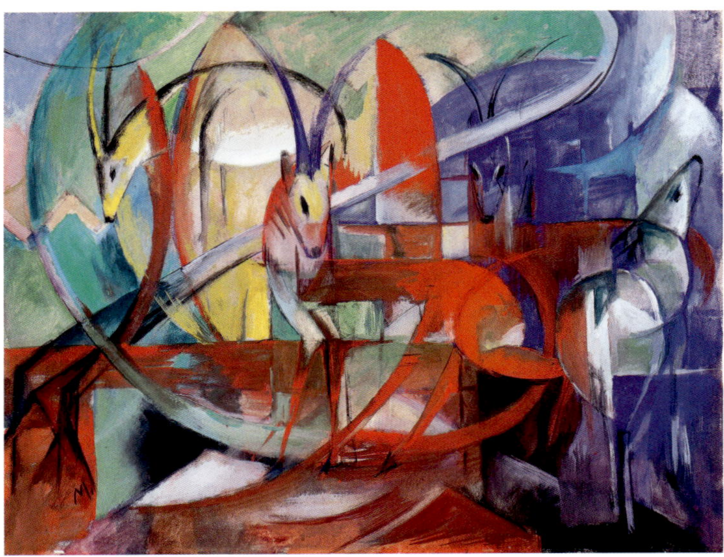

Fig. 6 Franz Marc, *Gazellen* (*Gazelles*), 1913–14, tempera on cardboard, 55.5 x 71.3 cm, Franz Marc Museum, Kochel am See, on loan from a private collection

> *As long as we only consider art that which appears as art to our eye, the eye must prove worthy of its role and learn to apprehend. Yet we Germans suffer from the error of thinking art instead of contemplating it. We project our soul into it instead of allowing ourselves to be inspired by it, and we pay no attention to whom we follow when our compulsion to interpret finds satisfaction in a work, no matter how cheap.*[28]

This amounted to a reversal of Marc's judgement. Meier-Graefe viewed French art appreciation, based on sensory perception, as positive, whereas the German compulsion to interpret risked misjudging the true value of a work of art. Insofar as his *Entwicklungsgeschichte der modernen Kunst* saw modernism as being rooted in Impressionism, his weighting of its importance appeared logical. Macke lent Marc the book in 1910, shortly after the two artists had first met.[29] The categorical difference between the "Romanic" Macke and the "Germanic" Marc, emphasized by the latter in 1914, would not crystallize until the ensuing years. At first, their shared themes were more important: artistic issues such as research on autonomous color, the struggle to find opportunities to show and sell their work, and the *Blaue Reiter* project. Their patron, Koehler—who generously supported both artists who, in turn, advised him regarding his acquisitions—was a further link in their friendship.

The difference that Marc later so clearly defined had become apparent much earlier. Whereas he attempted to derive the coloration in a "New Painting" from symbolic categories, Macke established a connection between painting and music, as had been propagated by French exponents of colorism since the eighteenth century.[30] With the reproduction of only two of his works and a belated request for an article, *Der Blaue Reiter* almanac devoted little space to Macke. Macke was no longer in agreement with the views of the editors Kandinsky and Marc, as he later wrote to Koehler.[31] Furthermore, Macke thought he was insufficiently represented in the first show of the *Blaue Reiter* editorship. "And the two gentlemen do not even think it necessary to ask me. The Epoch of the Great Spirituality can get underway, as far as I'm concerned," he wrote, with disgruntled irony, to Koehler.[32] What was crucial for Macke was not spiritual essence, but form, because "forms are powerful expressions of powerful life," as he stated in the almanac.[33] Marc, by contrast, viewed "mystical inner construction" as the "great problem of our generation."[34]

1 Elisabeth Erdmann-Macke, *Erinnerung an August Macke,* with an essay by Lothar Erdmann (Frankfurt am Main, 1994), p. 275.
2 Annegret Hoberg, "Chronologie der Freundschaft," in *August Macke und Franz Marc: Eine Künstlerfreundschaft,* ed. Volker Adolphs and Annegret Hoberg, exh. cat. Kunstmuseum Bonn; Städtische Galerie im Lenbachhaus and Kunstbau, Munich (Ostfildern, 2014), pp. 320–42, here p. 339.
3 August Macke, letter to Bernhard Koehler, November 30, 1913, in August Macke, *Briefe an Elisabeth und die Freunde,* ed. Werner Frese and Ernst-Gerhard Güse (Munich, 1987), p. 315. Bernhard Koehler supported not only Macke but also Marc, whom he met in 1911. Koehler was an important patron of the Blaue Reiter; without his support neither the almanac (1912) nor the *Erste Grosse Herbstsalon* (First large autumn salon) in Berlin (1913) would have come about. See Silvia Schmidt-Bauer, "Bernhard Koehler: Ein Mäzen und Sammler August Mackes und der Künstler des Blauen Reiters," *Zeitschrift des deutschen Vereins für Kunstwissenschaft,* N.F. 42, no. 3 (1988), pp. 76–91. This publication contains a complete list of Koehler's collection, including acquisition dates. See also Schmidt-Bauer, "Werke der 'Neuen Künstlervereinigung München' und des 'Blauen Reiter' in der Sammlung Bernhard Koehler," in *Der Blaue Reiter und das Neue Bild: Von der "Neuen Künstlervereinigung München" zum "Blauen Reiter,"* ed. Annegret Hoberg and Helmut Friedel, exh. cat. Städtische Galerie im Lenbachhaus, Munich (Munich and New York, 1999), pp. 307–14; and Schmidt-Bauer, "Die Sammlung Bernhard Koehler," in *Die Moderne und ihre Sammler: Französische Kunst in deutschem Privatbesitz vom Kaiserreich zur Weimarer Republik,* ed. Andrea Pophanken and Felix Billeter (Berlin, 2001), pp. 267–84.
4 Paul Signac's pioneering essay "D'Eugène Delacroix au néo-impressionnisme" was first published in German translation in the journal *Pan* 4 (1898), pp. 55–62.
5 See Françoise Cachin, "Catalogue des écrits de Félix Fénéon sur l'art," in Félix Fénéon, *Au-delà de l'impressionnisme* [1886], ed. and annotated by Françoise Cachin (Paris, 1966), pp. 177–82.
6 Erdmann-Macke 1994 (see note 1), p. 136.
7 The important influence of Seurat on Macke's works of 1913–14 has scarcely been discussed to date. In her catalogue raisonné of the paintings, Ursula Heiderich only briefly mentions the significance that Macke's 1908 stay in Paris had on his later development: Ursula Heiderich, *August Macke: Gemälde: Werkverzeichnis* (Ostfildern, 2008), p. 32. The first detailed discussion of this issue is found in Maria Saal, *Figur, Raum und Licht: August Mackes Begegnung mit dem Werk Georges Seurats 1908 in Paris,* MA thesis, Ludwig-Maximilians-Universität München, Munich, 2011.
8 During his visit to Berlin, Fénéon was able to see some ten paintings by Macke in the Koehler Collection, which ushered in the German artist's stylistic phase influenced by Seurat and Delaunay. See Schmidt-Bauer 1988 (see note 3), nos. 26–36.

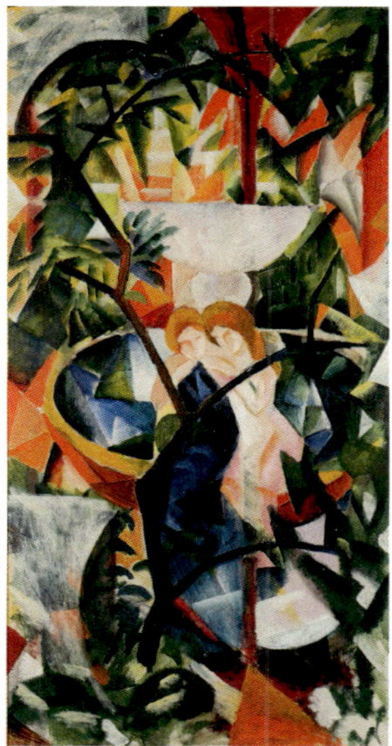

Fig. 7 August Macke, *Mädchen vor dem Springbrunnen* (*Girls at the Fountain*), 1914, oil on canvas, 142 x 73.5 cm, LWL-Museum für Kunst und Kultur (Westfälisches Landesmuseum), Münster

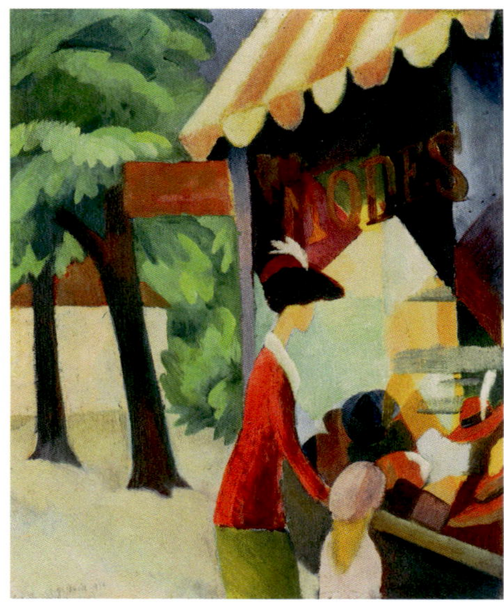

Fig. 8 August Macke, *Vor dem Hutladen* (*Frau mit roter Jacke und Kind*) (*Before the Milliner's Shop [Woman with Red Jacket and Child]*), 1913, oil on canvas, 54.5 x 44.5 cm, private collection

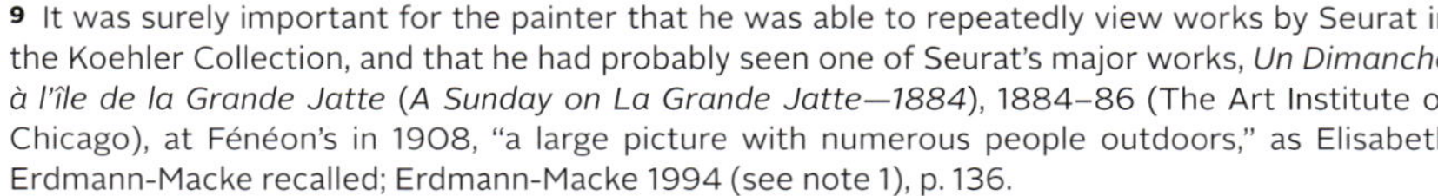

9 It was surely important for the painter that he was able to repeatedly view works by Seurat in the Koehler Collection, and that he had probably seen one of Seurat's major works, *Un Dimanche à l'île de la Grande Jatte* (*A Sunday on La Grande Jatte—1884*), 1884–86 (The Art Institute of Chicago), at Fénéon's in 1908, "a large picture with numerous people outdoors," as Elisabeth Erdmann-Macke recalled; Erdmann-Macke 1994 (see note 1), p. 136.
10 "Except for a few days spent in Berlin, he was still in Frankfurt am Main, and in the autumn spent eight days with the Marcs in Paris, where they met Delaunay and Henri Le Fauconnier and went to see the art dealers Eugène Druet, Bernheim-Jeune, Fénéon, and Ambroise Vollard." Trans. from Erdmann-Macke 1994 (see note 1), p. 256.
11 August Macke, letter to Bernhard Koehler, March 17, 1913, in Macke 1987 (see note 3), p. 298.
12 See Susanne Meyer-Büser, "Marc, Macke und Delaunay: Ein Dreigestirn auf Zeit," in *Marc, Macke und Delaunay: Die Schönheit einer zerbrechlichen Welt (1910–1914),* ed. Susanne Meyer-Büser, exh. cat. Sprengel Museum, Hannover (Hannover and Cologne, 2009), pp. 12–26, here p. 17.
13 *Tour Eiffel,* 1911, oil on canvas, formerly in the Koehler Collection, Berlin, destroyed in 1945.
14 Franz Marc, "Die neue Malerei" [1912], in Franz Marc, *Schriften,* ed. Klaus Lankheit (Cologne, 1978), pp. 101–04.
15 Franz Marc, letter to August Macke, June 12, 1914, in August Macke and Franz Marc, *Briefwechsel 1910–1914,* ed. Karl-Maria Guth, complete new ed. (Berlin, 2014), p. 158.
16 *Der Sturm: Wochenschrift für Kultur und die Künste* 3, nos. 144–45 (January 1913), columns 255–56. See Cathrin Klingsöhr-Leroy, "Licht oder Mysterium: Gedanken zum Briefwechsel zwischen Franz Marc und Robert Delaunay 1912/13," in Klingsöhr-Leroy, *Zwischen den Zeilen: Dokumente zu Franz Marc* (Ostfildern, 2005), pp. 146–53, here pp. 131, 137, 148.
17 "In perceiving colors . . . the eye can sensorily register a diverse relation and difference of a great variety of values . . . by perceiving what it itself engenders. It can experience in an image and as an image *la forme en mouvement statique—et dynamique* as a *simultanéité rythmique,* if the image provokes the eye with spectrum colors that are correspondingly related. But then too—and only then—the image will become a perceptional model of an intended reality, i.e. the vitality of the world imagined as a simultaneous action of division and unification. . . ."; quoted and trans. from Max Imdahl, *Farbe: Kunsttheoretische Reflexionen in Frankreich* (Munich, 1987), pp. 140–41.
18 Franz Marc, letter to Robert Delaunay, December 1912, in Klingsöhr-Leroy 2005 (see note 16), pp. 131, 148.
19 Franz Marc, "Die neue Malerei" and "Die konstruktiven Ideen der neuen Malerei" [1912], in Marc 1978 (see note 14), pp. 101–04, 105–08.
20 Ibid., pp. 102, 105.
21 Robert Delaunay, draft letter to Franz Marc, December 14, 1912, reproduced in Karl-Heinz Meissner, "Delaunay-Dokumente: Ausstellungen, Briefe, Rezensionen, Zitate," in *Delaunay und Deutschland,* ed. Peter-Klaus Schuster, exh. cat. Staatsgalerie moderner Kunst im Haus der Kunst, Munich (Cologne, 1985), pp. 482–531, here p. 498.
22 August Macke, letter to Bernhard Koehler, June 18, 1907, in Macke 1987 (see note 3), pp. 125–26.
23 August Macke, letter to Bernhard Koehler, March 10, 1913, in ibid., p. 296.
24 Franz Marc, "Französisches Tagebuch," June 9, 1903, in Marc 1978 (see note 14), p. 81.
25 Franz Marc, letter to Maria Franck, end of March 1907, in Franz Marc, *Briefe, Schriften und Aufzeichnungen,* ed. Günter Meissner (2nd ed.; Leipzig, 1989), p. 25.
26 See notes 14 and 19.
27 Thomas Mann's "*Gedanken im Kriege*" (Thoughts in war) was published in 1914. Marc was probably referring to this essay in his letter from the front to Maria on October 6, 1915; Franz Marc, *Briefe aus dem Feld: 1914–1916,* with an introduction by Cathrin Klingsöhr-Leroy (Munich, 2014), p. 112. In 1918, at the end of the war, Mann published *Betrachtungen eines Unpolitischen* (*Reflections of a Nonpolitical Man*). Articulated here is the notion of a German "*Volksgeist*" ("national spirit") opposed to Western civilization, which adopted a view that differentiated between German and French culture and was current in Germany before World War I. See Hanno Helbling, "Vorwort zu Thomas Mann," in *Betrachtungen eines Unpolitischen* (Frankfurt am Main, 2004), p. 9. See also Maria Stavrinaki, "Le Prédicat selon Marc: De l'ensauvagement à l'ascèse," introduction to Franz Marc, *Écrits et correspondances,* ed. Maria Stavrinaki (Paris, 2006), pp. 9–57, here pp. 36–43.
28 Julius Meier-Graefe, introduction to the first edition of *Entwicklungsgeschichte der modernen Kunst* [1904], rev. and with an afterword by Hans Belting (Munich, 1987), vol. I, foreword, p. 14. Engl. ed. [no foreword]: *Modern Art: Being a Contribution to a New System of Aesthetics,* trans. Florence Simmonds and George W. Chrystal, vol. I (London and New York, 1908).
29 Macke's recommendation of the book to Koehler on March 24, 1908, indicates the importance he attached to Meier-Graefe's discussion: "To be honest, this book completely opened my eyes to art for the first time." In Macke 1987 (see note 3), p. 174.
30 See Max Imdahl, "Kunstgeschichtliche Exkurse zu Perraults 'Parallèle des anciens et des modernes,'" introduction to facsimile edition of Charles Perrault, *Parallèle des anciens et des modernes en ce qui regarde les arts et les sciences* (Munich, 1964); Bernard Teyssèdre, *Roger de Piles et les débats sur le coloris au siècle de Louis XIV* (Paris, 1965).
31 August Macke, letter to Bernhard Koehler, October 16, 1913. "My views on art are different from Kandinsky's and Marc's. Now I feel responsible for myself alone." In Macke 1987 (see note 3), p. 313.
32 Ibid., p. 278.
33 August Macke, "Die Masken," in *Der Blaue Reiter,* ed. Wassily Kandinsky and Franz Marc (Munich, 1912), pp. 21–26, here p. 24; English ed.: "Masks," in *The Blaue Reiter Almanac,* ed. Wassily Kandinsky and Franz Marc, documentary edition, ed. and with an introduction by Klaus Lankheit, trans. Henning Falkenstein with the assistance of Manug Terzian and Gertrude Hinderlie (London, 1974; repr. Boston, 2005), pp. 83–89, here p. 88.
34 Franz Marc, "Geistige Güter," in Kandinsky and Marc 1912 (see note 33), pp. 1–4, here p. 3; English ed.: "Spiritual Treasures," in Kandinsky and Marc 2005 (see note 33), pp. 55–60, here p. 59.

DER BLAUE REITER: A CHRONOLOGY

COMPILED BY FIONA HESSE

1908

June Following years of travel, including protracted stays in Rapallo, Paris, and Berlin, Wassily Kandinsky and Gabriele Münter return to Munich. In late summer Kandinsky moves into an apartment at Ainmillerstrasse 36, in the Schwabing district.

Mid August—End of September Kandinsky, Münter, Alexei von Jawlensky, and Marianne von Werefkin spend a few weeks working in Murnau, on Lake Staffel. The experience of the Alpine foothills and Upper Bavarian folk art lead, especially for Kandinsky, Münter, and Jawlensky, to a turn to stronger colors and an emphasis on the plane: "After a short period of agony I took a great leap forward, from copying nature—in a more or less Impressionist style—to feeling the content of things—abstracting—conveying an extract. . . . All 4 of us were keenly ambitious and each of us made progress," as Münter recalled in a diary entry for 1908.

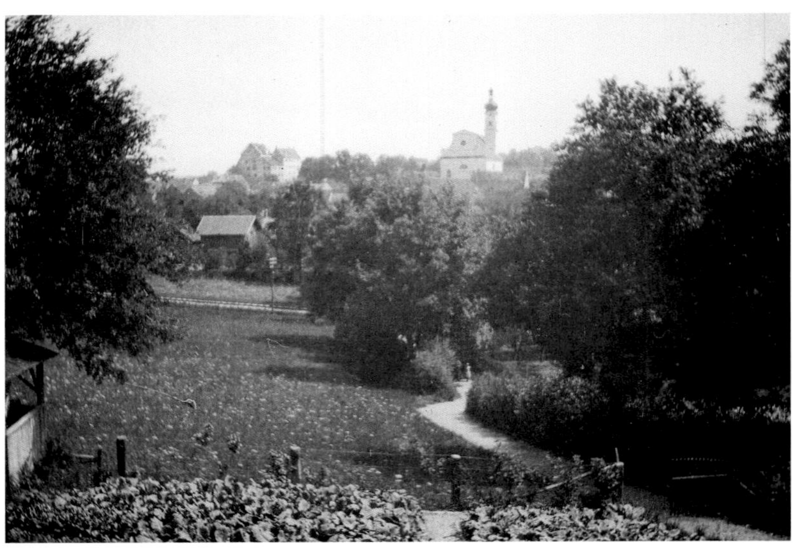

View of the garden of Gabriele Münter's house toward the castle and church hill in Murnau, ca. 1909, photograph by Gabriele Münter, Gabriele Münter- und Johannes Eichner-Stiftung, Munich

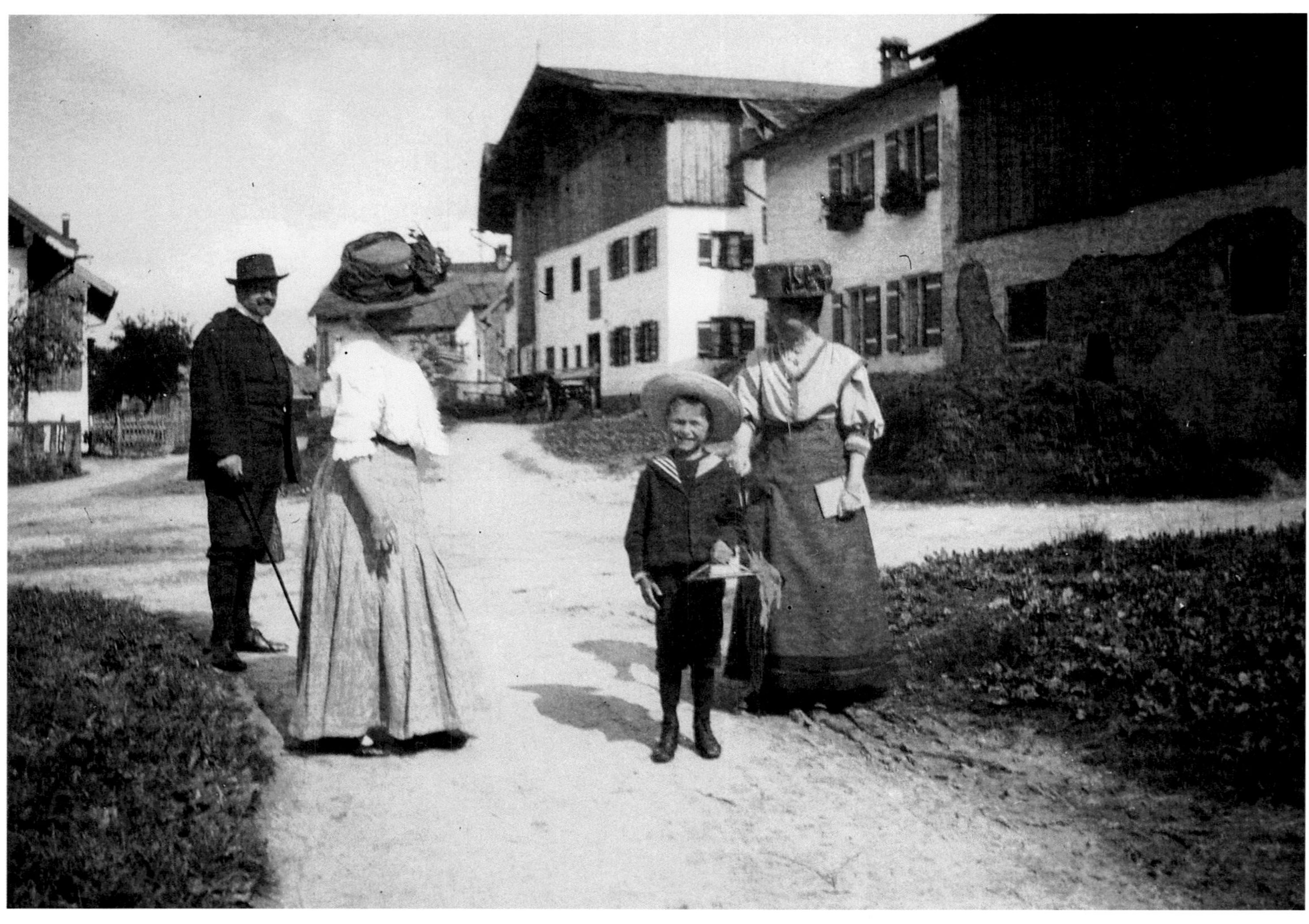

Alexei von Jawlensky, Marianne von Werefkin, Andreas Jawlensky, and Gabriele Münter in Murnau, ca. 1909, photograph by Wassily Kandinsky, Gabriele Münter- und Johannes Eichner-Stiftung, Munich

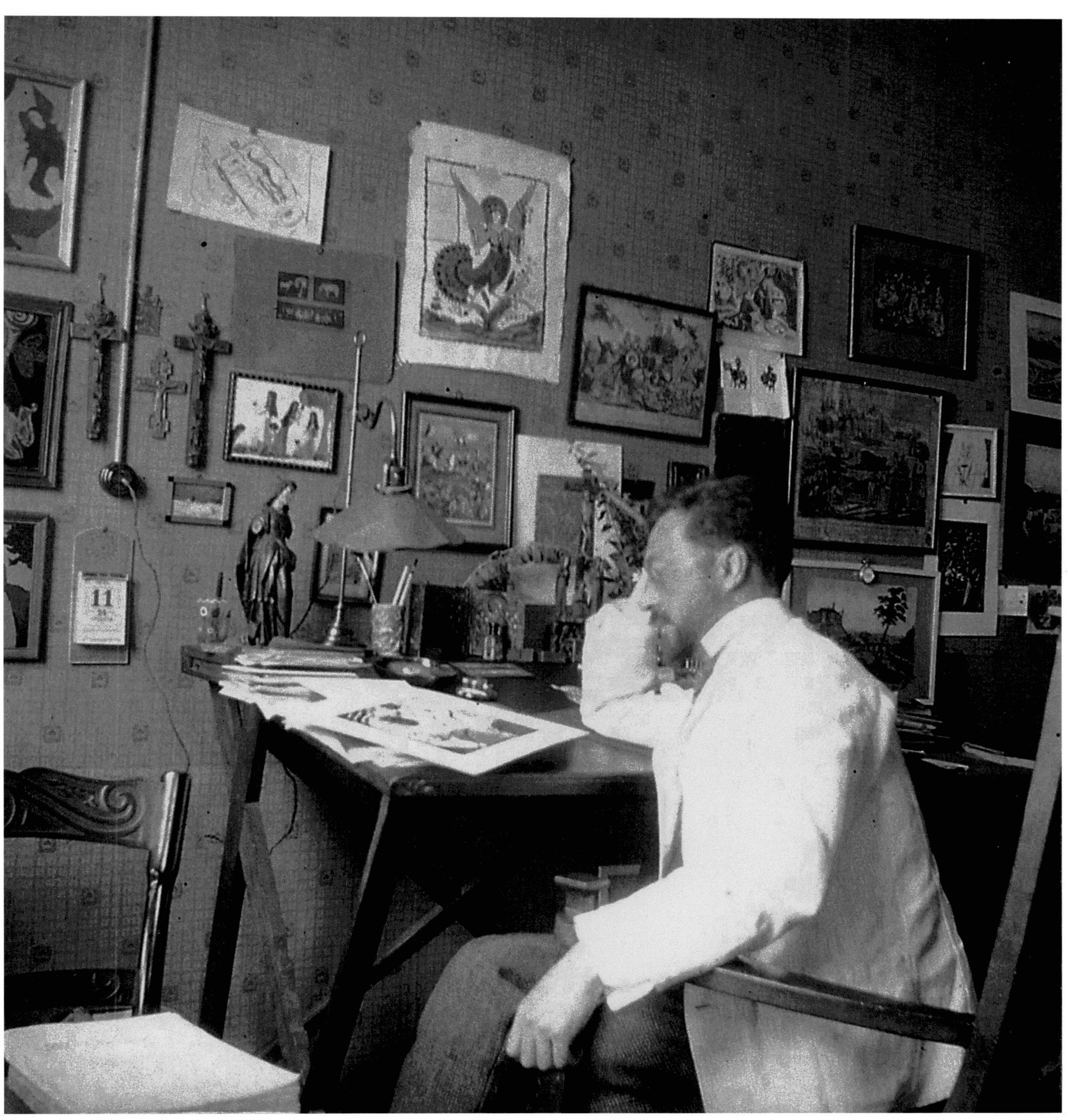

Wassily Kandinsky seated at the desk in his apartment at Ainmillerstrasse 36, Munich, June 1911, photograph by Gabriele Münter, Gabriele Münter- und Johannes Eichner-Stiftung, Munich

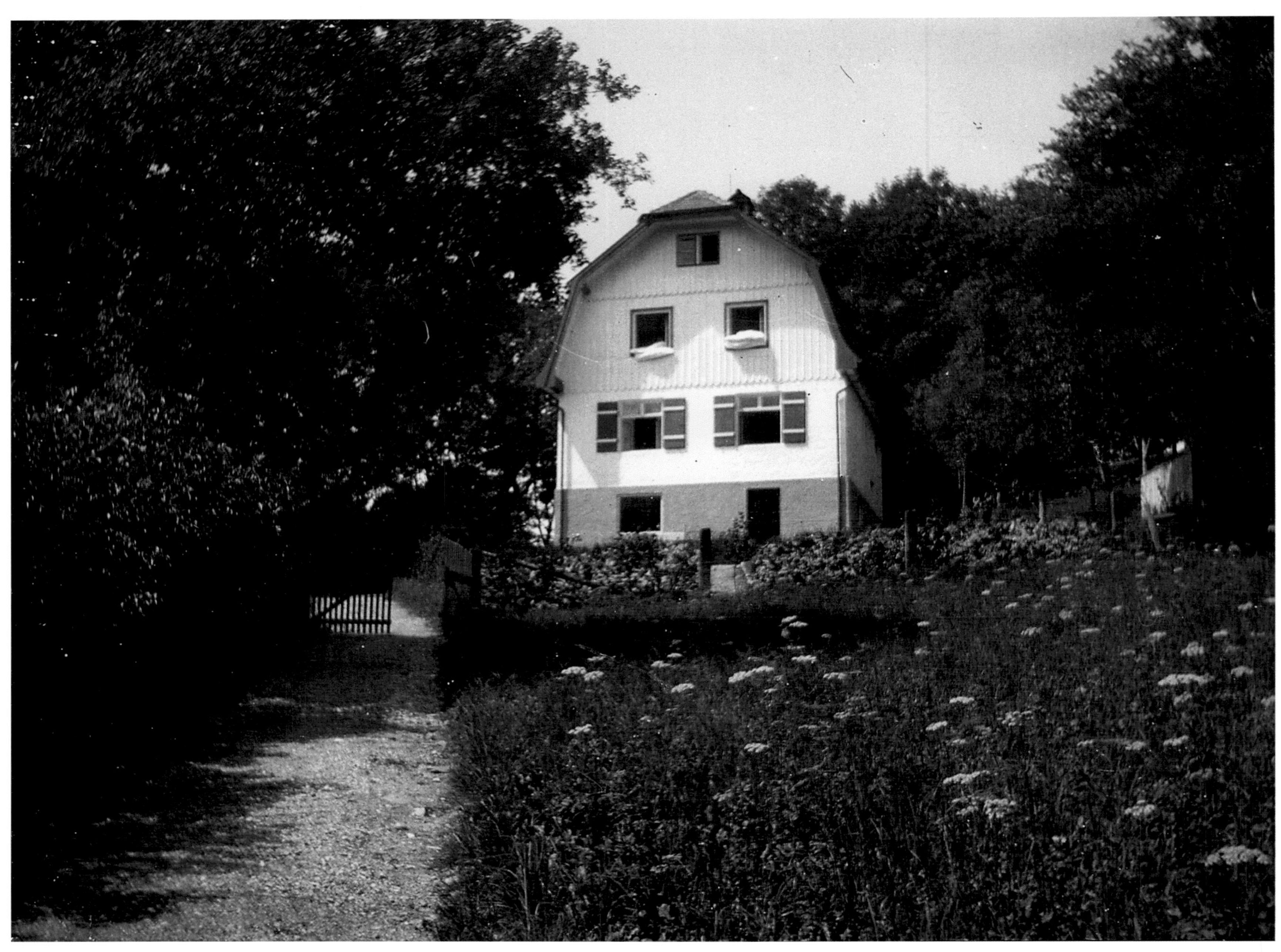

Gabriele Münter's house in Murnau, view from the garden, 1909, photograph by Gabriele Münter, Gabriele Münter- und Johannes Eichner-Stiftung, Munich

1909

January 22 The Neue Künstlervereinigung München (NKVM; New Artists' Association Munich) is founded by Kandinsky (chairman) and Jawlensky (vice chairman), along with others, including Münter, Werefkin, Alfred Kubin, Adolf Erbslöh, Alexander Kanoldt, and the composer Thomas von Hartmann.

June Münter and Kandinsky rent a small *Jugendstil* villa on a hill in the western part of Murnau. On August 21, Münter buys what becomes known as the Russian House, where she and Kandinsky spend especially the summer months until 1914. The Murnau landscape, the house itself, the garden, and immediate surroundings become a key source of inspiration for the two artists. They frequently depict the view of the church and castle, as well as the mountains, from the window.

December 1–15 The first exhibition of the NKVM takes place at Galerie Thannhauser in Munich. Seeing the highly controversial show inspires Franz Marc to develop his own ideas and emerge from his artistic isolation.

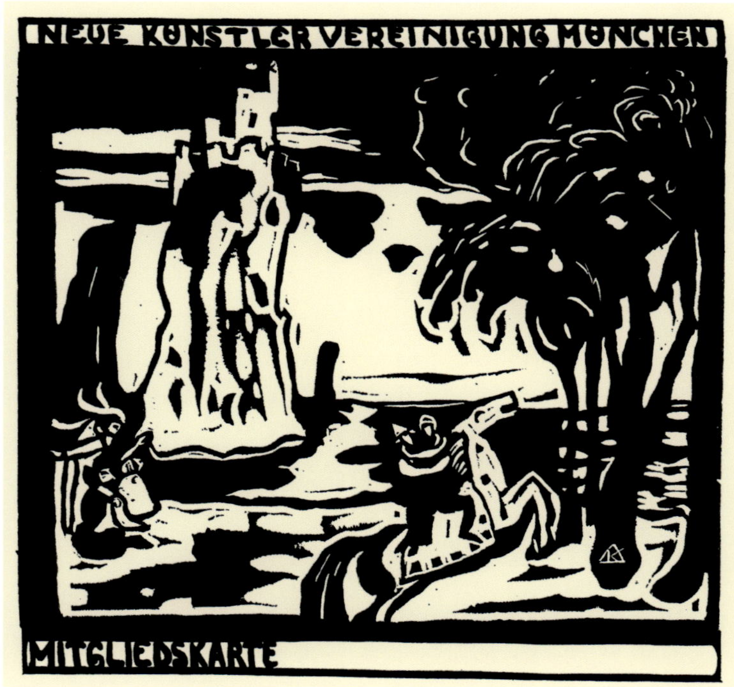

Membership card for the Neue Künstlervereinigung München (New Artists' Association Munich) with Wassily Kandinsky's woodcut *Felsen,* 1909

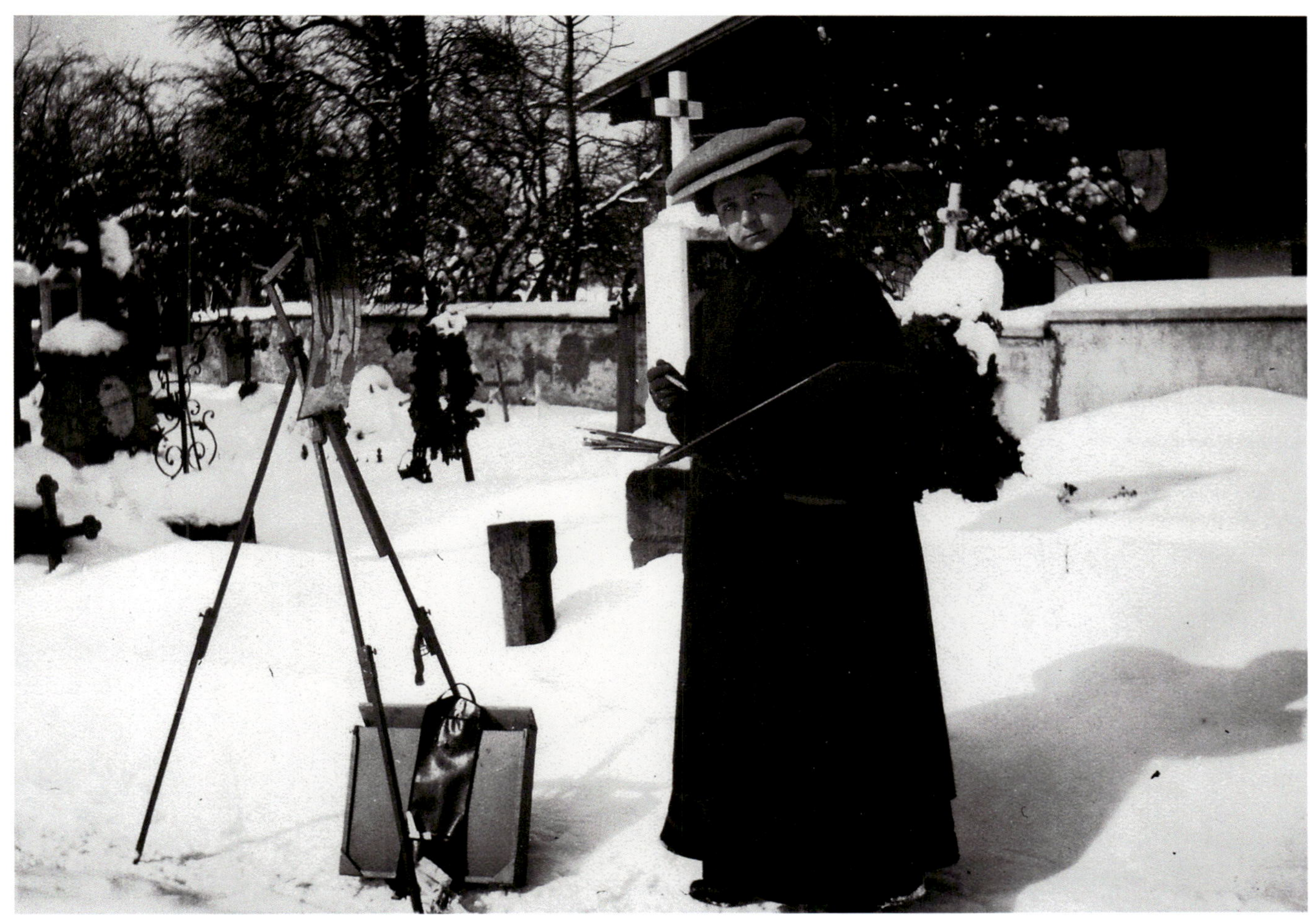

Gabriele Münter painting at the cemetery in Kochel, February 1909, photograph by Wassily Kandinsky, Gabriele Münter- und Johannes Eichner-Stiftung, Munich

1910

January 6 After viewing Marc's first solo show at the Brakl gallery, August Macke, along with his cousin Helmuth Macke and Bernhard Koehler Jr., pays a spontaneous visit to Marc in his studio. In a letter written that same day to his future wife, Maria, Marc predicts that his meeting with the "gentleman from Berlin [i.e., Koehler, son of the prosperous entrepreneur and art collector Bernhard Koehler Sr.] will be promising." In fact, over the coming years, the elder Koehler would not only support the publication of the *Blaue Reiter* almanac but would also help Macke, the future husband of his niece, Elisabeth, and Marc in particular.

September 1–14 Second exhibition of the NKVM takes place, again at Galerie Thannhauser. It, too, draws vitriolic and in part devastating criticism.

October After seeing the NKVM show, Marc writes one of the few positive reviews and sends it to the gallery owner, who publishes it as a catalogue supplement. As a result, Marc meets the NKVM members, except for Kandinsky, who is out of town.

November At the residence of Jawlensky and Werefkin, Marc introduces Macke to the NKVM circle.

Poster for the first exhibition of the Neue Künstlervereinigung München (New Artists' Association Munich), with a color lithograph by Wassily Kandinsky, 1909

1911

January 1 Kandinsky and Marc first meet at the New Year's reception held at Werefkin's residence at Giselastrasse 23. Münter is also present.

January 2 Along with Jawlensky and Helmuth Macke, Kandinsky and Marc attend a concert of Arnold Schoenberg's compositions in Munich. After the concert, Kandinsky and Schoenberg begin a lively correspondence.

January 10 After protracted disagreements with the NKVM, Kandinsky relinquishes his chairmanship.

February 5 Marc receives a telegram from the NKVM to the effect that he has been "unanimously named a member and third chairman." His anticipation of an inspiring artistic exchange is expressed in a letter to Maria of the same day: "Now it has come about, and I'm glad. . . . I'm fed up with being out of things. Now it's a common cause."

June 19 Kandinsky tells Marc about his idea of publishing a book in the form of an almanac. "Well, I have a new idea. Piper must be the publisher and the two of us the editors. A kind of almanac (yearbook) with reproductions and articles . . . and a *chronicle*!!" The two develop this plan in the course of the summer.

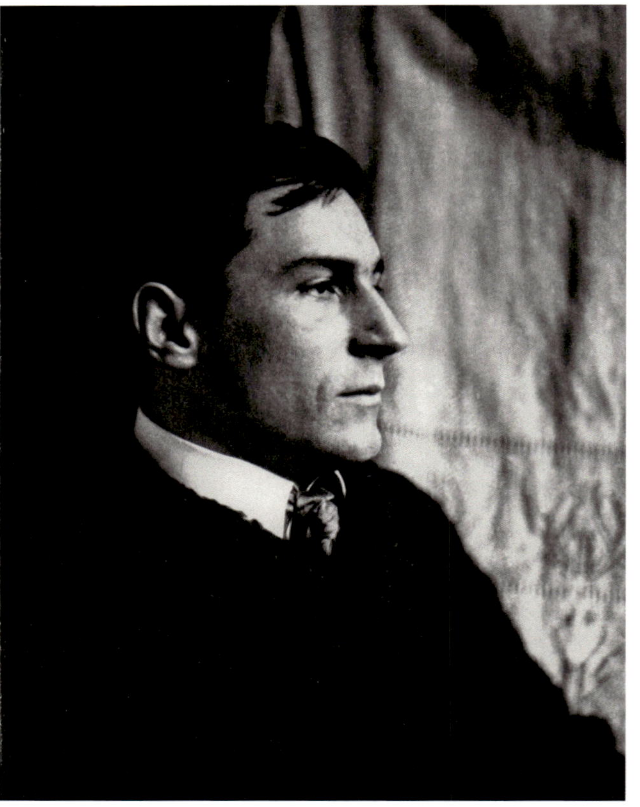

Franz Marc, ca. 1913

September In Sindelsdorf and Murnau, Kandinsky and Marc prepare the *Blaue Reiter* almanac.

October 24–25 The editing work continues apace, assisted by Macke, who has arrived from the Rhineland. As Elisabeth Erdmann-Macke recalled: "Those were unforgettable hours as each of the men worked out his manuscript, polished and altered it. . . . Everything was reviewed, discussed, accepted or rejected, not without little quarrels and frictions. . . . Despite everything, those days were incredibly exciting. . . ."

December 2 The jury of the third NVKM exhibition rejects Kandinsky's painting *Composition V* for formal reasons, citing the association statutes. Kandinsky and Marc leave the association, followed by others, including Münter, Kubin, and von Hartmann. Jawlensky and Werefkin support Kandinsky while remaining members for the time being.

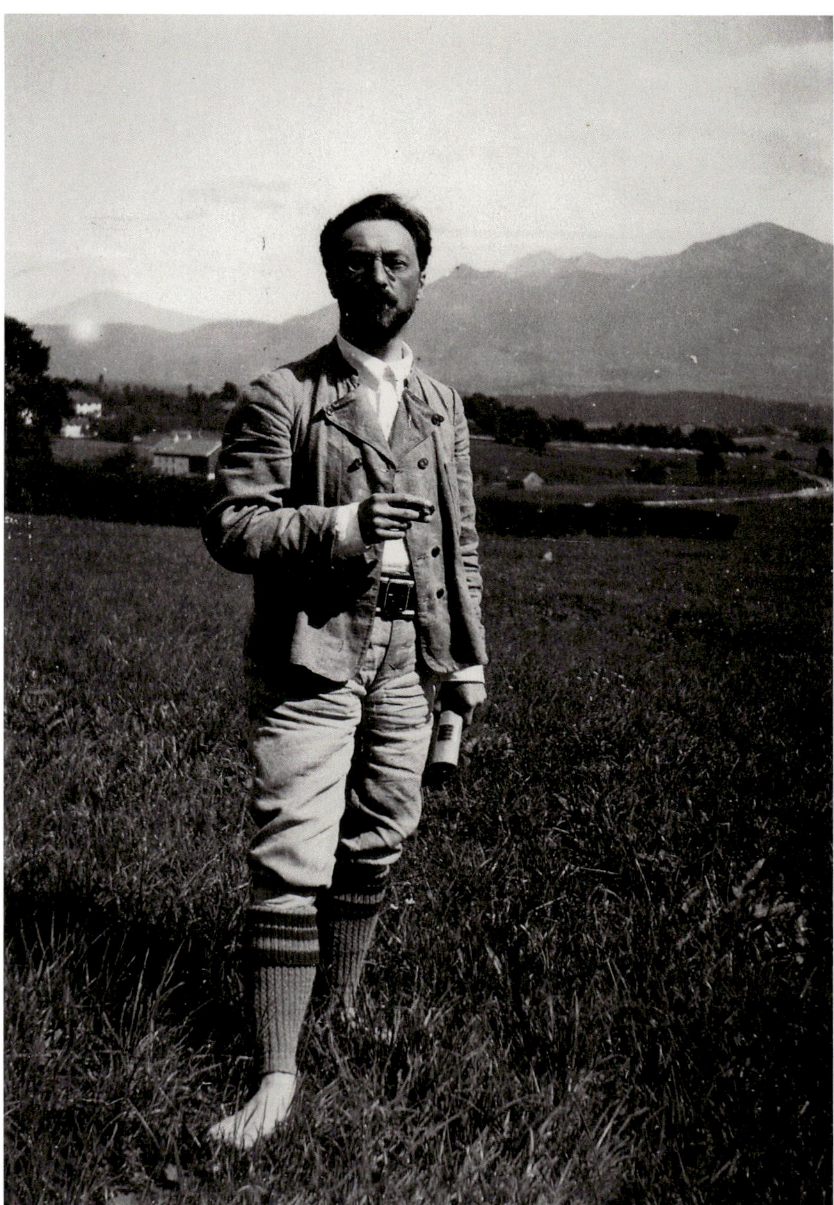

Kandinsky in a meadow near Murnau, ca. 1910, photograph by Gabriele Münter, Gabriele Münter- und Johannes Eichner-Stiftung, Munich

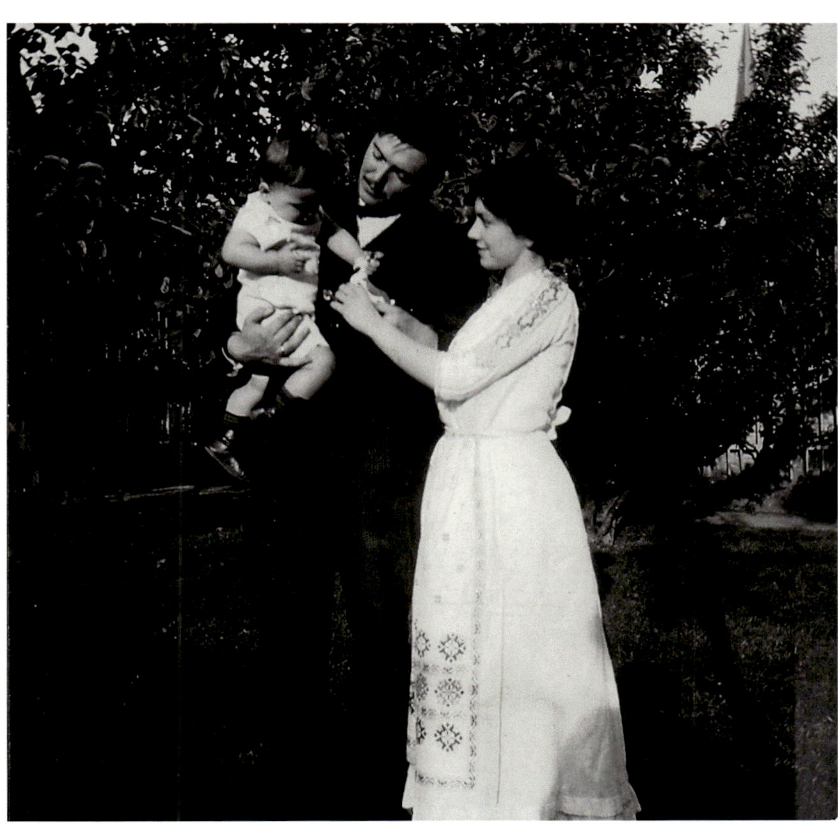

August and Elisabeth Macke with son Walter in their garden in Bonn, summer 1911, photograph by Gabriele Münter, Gabriele Münter- und Johannes Eichner-Stiftung, Munich

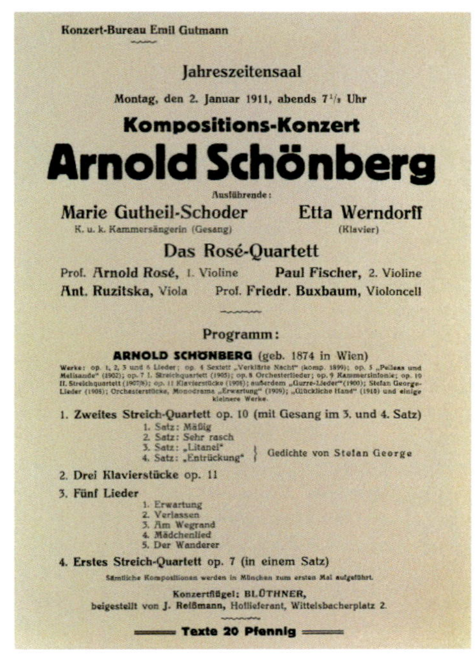

Konzert-Bureau Emil Gutmann

Jahreszeitensaal

Montag, den 2. Januar 1911, abends 7 1/2 Uhr

Kompositions-Konzert

Arnold Schönberg

Ausführende:

Marie Gutheil-Schoder K. u. k. Kammersängerin (Gesang)

Etta Werndorff (Klavier)

Das Rosé-Quartett

Prof. **Arnold Rosé,** 1. Violine — **Paul Fischer,** 2. Violine

Ant. Ruzitska, Viola — Prof. **Friedr. Buxbaum,** Violoncell

Programm:

ARNOLD SCHÖNBERG (geb. 1874 in Wien)

Werke: op. 1, 2, 3 und 6 Lieder; op. 4 Sextett „Verklärte Nacht" (komp. 1899); op. 5 „Pelleas und Melisande" (1902); op. 7 I. Streichquartett (1905); op. 8 Orchesterlieder; op. 9 Kammersinfonie; op. 10 II. Streichquartett (1907/8); op. 11 Klavierstücke (1908); außerdem „Gurre-Lieder" (1900); Stefan George-Lieder (1908); Orchesterstücke, Monodrama „Erwartung" (1909); „Glückliche Hand" (1910) und einige kleinere Werke.

1. **Zweites Streich-Quartett** op. 10 (mit Gesang im 3. und 4. Satz)
   1. Satz: Mäßig
   2. Satz: Sehr rasch
   3. Satz: „Litanei" } Gedichte von Stefan George
   4. Satz: „Entrückung" } Gedichte von Stefan George
2. **Drei Klavierstücke** op. 11
3. **Fünf Lieder**
   1. Erwartung
   2. Verlassen
   3. Am Wegrand
   4. Mädchenlied
   5. Der Wanderer
4. **Erstes Streich-Quartett** op. 7 (in einem Satz)

Sämtliche Kompositionen werden in München zum ersten Mal aufgeführt.

Konzertflügel: BLÜTHNER,
beigestellt von J. Reißmann, Hoflieferant, Wittelsbacherplatz 2.

Texte 20 Pfennig

Announcement for a concert of compositions by Arnold Schoenberg in Munich, 1911

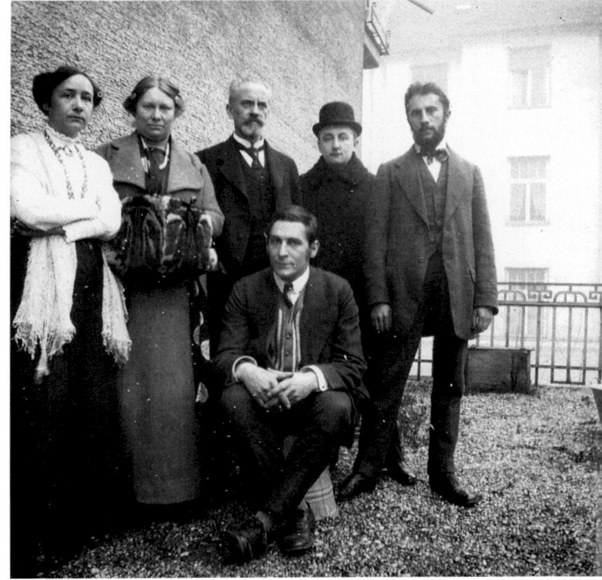

Gabriele Münter, Maria Marc, Bernhard Koehler, Thomas von Hartmann, Heinrich Campendonk, and (seated) Franz Marc on the terrace at Ainmillerstrasse 36, Munich, 1911, photograph by Wassily Kandinsky, Gabriele Münter- und Johannes Eichner-Stiftung, Munich

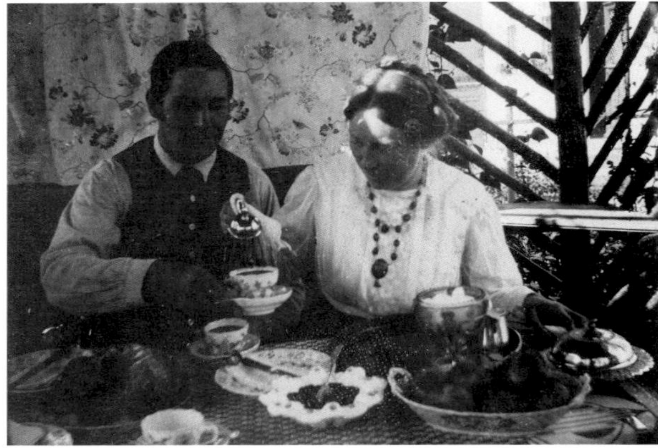

Franz and Maria Marc in their garden gazebo, Sindelsdorf, summer 1911, photograph by Wassily Kandinsky, Gabriele Münter- und Johannes Eichner-Stiftung, Munich

December 3 "The editors of the *Blaue Reiter* now become the point of departure for new exhibitions. . . . We will attempt to become the center of the modern movement," Marc writes to his brother, Paul.

December 9 Kandinsky's art theory manuscript, *Über das Geistige in der Kunst* (*On the Spiritual in Art*), is published by Piper Verlag, Munich (dated 1912).

December 18, 1911–January 3, 1912 In the space of only two weeks, Kandinsky and Marc organize their own exhibition, *Die Erste Ausstellung der Redaktion Der Blaue Reiter* (*First Exhibition of the Editors of Der Blaue Reiter*), presented at Galerie Thannhauser concurrent to the NKVM show. The catalogue lists forty-three paintings by fourteen artists, including Henri Rousseau and Robert Delaunay (see p. 160, fig. 4).

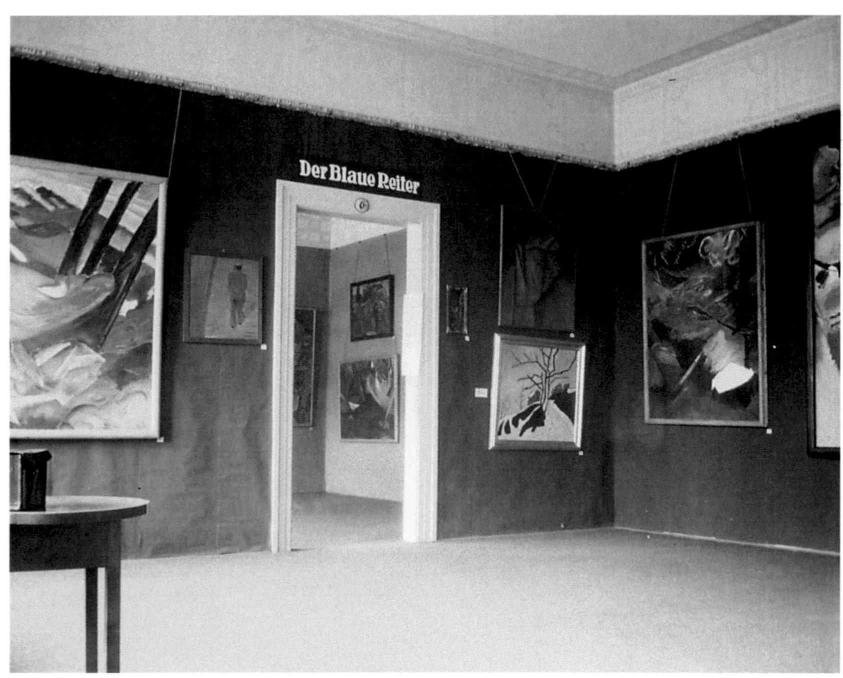

Die Erste Ausstellung der Redaktion Der Blaue Reiter (*First Exhibition of the Editors of Der Blaue Reiter*), Galerie Thannhauser, Munich, 1911–12, Room 2 with works by Franz Marc (*Die gelbe Kuh* [*Yellow Cow*]), Arnold Schoenberg, Wassily Kandinsky, Wladimir Burliuk, Gabriele Münter, Marc (*Reh im Walde I* [*Deer in the Woods I*]), and Kandinsky, photograph by Gabriele Münter, Gabriele Münter- und Johannes Eichner-Stiftung, Munich

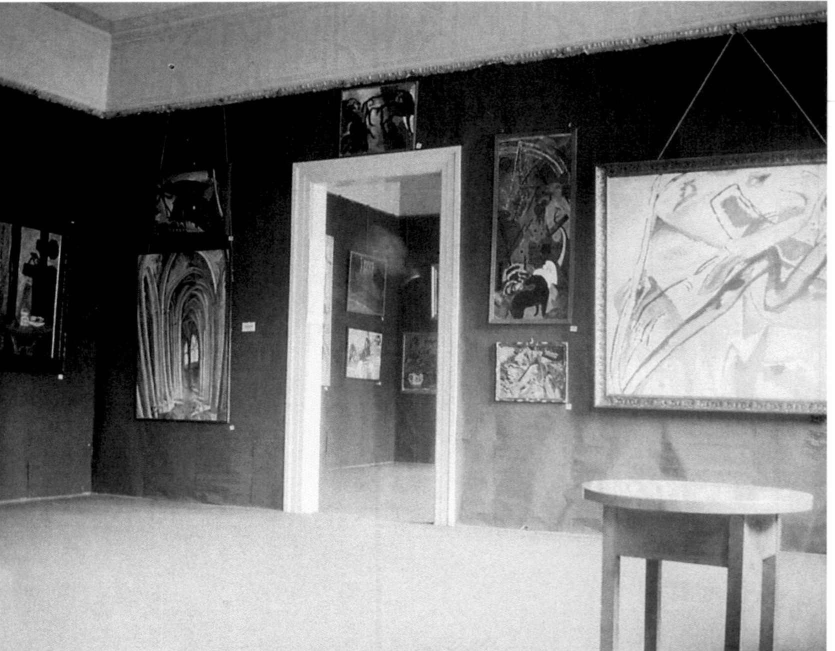

Die Erste Ausstellung der Redaktion Der Blaue Reiter (*First Exhibition of the Editors of Der Blaue Reiter*), Galerie Thannhauser, Munich, 1911–12, Room 2 with works by Münter, August Macke, Robert Delaunay, David Burliuk, Marc, and Kandinsky, photograph by Gabriele Münter, Gabriele Münter- und Johannes Eichner-Stiftung, Munich

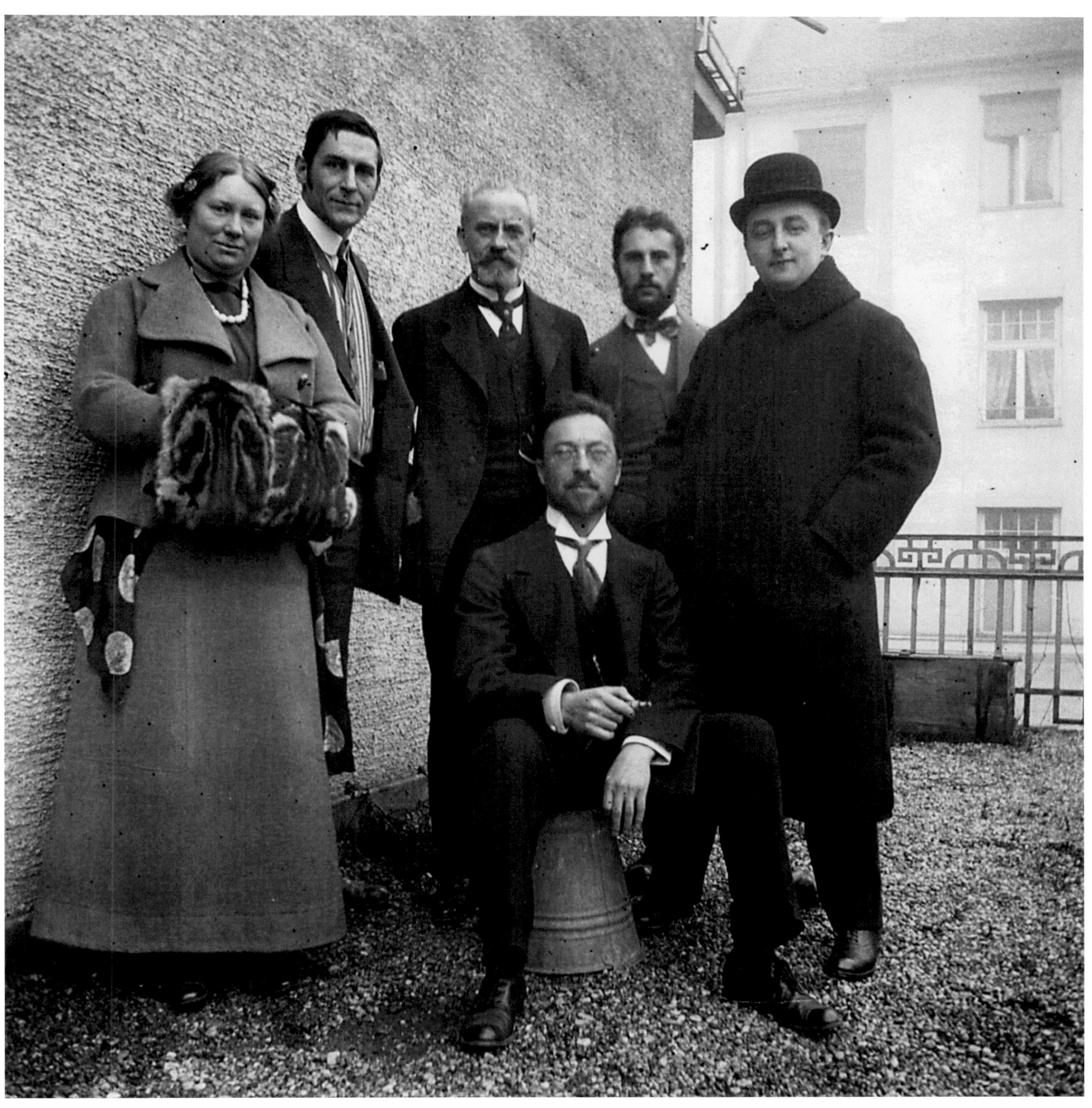

Maria and Franz Marc, Bernhard Koehler, Heinrich Campendonk, Thomas von Hartmann, and (seated) Wassily Kandinsky on the terrace at Ainmillerstrasse 36, Munich, 1911, photograph by Gabriele Münter, Gabriele Münter- und Johannes Eichner-Stiftung, Munich

1912

January–October Following the Munich premiere, *Die Erste Ausstellung* travels to Cologne, Berlin, Bremen, Hagen, Frankfurt am Main, and Hamburg. It tours through a total of eleven European cities until 1914.

February 12–March 18 *Die Zweite Ausstellung der Redaktion Der Blaue Reiter: Schwarz-Weiss* (*Second Exhibition of the Editors of Der Blaue Reiter: Black and White*), held at Galerie Goltz, Munich, focuses on drawing and prints.

February The almanac is announced together with a four-page subscription brochure, which attracts considerable interest. The edition is increased to 1,200 copies.

March 12–April 10 Herwarth Walden takes over *Die Erste Ausstellung* as the inaugural show for his gallery, Der Sturm, in Berlin: *Der Blaue Reiter, Franz Flaum, Oskar Kokoschka, Expressionisten.*

April The second edition of Kandinsky's *Über das Geistige in der Kunst* is published.

April 11 At the behest of Kandinsky, Paul Klee visits Robert Delaunay in Paris. Klee translates Delaunay's programmatic essay "La Lumière" (Light) into German for Walden's journal *Der Sturm*.

May 11 The *Blaue Reiter* almanac is published by Piper, with the financial support of Bernhard Koehler. Kandinsky has made eleven different designs for the cover. Reinhard Piper requests that Kandinsky delete the word "Almanac" from the block of the woodcut selected, in order to avoid being committed to an annual publication (see p. 159, fig. 2). Preparations for a second volume take place concurrently.

May 25–September 30 Since not all of the works of the Blaue Reiter artists are shown at the *Internationale Kunstausstellung des Sonderbundes* (*International Exhibition of the Sonderbund*), in Cologne, Marc arranges an alternative show, *Refüsierte des Sonderbundes* (*Sonderbund Rejects*), held from June 16 to the end of July at Der Sturm Gallery, in Berlin.

Autumn The third edition of Kandinsky's *Über das Geistige in der Kunst* is published.

November *Das neue Bild* (The new image), a book by the art historian and NKVM member Otto Fischer, sparks a controversy that ultimately prompts Werefkin and Jawlensky to resign from the association.

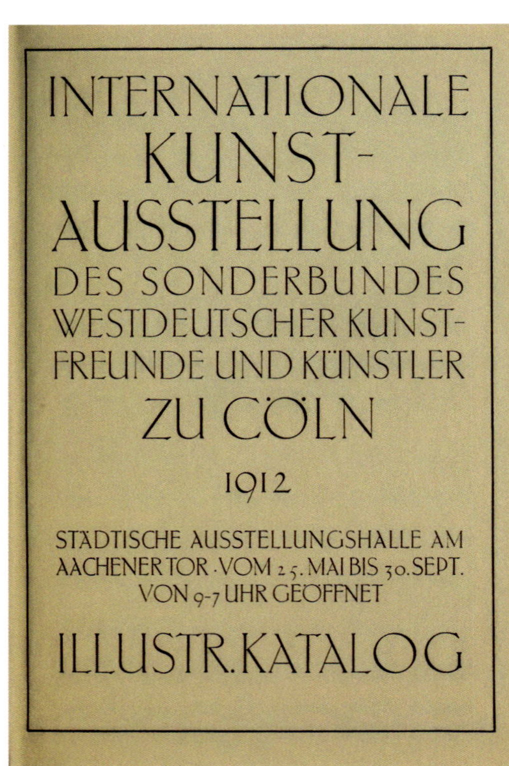

Catalogue accompanying the *Internationale Kunstausstellung des Sonderbundes* (*International Exhibition of the Sonderbund*), Cologne, 1912

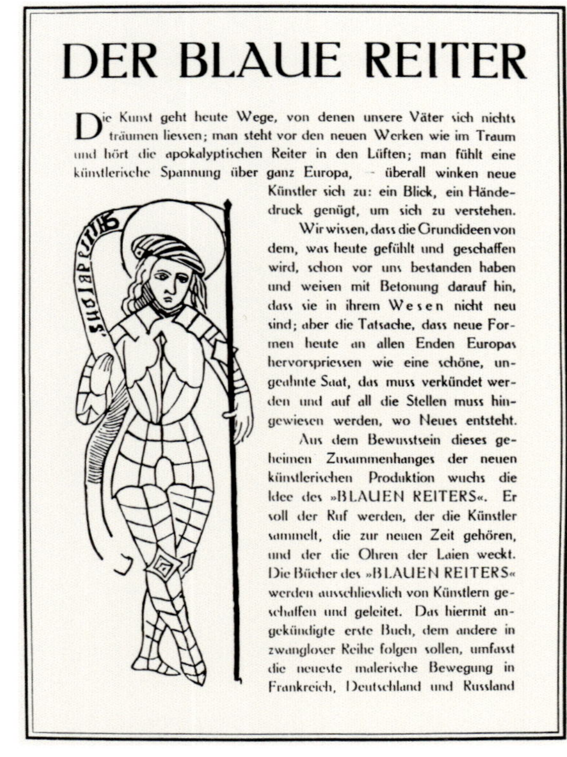

DER BLAUE REITER

Die Kunst geht heute Wege, von denen unsere Väter sich nichts träumen liessen; man steht vor den neuen Werken wie im Traum und hört die apokalyptischen Reiter in den Lüften; man fühlt eine künstlerische Spannung über ganz Europa, – überall winken neue Künstler sich zu: ein Blick, ein Händedruck genügt, um sich zu verstehen.

Wir wissen, dass die Grundideen von dem, was heute gefühlt und geschaffen wird, schon vor uns bestanden haben und weisen mit Betonung darauf hin, dass sie in ihrem Wesen nicht neu sind; aber die Tatsache, dass neue Formen heute an allen Enden Europas hervorspriessen wie eine schöne, ungeahnte Saat, das muss verkündet werden und auf all die Stellen muss hingewiesen werden, wo Neues entsteht.

Aus dem Bewusstsein dieses geheimen Zusammenhanges der neuen künstlerischen Produktion wuchs die Idee des »BLAUEN REITERS«. Er soll der Ruf werden, der die Künstler sammelt, die zur neuen Zeit gehören, und der die Ohren der Laien weckt. Die Bücher des »BLAUEN REITERS« werden ausschliesslich von Künstlern geschaffen und geleitet. Das hiermit angekündigte erste Buch, dem andere in zwangloser Reihe folgen sollen, umfasst die neueste malerische Bewegung in Frankreich, Deutschland und Russland

Title page of the four-page subscription prospectus for *Der Blaue Reiter* almanac, with a text written by Franz Marc, February 1912

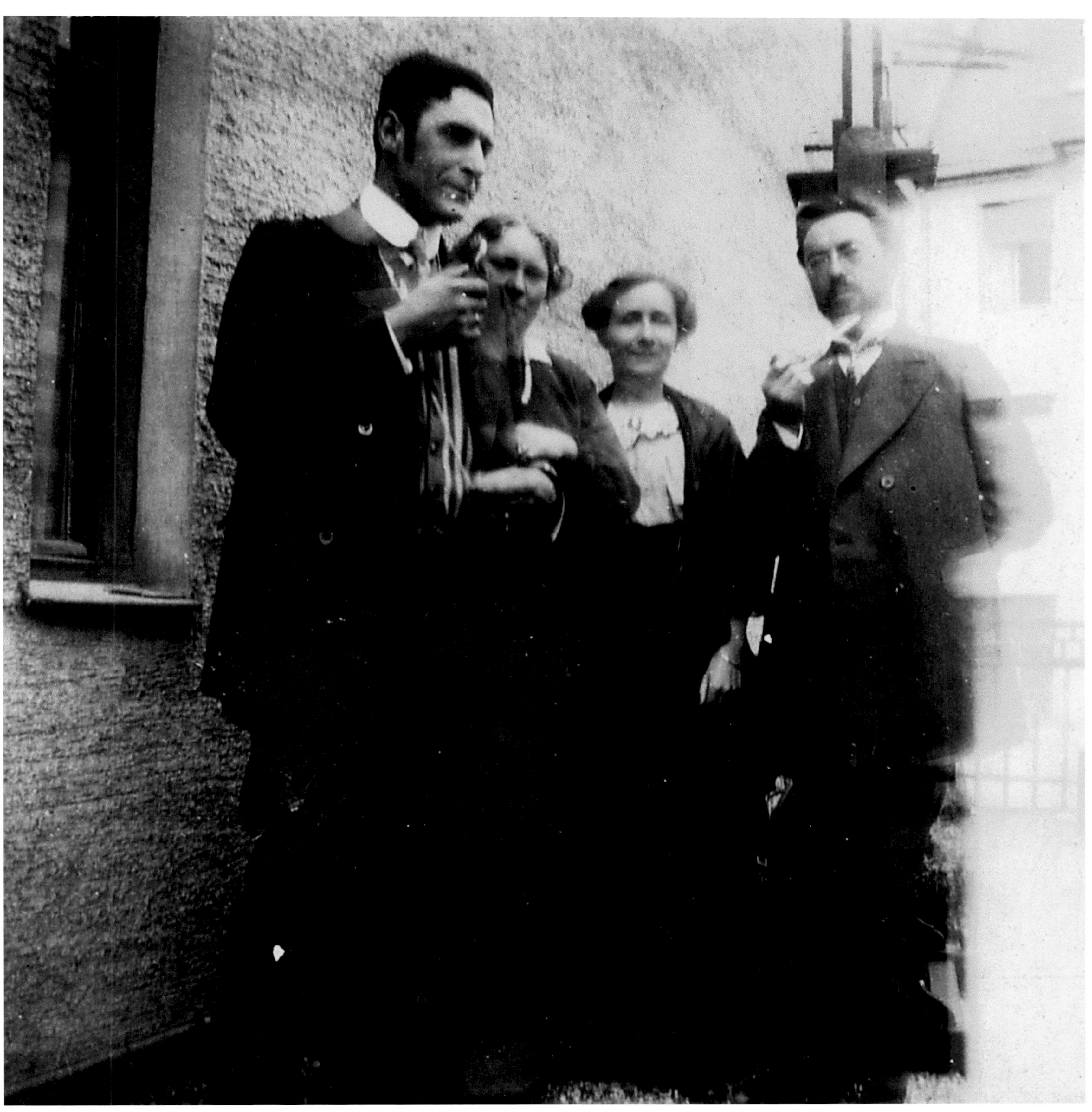

Franz and Maria Marc, Gabriele Münter, and Wassily Kandinsky on the terrace at Ainmillerstrasse 36, Munich, 1911–12,
Gabriele Münter- und Johannes Eichner-Stiftung, Munich

1913

May This year *Die Erste Ausstellung* travels solely to Budapest. Very few press reviews have survived.

June 5 Kandinsky and Marc continue to discuss a second volume of the almanac. Kandinsky predicts a publication delay, writing, "I believe that we will scarcely be able to come out with the second volume next winter."

September 20–December 1 At the Sturm Gallery, Walden shows the *Erste Deutsche Herbstsalon* (*First German Autumn Salon*), which includes all of the Blaue Reiter artists. Marc and Macke help to hang the show, which is now considered to be the most significant gallery exhibition held prior to World War I.

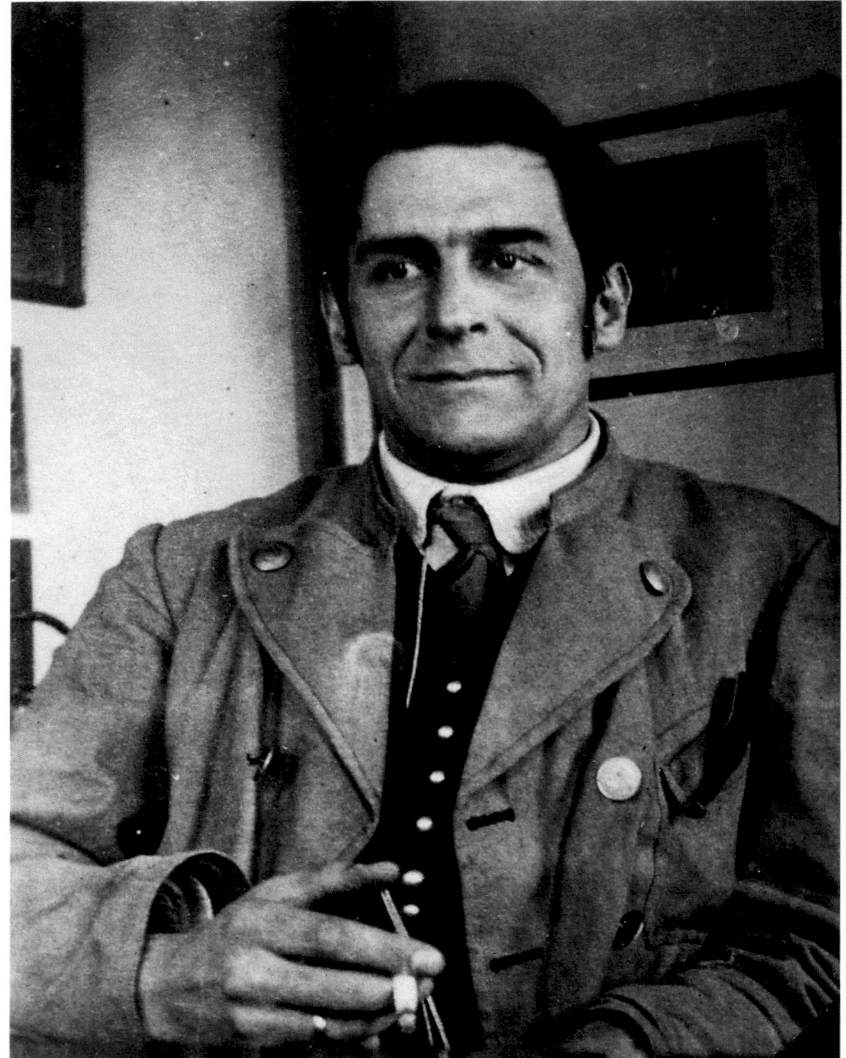

Franz Marc in Ried, spring 1914, photograph by Gabriele Münter, Gabriele Münter- und Johannes Eichner-Stiftung, Munich

1914

January–July *Die Erste Ausstellung* travels to Oslo, Helsinki, Trondheim, and Göteborg.

March The second edition of the *Blaue Reiter* almanac appears.

April Macke travels with Klee and his friend Louis Moilliet to Tunis. The trip has a lasting impression on all of them, as Macke writes to his wife Elisabeth on April 10: "We are lying in the sun, eating asparagus, etc. You only have to turn around and you have thousands of motifs. I must have already made fifty sketches today. Twenty-five yesterday. Things are going like the devil, and I am enjoying my work as never before."

August 1 World War I breaks out. Kandinsky, Jawlensky, and Werefkin are classed as enemy aliens and forced to leave Germany. Marc and Macke are inducted into the army as soon as the conflict begins. All activity of the Blaue Reiter comes to an abrupt end.

August 3 Kandinsky and Münter initially emigrate to Switzerland.

September 26 Macke is killed near Perthes-lès-Hurlus, France, on the Western Front.

October 24 Marc writes to Kandinsky, "I have the sad feeling that this war is flowing between us like a great flood that separates us; each of us can hardly see the other on the far shore."

October 25 Marc, shaken, writes an obituary for Macke: "Anyone who has concerned themselves with the new German art during these past eventful years, anyone who has anticipated our artistic future, knew Macke. And those who [knew him and] worked with him, his friends, knew what covert future this brilliant man held within himself. With his death, one of the finest and most audacious curves in our German artistic development abruptly breaks off; none of us is capable of continuing it. Each of us goes his own way, and wherever we may meet someday, he will always be missed."

November 25 Kandinsky leaves for Russia and first returns to Germany in 1921.

1916

March 4 Marc is fatally injured by shrapnel while engaged in mounted reconnaissance near Verdun.

March After a final meeting in Stockholm, Kandinsky's and Münter's lives separate for good.

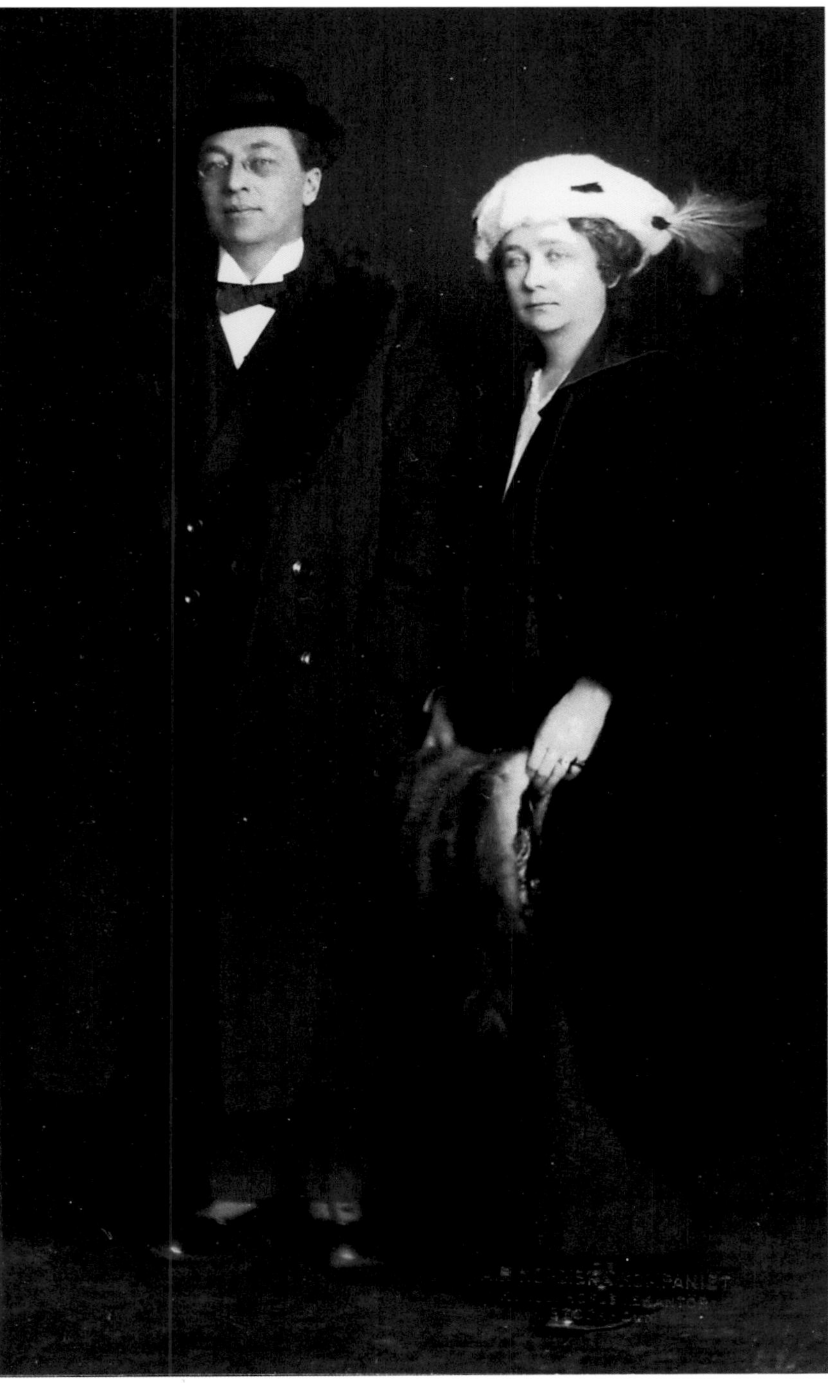

Wassily Kandinsky and Gabriele Münter in Stockholm, 1916, Photo studio of the Nordiska Kompagniet, Gabriele Münter- und Johannes Eichner-Stiftung, Munich

After the First World War

Kandinsky never returns to Munich or Murnau again. He becomes one of the leading instructors at the Bauhaus and emigrates to France in 1933, where he dies in 1944. Münter returns to Murnau in 1931, which becomes her main residence until her death in 1962. In 1957 she donates major portions of her unique collection of her own works, those of Kandinsky, and other Blaue Reiter protagonists to the Städtische Galerie im Lenbachhaus in Munich. Her residence is restored to its state between 1909 and 1914 and becomes a museum.

The original quotations are taken and in part translated from the following sources:
Elisabeth Erdmann-Macke, *Erinnerung an August Macke,* with a biographical essay by Lothar Erdmann (Frankfurt am Main, 1994); Annegret Hoberg, ed., *Wassily Kandinsky and Gabriele Münter: Letters and Reminiscences, 1902–1914* (Munich and New York, 1994); Andreas Hüneke, ed., *Der Blaue Reiter: Eine Geschichte in Dokumenten* (Stuttgart, 2011); Wassily Kandinsky and Franz Marc, eds., *The Blaue Reiter Almanac,* documentary edition, ed. and with an introduction by Klaus Lankheit, trans. Henning Falkenstein with assistance of Manug Terzian and Gertrude Hinderlie (New York, 1974; repr. Boston, 2005); Wassily Kandinsky and Franz Marc, *Briefwechsel: Mit Briefen von und an Gabriele Münter und Maria Marc,* ed., introduction, and annotation by Klaus Lankheit (Munich, 1983); August Macke, *Briefe an Elisabeth und die Freunde,* ed. Werner Frese and Ernst-Gerhard Güse (Munich, 1987); Franz Marc, *Briefe, Schriften und Aufzeichnungen,* ed. Günter Meissner (2nd ed., Leipzig, 1989); Franz Marc, *Schriften,* ed. Klaus Lankheit (Cologne, 1978).

LIST OF EXHIBITED WORKS

ARTISTS OF DER BLAUE REITER AND THEIR CIRCLE

WLADIMIR BURLIUK 1886–1917

Bäume, 1911
The Trees
Oil on canvas, 64 x 84 cm
Gabriele Münter- und Johannes Eichner-Stiftung, Munich
Page 42

Landschaft (Blühende Bäume im Frühling), 1911
Landscape (Blossoming Trees in Spring)
Oil on canvas, 73.2 x 92.5 cm
Private collection
Page 43

HEINRICH CAMPENDONK 1889–1957

Der Balkon, 1913
The Balcony
Oil on canvas, 87.5 x 76 cm
Merzbacher Kunststiftung
Page 119

ROBERT DELAUNAY 1885–1941

La Ville No. 2, 1910
The City No. 2
Oil on canvas, 146 x 114 cm
Musée national d'art moderne, Centre Pompidou, Paris, purchase, 1947
Page 39

ALEXEI VON JAWLENSKY 1864–1941

Herbst in Murnau, 1909
Autumn in Murnau
Oil on cardboard, 33 x 42.7 cm
Sprengel Museum Hannover
Page 79

Murnau—Landschaft, orange Wolke, ca. 1909
Murnau—Landscape, Orange Cloud
Oil on cardboard, 33 x 40 cm
Private collection
Page 81

Die Fabrik, 1910
The Factory
Oil on cardboard on wood, 72 x 85.7 cm
Private collection, Switzerland
Page 83

EUGEN VON KAHLER 1882–1911

Liebesgarten, 1910–11
Love Garden
Opaque colors and India ink on paper (on cardboard), 19 x 27 cm
Städtische Galerie im Lenbachhaus, Munich
Page 41

WASSILY KANDINSKY 1866–1944

Lanzenreiter in Landschaft, 1908
Lancer in Landscape
Oil on cardboard on panel, 63 x 81 cm
Merzbacher Kunststiftung
Page 63

Murnau—Dorfstrasse, 1908
Murnau—Village Street
Oil on cardboard (on wood), 48 x 69.5 cm
Merzbacher Kunststiftung
Page 70

Murnau—Kohlgruberstrasse, 1908
Oil on cardboard, 71.5 x 97.5 cm
Merzbacher Kunststiftung
Page 67

Murnau—Obermarkt mit Gebirge, 1908
Murnau—Obermarkt with Mountains
Oil on cardboard, 33 x 41 cm
Private collection
Page 69

Murnau—Schlosshof I, 1908
Murnau—Castle Courtyard I
Oil on cardboard, 33 x 44 cm
The State Tretyakov Gallery, Moscow
Page 71

Der blaue Berg, 1908–09
Blue Mountain
Oil on canvas, 106 x 96.6 cm
Solomon R. Guggenheim Museum, New York, Solomon R. Guggenheim Founding Collection, By gift
Page 65

Dünaberg, 1909
Oil on cardboard, 33 x 45 cm
Private collection
Page 75

Landschaft bei Murnau mit Lokomotive, 1909
Landscape near Murnau with Locomotive
Oil on cardboard, 50.4 x 65 cm
Solomon R. Guggenheim Museum, New York
Page 73

Studie zu Improvisation 3, 1909
Study for Improvisation 3
Oil and gouache on cardboard, 44 x 64 cm, with frame painted by the artist
Private collection
Page 64

Studie zu Murnau—Landschaft mit Kirche, 1909
Study for Murnau—Landscape with Church
Oil on cardboard, 33 x 45 cm
Stiftung Im Obersteg, on loan to the Kunstmuseum Basel
Page 68

Zwei Reiter und liegende Gestalt, 1909–10
Two Riders and Reclining Figure
Oil on cardboard, 70.4 x 70.1 cm
Merzbacher Kunststiftung
Page 92

Fragment zu Komposition II, 1910
Fragment for Composition II
Oil on cardboard, 57 x 47.5 cm,
with frame painted by the artist
Merzbacher Kunststiftung
Page 87

Improvisation 7, 1910
Oil on canvas, 131 x 97 cm
The State Tretyakov Gallery, Moscow
Page 93

Improvisation 10, 1910
Oil on canvas, 120 x 140 cm
Fondation Beyeler, Riehen/Basel, Beyeler Collection
Page 97

Improvisation 12, 1910
Oil on canvas, 97 x 106.5 cm
Bayerische Staatsgemäldesammlungen, Munich
Page 91

Improvisation 13, 1910
Oil on canvas, 120 x 140 cm
Staatliche Kunsthalle Karlsruhe
Page 95

Kahnfahrt, 1910
Boat Trip
Oil on canvas, 97.5 x 106.5 cm
The State Tretyakov Gallery, Moscow
Page 94

Murnau—Garten I, 1910
Murnau—The Garden I
Oil on canvas, 66 x 82 cm
Städtische Galerie im Lenbachhaus, Munich
Page 88

Murnau—Garten II, 1910
Murnau—The Garden II
Oil on cardboard, 67 x 51 cm
Merzbacher Kunststiftung
Page 89

Reiter und Apfelpflückerin, 1911
Rider and Woman Picking Apples
Reverse glass painting, 15.5 x 16 cm,
with frame painted by the artist
ahlers collection
Page 62

Improvisation Sintflut, 1913
Improvisation Deluge
Oil on canvas, 95 x 150 cm
Städtische Galerie im Lenbachhaus, Munich
Pages 150–51

Komposition VII, 1913
Composition VII
Oil on canvas, 200 x 300 cm
The State Tretyakov Gallery, Moscow
Pages 154–55

Landschaft mit Regen, 1913
Landscape with Rain
Oil on canvas, 70.2 x 78.1 cm
Solomon R. Guggenheim Museum, New York, Solomon R. Guggenheim Founding Collection
Page 149

Bild mit drei Flecken, 1914
Painting with Three Spots
Oil on canvas, 121 x 111 cm
Museo Thyssen-Bornemisza, Madrid
Page 153

Fuga, 1914
Fugue
Oil on canvas, 129.5 x 129.5 cm
Fondation Beyeler, Riehen/Basel, Beyeler Collection
Page 157

Improvisation 35, 1914
Oil on canvas, 110.3 x 120.3 cm
Kunstmuseum Basel,
Gift of Hans Arp 1966
Page 152

AUGUST MACKE 1887–1914

Paar im Wald, 1912
Couple in the Forest
Oil on canvas, 100 x 100 cm
Private collection
Page 124

Spaziergang in Blumen, 1912
Walk amongst Flowers
Oil on canvas, 63.5 x 48.5 cm
Staatliche Museen zu Berlin, Nationalgalerie, acquired 1949 through the State of Berlin
Page 125

Walterchens Spielsachen, 1912
Little Walter's Toys
Oil on canvas, 50 x 60 cm
Städel Museum, Frankfurt am Main
Page 122

Ausreitende Husaren, 1913
Hussars on a Sortie
Oil on canvas, 37.5 x 56.1 cm
Museo Thyssen-Bornemisza, Madrid
Page 123

Waldspaziergang, 1913
Forest Walk
Oil on canvas, 81 x 105.5 cm
Private collection
Pages 126–27

Grosse Promenade: Leute im Garten (Predigtamtskandidat), 1914
Great Promenade: People in the Garden
Oil on canvas, 74 x 105 cm
Franz Marc Museum, Kochel am See, loan from a private collection
Pages 128–29

FRANZ MARC 1880–1916

Pferd in Landschaft, 1910
Horse in a Landscape
Oil on canvas, 85 x 112 cm
Museum Folkwang, Essen
Page 101

Liegender Hund im Schnee, 1910–11
Dog Lying in the Snow
Oil on canvas, 62.5 x 105 cm
Städel Museum, Frankfurt am Main, property of the Städelscher Museums-Verein e. V.
Page 109

Blauschwarzer Fuchs, 1911
Blue-Black Fox
Oil on canvas, 50 x 63 cm
Von der Heydt-Museum Wuppertal
Page 107

Die gelbe Kuh, 1911
Yellow Cow
Oil on canvas, 140.5 x 189.2 cm
Solomon R. Guggenheim Museum, New York, Solomon R. Guggenheim Founding Collection
Pages 110–11

Die grossen blauen Pferde, 1911
The Large Blue Horses
Oil on canvas, 105.7 x 181.1 cm
Collection Walker Art Center, Minneapolis, Gift of the T. B. Walker Foundation, Gilbert M. Walker Fund, 1942
Pages 104–05

Reh im Walde I, 1911
Deer in the Woods I
Oil on canvas, 129.5 x 100.5 cm
Private collection
Page 133

Der Stier, 1911
White Bull
Oil on canvas, 100 x 135.2 cm
Solomon R. Guggenheim Museum, New York
Page 50

Die Angst des Hasen, 1912
The Fear of the Hare
Oil on canvas, 76.5 x 137 cm
Private collection, Courtesy Peter Eltz GmbH, Salzburg
Pages 138–39

Drei Tiere (Hund, Katze und Fuchs), 1912
Three Animals (Dog, Cat, and Fox)
Oil and tempera on canvas, 80 x 105 cm
Kunsthalle Mannheim
Page 108

Stute mit Fohlen, 1912
Mare with Foals
Oil on canvas, 76 x 90 cm
Private collection
Page 103

Der Traum, 1912
The Dream
Oil on canvas, 100.5 x 135.5 cm
Museo Thyssen-Bornemisza, Madrid
Pages 114–15

Der Wasserfall (Frauen unter einem Wasserfall), 1912
The Waterfall (Women under a Waterfall)
Oil on canvas, 164 x 158 cm
Private collection
Page 117

Drei Pferde II, 1913
Three Horses II
Oil on canvas, 59 x 80.5 cm
Staatliche Kunstsammlungen Dresden, on permanent loan to the Galerie Neue Meister
Page 137

Eber und Sau (Wildschweine), 1913
Boar and Sow (Wild Boar)
Oil on canvas, 73.5 x 57.5 cm
Museum Ludwig, Cologne
Page 143

Kleine Komposition I, 1913
Small Composition I
Oil on canvas, 46.5 x 41.5 cm
Private collection, Switzerland, on permanent loan to the Zentrum Paul Klee, Bern
Page 142

Stallungen, 1913
Stables
Oil on canvas, 73.6 x 157.5 cm
Solomon R. Guggenheim Museum, New York, Solomon R. Guggenheim Founding Collection
Pages 144–45

Die Weltenkuh, 1913
The World Cow (Bos Orbis Mundi)
Oil on canvas, 70.7 x 141.3 cm
The Museum of Modern Art, New York, Gift of Mr. and Mrs. Morton D. May, and Mr. and Mrs. Arnold H. Maremont (both by exchange), 1988
Pages 140–41

Die Wölfe (Balkankrieg), 1913
The Wolves (Balkan War)
Oil on canvas, 70.8 x 139.7 cm
Collection of the Albright-Knox Art Gallery, Buffalo, New York, Charles Clifton, James G. Forsyth, and George W. Goodyear Funds, 1951
Pages 134–35

WATERCOLORS AND PRINTS

Zwei blaue Fohlen, 1911
Two Blue Foals
Watercolor and pencil, 44.7 x 39.7 cm
Private collection
Page 102

Fabeltier, 1912
Fabulous Beast
Color woodblock print, 14.5 x 21.7 cm
Private collection, Switzerland
Page 30

Liegender Hirsch, 1913
Lying Stag
Postcard to Bernhard Koehler
Watercolor, India ink, and collage (gold foil) on cardboard, 9 x 14 cm
ahlers collection
Page 113

Pferd und Haus mit Regenbogen, 1913
Horse and House with Rainbow
Postcard to Paul Klee
Watercolor and India ink on cardboard, 14 x 9.1 cm
ahlers collection
Page 112

Vier Füchse, 1913
Four Foxes
Postcard to Wassily Kandinsky
Watercolor, gouache, and India ink on cardboard, 14 x 9 cm
Städtische Galerie im Lenbachhaus, Munich
Page 112

Zwei Katzen, 1913
Two Cats
Postcard to Lily Klee
Gouache and India ink on cardboard, 9 x 14 cm
ahlers collection
Page 113

Zwei Tiere, 1913
Two Animals
Postcard to Wassily Kandinsky
Watercolor, pencil, and India ink on cardboard, 9.1 x 14 cm
Städtische Galerie im Lenbachhaus, Munich
Page 113

GABRIELE MÜNTER 1877–1962

Landschaft mit Hütte im Abendrot, 1908
Landscape with Cabin at Sunset
Oil on paper on cardboard, 33 x 40.8 cm
Kunstsammlungen Chemnitz, Museum Gunzenhauser
Page 74

Garten in Murnau, 1910
Garden in Murnau
Oil on cardboard, 37.5 x 46 cm
Museum Wiesbaden, donated by M. and W. Rick, 2013
Page 77

Herbstliche Landstrasse, 1910
Country Road in Autumn
Oil on cardboard, 33 x 41 cm
Private collection
Page 78

Strassenbahn in München, 1910–12
Streetcar in Munich
Oil on cardboard, 40 x 31.5 cm
Private collection
Page 76

ARNOLD SCHOENBERG 1874–1951

Vision (Selbstportrait), 1910
Vision (Self-Portrait)
Oil on cardboard, 32 x 20 cm
Music Division, Library of Congress, Washington, DC
Page 48

MARIANNE VON WEREFKIN 1860–1938

Tragische Stimmung, 1910
Tragic Mood
Tempera on paper on cardboard, 46.8 x 58.2 cm
Museo Comunale d'Arte Moderna, Commune of Ascona
Page 82

WASSILY KANDINSKY AND FRANZ MARC
DER BLAUE REITER ALMANAC

Wassily Kandinsky, Vignette for *Der Blaue Reiter* almanac, 1911
Print on paper (chemitype) after an India ink drawing, 14.5 x 10.7 cm
Musée national d'art moderne, Centre Pompidou, Paris, Bequest of Nina Kandinsky, 1981
Page 28

Wassily Kandinsky, Final drawing for the "Der Blaue Reiter" signet, 1912
India ink on cardboard, 14.8 x 12 cm
Musée national d'art moderne, Centre Pompidou, Paris, Bequest of Nina Kandinsky, 1981
See half title

Der Blaue Reiter almanac, Munich, 1912
First standard edition, in board covers with the galvano print of the color woodcut in blue and black on the front cover and the vignette on the back, 29.5 x 22.3 cm
ahlers collection
Page 29

Der Blaue Reiter almanac, Munich, 1912
First standard edition, bound in cloth with the galvano print of the color woodcut in red, blue, and black on the front cover and the vignette on the back, 29.5 x 23 cm
ahlers collection
Page 28

Der Blaue Reiter almanac, Munich, 1912
Deluxe first edition (no. 13 of 50), bound in blue morocco with the vignette tooled in gold on the front cover, 29 x 22.2 cm
Private collection, Switzerland

Der Blaue Reiter almanac, Munich, 1912
Deluxe first edition (no. 21 of 50), bound in blue morocco with the vignette tooled in gold on the front cover, 29 x 22.2 cm
ahlers collection
Page 28

Der Blaue Reiter almanac, Munich, 1914
Second standard edition, bound in cloth with the galvano print of the color woodcut in red, blue, and black on the front cover and the vignette on the back, 29.5 x 23 cm
ahlers collection

Der Blaue Reiter almanac, Munich, 1914
Second standard edition, bound in cloth with the galvano print of the color woodcut in red, blue, and black on the front cover and the vignette on the back, 29.5 x 23 cm
Fondation Beyeler, Riehen/Basel

ALMANAC WORKS APART FROM THE BLAUE REITER

EUROPE

HANS BALDUNG GRIEN 1484/1485–1545
Kämpfende Hengste inmitten einer Herde von Wildpferden im Walde, 1534
Fighting Horses in a Forest Clearing
Woodcut on handmade paper, 21.3 x 32.1 cm
ahlers collection
Page 37

Votive painting donated by Anton Kapfer to the Murnau Lady of Sorrows church, ca. 1756–66
Oil on canvas, 50 x 50 cm
Katholische Kirchenstiftung St. Nikolaus, Murnau
Page 44

Death of Saint Joseph, Raimundsreut (Bavaria), 1775–1800
Mirror painting, 32.6 x 22.8 cm
Oberammergau Museum
Page 33

Stigmatization of Saint Francis of Assisi, Raimundsreut (Bavaria), 1775–1800
Mirror painting, 32.4 x 22.5 cm
Oberammergau Museum
Page 53

Descent of the Holy Ghost, Staffelsee region (Bavaria), 1800–50
Reverse glass painting, 28.5 x 18.4 cm
Oberammergau Museum
Page 47

HENRI ROUSSEAU 1844–1910
La Basse-Cour, 1896–98
The Poultry Yard
Oil on canvas, 24.6 x 32.9 cm
Musée national d'art moderne, Centre Pompidou, Paris, Bequest of Nina Kandinsky, 1981
Page 49

AFRICA

Horse with Groom, Egyptian shadow play, 14th–18th century
Vellum and colored fabric, 63 x 69.5 cm
Münchner Stadtmuseum, Collection Puppentheater/Schaustellerei
Page 51

Face mask, *okuyi/mukuyi,* Punu region, Gabon, before 1889
Painted wood, 34 x 21 x 16 cm
Bernisches Historisches Museum, Bern
Page 54

ASIA

Mythical Creatures, China (?), 18th–19th century
Gouache on paper, 20.5 x 33 cm
Franz Marc Museum, Kochel am See, Franz Marc Stiftung, on permanent loan from the community of Maria Marc's heirs
Page 31

UTAGAWA KUNIYOSHI 1798–1861
Two Fishermen (detail from the triptych *The Humility of Kanshin*), Japan, ca. 1835
Color woodcut, 36.1 x 24.5 cm
Franz Marc Museum, Kochel am See, Franz Marc Stiftung, on permanent loan from the community of Maria Marc's heirs
Page 57

Female figure, Gianyar, Bali, ca. 1900
Painted wood, 31.5 x 9 x 9 cm
Bernisches Historisches Museum, Bern
Page 35

Male figure, Gianyar, Bali, ca. 1900
Painted wood, 33 x 8.5 x 8.5 cm
Bernisches Historisches Museum, Bern
Page 35

Mother and child, Gianyar, Bali, ca. 1900
Painted wood, 53.7 x 28.5 x 19 cm
Bernisches Historisches Museum, Bern
Page 36

Ancestral figure of the Dayak, South Borneo, ca. 1900
Palisander, 190 x 39 x 33 cm
Bernisches Historisches Museum, Bern
Page 34

PHOTO CREDITS

The Fondation Beyeler wishes to thank the public institutions and private collectors named in the captions for providing the photographs reproduced here. Additional providers of photographs, copyright holders, individual photographers, and photography studios are as follows:

© Maurice Aeschimann: pp. 117, 124, 126–27

akg-images: pp. 48 top, 78, 81

© 2016. Albright Knox Art Gallery/Art Resource, NY/Scala, Florence: pp. 134–35

Alexej von Jawlensky-Archiv S.A.: p. 83

© The Art Institute of Chicago: p. 166 left

© Artothek: pp. 15, 103; Blauel/Gnamm: pp. 138–39, 161, 169 right; photo Hans Hinz: pp. 14, 102; © Museum Folkwang Essen: p. 101; © Städel Museum: p. 109; © Städel Museum, photo U. Edelmann: p. 122

Robert Bayer, Basel: p. 157

Walter Bayer, Munich: pp. 31 top, 57, 128–29, 167 left, 168

Bernisches Historisches Museum, Bern, photo Stefan Rebsamen: pp. 34 left, 35 top left and right, 36 right, 54

bpk, Berlin, for the Bayerische Staatsgemäldesammlungen: p. 91; for the Musée national d'art moderne – Centre de création industrielle: p. 49, photo Philippe Migeat: p. 39; for the Museum der bildenden Künste, Leipzig, Bertram Kober (Punctum Leipzig): p. 10; for the Nationalgalerie, SMB, photo Jörg P. Anders: pp. 125, 137; for the Sprengel Museum Hannover, photo Michael Herling/Aline Gwose: p. 79; for the Staatliche Kunsthalle Karlsruhe, photo Annette Fischer/ Heike Kohler: p. 95

Bridgeman images, © SZ Photo: p. 174 right

© Centre Pompidou, Musée national d'art moderne – Centre de création industrielle, Dist. RMN-Grand Palais: half title; Georges Meguerditchian: p. 28 left top; Adam Rzepka: pp. 9 right, 12 left and right

2004 Christie's Images Limited: p. 75

Gabriele Münter- und Johannes Eichner-Stiftung: pp. 76, 159 right, 160 right, 170–72, 173 bottom, 175 left and right top, 176–77, 179, 180–81

Thomas Ganzenmüller, Hannover: pp. 28 left bottom and right, 29, 37 top, 62, 112 right, 113 top and center

Kunsthalle Mannheim, Cem Yücetas: p. 108

Kunstmuseum Basel, Martin P. Bühler: pp. 68, 152

© Medienzentrum, Antje Zeis-Loi/Von der Heydt-Museum Wuppertal: p. 107

© Museo Thyssen-Bornemisza, Madrid: pp. 114–15

© 2016. Digital image, The Museum of Modern Art, New York/Scala, Florence: pp. 140–41

Mark Niedermann, Riehen/Basel: pp. 19, 31 bottom, 32, 34 right, 35 bottom, 36 bottom left, 37 bottom, 38, 40, 43 bottom, 45 top, 46, 48 bottom, 50 bottom, 51 bottom, 52, 55 top, 56

PUNCTUM / Bertram Kober: p. 74

Rheinisches Bildarchiv Köln, Cologne: p. 143

Peter Schälchli, Zurich: p. 64

Peter Schibli, Basel: pp. 97, 165

Irmgard Schnell-Stöger: p. 44

© The State Tretyakov Gallery, Moscow: pp. 71, 93, 94, 154–55

Stadtarchiv München, Munich: p. 163 right

© Warburg Institute, London: p. 21

Zentrum Paul Klee, Bern, Bildarchiv: p. 142

Exhibition
Kandinsky, Marc & Der Blaue Reiter

Fondation Beyeler, Riehen / Basel
September 4, 2016–January 22, 2017

Director
Samuel Keller

Managing director
Ulrike Erbslöh

Curator of the exhibition
Ulf Küster

Assistant curator, Curatorial assistant
Fiona Hesse, Lara Rath

Registrars
Matthias Fellmann, Nora Gassner, Nadine Koller, Tanja Narr

Conservators
Markus Gross, Anne Schmid, Friederike Steckling

Exhibition services
Michael Babics, Ben Ludwig, David Vogt

Art education
Julianna Filep, Daniel Kramer, Jana Leiker, Flavia Mayer, Christina Müller, Janine Schmutz

Communication, Public relations
Mirjam Baitsch, Elena DelCarlo, Sonja Dörig, Chiara Kettmeir, Elena Vittoria Kuznik, Jan Sollberger

Events, Fundraising
Angelika Bühler, Charlotte Ernst, Michael Gass, Blanca Hernandez, Bianca Lauscher, Julia Meyer, Nathalie Meyer, Myriam Rüegsegger

Controlling
Dorothea Merz

Further assistance
Bruno Anceschi, Raphaël Bouvier, Linda Briem, Simon Crameri, Michael Hunn, Ljiljana Jovic, Michiko Kono, Pascal Steiner, Anna Szech, Theodora Vischer, Andreas Widmer

Catalogue
Kandinsky, Marc & Der Blaue Reiter

Edited by
Ulf Küster for the Fondation Beyeler

Catalogue management and editing
Delia Ciuha and Franziska Stegmann, Fondation Beyeler

Copyediting
Joann Skrypzak-Davidsmeyer, Cologne

Translations
John Gabriel, Worpswede (essays Bätschmann, Beyer, Klingsöhr-Leroy, introductory texts Küster, timeline)
Jenny Dodman, Madrid (essay Ruiz del Árbol)

Graphic design
Heinz Hiltbrunner, Munich

Typesetting
Daniel Sieber, das formt, Munich

Typeface
Alright Black, Alright Regular

Production
Christine Stäcker, Hatje Cantz

Reproductions
Dr. Cantz'sche Druckerei Medien GmbH, Ostfildern

Printing
Offsetdruckerei Karl Grammlich GmbH, Pliezhausen

Paper
LuxoArtSamt, 170 g/m²

Binding
Josef Spinner Grossbuchbinderei GmbH, Ottersweier

A publication of the Fondation Beyeler
Baselstrasse 101
4125 Riehen / Basel
Switzerland
Tel. +41 61 6459-700
Fax +41 61 6459-719
www.fondationbeyeler.ch
info@fondationbeyeler.ch

ISBN 978-3-906053-34-9 (English museum edition)
ISBN 978-3-906053-33-2 (German museum edition)

Trade edition
Hatje Cantz Verlag
Mommsenstrasse 27
10629 Berlin
Germany
Tel. +49 30 3464678-00
www.hatjecantz.com
A Ganske Publishing Group company

ISBN 978-3-7757-4169-9 (English trade edition)
ISBN 978-3-7757-4168-2 (German trade edition)

Hatje Cantz books are available internationally at selected bookstores. For more information about our distribution partners, please visit our homepage at www.hatjecantz.com

Printed in Germany

Half title
Wassily Kandinsky, Vignette for the *Blaue Reiter* almanac, 1911

Cover illustration
Franz Marc, *The Large Blue Horses*, 1911
(cat. pp. 104–05)